Isaac Cruikshank and the Politics of Parody

Watercolors in the Huntington Collection

Fisher Gallery, University of Southern California
Los Angeles

Huntington Library Press
San Marino, California

Fisher Gallery, University of Southern California
University Park, Los Angeles, California 90089-0292

Henry E. Huntington Library and Art Gallery
1151 Oxford Road, San Marino, California 91108-1299

This publication documents the Huntington collection of Cruikshank watercolors and an exhibition at Fisher Gallery (March 2 to April 16, 1994).

Library of Congress Cataloging-in-Publication Data

Cruikshank, Isaac, 1756? - 1811.
Isaac Cruikshank and the politics of parody: watercolors in the Huntington collection / edited by Edward J. Nygren.
p. cm.

1. Cruikshank, Isaac, 1756?-1811—Themes, motives—Exhibitions. 2. Theater—England—History—18th century—Caricatures and cartoons—Exhibitions. 3. Great Britain—Social life and customs—18th century—Caricatures and cartoons—Exhibitions. 4. English wit and humor, Pictorial—Exhibitions. 5. Caricatures and cartoons—California—San Marino—Exhibitions. 6. Henry E. Huntington Library and Art Gallery—Exhibitions. I. Nygren, Edward J. II. Henry E. Huntington Library and Art Gallery. III. Fisher Gallery (University of Southern California) IV. Title.
NC1479.C94A4 1994
741.5'942—dc20 94-2794
CIP

ISBN 0-87328-147-0

Designer: Avelina Moeller
Editor: Susan Green
Printer: Pace Lithographers, Inc.

Isaac Cruikshank and the Politics of Parody

Table of Contents

Foreword 1

Acknowledgments 3

Introduction 5

Playing to the House: Cruikshank and the Theater
Edward J. Nygren

Chronology 15

Note on the Catalogue 19

Catalogue Entries, 1 – 117 21

Co-curators

Mari-Tere Alvarez
Maria L. Brendel
Danna Freedy
Rhonda Howard
Julie Joyce
Jennifer Katell
Kathleen Kelly
Mary-Kay Lombino
Mar Martinez-Perez
Deanne Shey
Tim D. Wright

Foreword

Isaac Cruikshank and the Politics of Parody is the result of a major collaborative effort between the Huntington and Fisher Gallery, the museum of the University of Southern California. This collaboration, an event to be warmly celebrated, is unusual for several reasons. It produced both an exhibition and a catalogue raisonné of the watercolors by Isaac Cruikshank in the Huntington's collection. Both are the work of graduate students in USC's Museum Studies Program, who are training to become curators while earning a master's degree in art history. The project is also unusual in that, for the first time, a part of the Huntington's British art collection is being shown at another institution.

In this dual host-and-venue endeavor, the students began work on the Huntington's extensive collection of Cruikshank material in a seminar held there during the spring of 1993. They were involved in the development of the project from selection of the topic to writing of the catalogue entries on individual works, from exploring funding possibilities to planning and promoting the exhibition and its programs. The soundness of their work is measured by the publication's dual achievement; it simultaneously commemorates the display at Fisher Gallery and documents a rich resource at the Huntington. With its insightful commentaries on these humorous and occasionally problematic images from the late Georgian period, the catalogue will be of lasting interest to the scholarly community.

The project provided the students in the Museum Studies Program with a special challenge: curating an exhibition on a little-known eighteenth-century figure that still had to appeal to a diverse contemporary audience. In order to make Cruikshank's social satires intelligible, apart from the broadest comic characterizations, the students had to reconstruct their historical background. They were fortunate to be able to draw on a body of scholarship on eighteenth-century England that is remarkable in both quality and scope. They explore here the targets of Cruikshank's parody and the wit underlying the depictions of ordinary objects and incidents. While sometimes remote from twentieth-century experience, the allusions and nuances of meaning they have discovered suggest the connection that can exist in all periods between social attitudes and comic art. Cruikshank's intention to engage with specific political issues in these watercolors is still open to debate, but the way in which his work inevitably conveys its political background is taken as the basis of the exhibition.

We are delighted that the Huntington and Fisher Gallery have been able to join in this effort. Together, we salute the students who made it possible. The production of the catalogue and the mounting of the exhibition have required them to hone skills that will be of use to them as they pursue their careers in art museums around the globe. It gives us great pleasure to have been part of the process of educating another generation of museum professionals.

Selma Holo
Director, Fisher Gallery and
Museum Studies Program

Edward J. Nygren
Director of the Art Collections
The Huntington

Acknowledgments

As members of the Museum Studies Class of 1995, we wish to express our gratitude and heartfelt appreciation to a number of individuals and institutions who contributed to the realization of *Isaac Cruikshank and the Politics of Parody.*

This exhibition would not have been possible without the generosity and cooperation of the Henry E. Huntington Library and Art Gallery, who loaned the works to Fisher Gallery as part of an unprecedented collaboration between these two institutions. We have been extremely fortunate to have had the opportunity to be a part of this joint undertaking.

We owe our deepest gratitude to Dr. Selma Holo, director of the Museum Studies Program and Fisher Gallery at the University of Southern California. Dr. Holo has continued to guide and support us throughout this endeavor. Her vision and enthusiasm have been an inspiration to all of us.

Dr. Edward Nygren, director of the Art Collections at the Huntington, introduced us to this rich body of Isaac Cruikshank's work and imparted to us his wealth of knowledge on eighteenth-century British art and culture. Dr. Nygren's expertise and high standards were of the utmost importance in guiding our work on both the exhibition and the catalogue.

We wish to note here the special participation of Sherrie Ray, education coordinator at Fisher Gallery who, as the liaison between the Museum Studies Program and the Huntington, held the pieces of this complex project together. The installation of the exhibition itself was possible because of the patient guidance of the other members of the staff of Fisher Gallery—Kay Allen, associate director, Jennifer Jaskowiak, exhibitions coordinator, and Gymeka Williams, administrative assistant.

We are greatly indebted to Susan Green and Avelina Moeller of the Huntington Library Press for their work on the editing and design of this catalogue. We are also especially thankful for the efforts of Eric Lutz and Jacqueline Dugas, who arranged for the preparation of the watercolors for exhibit and their transportation from the Huntington to Fisher Gallery. Linda Zoeckler, art reference librarian, aquainted us with the research materials at the Huntington.

Finally we wish to acknowledge the following individuals and institutions for their various contributions: Jan Blair, Photo Lab, USC; Professor Ed Gray, School of Journalism, USC; Professor Lynn Matteson, School of Fine Arts, USC; Dean Robert Scales, School of Theater, USC; Department of Education and Academic Affairs, the J. Paul Getty Museum; John Bidwell, reference librarian, William Andrews Clark Library, UCLA; Linda Katell; David Rodes, Susan Lockhardt, and the staff of the Grunwald Center for Graphic Arts at UCLA.

Museum Studies Class of 1995, USC

Introduction

Playing to the House: Cruikshank and the Theater

Like his contemporaries Thomas Rowlandson and James Gillray, Isaac Cruikshank turned to the life and politics of the late Georgian period for his subject matter. His oeuvre includes traditional illustrations, sentimental subjects, and political caricatures, as well as social satires. The Huntington's 117 watercolors, undoubtedly the largest group of his works in that medium in a single collection, belong almost entirely to the last category, known at the time as "drolls" for their humorous subject matter.[1] Produced between 1790 and 1804, they are surprisingly devoid of specific references to the major events of the period—the French Revolution, the wars with France, parliamentary arguments, the problems of the royal family. These subjects were dealt with by Cruikshank in his political caricatures. Rather, the drolls focus on social activities and attitudes—on romantic and sexual encounters, ethnic and class differences, fashion and custom, gambling and drinking, venality and incompetence in the professions—in short, on the human condition in general.

Cruikshank was one of a group of satirists, including Rowlandson and Gillray, who shaped the character of comic art at the end of the eighteenth century. Of the three, he remains the least known. The few facts established about his life are covered in Robert Wark's study of the Huntington collection, published twenty-five years ago, and in E. B. Krumbhaar's catalogue raisonné from the same period.[2] Additional information, especially on Cruikshank's marriage and death, was brought to light by John Wardroper a decade later.[3] The purpose of this introductory essay is, therefore, not biographical (a chronology, beginning on page 11 in this volume, places his career in a historical context). Rather, it will focus on one part of Cruikshank's life that, in my view, helped shape his aesthetic vision—his involvement with popular entertainment in general and with the theater in particular. Tied as his designs frequently are in theme as well as composition to the world of the Georgian stage, they are simultaneously visually accessible and contextually complex. Often a marriage of word and image, they rely, as did the theatrical farces with which they have so much in common, on stereotypes, on stock characters and burlesque situations that may in some instances strike the modern viewer as more offensive than humorous.

The late eighteenth century in England was not a memorable period for playwriting, with the possible exception of comedies by Thomas Brinsley Sheridan and Oliver Goldsmith. It was, however, an age that saw the rebuilding and enlarging of theaters, an expansion of the type of entertainment provided, and an increase in the audience, especially among the middle and lower-middle classes.[4] The theater was an arena where various levels of society congregated; where people came to be seen as well as to see; and where upwardly mobile members of the lower orders aped the actions and manners of their betters.[5] The theater "occupied a more prominent place in the social life of London then than at any other time."[6]

The Licensing Act of 1737 had restricted dramatic presentations in London to two major houses, Drury Lane and Covent Garden. Their companies presented plays in repertory. Productions of works by the masters of the past, from Shakespeare to Fielding, were mounted along with new comedies and tragedies. Performances did, however, take place elsewhere, particularly in smaller theaters removed from the center of the city or, like the Haymarket, with only a summer season.

Although the Licensing Act was not eliminated until 1843, theatrical entertainment in London underwent a change around the turn of the century. A number of smaller theaters opened their doors, and several new kinds of shows were offered: aquatic spectacles, musicals, dances, one-person presentations, pantomimes. The Licensing Act had come about, in part, to curb indecency in the theater, and as the century progressed the plays became increasingly circumspect. Restoration comedies, considered especially risqué, were cleaned up. A few, such as Edward Ravenscroft's *The London Cuckolds,* which had been performed every year on Lord Mayor's Day for decades, were dropped entirely from the repertory. Sentimental plays containing moral lessons became standard fare. This shift has been partially attributed to (perhaps *blamed on* expresses the modern judgment more accurately) to the expansion of the middle classes.[7]

Although little information about Cruikshank's life has been discovered, his ties to the theater are easily established. According to John Wardroper, he "was a member of a club of press and theatre men, The Brilliants, who met at the Swan, Chandos Street, Charing Cross, after curtain-fall, and sat drinking, reciting and singing until 4 or 5 a.m. The club chairman for many years was James Laurie of Laurie & Whittle."[8] The firm of Laurie & Whittle was one of Cruikshank's major publishers after 1794. Wardroper also notes that Isaac's son George, who was to become a more famous illustrator and caricaturist than his father, had contemplated early in his life a career in the theater, first as an actor and then as a stage designer.[9] The family numbered among its friends prominent figures in the theater, including the young actor Edmund Kean.

In turning to the stage for inspiration and employment, Cruikshank was operating within an established tradition in British art. Earlier in the century, William Hogarth had produced a number of works—including such serial images as *The Harlot's Progress, The Rake's Progress,* and *Marriage a la Mode*—the narratives of which unfold in stage-like compositions with gesticulating characters like so many scenes in a play.[10] And the many versions of *The Beggar's Opera,* as well as theatrical portraits such as *David Garrick as Richard III* and *The Farmer's Return,* attest to Hogarth's attachment to the theater. Artists such as Sir Joshua Reynolds, Johan Zoffany, Samuel de Wilde, Sir Thomas Lawrence, to name just a few, also produced portraits of actors and actresses in roles associated with them. Painters such as John Inigo Richards and Philip de Loutherbourg executed scenery for the theater in addition to easel landscapes. There were numerous editions of plays, many with illustrations of scenes, actors, or authors. Even the establishment of Boydell's Shakespeare Gallery in 1789, which stimulated the creation of history paintings derived from the master's plays, underscored through its theatrical subjects the vital connection between drama and art at the time.

The ties between the world of entertainment and the popular prints designed by Cruikshank and his contemporaries were equally strong. As Shirley Strum Kenny has observed, "For Hogarth and increasingly for later satirists such as Thomas Rowlandson and James Gillray, the theatre became a microcosm for depicting the follies of the British, in taste, in affectations, even in politics and social theory. . . . The centrality of theatre in British cultural life and the marketability of prints based on theatrical scenes continued to encourage artists to produce prints based on the theatre, even if the prints had little to do with actual productions."[11] Cruikshank was part of this development. As will be evident in the following discussion, unlike the theatrical conversation-piece portraits of Hogarth and Zoffany, his compositions are rarely related to specific performances, even when public recognition of the name of a performer or play may have been critical to the print's commercial success.

The strongest evidence of Cruikshank's familiarity with the theater exists in the works themselves. The most obvious examples are the illustrations he created for books and publications specifically related to plays and the theater. Among these are a frontispiece for *Falstaff Alive Again; or a choice Collection of Jests* (1794) and a design for John Roach's *New and Complete History of the Stage* (1796), in which the Graces are shown watering a monument to Shakespeare. In 1796, Cruikshank also etched compositions by Woodward derived from Thomas Holcroft's *Road to Ruin,* which might well have influenced his own interpretation of a related subject some years later (see *Will O' the Wisp,* 66). About the same time, he executed several engravings illustrating Allan Ramsay's pastoral comedy, *The Gentle Shepherd.*[12] Toward the end of his career, in November of 1809, he produced a frontispiece for *The Life of John Philip Kemble.* Kemble, an actor who was also the manager of Covent Garden, is shown on stage, being confronted by a protesting audience. This work was just one of a number of images Cruikshank created in the autumn of 1809 dealing with popular reaction to the increase in ticket prices when the new Covent Garden opened on September 18.

Like many caricaturists, Cruikshank occasionally placed his political satires in settings referring to specific plays. In *Shakespeare's Prophecy* of February 19, 1795, George III is Prospero and a number of political figures—Pitt, Fox, Sheridan—are depicted as other characters from *The Tempest.*[13] *A Scene in "The School for Scandal,"* published on July 18, 1786, deals with expense cutting by the Prince of Wales.

Several of the watercolors in the Huntington's collection were specifically designed as headpieces for songs, verse, or tales performed or recited in theaters.[14] Such one-person shows and afterpieces had become commonplace by the late eighteenth century,[15] and as early as 1790 Cruikshank began to work in this specialized area. The following year he produced such illustrations for *Bachelor's Hall* and *The Greenwich Pensioner* by Charles Dibdin, one of the popular writers of the day. Dibdin and his son Thomas figured prominently in the artist's career (see *Captain Wattle and Miss Roe,* 82). Representative watercolors at the Huntington include designs for two theatrical pieces by John Taylor—*Monsieur Tonson* (56) and *Frank Hayman* (76). The former was recited by John Fawcett, a leading comedian, at Covent Garden, and the latter at the Haymarket. The composition of these two watercolors, like that found in many of Cruikshank's designs, is conceived dramatically—the characters, turned almost frontally toward an imaginary audience to provide a maximum view of their actions, are arrested in movement, as if caught in a specific moment in the scene. The broad gestures and expressions of the figures add to the theatricality of the presentation.

Cruikshank continued to produce headpieces for songs, verse, and tales virtually until the end of his career (the Huntington owns only one original watercolor produced for the later broadsides). His productivity in this area in the later part of his career suggests that he (and later his sons George and Robert) came to be recognized as a specialist in the field and therefore received many commissions for this kind of work.

The rush of activity begins in 1804 with *Unfortunate Miss Bailey* (116), a song integral to the plot of George Colman's *Love Laughs at Locksmiths,* presented, according to the legend on the print, by Charles Mathews at the Haymarket and by John Fawcett at Covent Garden. The next five years saw Cruikshank creating more than two dozen such designs for material performed by about as many actors and actresses,[16] in a variety of London theaters—Covent Garden, Crotchet Lodge, Drury Lane, Haymarket, Lyceum, Royal Circus, Sadler's Wells. Not surprisingly given James Laurie's association with The Brilliants, these prints were published by Laurie & Whittle.

These compositions did not depict specific performances or performers, even when the composition illustrated a particular moment in the text, or when the text mentioned specific actors or singers. Not infrequently, the legend would proclaim that the presentation had been greeted "with unbounded applause," or that the piece was for a "popular farce" or "popular entertainment."[17] Such phrases were calculated to promote a particular song, play, or performer as well as to help sell the broadsheet, a kind of low-key advertisement that might also make a bit of money. Cruikshank's illustration no doubt made the package more appealing.

Although the artist probably selected the moment in the story to be depicted, this type of commission was basically hackwork, and in his headpieces he was obviously designing an illustration for someone else. While it is impossible to determine the extent of Cruikshank's role in choosing the text or subject of other kinds of compositions, it seems likely that he was at least an equal participant in the creative process. Even when he was employing his talents for commercial purposes of a not-very-high order, however, the deft handling of line and color attests to Cruikshank's skill as an artist.

Cruikshank tapped the public's awareness of the theater not only in illustrations or headpieces but in many individual prints. This is particularly evident in his use of titles and in the situations he depicted. Works such as *Poor Snip and Family Frightened by a Thunderstorm* (12), *The Recruiting Serjeant Taken In* (13), *The Absent Man* (15), *The Man Milliner* (25), *A Box-Lobby Challenge* (34), *The Farmer's Return* (38), *Claiming the Flitch of Bacon* (60), and *True Blue* (94) all make use of the titles of well-known comedies or the names of popular characters to arouse the interest of a potential purchaser. While a composition could reflect the general subject or farcical tone of the play, it sometimes had little more than a title in common with it.[18] In effect, the artist (or his publisher) was exploiting a would-be buyer's personal knowledge of the comedy or at least a general familiarity with its content to elicit a humorous response to the image.

Unlike political caricatures, with their timely subject matter that soon made them out-of-date, Cruikshank's satirical prints, when they had theatrical associations, could enjoy a long life over many seasons. The short farces that often served as afterpieces for the major attraction of the evening were usually produced several times within a given season and, if successful, they could be in repertory for years. The audience for both play and print could, in fact, grow, especially if the play was produced at Covent Garden or Drury Lane, each of which had a seating capacity of over three thousand.

In a few of Cruikshank's designs, internal elements enrich the theatrical allusions and further document the artist's intimate knowledge of the contemporary stage. *A Spouting Club* (28), published on May 12, 1794, refers to the infatuation of the lower orders with the theater, which was lampooned in *The Apprentice* by Arthur Murphy, performed regularly from 1756 into the next century.[19] However, the quotation from *Macbeth* delivered by the gesticulating barber—"Is that a dagger I see before me . . . "—was undoubtedly also an allusion to the first production mounted in the new Drury Lane just weeks before the print was issued, a theater-goer's inside joke. So, too, in *A Box-Lobby Challenge,* published in May of 1794, a few months after the play of that name was first performed, the reference on the billboard, at least in the watercolor, to *Richard Coeur de Lion* by John Burgoyne, which debuted in 1786, contributes to the irony of the composition and enhances the image's meaning.

The formal aspects of Cruikshank's compositions also suggest the impact of the theater on his aesthetic vision. From *Courting Couple* (1) to *Charms of Precedence* (51) to *Fellow Feeling* (108), virtually all of the works in the Huntington's collection contain elements which seem to correspond to the physical features of the stage itself. Such compositions, in which the figures are caught in a climactic but transitory moment, parody typical scenes from plays. A small group of dramatis personae—most often two or three but seldom more than six or seven main characters (the size of most casts)—are placed in a shallow picture plane suggestive of a stage. The characters engage in a verbal exchange or establish the dramatic situation with their gestures and expressions. Attention is focused on an activity in the center with figures or design elements bracketing the scene like the wings of a set. The presentation also defines the viewer's relationship to the image by situating him in front of the picture plane as a member of a fictive audience.

Occasionally, as in *New Boots* (8), *The Rabbits* (21), or *Loo* (61), one of the characters looks out of the composition, as if to make an aside to the viewer/audience, to clue us in, a dramatic device popular from Shakespeare onward. For the most part, however, the figures are portrayed as completely absorbed in the action depicted, even to the point of spilling their drinks (see 38). The deliberate disregard of the audience was a formal device in keeping with the tendency toward realism in eighteenth-century theater, and this conceit was also applied to the visual arts.[20]

At times, Cruikshank introduces onlookers to an event into the composition (see 34 and 62). Like actual theater-goers in the boxes that overhung the stages of the period, these figures are at the periphery of the scene, but so close as to become witnesses to the action. Such onlookers also serve as the viewer's surrogate. In *The Theory of Moral Sentiments* (1759), Adam Smith reflected on the impartial spectator as someone who influences the viewer's reactions by encouraging or discouraging "fellow-feeling."[21] Cruikshank's internal spectators encourage the viewer of the composition to identify with the action or sentiments depicted. In the work called *Fellow Feeling* (108), undoubtedly an ironic allusion to Smith's theory and perhaps to the prevailing taste for sentimental comedies, the artist plays with the concept by introducing figures who are not impartial and clearly have more sympathy for their pets than they do for a fellow human being.

Cruikshank's compositions are theatrical in other ways. Recurring themes in his works often have their counterparts on the stage. Although by the end of the century cuckoldry did not command quite the dramatic attention it had earlier, when unexpurgated Restoration comedies were still performed, the subject was a popular one because of its comic potential and would have been familiar to many theater-goers. Several of Cruikshank's compositions exploit the idea that an old man who marries a young wife is a fool and will inevitably be a cuckold (5, 7, 72). The theme of the courtesan was also treated by Cruikshank on several occasions (4, 6, 43). If not a subject often undertaken on the contemporary stage (it probably would have made a young lady blush),[22] prostitution was certainly a feature of Georgian life, and the attendance of prostitutes at performances increased considerably toward the end of the century.[23]

Like many of the comedies and farces of the period, Cruikshank's compositions rely on stock characters, cultural stereotypes as it were, for their comic effect.[24] But his figures, while broadly conceived, are comic representations rather than caricatures, a distinction current in the eighteenth century. In the "Author's Preface" to *Joseph Andrews* (1742), Henry Fielding differentiates between comic history-painting and caricature: "[W]e shall find the true excellence of the former [comic history-painting] to consist in the exactest copying of nature insomuch that a judicious eye instantly rejects anything *outre*, any liberty which the painter hath taken with the features of that *alma mater.* Whereas in the *Caricatura* we allow all license. Its aim is to exhibit monsters, not men; and all distortions and exaggerations whatever are within its proper province."[25] Fielding established this dichotomy to define his own style and to contrast Hogarth's approach with *caricatura,* an art form recently imported from Italy, and it is also useful in understanding the difference between the robust, grotesque caricatures of Rowlandson and the restrained, naturalistic satires of Cruikshank. Cruikshank's figures are ordinary men and women whose failings get them into trouble or make them appear foolish. Their features and forms are not generally distorted for comic effect, even as the artist simplifies their characteristics. Country folk are presented as wholesome or simple (9, 37); urban bucks, as decadent and vain (51, 117). Doctors and parsons are ridiculed for their venality and materialism (77, 101). Social climbers are mocked for their pretensions (34, 63); women, for their romantic fantasies and belief in fortune-telling (3, 54). These are stock but not grotesque figures. Still, in Cruikshank's satires, the motivations of his one-dimensional characters are transparent, to convey quickly the inherent humor of the situation. Similar types populated the stage as well as contemporary fiction.[26]

It is in the portrayal of ethnic and racial types that Cruikshank's dependence on theatrical stereotypes is particularly evident. In *Cumberland's British Theatre,* the anonymous author ("D. G.") of "Remarks on 'The Irishman in London,'" a popular play, describes characters also encountered in Cruikshank's compositions: "It is amusing to contemplate the various singularities of men. . . . The *Welshman* enjoys his leek, his pedigree, and his toasted cheese. The *Irishman,* his brogue and his bulls. There is no fun about a *Scotchman;* unless (in the absence of a *post*) when he is excited to dance to his national *fiddle.* . . . These characteristics have not escaped the observation of dramatic writers; and abundant mirth has been derived for their exhibition."[27]

Despite his Scottish origins, Cruikshank's satires (52, 71, 107) reflect in their comic delineation of national traits the middle-class Englishman's point of view toward members of other social and ethnic groups. It was a time when increasing numbers of workers, especially from Ireland and Scotland, were seeking employment in the cities and factories of England.[28] Free blacks were also typecast and relegated to the lower echelons of society (21, 49).

Although Cruikshank's compositions do not directly document the tensions inherent in the movement of large numbers of people and the competition for menial jobs, they do, by their stereotyping, hold the lower orders and immigrants up to ridicule. But his exploitation of theatrical types was not confined to the working class. Equally telling are his representations of the Irish fortune-hunter (53), who by mid-century had become a standard character in comedies as well as in fiction.[29] And Cruikshank was as pointed in his portrayal of foreigners as he was in his treatment of British nationals. Singled out for particular attention were the Germans (67, 69) and, especially, the French, who sought refuge in England in the wake of the revolution (32, 95). The xenophobia and chauvinism evident in these images reflect the ongoing hostility between Britain and France in this period.

Although it is not known who actually bought Cruikshank's social satires, certain things about their intended audience can be deduced from the form as well as the content of his compositions. Never conceived as works of fine art, these prints, which sold for six pence plain and one shilling colored, were designed as commercial ventures for a broad clientele. The imagery had to be easily comprehended for a piece to be saleable and successful. The subject matter of a number of the watercolors in the Huntington's collection, particularly the sexually charged images, suggests that the prints after them were created primarily for a male audience. The potential purchaser was also probably middle class and English, given Cruikshank's ridicule of the lower orders and ethnic groups. Furthermore, while the prints were not expensive, the cost would have placed them beyond the means of the average clerk or skilled worker, whose daily salary was around three shillings.[30]

Cruikshank did not conceive his visual satires with one class or gender in mind, however. A few works, particularly those dealing with the absurdities of female fashion or romantic fantasies, may well have been intended for a female audience;

several, dealing with social events or public occasions, could have been enjoyed by both sexes. Many undoubtedly appealed to a large cross section of the population. Whether intended for men or women or both, image and text with their theatrical overtones depend on certain assumptions for their humorous effect—on common experiences, general knowledge, and recognizable stereotypes. In short, the audience for Cruikshank's images probably shared his social attitudes, many of which were reflected in contemporary plays, as well as his interest in the theater.

---

1. The Huntington owns many political prints by Isaac Cruikshank, but these are not part of this study. Significant collections of his prints are at the British Museum, the Lewis Walpole Library in Farmington, Connecticut, and in the Widener Collection at Harvard. Many printed works as well as original drawings are in private collections; see E. B. Krumbhaar, *Isaac Cruikshank: A Catalogue Raisonné with a Sketch of his Life and Work* (Philadelphia: University of Pennsylvania Press, 1966). M. Dorothy George, *Catalogue of Political and Personal Satires Preserved in the Department of Prints and Drawings in the British Museum,* vols. 6-8 ([London]: British Museum, 1938-47), is essential to the student of British caricature and Cruikshank. A group of watercolors was sold at Christie's in London on May 29, 1983 (lots 28-50); fifteen of these were put up at auction at Sotheby's in London on July 11, 1990 (lots 26, 54).

2. Robert R. Wark, *Isaac Cruikshank's "Drawings for Drolls"* (San Marino, Calif.: Huntington Library, 1968), pp. 5-18; Krumbhaar, *Catalogue Raisonné,* pp. 15-23.

3. John Wardroper, *The Caricature of George Cruikshank* (London: Gordon Fraser, 1977), esp. pp. 7-11.

4. Leo Hughes, *The Drama's Patrons* (Austin: University of Texas Press, 1971), discusses the change in audience, particularly the increase of middle-class attendance (pp. 169-78); as does James J. Lynch, *Box Pit, and Gallery* (Berkeley and Los Angeles: University of California Press, 1953), pp. 201-5. Hughes also deals with the physical changes to the theaters designed to increase seating (pp. 180-87).

5. Hughes quotes from Thomas Holcroft's *Rival Queens* (1794) on why ladies went to the theater (*The Drama's Patrons,* p. 62; see also pp. 175, 177).

6. Charles Harold Gray, *Theatrical Criticism in London to 1795* (New York: Columbia University Press, 1931), p. 3.

7. For a discussion of this shift, see Lynch, *Box, Pit, and Gallery,* esp. pp. 264-70; see also Hughes, *The Drama's Patrons,* chap. 4, "Morality and Sensibility," pp. 120-53.

8. Wardroper, *The Caricature of George Cruikshank,* pp. 10-12.

9. Ibid., p. 11.

10. On Hogarth and the theater, see Ronald Paulson, *Hogarth: His Life, Art, and Times,* 2 vols. (New Haven and London: Yale University Press, 1971), 1:180-85. Like Hogarth, Cruikshank occasionally introduces images of works of art on the wall to help illuminate a subject (see 85 and 89).

11. Shirley Strum Kenny, "Theatre, Related Arts, and the Profit Motive: An Overview," in Kenny, ed., *British Theatre and the Other Arts, 1660-1800* (Washington, D.C.: Folger Shakespeare Library, 1984), p. 22.

12. Cruikshank's compositions are indebted to the designs of fellow Scotsman David Allan. See Krumbhaar, *Catalogue Raisonné,* p. 119 (890), for mention of the other prints in the series.

13. For another example, see *Prospero and Caliban on the Enchanted Island,* from December 6, 1798, in which Pitt is Prospero and Fox, Caliban.

14. Many of Cruikshank's published works of this type are reproduced in *The Cruikshankian Momus . . . Pictorial Broadsides and Humorous Song-Headings* (London: John C. Nimmo, 1892).

15. Lynch, *Box, Pit, and Gallery,* pp. 15, 239; see also Richard L. Klepoc, *Mr. Mathews at Home* (London: Society for Theatre Research, 1979), pp. 9, 11.

16. Among those who performed pieces illustrated by Cruikshank were Maria Bland, John Bannister, John Braham, William Dowton, John Emery, Henry Carey, John Fawcett, Joseph Grimaldi, Charles Incledon, John Johnstone, Mrs. Jordan, John Liston, Josh Major, John Moyne, Charles Mathews, Thomas Stewart, John Taylor, Miss Tyrer. Most of these actors and actresses are mentioned in *Roach's Authentic Memoirs of the Green Room* (1795), for which Cruikshank created a title page.

17. See Krumbhaar, *Catalogue Raisonné,* pp. 152-53 (1201-1214); alsop. 43 (118) and p. 57 (267).

18. For example, Isaac Bickerstaffe's *The Absent Man* (1768), a popular play dealing with an absent-minded suitor, had nothing at all to do with Thomas Paine, but the title of the print comments on the writer's absence from England in 1791 at the time of the publication of his book and his subsequent trial in absentia for treason, as well as on the absent-mindedness of the cleric who is in possession of Paine's treatise.

19. Murphy died in 1805. Editions of the play appeared as late as 1809 and 1815. Charles Beecher Hogan, ed., *The London Stage, 1660-1800,* pt. 5 (Carbondale: So. Illinois University Press, 1968), provides information on the date and location of performances from 1776 to 1800.

20. For a study of absorption as a theatrical and artistic concern in late eighteenth-century France, see Michael Fried, *Absorption and Theatricality* (Chicago: University of Chicago Press, 1980). It seems likely that similar attitudes would be reflected in British art of the same period.

21. For a discussion of Smith's theory and its impact on the theater, see David Marshall, *The Figure of Theater* (New York: Columbia University Press, 1986), chap. 7, "Adam Smith and the Theatricality of Moral Sentiments," pp. 167-92.

22. The heroine of Fanny Burney's *Evelina* blushed over Congreve's *Love for Love;* see Hughes, *The Drama's Patrons,* pp. 126-27.

23. Ibid., pp. 167-68.

24. In "Theatre and the Art of Caricature" (Kenny, ed., *British Theatre*), Leo Hughes comments on the "symbolic type-character" as "the dominant figure in much of English comedy in any age" (p. 219).

25. Henry Fielding, *Joseph Andrews* (Boston: Houghton Mifflin, 1961), p. 9.

26. Numerous examples could be cited. For example, see the character of Jemmy Jumps in *The Farmer* (1787) by John O'Keeffe, who returns home from a stay in London dressed in the extravagance of fashion, a description that brings to mind Cruikshank's *The Rustics Alarm'd at the Appearance of a London Buck* (9).

27. D____ G____, "Remarks on 'The Irishman in London,'" in *Cumberland's British Theatre* (London: John Cumberland, [1828]), 20:3.

28. For a discussion of immigrants see M. Dorothy George, *London Life in the Eighteenth Century* (1925; rpt., Chicago: Academy Publishers, 1984), pp. 116-57; and Linda Colley, *Britons: Forging the Nation, 1707-1837* (New Haven and London: Yale University Press, 1992), pp. 329-30.

29. One of the characters in Isaac Jackman's *All the World's a Stage* (1777) is an Irish clerk who runs off with an elderly lady worth fifty thousand pounds. Charles Macklin's *Love a-la-Mode* (1759; but first printed in full in 1793) satirizes several national types, including an Irishman and a Scot. Smollett's *Humphry Clinker* (1771) also has an Irish fortune-hunter as a minor character.

30. For a discussion of wages and living expenses of workers in the late eighteenth and early nineteenth centuries, see George, *London Life,* pp. 166-70.

Isaac Cruikshank: A Chronology

1764 **October 5** Born in Edinburgh, son of Andrew and Elizabeth, youngest of five children.

c. 1784 Moves to London.

1784 **January 30** Earliest signed and dated print, probably made in London.

S. W. Fores (one of Cruikshank's major publishers) sets up shop in Piccadilly.

History of the Westminster Election published, with plates by Thomas Rowlandson and Cruikshank.

Rowlandson exhibits *Vauxhall Gardens* at the Royal Academy.

1785 **April 5** First recorded print for William Holland.

1786 *Vathek* by William Beckford published.

James Gillray devotes himself exclusively to satire.

1788 **August 2** Thomas Gainsborough dies.

August 14 Marries Mary McNaughton of Perth.

November George III appears to become insane.

1789 **February** George III recovers.

May 4 John Boydell's Shakespeare Gallery opens.

Summer Exhibits *Return to Lochaber* at Royal Academy, from 1 St. Martin's Lane.

June 17 Haymarket Opera burns.

July 14 Fall of the Bastille.

September 27 Son Robert born.

November 26 First recorded collaboration as etcher, with George Woodward.

Songs of Innocence by William Blake published.

1790 **May 1** Several prints published by Robert Sayer, one of his first major publishers.

Summer Exhibits *Visit to the Cottage: vide Joe [sic] Thomson* at Royal Academy, from 7 St. Martin's Lane.

July 14 First recorded songhead, for *The British Tar's Laughing Stock.*

November 1 *Reflections on the French Revolution* by Edmund Burke published.

November 29 *Vindication of the Rights of Men* by Mary Wollstonecraft published.

John Boydell becomes Lord Mayor.

1791 **February 22** *Rights of Man* (pt. 1) by Thomas Paine published.

March 26 King's Theatre opens.

April 30 Headpiece for *Bachelor's Hall* by Charles Dibdin; first recorded collaboration with this author, published by Fores.

June 4 Old Drury Lane Theatre closes.

June 22 Louis XVI's flight and capture.

Autumn James Gillray in partnership with Hannah Humphrey.

Rowlandson illustrates Smollett and Fielding.

First recorded work for the publisher John Roach.

1792 Living at 203 High Holborn.

February 23 Sir Joshua Reynolds dies.

April 2 One of his first etchings after a work by John Nixon.

April 20 France declares war on Austria.

Summer Exhibits *The Distresses and Triumphs of Virtue: vide Curate of Elmwood* at Royal Academy.

September 22 French Republic established.

September 27 Son George born.

Covent Garden Theatre refurbished.

Vindication of the Rights of Woman by Wollstonecraft published.

1793 **January 21** Execution of Louis XVI.

February 1 France declares war on Britain.

July 16 Assassination of Marat.

October 16 Execution of Marie-Antoinette.

1794 Moves to 117 Dorset Street, Salisbury Square.

March 12 New Drury Lane Theatre opens.

May 12 Several works published by Laurie & Whittle, successor of Robert Sayer as one of his major publishers.

December Begins to illustrate *Roach's Beautiful Extracts of Prosaic Writers;* serialization continues into 1797.

America, Visions of the Daughters of Albion, Songs of Experience by William Blake published.

1795 **April 8** Prince of Wales marries Caroline of Brunswick.

First recorded headpiece for verse by John Taylor.

Letters to Literary Ladies by Maria Edgeworth published.

Laurie & Whittle issue a catalogue of prints with many by Cruikshank.

Rudolph Ackermann opens a shop in the Strand.

1796 **February 10** Frontispiece to *Roach's Authentic Memoirs of the Green Room.*

May 16 Frontispiece to *Roach's New and Complete History of the Stage.*

November 17 Catherine the Great dies.

Eccentric Excursions published with designs by Woodward, etched by Cruikshank.

1797 **March 12** Creates first British caricature of Napoleon.

April 27 Issues a series of five sentimental works called *Julia's Journey to London,* based on John William's Curate of Elmwood.

Gillray receives a pension from the Tories.

Sir Joshua Reynolds's *Discourses* published in their entirety.

Ackermann begins publishing works by Rowlandson.

1798 **April 4** First recorded collaboration with Thomas Dibdin.

August 2 Battle of Aboukir won by Nelson.

September 18 Lyrical Ballads by Samuel Coleridge and William Wordsworth published.

Fores publishes Rowlandson's illustrations for *The Comforts of Bath.*

1799 **December 12** Bonaparte made First Consul.

1800 **August 13** A songsheet published by Ackermann.

Rowlandson etches plates by Woodward for *Le Brun Travestied,* published by Ackermann.

1801 **January 1** Union with Ireland.

March 14 Pitt resigns over Catholic emancipation.

Summer France threatens to invade Britain.

1802 **March 27** Peace of Amiens.

August 2 Bonaparte made First Consul for life.

Walter Scott begins to publish *Minstrelsy of the Scottish Border.*

1803 **May 17** War with France.

April – September Threat of an invasion of Britain; Cruikshank creates many cartoons dealing with the subject.

1804 **May 12** Pitt made Prime Minister.

May 18 Napoleon proclaimed Emperor.

November 30 Society of Painters in Watercolours established.

December 2 Napoleon crowned.

1805 **June 4** British Institution founded.

October 21 Battle of Trafalgar and death of Lord Nelson.

Rhymes on Art by Martin Archer Shee published.

Creates many headpieces for songs, tales, and verse sung or performed in theaters (continues through 1810).

1806 **January 23** Pitt dies. Grenville made Prime Minister.

1807 **March 25** Abolition of Slave Trade.

March Grenville resigns over Catholic emancipation. Duke of Portland made Prime Minister.

The Caricature Magazine first published by Thomas Tegg.

1808 **September 20** Fire destroys Covent Garden Theatre.

Rowlandson begins to produce with A. C. Pugin *The Microcosm of London* for Ackermann.

1809 **February 24** Drury Lane Theatre destroyed by fire.

Spring *English Bards and Scotch Reviewers* by Lord Byron published.

September Portland resigns.

September 18 New Covent Garden Theatre opens.

September Creates several prints about the increase in theater prices and the reduction of seating for the general public.

November Frontispiece to *The Life of John Philip Kemble* published.

November George M. Woodward dies.

1810 **Late spring or early summer** Gillray insane.
September 6 Last known individual print.
November Death of Princess Amelia and madness of the King.

1811 **February 5** Regency established.
April 16 Cruikshank buried at St. Bride's, London.

Note on the Catalogue

In *Isaac Cruikshank's "Drawings for Drolls"* (1968), Robert Wark proposed a chronology for the Huntington's collection based on stylistic considerations, on dates for the published prints, and on the 1795 Laurie & Whittle catalogue. The present study generally follows his pioneering efforts; however, a few watercolors added to the collection have affected the sequence. Moreover, to the present cataloguers, several pieces seem stylistically earlier than Wark suggested. The placement of prints after these images in Laurie & Whittle's 1795 catalogue supports the idea that a half dozen or so were probably reissues, published in 1794, of works that originally appeared several years prior; all of the items in that catalogue or published subsequently by Laurie & Whittle are numbered in their order of publication. For the most part, the present chronological arrangement follows the Laurie & Whittle numbers when known.

Several points should be made about information at the top of each entry.

- If an image was published, the title given is that of the print; if no print after the image (or resembling it in most respects) is known, the title recorded on the verso of the original appears in quotation marks.
- The works included in the exhibition at Fisher Gallery are indicated by a dagger [†], following the title.
- The date given is that of execution. The date of publication, if any, appears a few lines below.
- In general, the medium is described as pen and either wash or watercolor. When there is evidence of an underdrawing in pencil, this is stated; however, in certain cases "pencil" is followed by (?) to indicate that the use of the medium is in question.
- All dimensions are given first in inches, then in centimeters, height preceding width.
- Texts that were printed with the image are included with the entry; the longer ones are found after the footnotes (some punctuation in texts has been modified for clarity).
- "Inscribed" is used only for words and numbers, including signature and date, written by the artist; "annotated" denotes information added by another, presumably later, hand.
- Original material by Cruikshank, such as pencil or ink drawings, occasionally appears on the verso of a sheet; this is described or illustrated.
- Virtually all of the watercolors enjoy the same provenance, having been purchased by Mr. Huntington in 1915. The history of this collection is given by Wark; therefore, the provenance of only four works acquired since 1915 is provided.
- Under "bibliography," accompanying each entry, references are to both the original watercolors (Wark) or to publications dealing with printed images after them (Laurie & Whittle, George, Momus, and Krumbhaar). Complete references to these works are given in the notes to the Introduction, above. References to the Laurie & Whittle catalogue are given with the publication date, if Laurie & Whittle originally published the image. Krumbhaar divides his listings into two basic categories; those numbers pre ceded by an "A" are to be found in a list of ascribed works.
- No attempt has been made to locate all impressions of a particular print; the collections cited represent major holdings or those easily accessible to the authors. They are: British Museum (BM); Lewis Walpole Library, Farmington, Connecticut (LWL); Widener Collection, Harvard College Library (WMC); and Grunwald Center, UCLA (GC).

1 "Courting Couple"

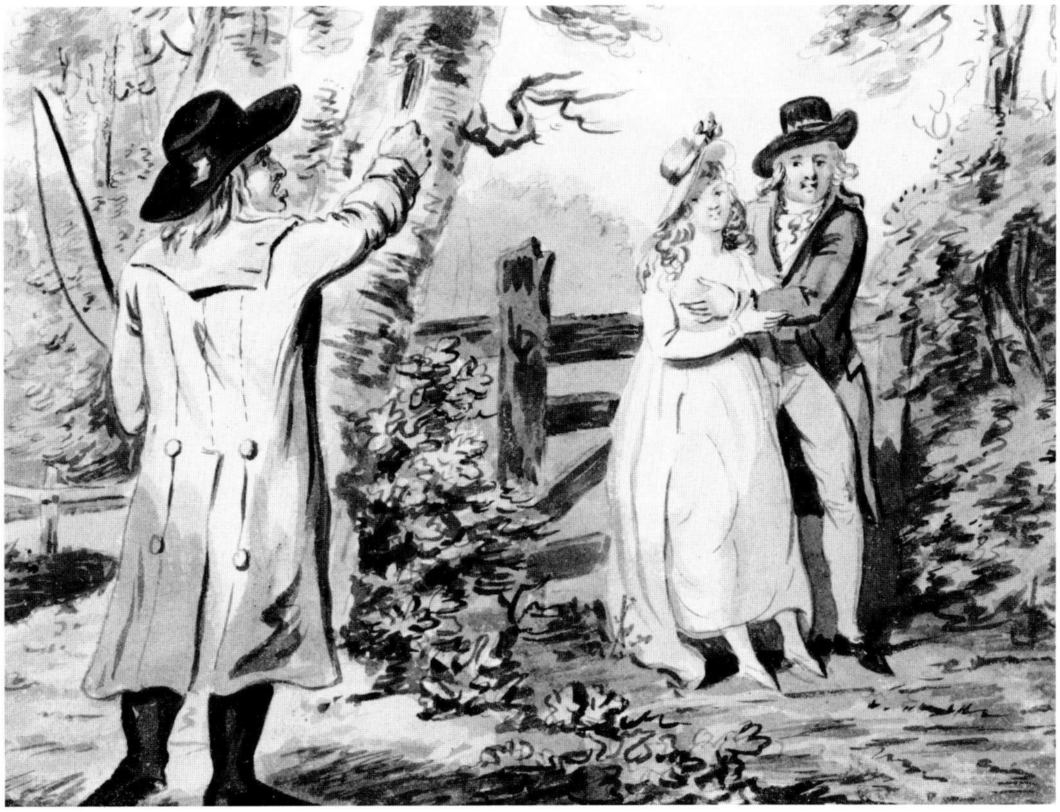

c. 1790
Watercolor over pencil
6⅞ x 9⅞ inches (17.6 x 24 cm.)
Annotated verso: collector's mark (Dr. J. Percy); 12
Provenance: Dr. J. Perry; L. G. Duke; with Fry, from whom purchased in 1970

On stylistic grounds, this work can be dated to the early 1790s. The use of color and line are similar to that in other compositions from the period, such as *A Fool and His Money's Soon Parted* (4), *Studying Politics* (10), and *A Sparring Match* (11).[1] Because no print after the composition has been identified, the exact subject is uncertain and any interpretation is conjectural. The title is traditional, referring simply to the relationship of the couple. The placement of the man's hand on the lady's breast speaks for their intimacy. They are confronted by an older man, whose fist is raised in anger. He may own the house depicted in the background, with which he is compositionally aligned. His plain dress—the long coat and large-brimmed hat—contrasts with the elegant attire of the young man and indicates that he is a Quaker.

The drama of the scene suggests its subject may have some connection with contemporary theater. Perhaps Cruikshank's composition alludes to Charles Dibdin's play *The Quaker*, performed every season between 1783 and 1792.[2] In the play, a young man returns to the house of his beloved after a short trip only to find that her mother will not admit him. She tells him that her daughter is to be wed the following day to an old and wealthy Quaker. The girl, however, is still in love with the young man. In the end, through a clever trick, the two are happily reunited, much to the satisfaction of all concerned. While the scene illustrated here does not occur in the play, the cast of characters is similar, hinting at a possible connection between Cruikshank's watercolor and Dibdin's play.

Jennifer Katell

1. Robert Wark, *Isaac Cruikshank's "Drawings for Drolls"* (San Marino, Calif.: Huntington Library, 1968), p. 16.
2. Ben Ross Schneider, Jr., comp., Index to *The London Stage, 1660-1800* (Carbondale: So. Illinois University Press, 1979), p. 238.

2 *Taking Water for Vauxhall*

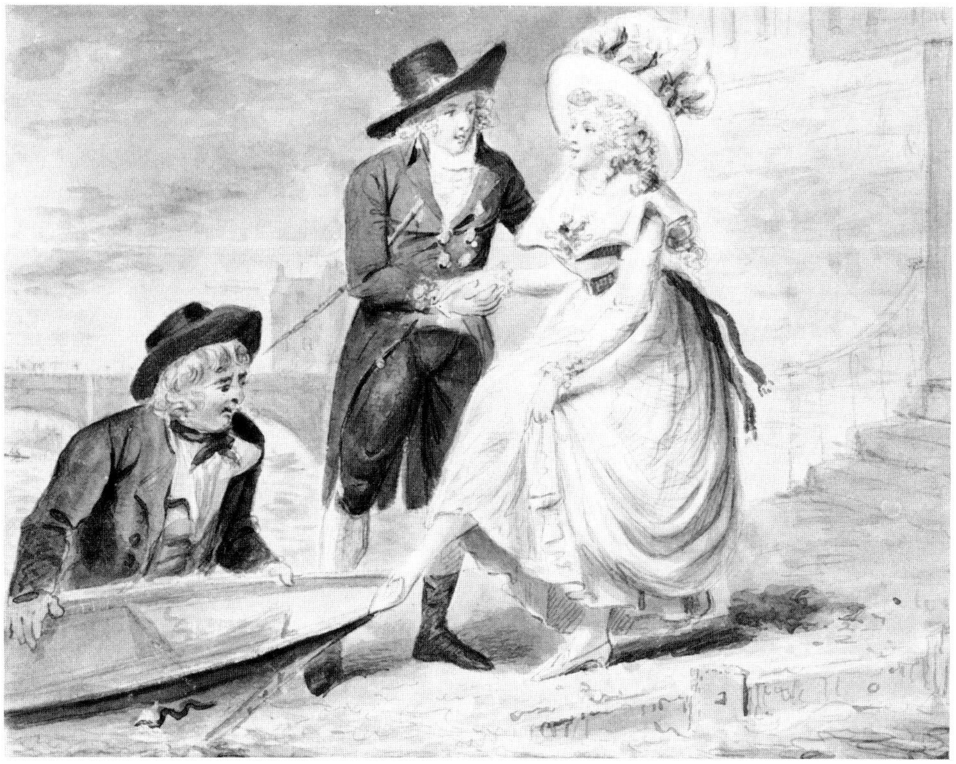

1790
Pen and watercolor over pencil
7 1/8 x 8 3/4 inches
(18 x 22.2 cm.)
Annotated verso: Taking water for Vauxhall / I. Cruikshanks
Published: 1790, by Robert Sayer; below the title is engraved: Be Cautious my Love —don't expose your leg.
Biblio: L & W, 56; George, 7801; Wark, 1
Impression: BM, LWL

Vauxhall, a popular tea and pleasure garden, was located upriver from Westminster in the parish of Lambeth. References to the pleasure garden at Lambeth are found as early as 1662 in the writings of Samuel Pepys, and it continued to be mentioned in English and European works throughout the seventeenth and early eighteenth centuries.[1] Originally called New Spring Garden, Vauxhall probably acquired its name from nearby Faulke's Hall manor in 1785.[2] Situated on the south bank of the Thames, the gardens featured attractions such as lawns, temples, and pavilions adorned with statues and paintings. "The whole [was] illuminated with an infinite number of lamps disposed in different figures and constellations," according to Lydia Melford in Tobias Smollett's *The Expedition of Humphry Clinker* (1771).[3]

Vauxhall was at the height of its popularity when Cruikshank executed this watercolor.[4] The journey there was most often undertaken by boat from Whitehall, Westminster, or Ranelegh, adding to the pleasure. Lydia Melford described such a trip in a letter to a friend: "At nine o'clock in a charming moonlight evening, we embarked at Ranelegh for Vauxhall in a wherry, so light and slender that we looked like so many fairies sailing in a nutshell."[5] This watercolor depicts a couple about to begin a similar boat ride. The young woman being helped into the wherry by her male companion lifts her dress, exposing her ankle and lower calf. The caption implies that it was not proper for the young lady to reveal her legs in public, no matter how innocent the circumstances. The waterman, holding the boat steady, stares at the exposed ankle. His gaze evidently prompts her male escort to warn her.

However pleasurable the boat ride, skipping in and out of wherries at Vauxhall stairs was sometimes fraught with misfortune. Such an incident was recounted by Horace Walpole: a duke almost drowned through the politeness of Lord Cathcart, who "stepping on the side of the boat to lend his arm, overset it, and both fell in the water up to their chins."[6]

Danna Freedy

1. James Granville Southworth, *Vauxhall Gardens: A Chapter in the Social History of England* (New York: Columbia University Press, 1941), p. 9.
2. George Rude, *Hanoverian London, 1714-1808* (Los Angeles: University of California Press, 1971), p. 73.
3. Smollett, *Humphry Clinker* (London: Oxford University Press, 1966), p. 93.
4. Rude, *Hanoverian London,* p. 73.
5. Smollett, *Humphry Clinker,* p. 92.
6. Quoted in Southworth, *Vauxhall Gardens,* p. 28.

3 *"Telling Fortunes in Coffee Grounds"* †

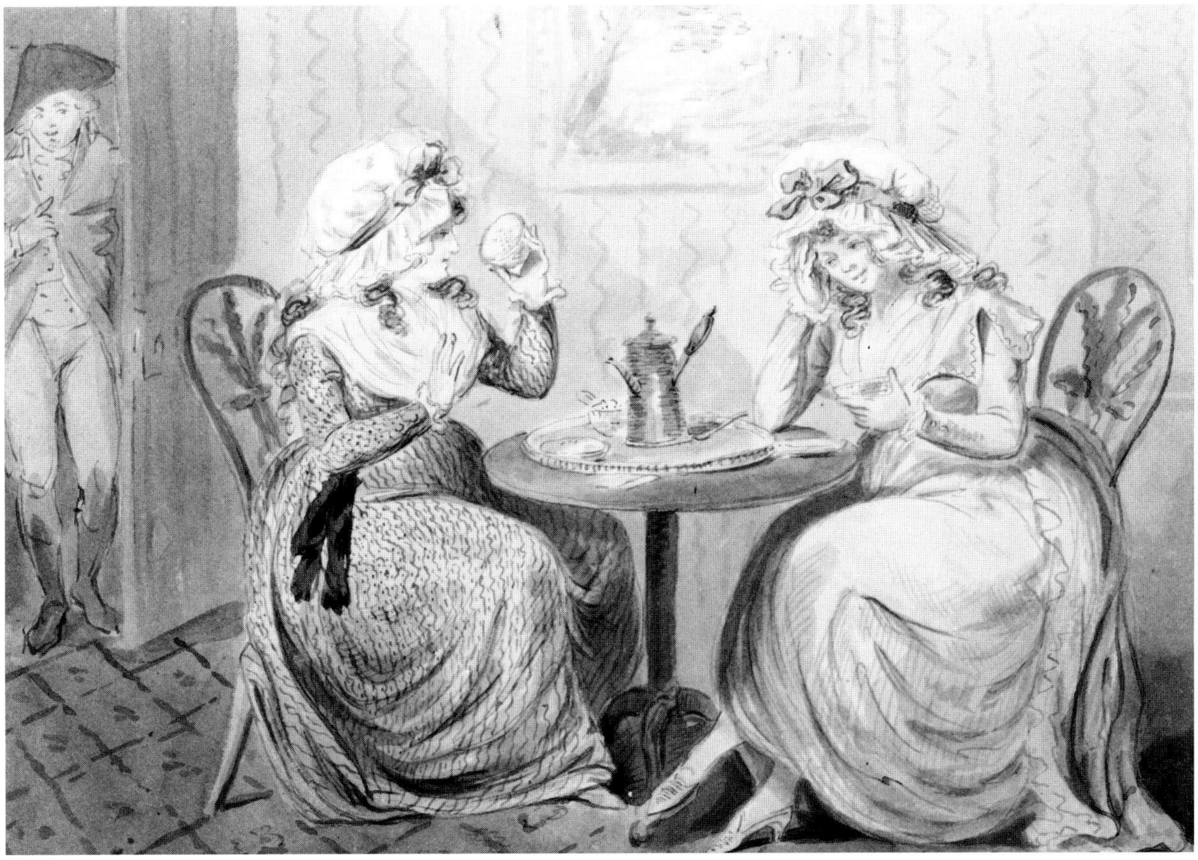

c. 1790
Pen and gray wash over pencil
7 x 8¾ inches (17.7 x 22.1 cm.)
Annotated verso: Telling Fortunes / I. Cruikshanks
Biblio: L & W, 57; Wark, 10

Although no print after this image has been located, a work of the same title is listed in the 1795 catalogue of Laurie & Whittle, among other images from 1790. This drawing is undoubtedly the model for that print.

Cruikshank used the subject of fortune-telling with coffee grounds in a pointed political satire called "Grounds of Fortune Telling or Princely Repast" (December 8, 1789). In that image, telling of fortunes was performed by an amateur. Here, while the satire is social rather than political, the two young women reading each other's futures are again clearly novices. The man entering the room is presumably the love interest of one of the ladies, perhaps the one on the left, who looks embarrassed and wistful. This image most likely was intended as a gentle satire on the diversions and superstitions of young ladies.

One of the most popular novels of the eighteenth century was Samuel Richardson's *Pamela* (1742), a moralistic tale of virtue rewarded, in which a beautiful young servant girl marries her master.[1] In Richardson's novel, Pamela visits a fortuneteller, who foresees the marriage to her master.

Although the fortune-teller in *Pamela* was a palm-reader, several other methods of divination were common at the time. In London, "wise women" engaged to foretell the amorous prospects of young ladies often resorted to reading coffee grounds. According to an eighteenth-century source, the belief was that "every cast of the cup is a picture of all one's life to come and every transaction and circumstance is delineated with the strictest certainty."[2]

Jennifer Katell

1. Robert Palfrey Utter and Gwendolyn Bridges Needham, *Pamela's Daughters* (New York: Macmillan Co., 1936), p. 7.
2. Quoted in Rosamund Bayne-Powell, *Eighteenth-Century London Life* (London: Butler and Tanner, Ltd., 1937), p. 251.

4 *A Fool and His Money's Soon Parted* †

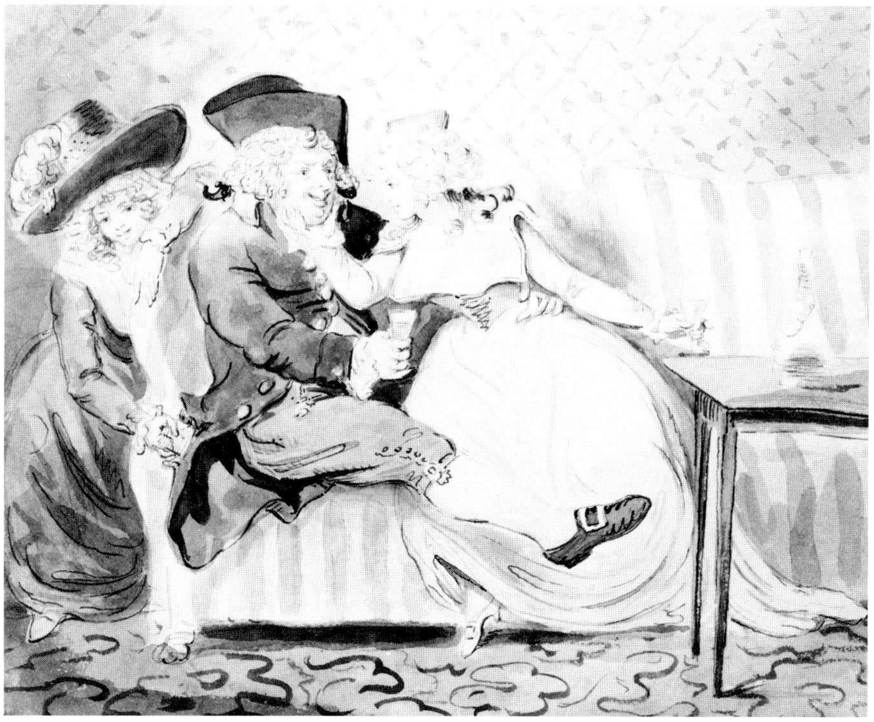

1790
Monochrome gray wash over pen
6 3/4 x 8 3/4 inches
(17 x 22.8 cm.)
Annotated verso: Love and Wine
Published: May 1, 1790, by Robert Sayer; below the title is engraved: The Old Booby half Muzzy to a Bagnio Reel'd / In hopes the sweet Kiss of delight to have seal'd / He sealed it ye Gods! Oh! to his Cost / His money was squander'd, & Pocket Book lost.
Biblio: L & W, 58; George, 7802; Krumbhaar, 385; Wark, 3
Impression: BM, LWL

The title is derived from a phrase coined in the seventeenth century.[1] Here it is used to describe the foolishness of an unsuspecting drunk whose pocket is being picked by one prostitute while he is entertained by another. Prostitution is a recurring subject of Cruikshank's satires in part because of its comic potential but also because it reflected the realities of Georgian England.[2] Prostitution was a fact of life; there was even a movement to legalize it. Some men argued that "prostitutes were necessary to protect respectable women from impropriety." They believed that it was desirable to sacrifice one part of womankind to preserve the other.[3] There were prostitutes, or courtesans, for every class in society: streetwalkers; those that operated out of brothels and coffee houses; and mistresses. Given the reference to a bagnio in the text, the location of this scene is presumably a brothel; however the decor of the room and the appearance of the courtesans suggest that the establishment is of a higher order.

The action depicted reflects specific attitudes held by Cruikshank and his contemporaries about women of this profession. Prostitutes were considered to be greedy and heartless. This view is conveyed by Cruikshank again in *Dividing the Spoils* (1796), a work dealing with much the same theme.[4] According to E. J. Burford, "Prostitutes at this time were frequently pickpockets, quite apart from the stealing of valuables from drunken or beaten-up clients. Fanny Murray's *Memoirs* mention her meeting every Saturday at Shakespeare's Head at the 'Whores' Club' . . . to divide the spoils."[5]

Danna Freedy

1. The phrase was first used by George Buchanan, tutor to James VI of Scotland, after winning a bet with a courtier over who could make the coarser verse; see Kate Louise Roberts, ed., *Hoyt's New Encyclopedia of Practical Quotations* (New York: Funk and Wagnalls, 1922), p. 523.
2. For other examples see *New Boots* (8) and *None But the Brave Deserves the Fair* (6).
3. Jacqueline Pearson, *The Prostituted Muse: Images of Women and Women Dramatists, 1642-1737* (New York: St. Martin's Press, 1988), p. 93.
4. Four prostitutes, gathered around a table laden with money and valuables, argue over the distribution of the objects collected. Other artists treated similar subjects, including John Collett in *Deceiptful Kisses of Pretty Plunderers*.
5. Burford, *Wits, Wantons, and Wenchers, London's Low Life: Covent Garden in the Eighteenth Century* (London: Robert Hale, 1986), p. 226. Fanny Murray (1729-78) was an infamous Covent Garden prostitute.

5 *Folly of an Old Man Marrying a Young Wife* †

1790
Pen and gray wash over pencil
7 x 8¾ inches
(18 x 22.2 cm.)
Inscribed recto:
I. Cruikshanks
Annotated verso: A Curtain Lecture
Published:
May 1, 1790, by Robert Sayer
Biblio: L & W, 59; George, 8407; Krumbhaar, 384; Wark, 9
Impression:
BM, LWL

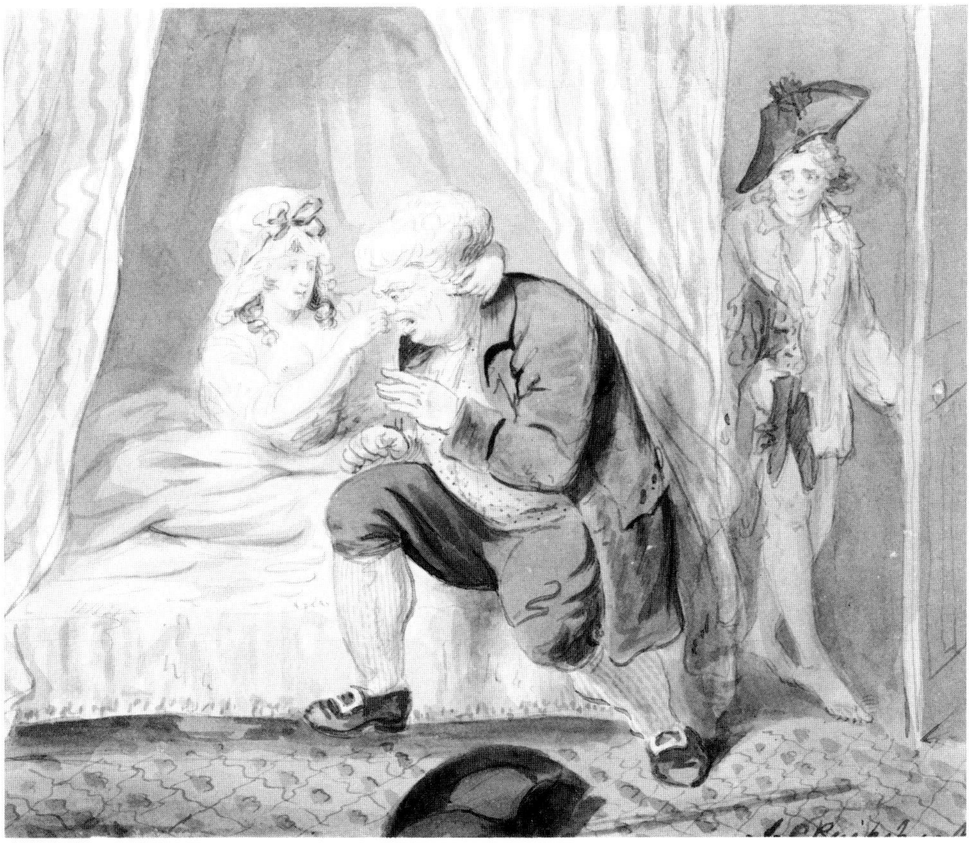

Cuckoldry and infidelity had been a source of humor in England since the Middle Ages. While a man's transgressions were expected, the infidelity of a wife undermined a man's masculinity, raising doubts about his ability to satisfy a woman. A man whose wife was known to be unfaithful became the laughing stock of the town and was even considered unfit to hold public office.[1]

Reports of the trials of adultery cases made for popular reading in the eighteenth century; they were the tabloid magazines of their day. The publication of such reports began as early as 1647, and by the 1770s this genre of literature was fully developed, as demonstrated by seven volumes entitled *Trials of Adultery or History of Divorce*.[2] Toward the end of the following decade, such books were illustrated by prints. While it is unlikely that this particular illustration had a direct link to trial reports, the popularity of these publications attests to the fascination with such subject matter. In this scene, the husband has just returned home unexpectedly to find his wife half-dressed in bed. Having barely managed to hide himself, her soldier lover has not had time to put on his pants and shoes. The wife distracts her husband by tweaking his nose and pinching his ear while her lover escapes.

Depictions of cuckolds were ubiquitous in Georgian art, on stage as well as in prints. In *Marriage a la Mode,* William Hogarth portrayed an unfaithful wife, mixing a moral with humor. Similar subjects were also treated by Cruikshank's contemporary, Thomas Rowlandson. Like Rowlandson, Cruikshank focused on the ribald humor of the event rather than on its moral implications.

Danna Freedy

1. Lawrence Stone, *The Family, Sex, and Marriage in England, 1500-1800* (New York: Harper and Row, 1977), pp. 503-4.
2. Peter Wagner, "Pornography in the Courtroom: Trial Reports About Cases of Sexual Delinquencies as a Genre of Eighteenth Century Erotica," in Paul-Gabriel Boucé, ed., *Sexuality in Eighteenth-Century Britain* (Totowa: Manchester University Press, 1982), pp. 128-29.

6 *None But the Brave Deserves the Fair* †

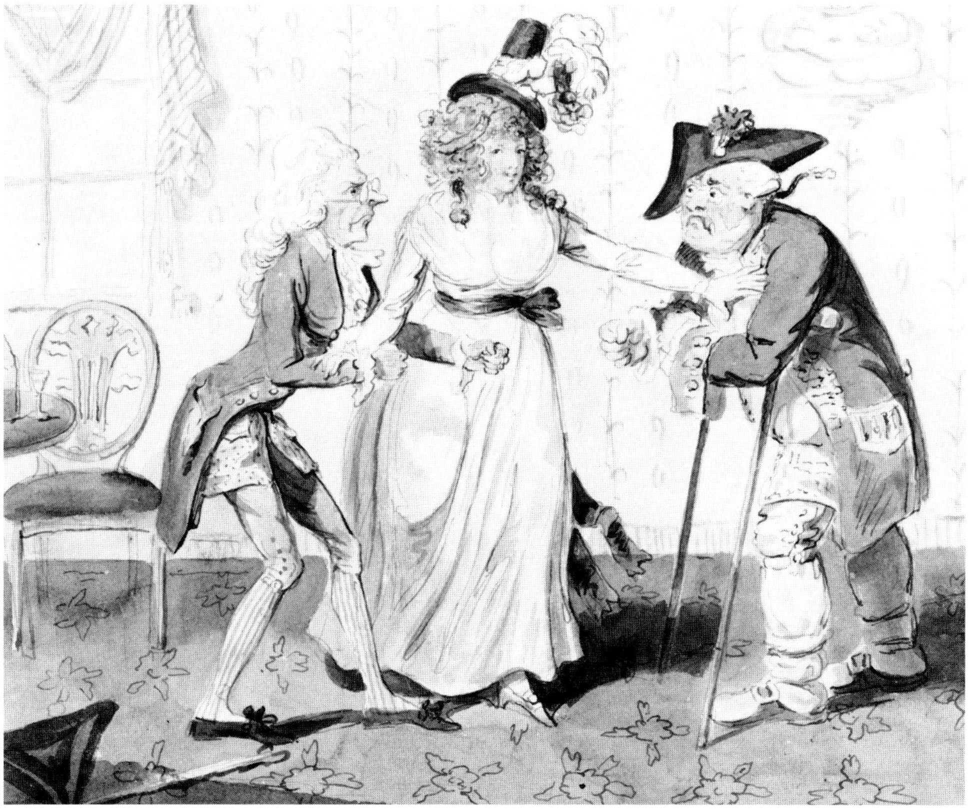

1790
Pen and watercolor over pencil
7 x 8 1/2 inches
(18 x 21.7 cm.)
Annotated verso: None but the Brave / Deserves the Fair / I. Cruikshanks
Published: May 1, 1790, by Robert Sayer
Biblio:
L & W, 60;
George, 7803;
Krumbhaar, 832;
Wark, 4
Impression:
BM, LWL, WMC

The title is taken from John Dryden's ode "Alexander's Feast" (1697); however, it had become a common expression by Cruikshank's time.[1] Used here, these words add a humorous note to the comical portrayal of a courtesan being fought over by two old gentlemen. The representation of a woman with outstretched arms holding apart her warring admirers is a clear reference to Satan, Sin, and Death from Milton's *Paradise Lost,* a subject frequently depicted by Cruikshank's contemporaries, including William Hogarth, Thomas Rowlandson, Henry Fuseli, and William Blake. Satan, on his way to undertake the temptation of Adam and Eve, is stopped by Death. They charge toward each other but are separated by Sin, represented as a woman with snake-like legs. Between 1790 and 1810, at least fifteen illustrated editions of *Paradise Lost* were published.[2] Cruikshank's audience would have immediately made the visual connection between his composition and depictions of Satan, Sin, and Death. In the watercolor, the artist reinforced the association by coloring the coat of the man on the left red for Satan and that of the man on the right black for Death.[3] The prostitute in the center is obviously equated with sin.

Old men visiting prostitutes was a common subject for satire because of the belief that they were lacking in virility. The anonymous author of *The Midnight Spy* observed: "As she is young and handsome, she is the flame of those old dotards who's *[sic]* desires outlive their ability and who always pay for what they cannot do."[4] The visual and literary references of this work heighten the humor of a conventional comic subject.

Danna Freedy

1. H. L. Mencken, ed., *A Dictionary of Quotations on Historic Principles* (New York: Alfred A. Knopf, 1942), p. 124.
2. Robert R. Wark, *Ten British Pictures, 1740-1840* (San Marino, Calif.: Huntington Library, 1972), pp. 79-80.
3. In the impression of the print at WML, the color association is not maintained: the black coat is changed to blue.
4. *The Midnight Spy, or A View to the Transactions of London and Westminster from Ten in the Evening till Five in the Morning* (London: Printed for J. Cook at Shakespeare's Head, 1756), p. 111.

7 The Husband Highly Delighted with His Supposed Fruits †

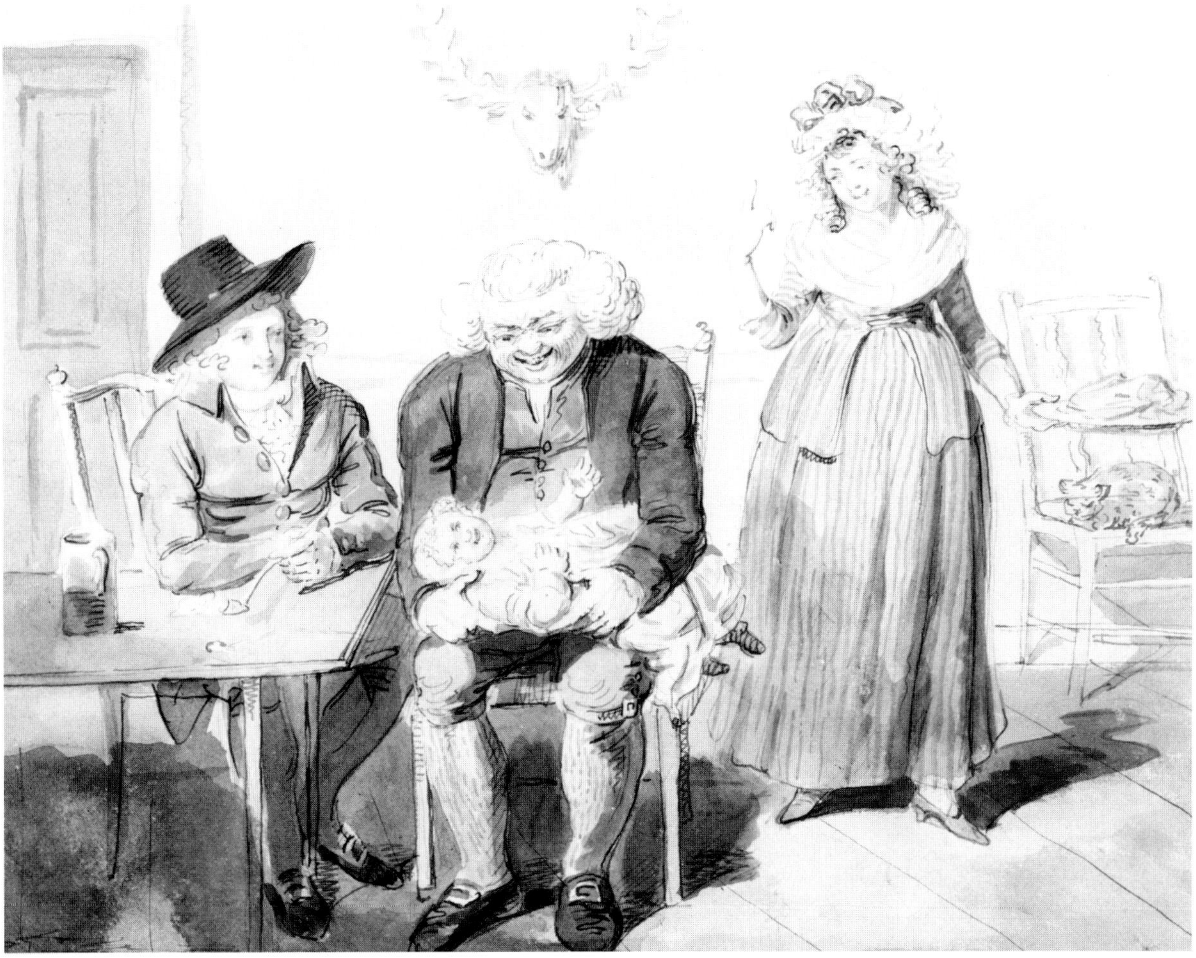

1790
Pen and gray wash over pencil
7 x 8⅞ inches (18 x 20 cm.)
Annotated verso: The Husband delighted with his supposed fruits / I. Cruikshanks
Published: May 1, 1790, by Robert Sayer
Biblio: L & W, 61; George, 7804; Wark, 5
Impression: BM, LWL

The situation depicted here is explained by the title as well as by visual clues (when this composition was made into a print, it was reversed). The old man holding the child is positioned directly underneath the deer's head mounted on the wall. His young wife points to the horned animal to indicate that her husband is a cuckold, that is, that she has been unfaithful to him. The younger man is presumably the young wife's lover and the real father of the baby. The joke is of course on the old man, who innocently dotes on his supposed offspring.

Cruikshank produced several images in which he poked fun at cuckolds, a subject familiar in the literature of the period.[1] In Cruikshank's portrayals, the men are often depicted as significantly older than their young wives, and he obviously believed them unfaithful to their husbands. Generally these marriages were arranged, or the young women may have married for money with no love involved. The results could be disastrous. Certainly such unions offered satirists, artists, and writers innumerable opportunities.

Danna Freedy

1. For other examples see *Folly of an Old Man Marrying a Young Wife* (5), *A Matrimonial Puzzle* (72), *A Bone to Pick* (74), and *Robin & Sue* (97).

8 *"New Boots"* †

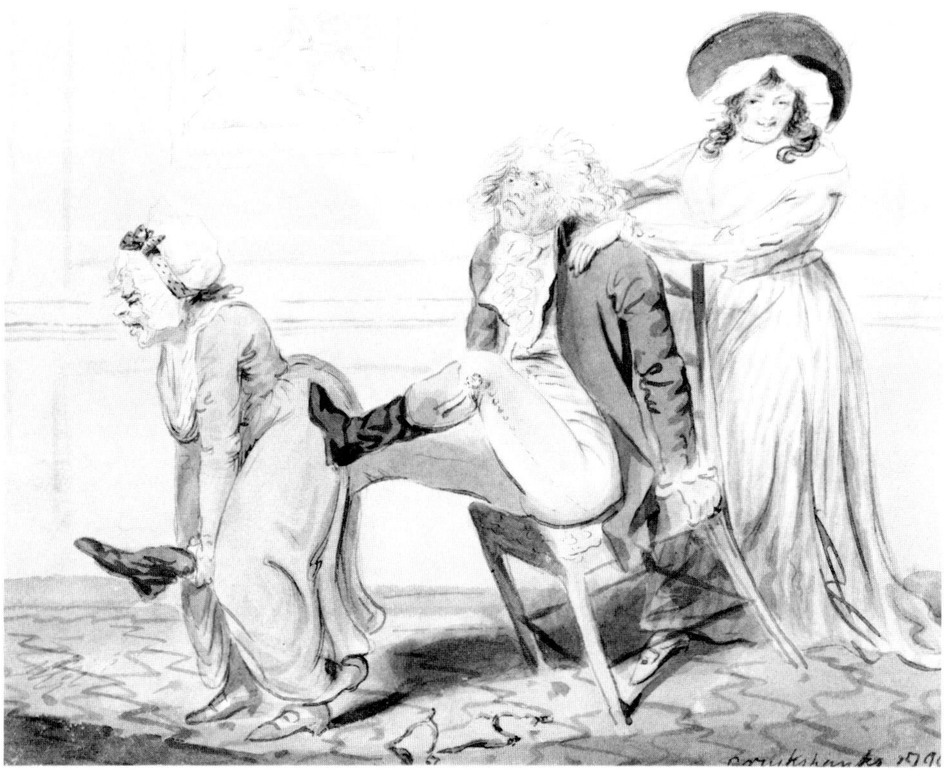

1790
Pen and gray wash over pencil with touches of color
7 x 8⁷/₈ inches (18 x 25 cm.)
Inscribed recto: Cruikshanks 1790
Annotated verso: Tight Boots / I. Cruikshanks
Biblio: L & W, 62 (?), Wark, 2

Although no print after this watercolor has been located, Robert Wark has suggested that it may be the design for *New Boots or the Old Buck in Distress,* listed by Laurie & Whittle in the 1795 catalogue. Certainly that title seems to describe this scene, in which a man is being helped to remove his obviously tight, new boots. The young woman on the right is undoubtedly a courtesan, while the old woman in the front is probably her maid.

The painting or print of a racehorse and jockey on the wall in the background suggests a connection between what is happening in the scene and horse racing, a sport closely identified with Georgian England.[1] During the racing season, many prostitutes came to London and the surrounding areas. There were even directories published (e.g., *Harris' List of Covent Garden Ladies*), in which the names and services of the women appeared along with their fees. According to these listings, many came to the city just for the season.[2] Given the drinking and celebration associated with racing, it is not surprising that women were looked to as well for entertainment.

The anonymous author of *The Midnight Spy* told a story about a man wearing boots in a "Night House": "He put on those boots, to impose on his family the pretense of going out of town; but this [the brothel] is the extent of his journey and if he rides, it will not be a quadrupede."[3] Cruikshank carries the story one step further. In this watercolor, the joke revolves around the man's frustration at being unable to remove his boots in preparation for a sexual encounter. The old woman calls to mind a jockey on a race horse.

The seductive glance of the prostitute invites the viewer to participate in the fun. The contrast between the beauty of youth and the ugliness of old age was a convention used by satirists, such as Cruikshank's contemporary Thomas Rowlandson, to suggest the ravages of time. The male audience for whom this work was intended would have enjoyed the allusions and innuendos of the composition.

Danna Freedy

1. J. H. Plumb, *Georgian Delights* (Boston: Little, Brown, and Co., 1978), p. 112.
2. Vern and Bonnie Bullough, *Prostitution: An Illustrated Social History* (New York: Crown Publishers, Inc., 1978), p. 162.
3. *The Midnight Spy,* p. 111.

9 *The Rustics Alarm'd at the Appearance of a London Buck* †

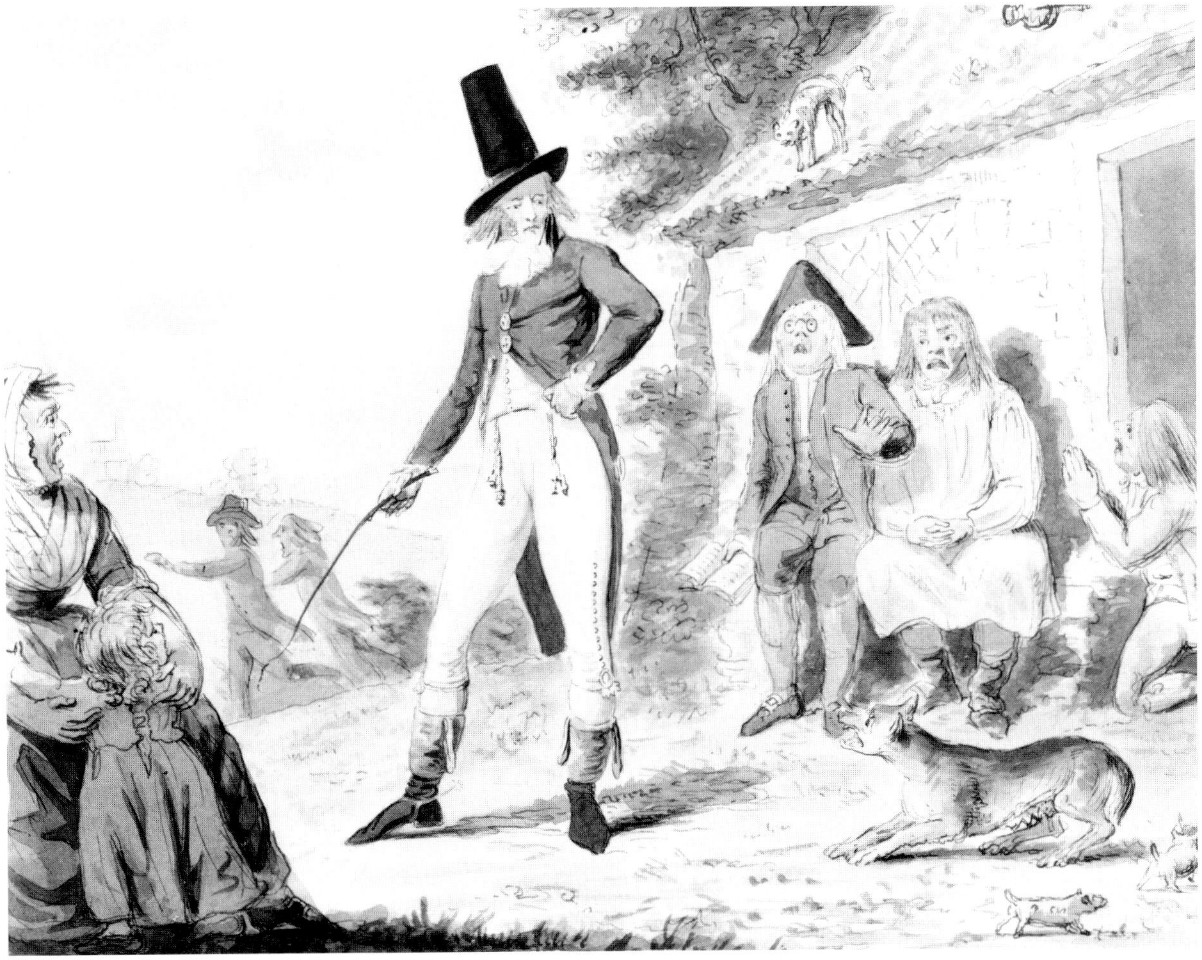

1790
Pen and watercolor over pencil
6 7/8 x 8 3/4 inches (17.5 x 22.2 cm.)
Annotated verso: The London Buck / I. Cruikshank
Published: July 27, 1790, by Robert Sayer
Biblio: L & W, 63; George, 7805; Krumbhaar, 1037; Wark, 6
Impression: BM, LWL

The word *buck*, meaning "dandy," is derived from *buckram*, a heavily sized fabric used to stiffen clothing in preparation for wear.[1] The young man in this humorous image is dressed in the most fashionable clothing from the year 1790. Here one can see the shift in fashion from lace and bows to more understated riding attire. He wears a tall round hat, a riding jacket, fob ribbons, high-waisted pantaloons, and French top boots with straps.

Cruikshank mocks the man further by portraying the country people as fearful of this strangely dressed figure. The young man seems quite pleased with himself as he frowns at the snarling bitch with pups. Even the cat on the roof is afraid. Cruikshank has portrayed the country people as plain in dress and homely in appearance, and the buck as a handsome man whose pretensions are exaggerated by his elongated form, which dominates the setting. Frightened of him, the country folk draw back in terror, pray, and run for their lives.[2]

Kathleen Kelly

1. Albert M. Hyamson, *The Dictionary of English Phrases* (London: George Routledge and Sons, 1922), p. 65.
2. Cruikshank took up this subject again in plate 7 of his illustrations for G. M. Woodward's *Eccentric Excursions* (London: Allen and West, 1796).

10 *Studying Politics, Or the Bon Companions* †

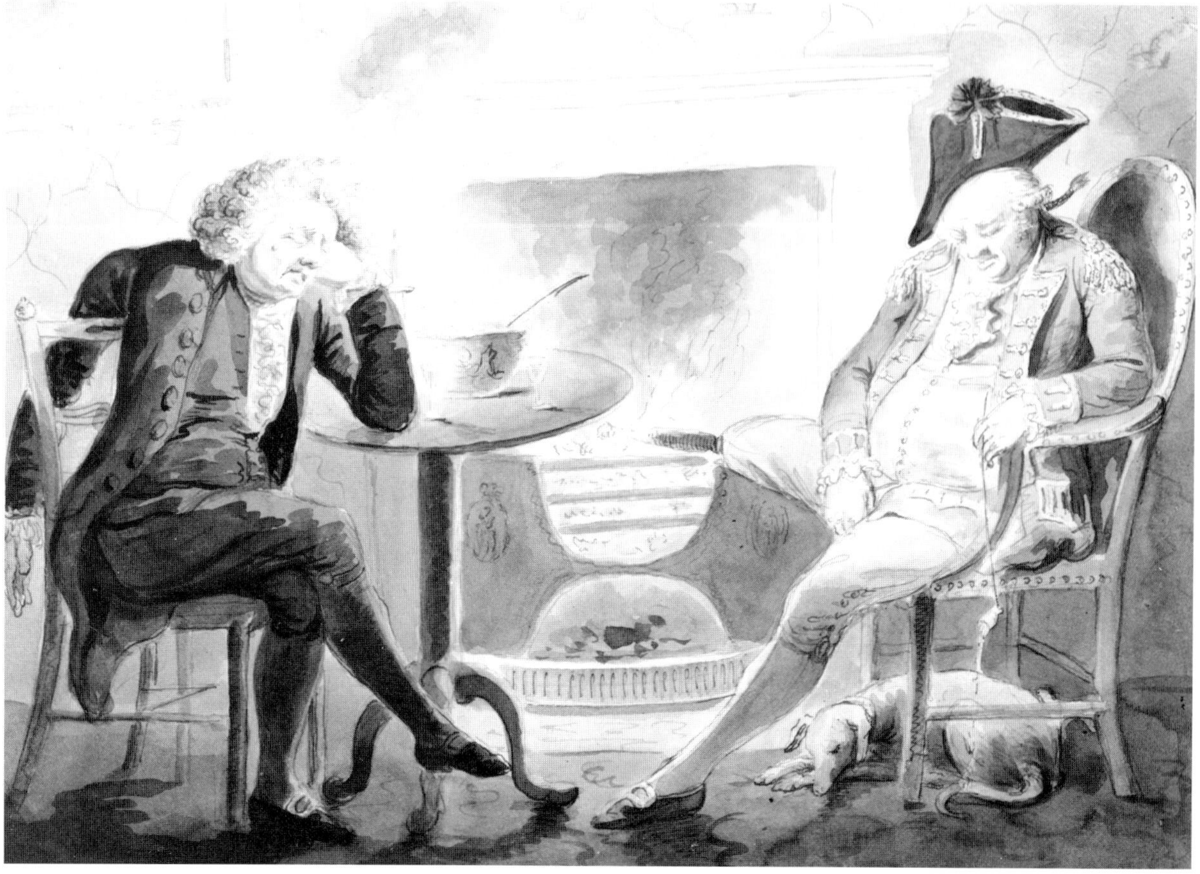

1790
Pen and monochrome gray wash over pencil
$6\frac{11}{16}$ x $8\frac{15}{16}$ inches (17 x 22.7 cm.)
Inscribed recto: Plan of London before the fire in 1666
Annotated verso: Flaming Politicians / I. Cruikshanks
Published: September 15, 1790, by Robert Sayer
Biblio: L & W, 65; George, 7806; Wark, 7
Impression: BM, LWL

These men are probably relaxing in their club. Drinking was the main order of business at such establishments, and thinking was usually deferred until a more convenient season.[1]

Overcome by alcohol from the punch, originally an Indian drink which by the eighteenth century had become part of everyday British life,[2] the gentleman on the left, who rests his head on his hand, is unaware that the candle's flame is singeing his wig. Sharing a similar drunken and incendiary fate, his companion, in military attire, inattentively supports his wooden leg on the fire grate. His relaxed hand causes his pipe to slip and spill hot ashes on the dog sleeping under his chair.

In the upper right corner a framed print of London is depicted, which gives the comic thrust to the image. It alludes to London before the Great Fire of 1666, which broke out in a baker's shop in the dead of night and, over a five-day period, devastated the city. While this reference does not appear in the final print, Cruikshank may well have created this image, published near the anniversary of the Great Fire, in part as a reminder of that catastrophe. Certainly the insignificance of the minor fires that will soon hurry these slumbering drunkards to their feet is being contrasted with the historic event of more than a century before. These "Bon Companions," who gathered to converse in an atmosphere of conviviality, are sleeping instead. Their imminent fates smolder before our eyes.

Tim D. Wright

1. John Timbs, *Club Life in London* (London: Richard Bentley, 1866), p. 22.
2. Louis C. Jones, *The Clubs of the Georgian Rakes* (New York: Columbia University Press, 1942), p. 5.

11 *A Sparring Match*

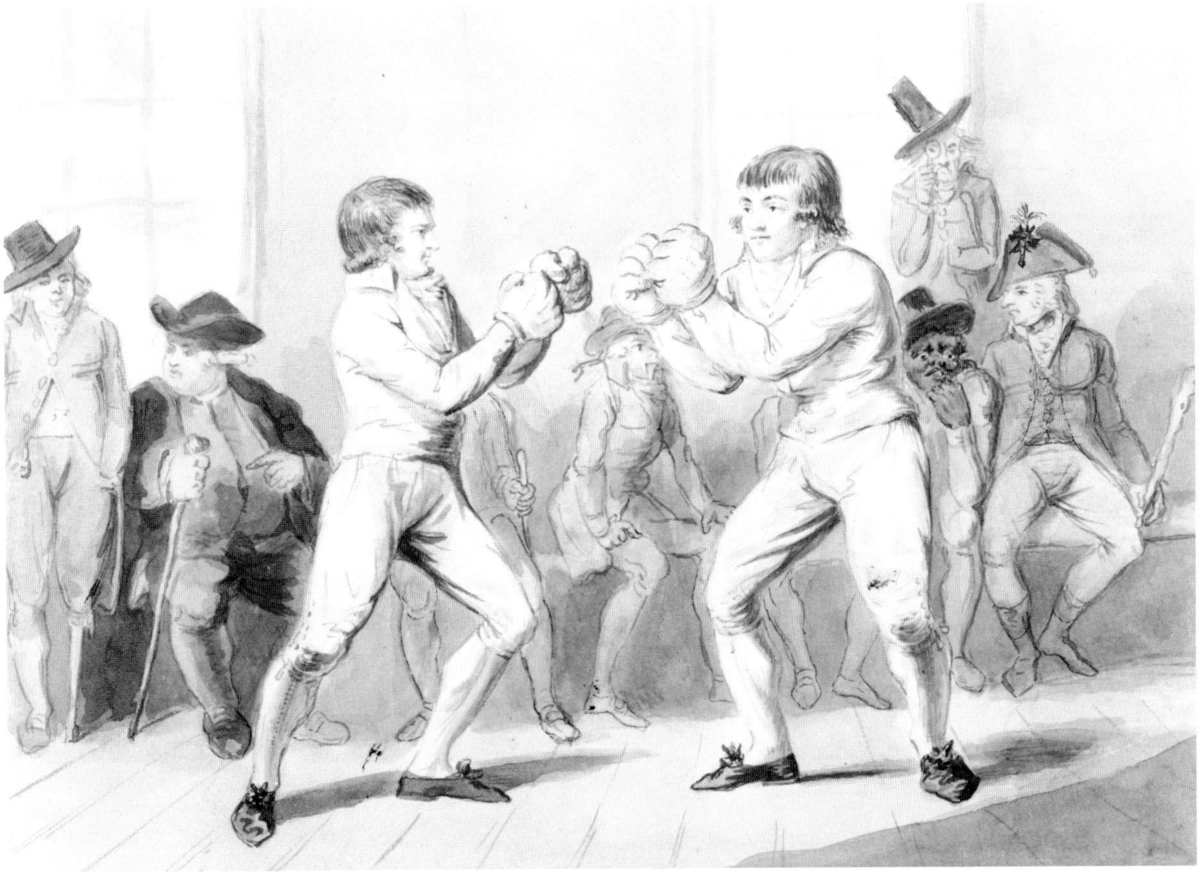

1790
Pen and gray wash over pencil
7 x 8¾ inches (17.8 x 22.2 cm.)
Annotated verso: A Sparring Match / I. Cruikshanks
Published: September 15, 1790, by Robert Sayer
Biblio: L & W, 66; George, 7807; Wark, 8
Impression: BM

The support that the Prince of Wales and his brother the Duke of Cumberland gave to prize-fighting in the 1780s transformed its reputation. Once considered a vulgar activity, it was now thought suitable for gentlemen. Thanks to fighters like "The Jew Mendoza," boxing became more civilized; rules were established and gloves were introduced.[1] Tours and sparring exhibitions popularized the sport and attracted individuals of many different backgrounds.

Boxing began to draw a large number of fashionable young men interested in exercise as well as in a change from lounging in clubs or card-rooms. Gentlemen began to spend more time hunting and driving, as well as boxing. It even became fashionable to dress in the manner of their grooms. Certain establishments offered instruction in boxing, such as John Jackson's at 13 Bond Street, or Fives Court in St. Martin's Street.[2] Well-known professionals and teachers gave exhibitions to audiences, who paid three shillings apiece.

In this drawing Cruikshank depicts two young athletes wearing boxing gloves and short jackets with high collars practicing what had come to be known as "the art of self-defense." The fact that they are wearing shirts and jackets indicates that this is a match for amateurs and not a professional one. Behind them, a group of men, clearly heterogeneous in social class, converse or watch activities taking place elsewhere within the club.

Kathleen Kelly

1. William B. Boulton, *The Amusements of Old London*, 2 vols. (London: John C. Nimmo, 1901), 2:97.
2. Ibid., p. 100.

 Poor Snip and Family Frightened by a Thunder Storm †

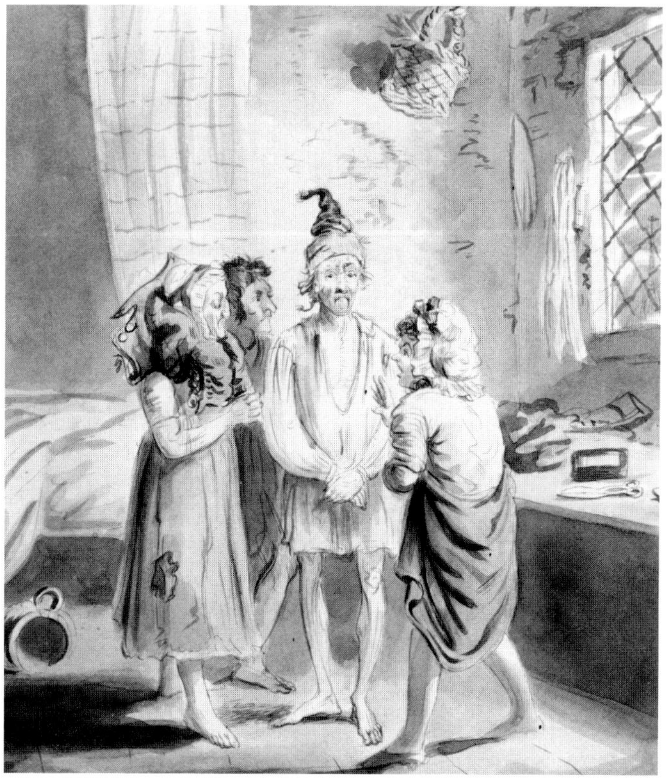

c. 1791 (?)
Pen and gray wash over pencil
8 3/8 x 6 7/8 inches (21.6 x 17.6 cm.)
Annotated verso: Poor Snip and Family in a Thunderstorm / I. Cruikshanks
Published: July 30, 1798, by Laurie & Whittle (67)
Biblio: Krumbhaar, A.78; Wark, 33
Impression: WMC

A major factor in shaping the perception of nature in the latter part of the eighteenth century was Edmund Burke's treatise on the sublime and the beautiful, published in 1757. Paintings with sublime themes, exploring the power of nature, became commonplace. One of Burke's observations was that light could be sublime, either by its magnificence or by horror; darkness even more so.[1] This night scene of four people illuminated by lightning can be seen in part as Cuikshank's response to contemporary aesthetic issues.

Snip, a tailor, as implied by his name and confirmed by the large scissors on the window sill,[2] is centrally placed in the composition. Positioned frontally, he stares out at the viewer with hands crossed. The rest of the family encircle him, casting shadows. Their faces are presented in profile, with the young man's face turned to almost a three-quarter view. Mrs. Snip, with the breeches around her neck representing the only comfort her husband can provide, has closed her eyes and folded her hands in prayer. Both son and daughter, although adults, beseech the bare-legged Snip for protection: the young woman, terror expressed through her raised hand and open mouth, seeks comfort that is obviously not forthcoming. "No passion," writes Burke, "so effectually robs the mind of all its powers of acting and reasoning as fear."[3] The father's weak state is further emphasized by his thin legs, one with a gnarled knee. Even his nightcap, which in defiance of gravity stands almost straight up, seems to express his fear.

The benighted Snip—a representative of the lower class—is also a passive touchstone for Romantic perceptions of nature, here being lampooned by Cruikshank. Despite the flash of lightning, Snip finds himself unable either to seek ecstasy in nature's sublimity or to resist heroically its dreadful powers. Snip's own light has yet to be turned on.

Presumably the subject was a popular one since the print was published at least twice. The drawing itself, to judge from the style and the monochromatic technique, was likely executed in 1791.[4] Moreover, in Laurie & Whittle's catalogue of 1795, it is listed with other works by Cruikshank issued in 1791. However, the impression at the Widener Collection bears a date of 1798, suggesting it was probably reissued in that year.

Maria L. Brendel

1. Edmund Burke, *A Philosophical Enquiry into the Origin of our Ideas of the Sublime and Beautiful* (London: Dodsley, 1757), pp. 41-42, 62.
2. Hyamson, *A Dictionary of English Phrases*, p. 321.
3. Burke, *The Sublime and Beautiful*, p. 42.
4. Wark, *"Drawings for Drolls,"* p. 16.

13 *The Recruiting Serjeant Taken In, Or All Fair Above Board* †

1791
Pen and gray wash over pencil
6¾ x 8¾ inches (17.2 x 22.1 cm.)
Verso: a slight pencil sketch of the same subject
Annotated verso: The Recruiting Sergeant / I. Cruikshanks
Published: March 10, 1791, by Robert Sayer
Biblio: L & W, 70; George, 8034; Wark, 11
Impression: BM, LWL

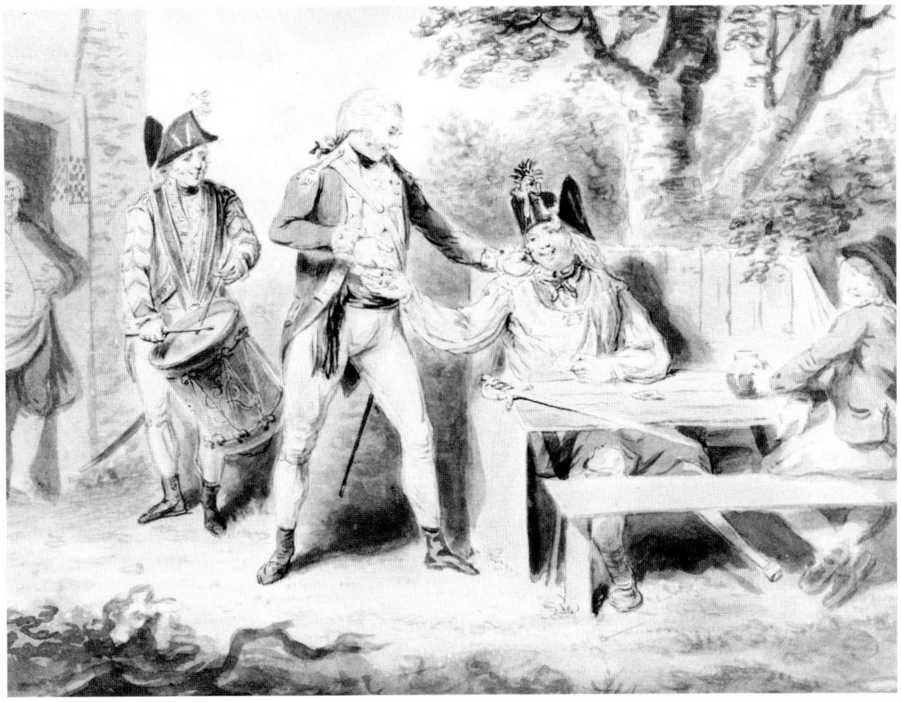

During the eighteenth century, England was at war more than it was at peace. Although 1791 saw a brief respite, the efforts of recruiting sergeants to trick naive countrymen into joining the army—typically through intoxication or promises of a better life— never ceased. Through stories and plays such as *The Recruiting Sergeant* by Isaac Bickerstaffe, performed repeatedly from 1706 to the end of the century, and *The Recruiting Officer* by George Farquhar, the *modus operandi* of the military recruiters became a familiar one. As in Farquhar's comedy, a sergeant would arrive in the center of town and announce: "If any prentices have severe masters; any children have undutiful parents; any servants have too little wages; or any husband too much wife: let them repair to the noble Sergeant."[1]

In Cruikshank's drawing, we are privy to such a comic drama. The recruiting sergeant stands, stage center, dropping coins into the hand of a new recruit—a countryman—who also dons the sergeant's hat with apparent enthusiasm. The sergeant, who attempts to draw the new recruit in further by gently touching the side of his face, might well be uttering at the same time, "the finest life that goes, free quarter's everywhere, wenches, girls love the red coats."[2] To the left is an infantry drummer, whose playing draws attention to the recruiter's presence.

To the far right sits the commentator on this farce. Looking at the viewer, he invites us to share in the joke: this time it is the recruit, with his wooden leg hidden from the sergeant's view by the table, who is hustling the sergeant. The viewer's eye is led to the peg leg by the tip of the sergeant's sword. Most likely familiar with his rustic patron, the innkeeper standing to the far left heartily enjoys the ruse. The recruiting sergeant is not so clever as he imagines.

Tim D. Wright

1. G. Farquhar, *The Recruiting Officer* (London: Ernest Benn, Ltd., 1977), p. 11.
2. Ibid., p. 14.

The Knowing Crops

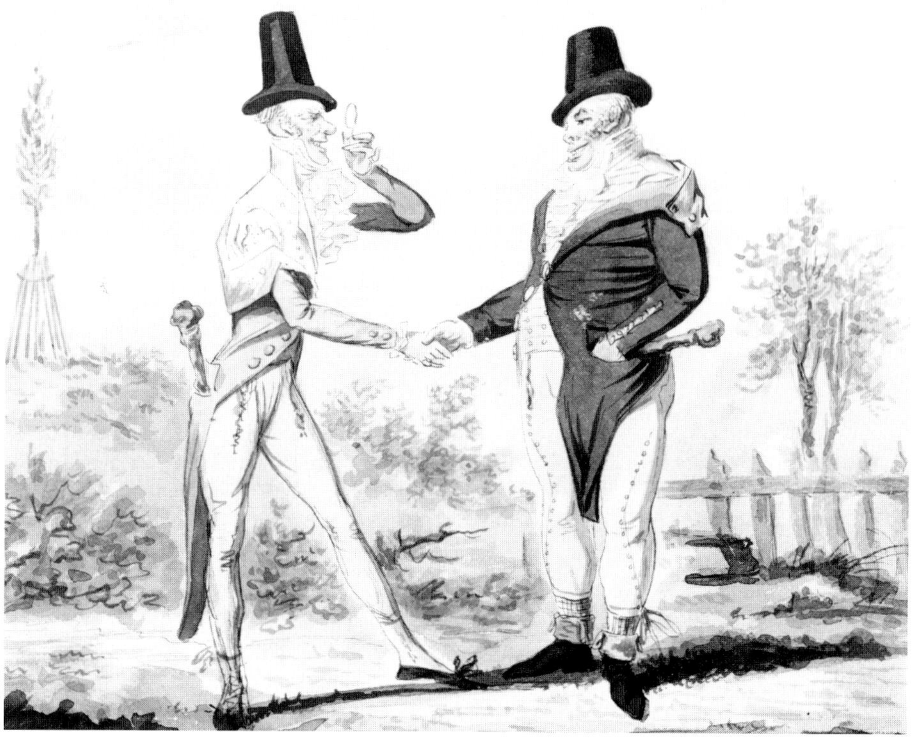

179[1?]
Pen and gray wash with watercolor over pencil
7 x 8⅝ inches (17.8 x 22 cm.)
Annotated verso: The Knowing Crops / I. Cruikshanks
Published: May 12, 179[4?], by Laurie & Whittle (72); below the image is engraved: Ha! Jack is it you. How are you dam-me.
Biblio: Wark, 23
Impression: LWL

Here Cruikshank satirizes men who have been carried away by the new fashions of the day. The figures are dressed quite formally for a stroll in the park. Both wear tall round hats, ruffled shirts, fashionable coats, and pantaloons. Cruikshank pokes fun at the overweight figure on the right, who wears tight breeches with buttons that go all the way up his legs and plaid socks that show above his short boots. The figure on the left is striking the affected pose one sees again and again in Cruikshank's representations of devotees of fashion.[1] Both figures have all of the accoutrements (and then some) of the fashionable men of the time, including fob ribbons and clubs.

The title is a play on the word *crop,* used of bucks because of their closely cropped hair, which both men have. According to the *Times* of 1795, "a club was formed called the Crop-Club, every member of which was obliged to have his head cropped . . . for the purpose of evading the tax on powdered heads."[2] *Crop* also, of course, could mean new growth or harvest.[3] In this case the word may have been an allusion to the nouveau riche, a merchant class whose numbers were increasing and who called attention to their new wealth with excessively stylish dress like that depicted here. Cruikshank's use of the word *crop* then would have been directed at both the new fashions and at the men who were reaping the benefit from the increased trade and economic boom. The young trees in the background reinforce this interpretation.

The publication date of this image is uncertain. Although Wark suggested it was issued on or about May 12, 1794, E. B. Krumbhaar included in his catalogue raisonné of the work of Isaac Cruikshank a representation of a single "crop" looking through a quizzing glass, dated September 1791.[4] In the Laurie & Whittle catalogue of 1795 the print after this image appears among works from mid-1791 to early 1792. It seems likely, therefore, that this piece was produced earlier in Cruikshank's career and reissued by Laurie & Whittle in 1994. A date of 1791 is here proposed.

Kathleen Kelly

1. See, for example, *Great Plenty and Little Waste* (36).
2. C. Willett Cunnington and Phyllis Cunnington, *Handbook of English Costume in the Eighteenth Century* (London: Faber and Faber, Ltd., 1957), p. 247.
3. Samuel Johnson and John Walker, *The People's Pronouncing and Defining Dictionary* (Philadelphia: Wm. T. Ames, 1879), p. 270.
4. E. B. Krumbhaar, *Isaac Cruikshank: A Catalogue Raisonné with a Sketch of his Life and Work* (Philadelphia: University of Pennsylvania Press, 1966), p. 52 (219). Krumbhaar lists a print of a related subject, also dated 1791 (220).

15 *The Absent Man* †

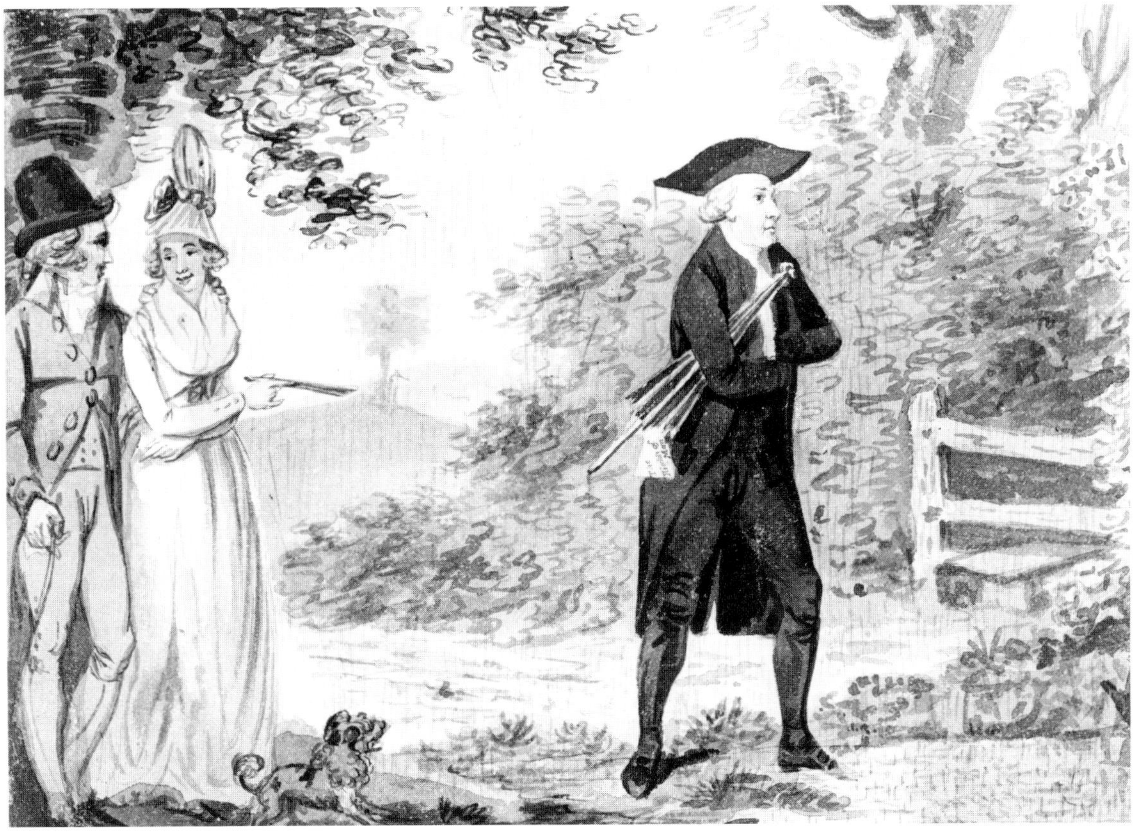

1791
Pen and gray wash over pencil
6 7/8 x 9 1/4 inches (17.7 x 23.4 cm.)
Annotated verso: The Misanthrope / I. Cruikshanks / 1791
Published: January 10, 1792, by Robert Sayer
Biblio: L & W, 75; George, 8212; Wark, 12
Impression: BM, LWL

A fashionably dressed young couple stands on the left under a tree, protecting themselves from the rain, while their little dog barks at a man on the right dressed in black. They look at each other with smiles on their faces as the woman points with her fan to the solitary figure, who holds an umbrella under his arm despite the downpour. A paper inscribed "The Rights of Man" projects from his pocket. He is so absorbed in his thoughts that he is oblivious to the rain and to the puddle in which he is standing.

The drawing is a topical satire on the supporters of the French Revolution. *The Rights of Man* (1791) was authored by the Englishman Thomas Paine, a political writer and an influential voice for the American cause during the Revolutionary War.[1] Penned in response to the French Revolution, the book had a great impact on Britain's urban working class. In it, Paine expounded on the rights of men in a free society.

Here Cruikshank expresses his support of the sentiments of the ruling class, then customarily anti-revolutionary.[2] The composition underscores the differences between the couple on the left and the individual on the right. By taking refuge under the tree, the fashionable pair show that they are aware of their surroundings, a metaphor for their practicality and knowledge of the political situation. However, the reader of *The Rights of Man* is clearly impractical and oblivious to life around him; he is lacking minimal "common sense," the title of another work by Paine written in support of the American cause.

Mar Martinez-Perez

1. James Walvin, *English Urban Life, 1776-1851* (London: Hutchinson and Co., 1984), p. 95.
2. Thomas Wright, *Caricature History of the Georges* (London: Chatto and Windus, 1876), pp. 476-78.

16 *The Merry Thought*

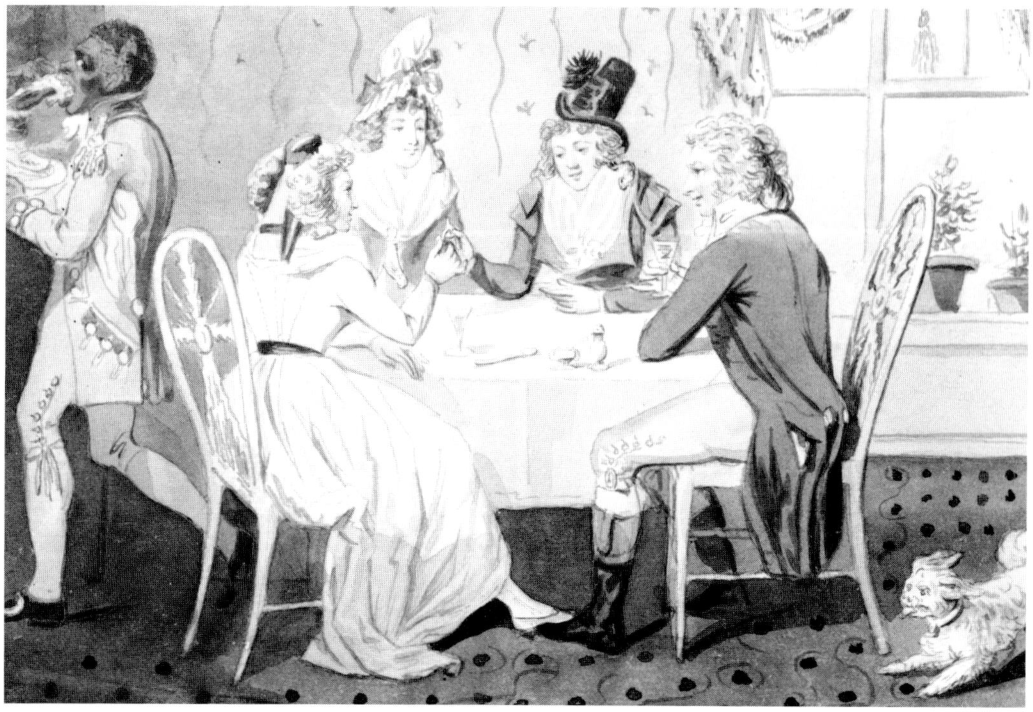

c. 1792
Pen and gray wash over pencil
6⅝ x 9 inches (16.9 x 23.0 cm.)
Annotated verso: The Merry Thought / I. Cruikshanks
Published: May 12, 1794, by Laurie & Whittle (78)
Biblio: Wark, 24
Impression: LWL

Following dinner, three women and a man engage in a little entertainment—breaking the wishbone. Before breaking the bone, each participant makes a wish that supposedly will be granted to the one with the larger half. The lady wearing the tall black hat focuses intently on the bone, while her opponent smiles guilefully. The gentleman exchanges glances with the lady on his left, whose foot seems to rest next to or on top of his. In the event of her victory, her "merry thought" may well involve her seemingly receptive male companion.

Black servants, like the one depicted here, were not uncommon in eighteenth-century London and, for the most part, they were sought after. Many masters and mistresses found them not only exotic but faithful as well as hard-working.[1] Others, however, believed blacks to be drunkards and lechers, with little sense of responsibility or loyalty,[2] and treated them with no more respect than they would a household pet.

Here, Cruikshank visually equates a servant and a dog by using them as balancing compositional elements, flanking the central action. The black servant on the left devours a plate of food he has just cleared from the table. As a footman, he was ranked beneath the steward and maid in the household hierarchy. This inferior status often resulted in having less to eat than the upper servants, who often managed to take food to their friends and family. Therefore, he was occasionally obliged to eat scraps from his master's or mistress's plate to supplement his meager meals.[3]

The style of this wash drawing suggests it may have been executed two years before its publication in 1794 by Laurie & Whittle. The print is listed with other works of that date in the 1795 catalogue. It is possible that the work was reissued by Laurie & Whittle after the firm took over from Robert Sayer, one of Cruikshank's publishers, who died in 1794.

Rhonda Howard

1. Bayne-Powell, *Eighteenth-Century London Life*, p. 327.
2. J. Jean Hecht, "Continental and Colonial Servants in Eighteenth-Century England," *Smith College Studies in History* (Northampton, Mass.: Department of History, Smith College, 1954), p. 43.
3. Ibid., p. 12.

17 *Point of Honour*†

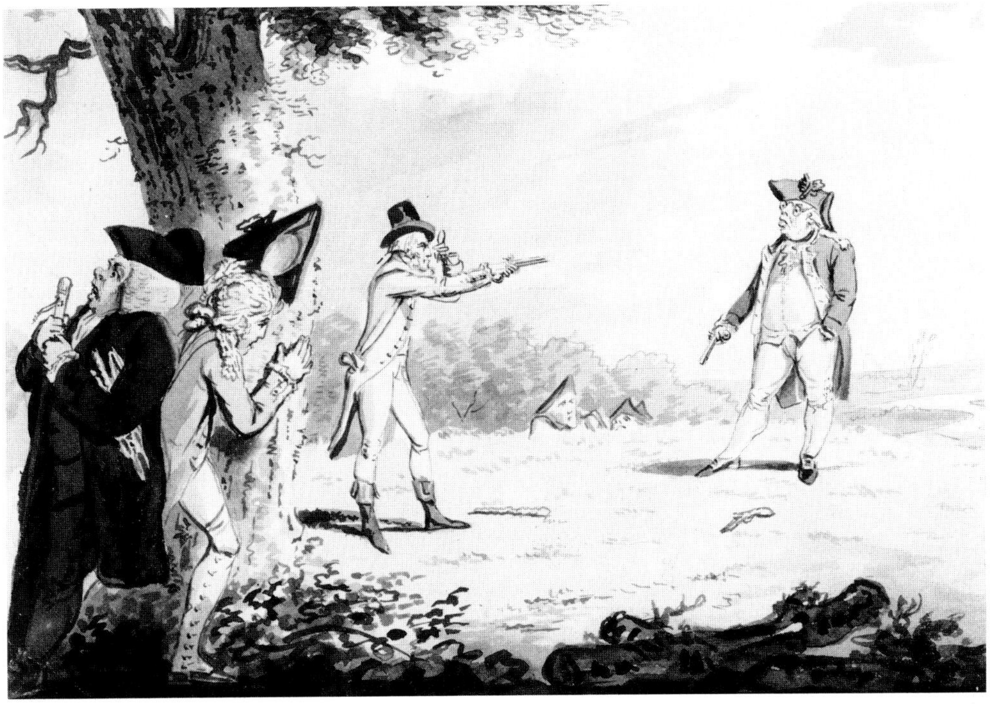

1792
Pen and gray wash over pencil
6⅝ x 8¾ inches (16.8 x 22.2 cm.)
Annotated verso: A Point of Honor / I. Cruikshanks
Published: July 10, 1792, by Robert Sayer
Biblio: L & W, 82; George, 8214; Wark, 13
Impression: BM, LWL

Dueling was an act originally intended to validate honor and demonstrate courage.[1] In this case, neither participant displays valor, and the humor lies in the absurdity of the confrontation. The man to the left, who brings undue attention to himself by his manner of dress and the use of an eyeglass to improve his aim, is a dandy. Although he shoots with his right hand, his body remains in a frontal position, exposing his heart, and his weight rests incorrectly on his left leg. His well-fed opponent wears the hat and plume of a military officer.[2] With his left hand in his pocket, his right uselessly pointing the gun at the ground and his mouth partially open, this officer parodies the pretense of military preparedness.

By placing these ridiculously matched duelists at unrealistically close range, Cruikshank heightens the comical situation. Hiding behind the tree are their nervous seconds, who were there to serve as witnesses. Usually friends of the antagonists, seconds shared any legal penalties incurred, which may explain why the doctor, clutching his instruments, and the younger man, dressed in regimentals, appear anxious. Crouched in the background are two observers.

Although duels such as the one Cruikshank depicted were legal (they were prohibited in 1819) and not uncommon, he may have been particularly inspired by a widely publicized fight involving a "point of honor" that took place between Captain Cothbert and Lord Lansdale one month prior to the date of this image.[3] While attempting to suppress a brawl that had erupted on Mount street, Captain Cothbert halted all traffic, including the carriage of a very irritated Lord Lansdale. Finding this impediment intolerable, Lord Lansdale reprehended Captain Cothbert in an insulting manner. A verbal altercation ensued, and to settle the matter a duel was arranged for the next morning.

Tim D. Wright

1. J. G. Millinger, *The History of Duelling* (London: Richard Bentley, 1841), p. 88.
2. W. Y. Carman, *British Military Uniforms* (London: Leonard Hill Books, Ltd., 1957), p. 91. The absence of any color prevents identification of the officer's rank.
3. Millinger, *History of Duelling*, pp. 143-44.

The Polite Alderman, Advancing to Future Happiness

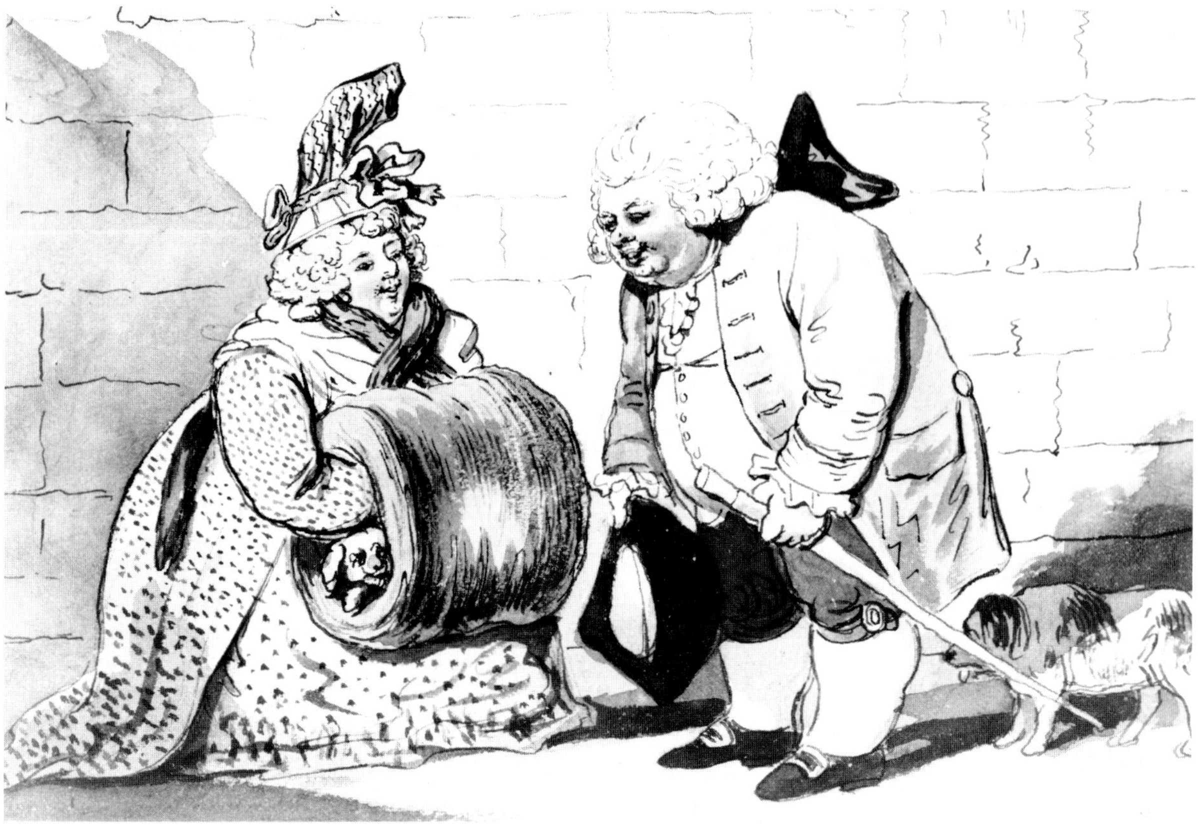

1792
Pen and gray wash over pencil
6¾ x 8⅝ inches (17.1 x 21.8 cm.)
Annotated verso: The polite Alderman / I. Cruikshanks
Published: August 1, 1792, by Robert Sayer; below the title is engraved: Madam will you honor me with your hand at the Lord Mayor's Ball – With a great Deal of pleasure Mr. Alderman.
Biblio: L & W, 83; George, 8215; Krumbhaar, 903; Wark, 14
Impression: BM, LWL

An alderman, who was a magistrate of the city of London, was elected to serve for life. The Lord Mayor was elected annually from the Court of Alderman on Michaelmas Day (September 29).[1] On Lord Mayor's Day, celebrated annually on November 9, the new mayor was sworn in at Westminster.[2] Traditionally, this day had been the occasion for an extravagant celebration; however, by the middle of the eighteenth century, it had become a more modest affair.

Cruikshank's image, published several months before Lord Mayor's Day, obviously was issued in anticipation of the occasion. A banquet, during which a ball presumably took place, was one of the events associated with the celebration. In the text accompanying the image, a stout alderman invites an equally plump lady to attend the ball; she accepts. Both their dress and size comment on their prosperity and, by implication, on their stature in society. Each figure is accompanied by a dog that seems to mirror his or her owner's attitude. The alderman's, as rotund as he, stands dutifully behind; the lady's, peering out from inside her enormous muff, hints at the pampered life of her mistress.

A print published in 1790, *Lord Mayor's Day Pickings* (George, 7757), shows the guests at the banquet eating ravenously. The accompanying verse reads: "Each squeezing, puffing, *panting* to be *first,* / To gormandize and cram till all their *waistcoats* burst." The illustration clearly satirizes the eating habits of the prosperous. A similar sentiment may well be behind this image of well-fed figures.

Jennifer Katell

1. E. N. Williams, *Life in Georgian England* (London: B. T. Batsford, Ltd., 1962), p. 26.
2. J. H. Plumb, *The Pursuit of Happiness* (New Haven, Conn.: Yale University Press, 1977), p. 53.

19 *Concert of Vocal and Instrumental Music, Or The Rising Generation of Orpheus* †

c. 1792
Pen and gray wash over pencil
6 1/2 x 8 3/8 inches (16.5 x 21.3 cm.)
Annotated verso: A family Concert / I. Cruikshanks
Published: May 12, 1794, by Laurie & Whittle (84); below the title are engraved 11 lines of verse.
Biblio: Wark, 25
Impression: LWL

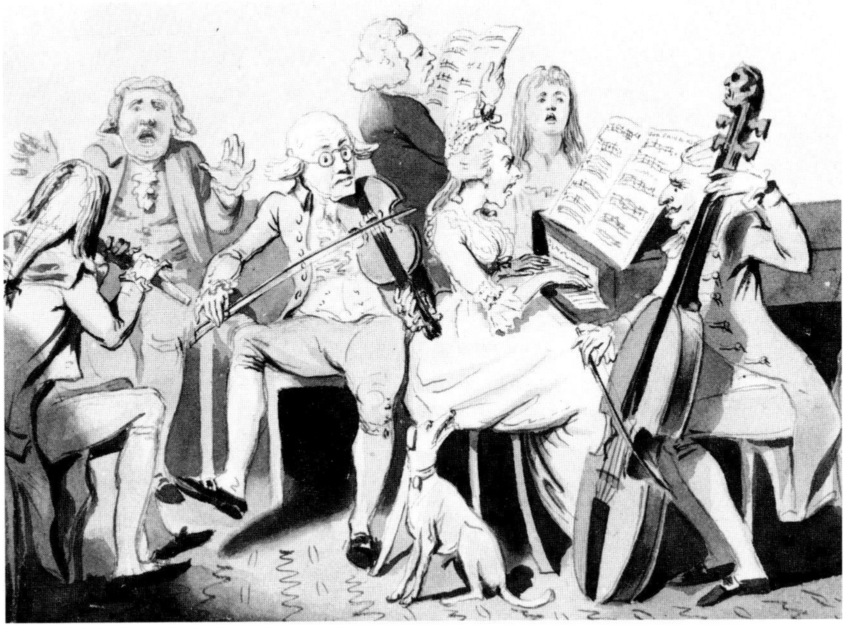

This music-making group clearly is a study in dissonance. Each player saws away independently instead of working as part of an ensemble. Even the dog joins in, howling piteously. A bewildered-looking violin player, likely the lead musician, is stamping his foot in an attempt to keep time, while his excessively long bow threatens to strike someone. The cello player, with an instrument too large and narrow, seems to express through his grimace his indifference to this ordeal. The carved head of his cello echoes the expression of the woman at the keyboard, who shrieks as she plays "God Save the King." The singers add their voices to the confusion as the flutist, his back to us, taps away. Cruikshank complements the impression of aural chaos with facial distortions and figural gestures. A composition by George Woodward, *The Musical Murder*, very close to this one in subject and medium, is also in the Huntington collection.

The engraved text refers to the music of Orpheus, who charmed all listeners, even trees and animals, with his performance. Such clearly is not the case with this group, where cacophony prevails. Obviously, this amateur group is not representative of the high standard of musical performance achieved in this era; rather, it suggests the domestic role played by music among certain classes in Georgian England.[1] Judging by the group's clothing, wigs, and silver-buckled shoes, the ensemble is representative of the upper middle class.

The music being attempted by these "musicians" may be a version of Handel's "God Save the King." During the periodic illnesses of George III, in particular during the season of 1788-89, theaters and music halls often played this tune in respect for the monarch.[2] The lyric refrain of "God Save the King" may have had an even more particular meaning in 1794, following the execution of the French king a year earlier.

The style of this wash drawing suggests it was executed in 1792, two years before its publication by Laurie & Whittle. The print is listed with other works from that year, indicating that the image may have been reissued at the time the firm took over on the death of Cruikshank's publisher, Robert Sayer.

Maria L. Brendel

1. Plumb, *Pursuit of Happiness*, pp. 17, 28.
2. Charles Beecher Hogan, ed., *The London Stage, 1660-1800*, pt. 5, *1776-1800* (Carbondale: So. Illinois University Press, 1968), p. 1087.

Orpheus was Music Master of the woods,
Groves a Gamut, put in tune the floods.
He made tall-trees a minuet step advancing,
Taught hedges hornpipes, shrubberys country dancing.

For every reptile he had Songs and Jiggs,
And Symphonies composed for Guinea Piggs.
For Weasels & Rats, he had both Sharps, and flats
For Cats—catawauling Arpegio.

He found D in Cocks crow,
Bulls sound G below
And sucking Pigs squeaked out Adagio.

20 *The Wedding*

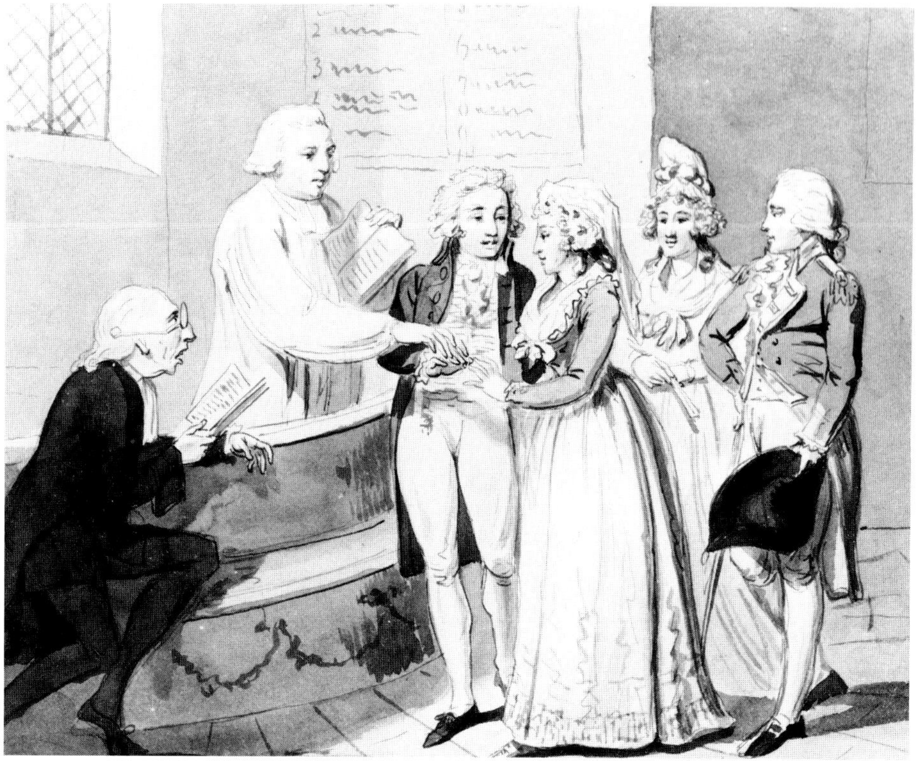

c. 1792
Pen and gray wash over pencil
6¾ x 9⅜ inches
(17.1 x 23.8 cm.)
Annotated verso: The Wedding / I. Cruikshanks
Published: May 12, 1794, by Laurie & Whittle (85)
Biblio: Wark, 26
Impression: LWL

To depict a wedding in monochromatic tones, especially for Cruikshank, who excelled as a colorist, is unusual. Also striking is the small crowd, with only one couple in attendance besides the clergy. The gray wash and limited group suggest the simplicity and solemnity of the ceremony. The wedding is taking place in an Anglican church, as indicated by the military officer's uniform; dissenters could not hold a commission in the army or navy.[1]

The scene depicts the high point of this wedding. The groom's hand is guided by the priest as he places a ring on the bride's finger. In the sketch the sunshine coming through the window (this light source is omitted in the print) seems almost to bless the event. Glances are directed by the two young gentlemen toward the ladies while the priest, aware of the sacredness of this moment, with lips slightly parted and eyes fixed on the hands, seals the union. The only comic element in the composition is the bespectacled cleric, whose exaggerated facial features and open mouth suggest that his voice is raised in song. Dressed in a black frock, the precentor is providing simple musical accompaniment to the nuptials. The writing on the board placed against the wall, most likely the Ten Commandments, stresses the religious nature of the event although this detail does not appear in the print.

Modest as this ceremony appears, all the men are wearing wigs. Cruikshank underscores the formality of the event by including an architectural device, the high-based column bathed in light, to frame the composition. In the print the column extends to the bottom of the sheet, emphasizing even further its importance compositionally and perhaps theologically.

Published in 1794, this wash drawing may well have been created as early as 1792. Its style suggests this date. Moreover, the print after it is listed with other works from that year in the Laurie & Whittle catalogue. The print could have been reissued when the firm became Cruikshank's primary publisher. At the time, the war with France undoubtedly occasioned many simple and hastily arranged weddings like this one.

Maria L. Brendel

1. Sir W. Besant, *London in the Eighteenth Century* (London: A. and C. Black, 1925), pp. 169-70.

21 *The Rabbits* †

1792
Pen and watercolor over pencil
8 7/8 x 6 1/2 inches (22.7 x 16.7 cm.)
Annotated verso: Buying Rabbits / I. Cruikshanks / Buckra
Published: October 8, 1792, by Robert Sayer; below the title is engraved: Miss – O la how it smells, sure its not fresh – Mungo – Be gar Misse dat no fair. If Blacke Man take you by Leg so, you smell too.
Biblio: L & W, 87; George, 8217; Wark, 1
Impression: BM, LWL

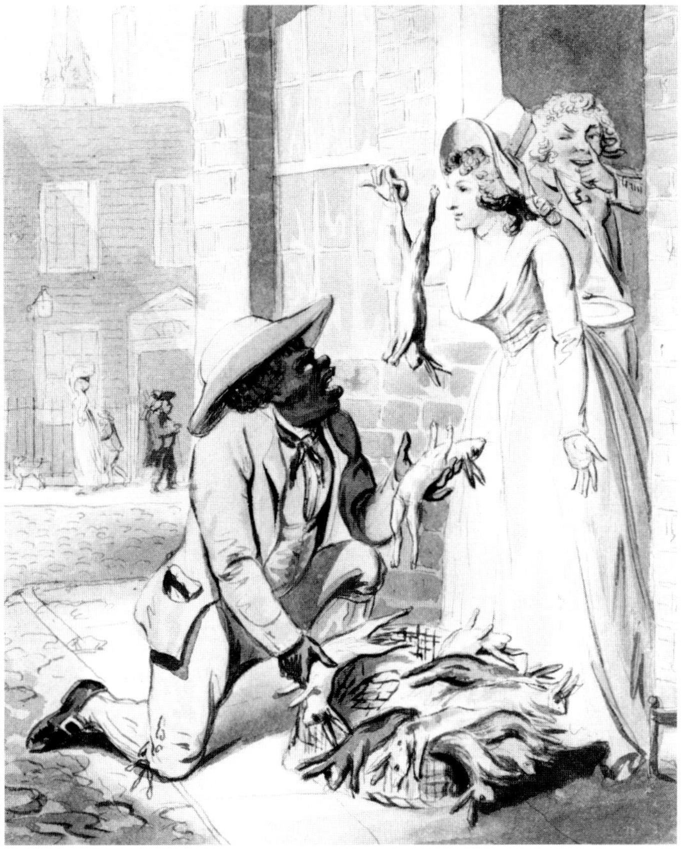

The streets of eighteenth-century London were filled with street vendors who carried their stock of fish, fowl, fruit, vegetables, or other foods on their heads, in baskets, on asses, in small carts, or off of poles. These criers—so named because they would call out their wares as they made their way—purchased goods from wholesale markets and then journeyed to other parts of London to sell the merchandise for a small profit.[1]

Seen here in an affluent neighborhood are two street criers. In the background is a woman with a basket on her head and in the foreground a rabbit vendor. Black criers, often called "St. Giles Blackbirds" because of their residence in that parish, were common toward the end of the eighteenth century.[2] With the decision of the Somerset case in 1772, initiating the move toward the abolition of slavery, many blacks left their masters' homes in search of freedom in the streets.[3] Then in 1784, following the War of Independence, a flow of refugees from North America, including blacks, arrived in London.[4] Only two types of jobs were generally available to blacks: servant or street crier.

The black crier, identified in the text as Mungo (a generic name for blacks at the time), is desperately trying to sell his stock of rabbits. At the door of a house, he kneels next to his basket before a woman who has just stepped out. Despite her attire, the woman is a domestic. Not only does her dialect suggest this, but she is identified as a "servant girl" in the Laurie & Whittle catalogue of 1795. With a rabbit in each hand, the crier solicits the woman to purchase a "fresh" rabbit. She holds it daintily in front of her by a hind foot, remarking that the animal smells spoiled. He tries to persuade her to buy it by crudely suggesting that she would smell too if he held her up that way. In the doorway a male servant smiles and supports the claim of the woman by placing his index finger to his nose.

Rhonda Howard

---

1. William Pyne, *Costume of Great Britain* (London: Howlett and Bruiner, 1804).
2. R. J. Mitchell and M. D. R. Leys, *A History of the English People* (London, New York, Toronto: Longmans, Green, and Co., 1950), p. 526.
3. Hecht, "Continental and Colonial Servants in Eighteenth-Century England," *Smith College Studies in History* (1954), p. 140.
4. Peter Fryer, *Staying Power: The History of Black People in Britain* (London and Sydney: Pluto Press Unlimited, 1984), p. 199.

22 *Ladies Ears Bored, Gratis* †

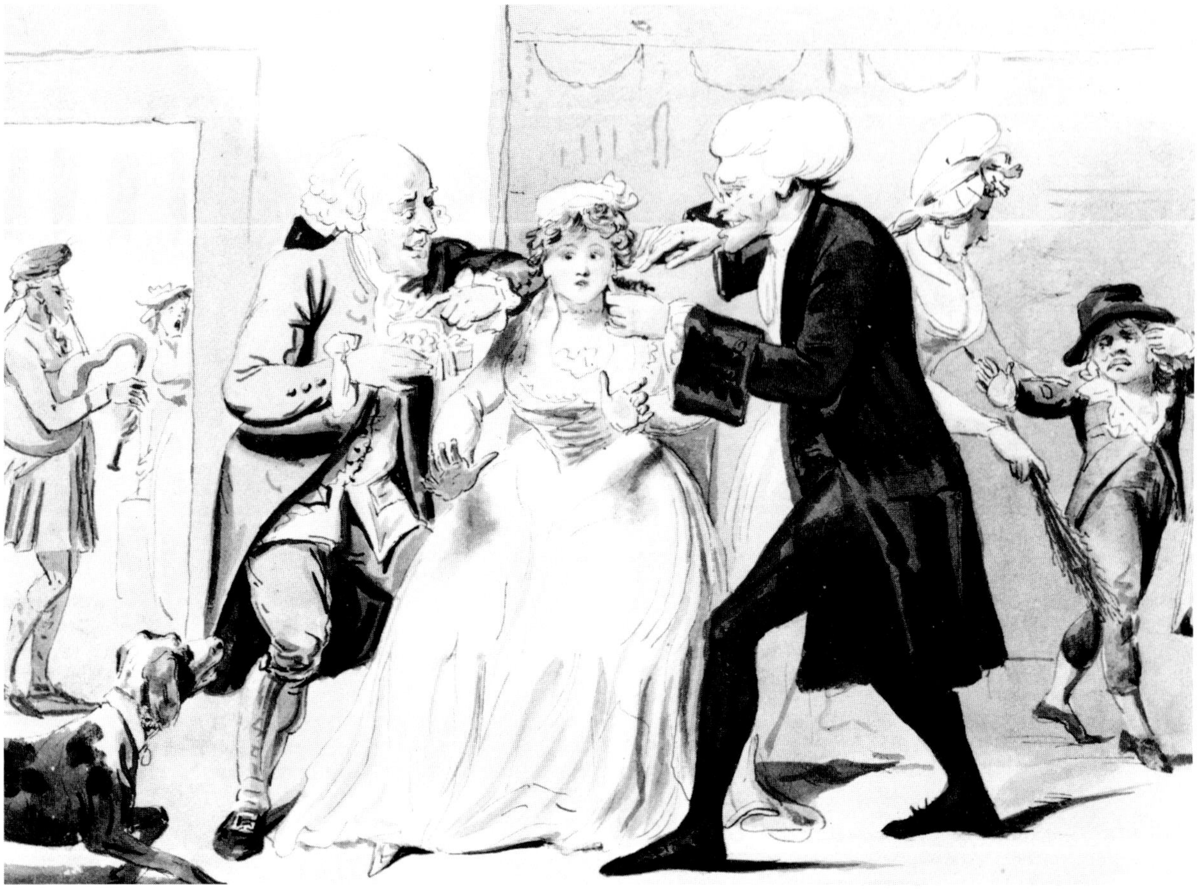

1793
Watercolor and pen
6¾ x 9 inches (17.2 x 22.9 cm.)
Annotated verso: Ladies' Ears Bored – gratis / I. Cruikshanks
Published: October 24, 1793, by Robert Sayer
Biblio: L & W, 90; George, 8408; Wark, 16
Impression: BM, LWL

A young woman sits in the center of a room, her face and hands expressing dismay as a man on the right prepares to bore her ear lobe. The man on the left points to a box of earrings he is holding. In the right background, a woman reprimands a boy who seems to wail as she birches him. Beyond the doorway on the left, a Highlander blows vigorously on bagpipes as a street crier selling milk seems to shriek with mouth agape. A dog in the foreground contributes to the cacophony.

Although the seated girl is ostensibly having her ears pierced for earrings, they are being pierced in other ways as well. The viewer can almost hear the pandemonium. Given the variety of sounds and episodes, the drawing may well be a general satirical comment on the noisy irritations of life.

Cruikshank's humorous depiction is part of a long tradition of the allegorical treatment of the senses.[1] However, compositions dealing with hearing usually portray auditory delights such as the playing of music. Cruikshank's parodic version gives a contemporary twist to the theme by focusing on the unpleasant aspects of aural experience. Through his association of hearing with crying, bagpipes, screeching, barking, and pain, sound becomes noise—an intrusion or irritant rather than a pleasurable diversion. These are the sounds the young woman is being subjected to free of charge.

Deanne Shey

1. For another parodic treatment of the tradition, see *The Senses* (30).

23 *Viewing the Transit of Venus* †

1793
Pen and watercolor over pencil
6 7/8 x 8 3/4 inches
(17.5 x 22.2 cm.)
Annotated verso: Viewing the Planet Venus / I. Cruikshanks
Published: December 16, 1793, by Robert Sayer
Biblio: L & W, 93; George, 8410; Wark, 17
Impression: BM, LWL

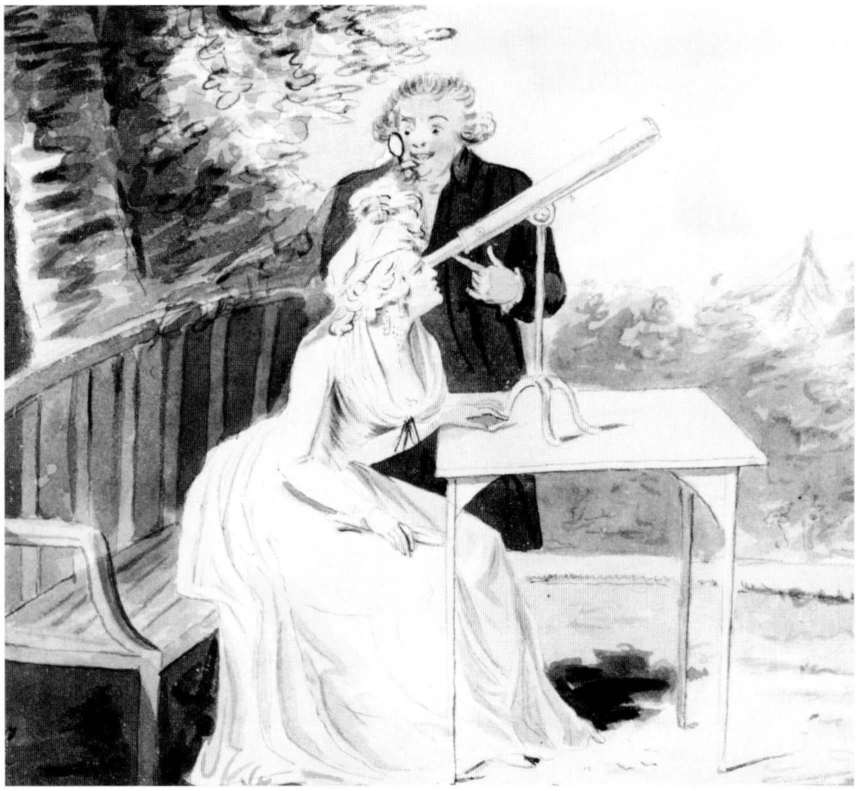

A beautiful lady sits on a garden seat, gazing earnestly through a telescope toward the heavens, while a grinning man, who directs her gaze by pointing the lens, ogles her through his own quizzing glass.[1] In the midst of the shrubbery in the background is a classical statue, typical of the picturesque garden decorations of the period. A woodland creature associated with Dionysus, the god of bacchanalian pleasures, the satyr embodies ideas of lust and sensuality. The statue's expression mirrors that of the man, thereby underscoring the sexual nature of the gentleman's stare.

Cruikshank presents the garden as a scene of love, a common conceit in eighteenth-century art, whether in French paintings or in Chelsea figurines. The pale-colored gown of the woman connects her via the direct axis of the telescope with the evening sky. Through his clever use of color and compositional arrangement, Cruikshank draws a distinction between the heavenly realm and man's earthly nature. The gentleman's dark coat links him with the shadowy foliage. Like the satyr, who is similarly surrounded by bushes, he is tied visually and psychologically to the natural world.

The reference to Venus adds to the humor of the piece. While the young woman is intent on observing the astronomical movement of the planet Venus, the ogler seems to be interested in a human manifestation of the goddess of love. Astronomy was often referred to as the most elevated field of scientific knowledge, and the laws of celestial movement were associated with the Divine.[2] The intentions of the man in Cruikshank's drawing are hardly spiritual. Moreover, the word "celestial" had other connotations at this time. In the phrase "celestial fire," for example, it was a metaphor for erotic passion.[3]

Deanne Shey

1. For other examples of ogling in Cruikshank's work, see *The Senses* (30) and *Billing and Cooing at the Jelly Shop* (84).
2. See, for example, William Whiston, *Astronomical Principles of Religion* (London: J. Senex, 1717).
3. Boulton, *Amusements of Old London*, 2:228.

24 "Mother and Child"

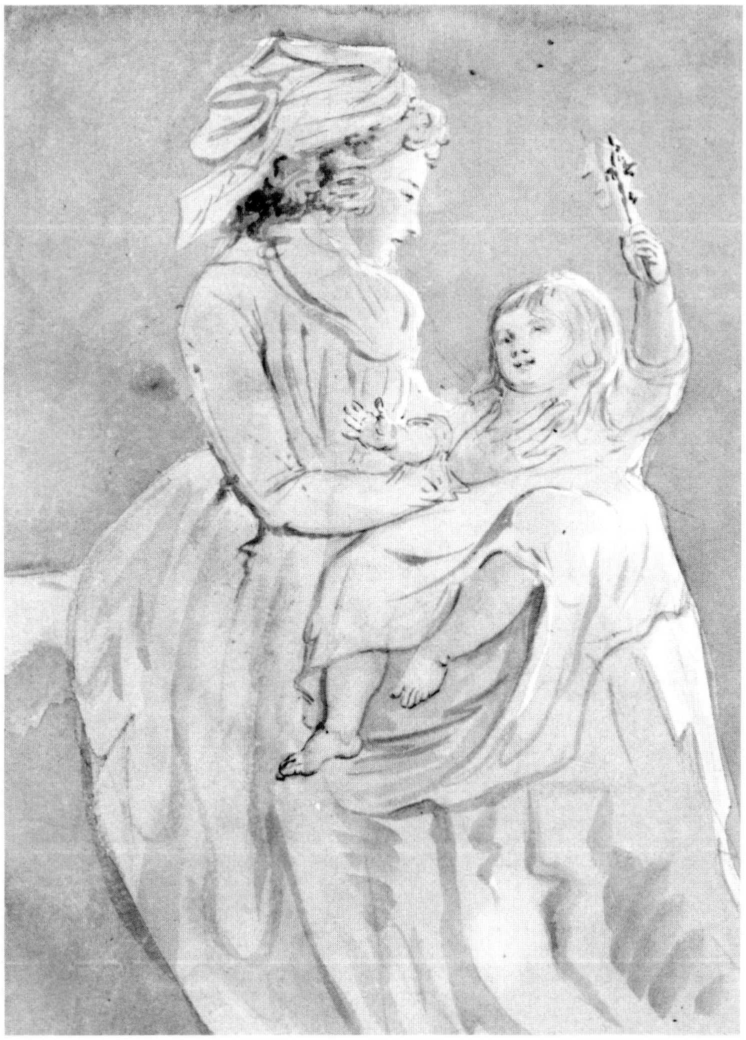

early 1790s
Gray wash over pencil
6 1/2 x 4 7/8 inches (16.5 x 12.3 cm.)
Provenance: with Covent Garden Gallery (London), from whom purchased in 1978

Although Cruikshank is best known for his humorous compositions, many of which were translated into prints, he created other kinds of works, including straight literary illustrations and portraits.[1] However, the present drawing is unusual in his known oeuvre for the intimacy of its subject matter and the sensitivity with which it captures the relationship between a mother and child.

While the composition recalls religious representations of the Madonna and child, there were many precedents for this kind of grouping in British portraiture. Sir Joshua Reynolds treated similar subjects on several occasions; his portrait *Georgiana, Duchess of Devonshire and Her Daughter*, exhibited at the Royal Academy in 1786, is a particularly animated portrayal of a mother playing with a child on her lap.[2] It is a composition Cruikshank could have known.

Spontaneous in feeling and natural in style, Cruikshank's tender interpretation of the theme suggests that it might be a portrait of his wife and one of their children, perhaps George, who was born in 1792. The manner of execution—the fluid handling of monochromatic washes—as well as the woman's attire support a date around that time.

Edward J. Nygren

1. See, for example, the many illustrations in *Roach's Beauties of the Poets*, 6 vols. (London: J. Roach, 1793-95).
2. For an illustration of this work, see Ellis K. Waterhouse, *Reynolds* (London: Kegan Paul and Co., Ltd., 1941), pl. 267.

25 *The Man Milliner*

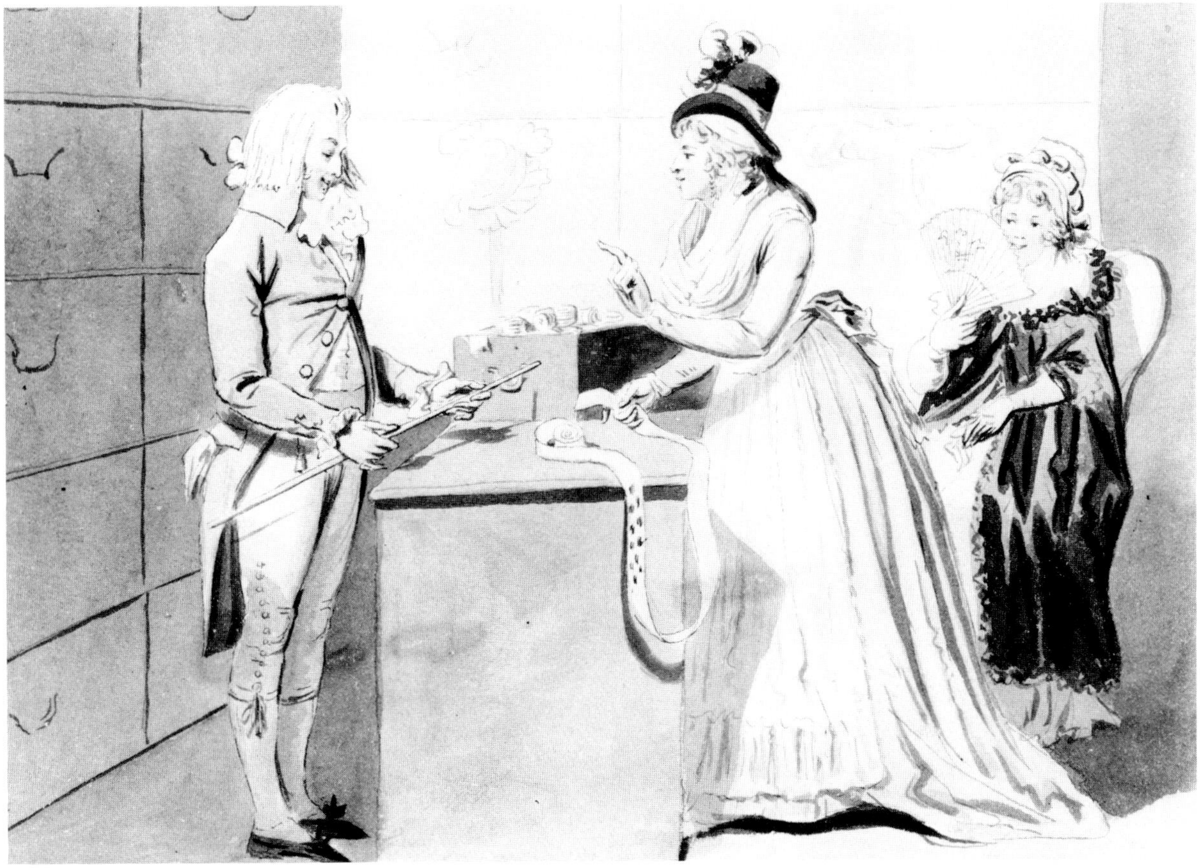

1793
Pen and watercolor over pencil
6¾ x 9 inches (17.0 x 22.7 cm.)
Annotated verso: The Man Milliner / I. Cruikshanks
Published: December 16, 1793, by Robert Sayer; below the image is engraved: Indeed Mr. Fribble I am not to be done in this manner, your Yard is to [*sic*] short by an Inch.
Biblio: L & W, 97; George, 8413; Wark, 18
Impression: BM, LWL

The milliner's shop, with its clearly defined interior space, including drawers, a busy counter, and shop windows displaying merchandise, is the setting for the reproach of Mr. Fribble. With sheepishly downcast eyes and a faint smile, he stands behind the counter holding a yardstick. A woman in profile faces him across the counter. Holding the end of a yellow ribbon, she raises her left hand in a gesture of admonition. The details of her costume, her fashionable hat and her apron, indicate her middle-class status. Her ample drapery and proud bearing suggest that she will brook no opposition. But another strategy is at work as well: leaning slightly toward the milliner, she displays the décolletage of her pink dress. Mr. Fribble avoids the woman's gaze as he fingers the measuring stick. His tight green coat, buttoned at the top, and a handkerchief hanging out of his pocket give him a slightly foppish air. In the background, a woman in a dark cape finds amusement, as might the viewer, in the exchange between customer and salesman.

The satire is carried by the figures' gestures, stances, and the way they direct their gaze. Their interaction suggests a narrative, yet it is the accompanying text that completes the context and adds sexual innuendo to the encounter. Members of the middle class were often the subjects of, and the audience for, Cruikshank's works. Here he satirizes the self-importance of the rising middle class, depicting the modest mercantile setting in which they exercised their new power.

Maria L. Brendel

26 *"The Water Party"* †

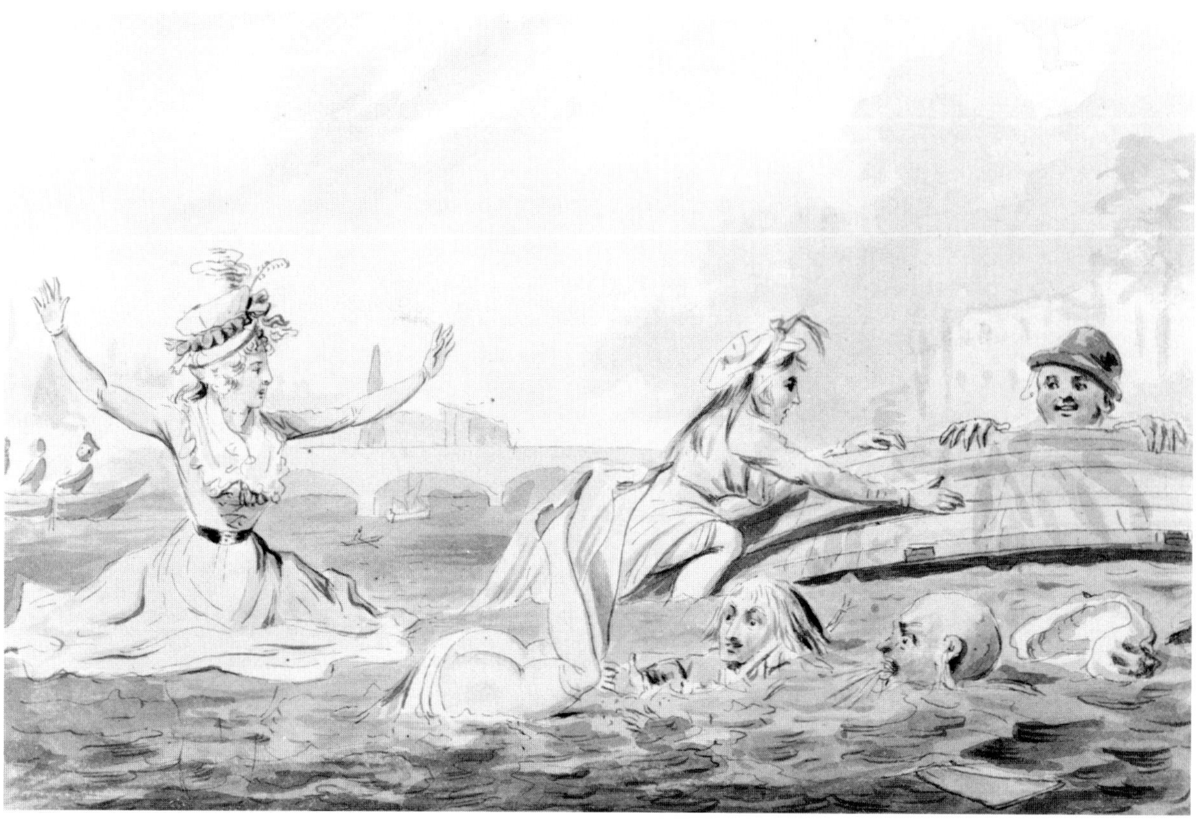

c. 1793
Pen and watercolor over pencil
6 1/2 x 9 inches (16.5 x 22.8 cm.)
Annotated verso: A Water Party / I. Cruikshanks
Biblio: L & W, 98 (?), Wark, 19

The British historian J. H. Plumb has characterized the Georgian period as one marked by the public pursuit of happiness: "Happiness became less private, less a state of the soul, a personal relationship with God, than something visible to one's neighbors."[1] One of the more popular leisure activities was the boat trip to the pleasure garden of Vauxhall. On summer evenings, ladies and gentlemen of the middle and upper classes would arrive at either Westminster or Whitehall stairs, where they would board barges bound for Vauxhall.[2] This journey by barge or wherry, as well as the time spent at the pleasure garden, was an opportunity to see and be seen in a fashionable setting.

Cruikshank's composition depicts a mishap that could have happened near Westminster Bridge during one such boat trip. Although no print after this watercolor has been located, Robert Wark has suggested that it may have been the design for a print entitled *A Serious Affair which Happened on the River Thames near Vauxhall,* listed by Laurie & Whittle in 1795 (98). Certainly the event depicted seems to substantiate this identification. The capsizing of the boat with its middle-class occupants is treated humorously. The woman partially submerged, with her legs and buttocks in the air, is the focus of the composition. Only the man holding on to the boat, possibly the waterman, seems to be enjoying himself, and his amusement was undoubtedly shared by Cruikshank's audience.

Danna Freedy

1. Plumb, *Georgian Delights,* p. 8.
2. Southworth, *Vauxhall Gardens,* p. 26.

27 *Smart Shoes Made to Fit – Without a Last* †

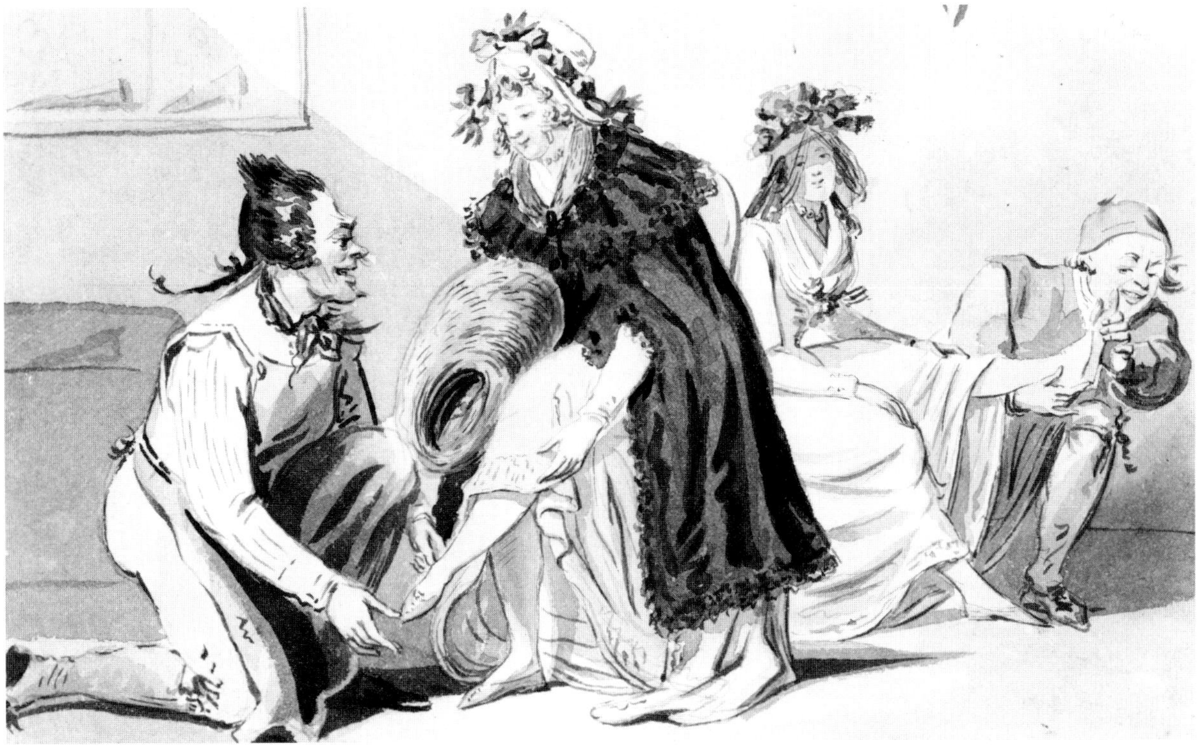

1794
Pen and watercolor over pencil
6 1/2 x 8 3/4 inches (16.7 x 22.5 cm.)
Annotated verso: Shoes made to fit without a Last / I. Cruikshanks
Published: January 15, 1794, by Robert Sayer; below the title is engraved:
Yes my Lady They sit neat about the Quarters, they only want a little Bobbing.
Biblio: L & W, 103; George, 8572; Krumbhaar, 1114; Wark, 20
Impression: BM, LWL

The composition of this drawing is dominated by a kneeling shoemaker, cast in shadow, with catlike features, and a woman who shows more of her leg than was considered proper as she tries on a pair of shoes.[1] Fashionably dressed, with pink ribbons on her hat and a coat adorned with lace, the lady holds a muff of bearskin.[2] To the right, a younger customer, seated, with features similar to those of the woman in the foreground, has a shoe tenderly fitted to her outstretched foot by a gnome of a man while she looks out, encouraging us to enjoy the view. His facial expression, like that of the shoemaker, suggests that thoughts besides shoe fitting may be occupying his mind.

Beautiful as the drawing is in its formal elements—the use of line, the rendering of texture, the tones of color, and the contrast of light and shadow—the text suggests the rather vulgar point of the satire. To Cruikshank's contemporaries, "bobbing" could mean opportunism, which in this context could be taken to mean that the shoemaker and his helper are taking advantage of the situation to steal a look at some anatomical delights. "Bobbing" also referred to an old dance;[3] certainly the two men could be seen as performing the opening steps to the oldest dance of all. Perhaps the most telling point is in the detached expressions of the two women, who cannot possibly be as unaware as they pretend of the clumsy caresses of these two buffoons.

Maria L. Brendel

---

1. D. Marshall, *Dr. Johnson's London* (New York: John Wiley and Sons, 1968), p. 150.
2. See D. Langley Moore and Sacheverell Sitwell, *Gallery of Fashion, 1790-1822* (London: B. T. Batsford, Ltd., 1949), p. 6, pl. 6.
3. Hyamson, *Dictionary of English Phrases,* p. 55.

28 *A Spouting Club* †

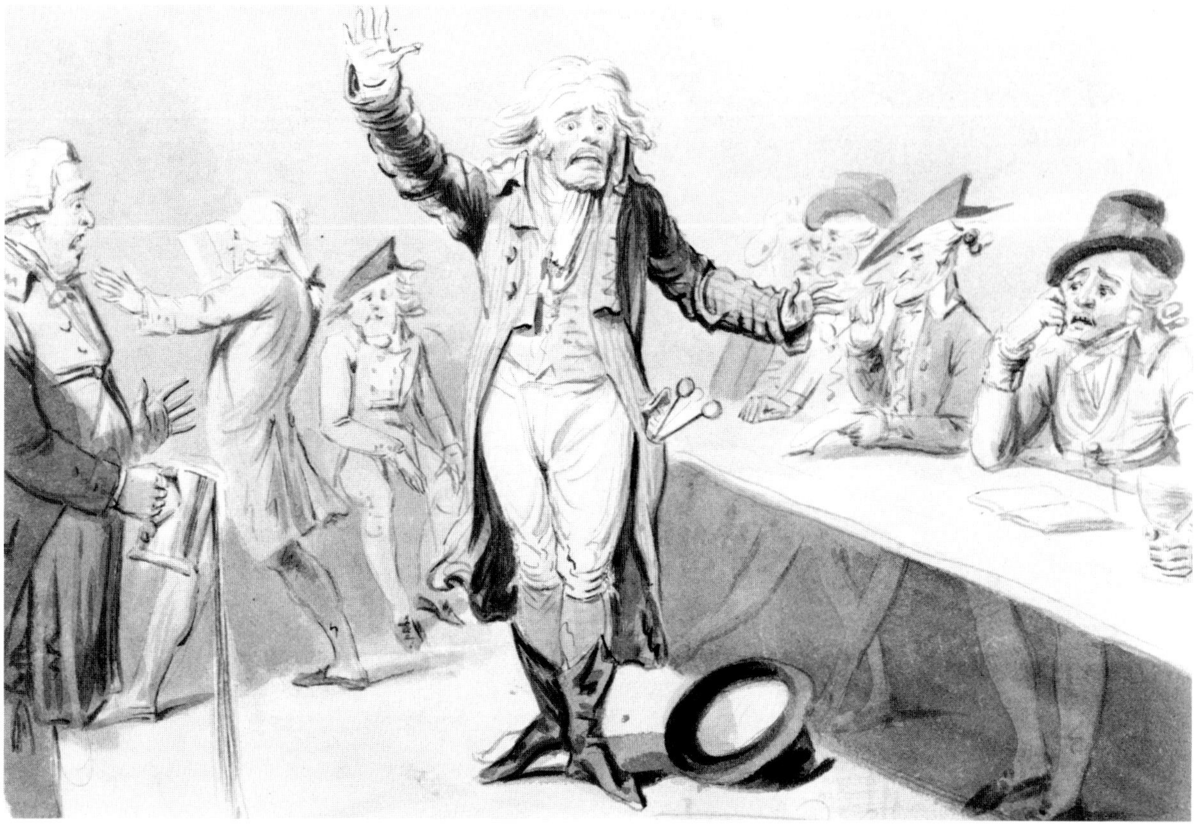

1794
Pen and watercolor over pencil
7 x 9 11/16 inches (18 x 24.6 cm.)
Annotated verso: The Spouter / I. Cruikshanks
Published: May 12, 1794, by Laurie & Whittle; below the title is engraved: "Is that a Dagger I see before me &tc. &tc."
Biblio: L & W, 101; Krumbhaar, A.96; Wark, 29
Impression: WMC

Spouting clubs were one of many types of men's clubs popular in eighteenth-century London.[1] A character in a 1756 play entitled *The Apprentice* explained their purpose and membership: "What's a spouting club? A meeting of prentices, clerks and giddy young men, intoxicated with plays, and so they meet in public-houses to act speeches; there they all neglect their business, despite the advice of their friends and think of nothing but to become actors."[2]

Cruikshank's watercolor clearly shows that he shared the low opinion of members of these clubs. Here the central figure, a barber with his curling iron hanging out of his pocket,[3] dashes down his hat and his pipe—which breaks—raises his right arm, and melodramatically delivers a line from *Macbeth*, "Is that a Dagger I see before me?" The familiar play was actually being performed in the Drury Lane Theatre on the day this watercolor was published.[4] The man on the left, who spills his beer and gasps, is moved—or at least startled—by this performance. In the background are two figures, one of whom sits passively looking on while the other declaims, oblivious to any competition. Two of the men at the table are absorbed in their conversation and ignore the declaimer, while a third man smokes his pipe. The man in the right foreground looks up from his book, presumably a play, to watch the theatrics.

Tim D. Wright

1. Jones, *Clubs of the Georgian Rakes*, p. 9.
2. Arthur Murphy, *The British Drama* (Philadelphia: M. Polock, 1853), p. 71.
3. James Stevens Cox, *All Illustrated Dictionary of Hairdressing and Wigmaking* (London: B. T. Batsford, Ltd., 1966), pp. 207, 265.
4. Schneider, comp., Index to *The London Stage*, p. 769.

29 *Justice Mittimus at a Loss How to Act in this Affair* †

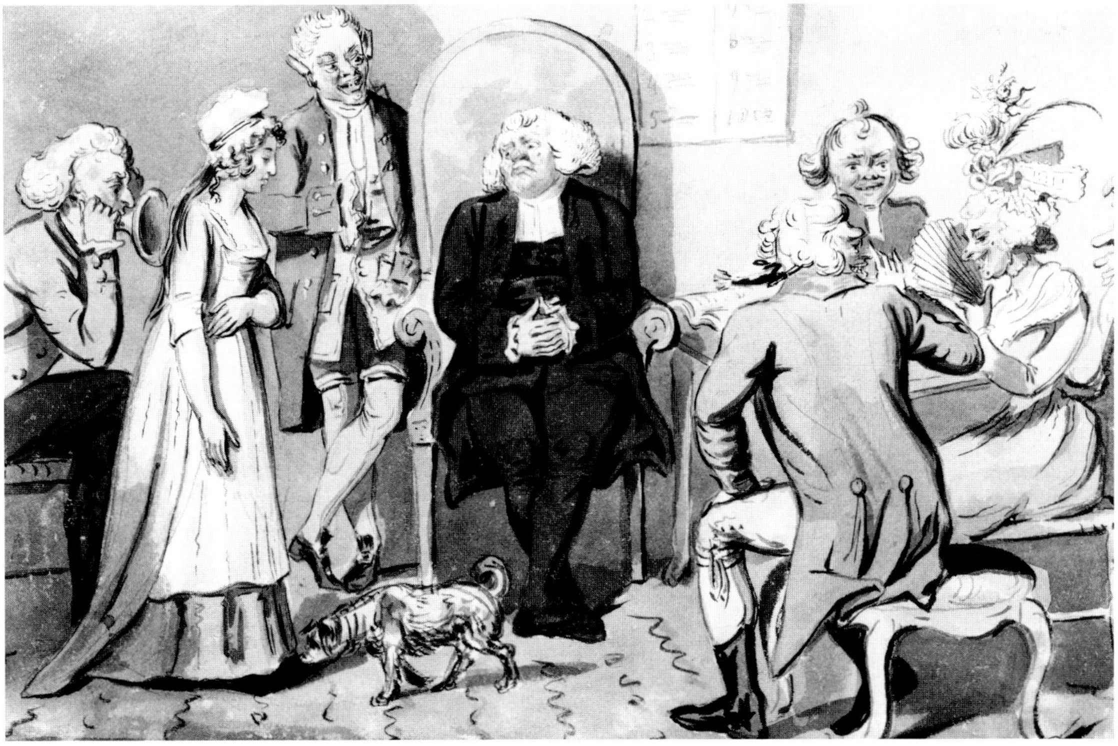

1794
Pen and watercolor over pencil
6 15/16 x 10 inches (17.6 x 25.4 cm.)
Annotated verso: I really don't know your Worship – Some ill Natured Pars – has raised this report – If I have done anything amiss sir, I am sure I was Dreaming / I. Cruikshanks
Published: May 12, 1794, by Laurie & Whittle (105); below the title is engraved: My Dear little Girl what have you been about, they say you are pregnant – I really dont know your Worship. Some Wicked Wretch is the Cause of this report. But if I have done any thing amiss Sir, I am sure I was Dreaming.
Biblio: George, 8575; Krumbhaar, 602; Wark, 27
Impression: BM, LWL

From the accompanying text, it would seem that this image deals with the issue of sexual morality, but it may well be an observation on gossip and slander. Justice Mittimus, the name perhaps signifying his duties, is clearly confronted with a difficult issue. The beautiful young woman professes her innocence in the presence of a few ugly and boisterous characters. Presumably she is being accused of moral laxity simply because of her youth and good looks. The dog's sad manner echoes that of the pretty defendant as it shrinks away from the scene.

A particular emphasis on ears and hearing at the left of the picture suggests that the charges may be based largely on hearsay. The curls on the man to the girl's left resemble long and pointed ears, recalling those of Envy in the famous theme of antiquity, the Calumny of Apelles. The subject of calumny, originating with the painting by the classical Greek artist Apelles, was widely treated in the art and literature of the Renaissance. According to Apelles, Truth is depicted in the form of a beautiful maiden led to the king by Envy, "a man with such a respectable length of ears, that they might be taken for those of Midas."[1] Often represented in compositions dealing with the subject are four other vices: Ignorance, Suspicion, Artifice, and Deceit. Any of these qualities could be ascribed to the remaining odd and conspiratorial characters on the right of Cruikshank's drawing. Above the judge's left shoulder is a tablet with numbers on it, suggesting the Ten Commandments. Two in particular may be relevant here: "Thou shall not commit adultery" and "Thou shall not bear false witness against thy neighbor."

Julie Joyce

1. For a study of the subject, see David Cast, *The Calumny of Apelles: A Study in the Humanist Tradition* (New Haven and London: Yale University Press, 1981); quotation on p. 3.

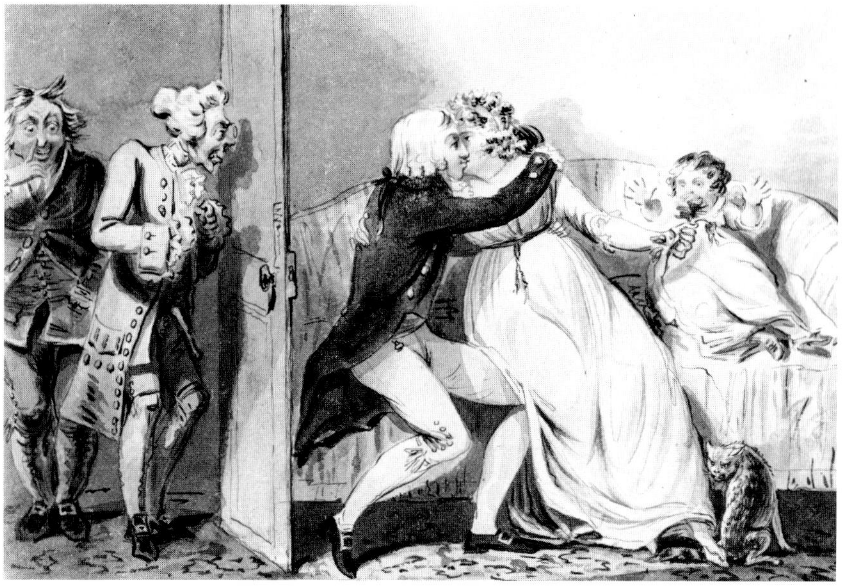

c. 1793/94
Pen and watercolor over pencil
7 x 9 3/8 inches
(17.8 x 23.8 cm.)
Annotated verso: The Senses / I. Cruikshanks
Biblio: Wark, 102

A young woman kisses a young man as she holds a bouquet of flowers under a surprised child's nose. At the same time she steps on the tail of a cat. Simultaneously, an older gentleman, perhaps her husband, spies the clandestine lovers through a peep-hole and is outraged, as is evident from his angry expression and clenched fists. Behind him, the servant grins as he touches the side of his nose with his finger, perhaps signifying that there is something rotten afoot.

Despite the fact that no print after this image has been located, the inscription on the verso provides a suitable title—The Senses. The servant *touches* his nose; the old husband *sees* his wife in the arms of a young lover, who *tastes* the lips of his beloved. The woman forces the child to *smell* the posies pushed under its nose, and the cat's cry will soon impinge upon the group's *hearing*. Finally, there is the notion not only of the physical senses but of the old man "coming to his senses" through a realization of all that has transpired.

There is precedent in early Dutch genre painting for sexually suggestive interpretations of the theme, for the senses were believed to be the avenues by which sin entered the soul.[1] In this drawing, Cruikshank burlesques traditional depictions of the senses by presenting the subject as a domestic farce, a quintessentially Georgian form of popular entertainment. It was during the late eighteenth century that light romantic comedies became a staple of theater and opera.[2]

As with other Cruikshank subjects, the dramatic action is presented in a highly theatrical manner. The artist has cleverly and almost seamlessly interwoven figurations of each of the senses into a coherent satirical narrative frieze.[3] It is the moment of dramatic climax that is captured in "The Senses." The drawing's frontality and lack of depth can be likened to the design of a stage set, while the sequential events have been conflated into a single representation. Each of the figures seems to be a stock character type that probably would have had a counterpart in the Georgian theater of the period.

Though the drawing was dated about 1800 by Robert Wark, it seems compositionally closer to Cruikshank's work of 1793 or '94.[4] The artist has employed the richer palette and careful draughtsmanship typical of other drawings from this period. While the costume of the older gentleman would naturally be less stylish than that of the younger beau, it is extremely old-fashioned for a date of 1800, the heavier topcoat and deeply buttoned cuffs having gone out of style some years earlier.[5]

Deanne Shey

1. An early and influential treatment is *The Five Senses*, engraved around 1595 by Jan Saenredam, after Hendrick Goltzius. See also Peter Sutton, *Masters of Seventeenth-Century Dutch Genre Painting* (Philadelphia: Philadelphia Museum of Art, 1984).
2. Elizabeth Burton, *The Pageant of Georgian England* (New York: Scribner, 1967), pp. 285-90.
3. For another example of a composition that has been temporally conflated to enhance dramatic appeal, see 53.
4. Wark, *"Drawings for Drolls,"* p. 16.
5. For more on costume and style, see Aileen Ribeiro, *A Visual History of Costume: The Eighteenth Century* (London: B. T. Batsford, Ltd., 1983).

31 *The Old Batchelor Alarmed by an Unexpected Present* †

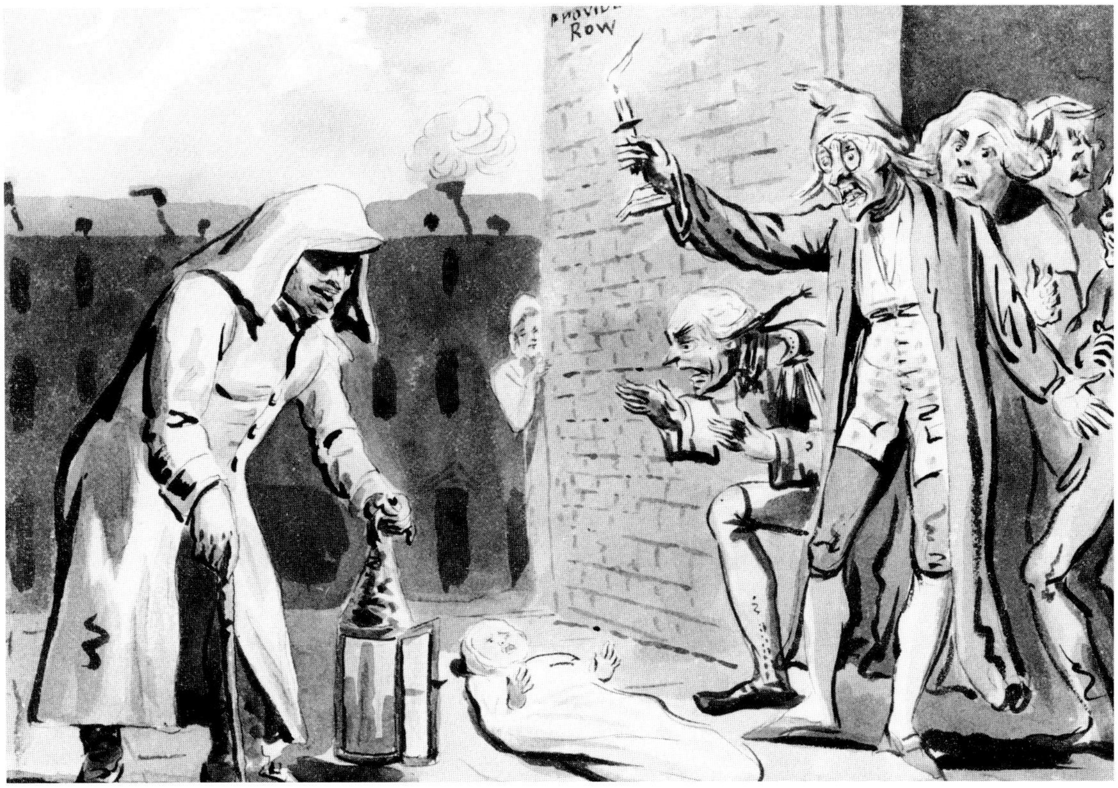

1794
Pen and watercolor over pencil
6½ x 8 15/16 inches (16.7 x 22.8 cm.)
Inscribed recto: Providence Row
Annotated verso: The Old Batchelor surprised / I. Cruikshanks
Published: May 12, 1794, by Laurie & Whittle (108)
Biblio: Wark, 22
Impression: LWL

There is, of course, nothing inherently amusing about the idea of abandoning a child. What alleviates the seriousness of such an event in Cruikshank's drawing is the varying responses of the household servants, along with the implication that the surprised old bachelor may in fact be the cause of his own predicament. The image also comments on attitudes toward prenuptial sexual relations in eighteenth-century England. A serious offense in English law, bastardy was also considered a grave moral and social crime. Much effort was expended to find the father and force him to marry the mother or maintain the child. Where marriage was out of the question, the equivalent of an affiliation order was imposed upon the father, if and when he admitted responsibility.[1]

The humor in this scene revolves around the central group—the night watchman, the baby, and the bachelor, the mother hovering in the background—and the play on words. Positioned prominently at the left, the night watchman, supposedly employed for his keen sight and attention through the night, is the picture of surprise and ineffectuality. The street sign "Providence Row" makes another witty comment on the figures. As defined in Samuel Johnson's dictionary, "providence" embodies, among other things, "foresight, timely care, forecast, the act of providing, divine superintendence and prudence."[2] The main characters in this scene seem devoid of these qualities. There may also be a play on the words in the title, between "old" and "present." "Old" is characteristic of the bachelor and the past; "present" could well refer to both time and the unexpected gift.

Julie Joyce

1. Paul Hair, *Before the Bawdy Court (Selections from church court and other records relating to the correction of moral offenses in England, Scotland and New England, 1300-1800)* (London: Paul Elek Ltd., 1972), pp. 236-38.
2. Samuel Johnson and John Walker, *The Peoples' Pronouncing and Expositor of the English Language* (London: J. Harned Morris, 1791).

32 A French Emigrant Cook Begging for a Slice of English Beef†

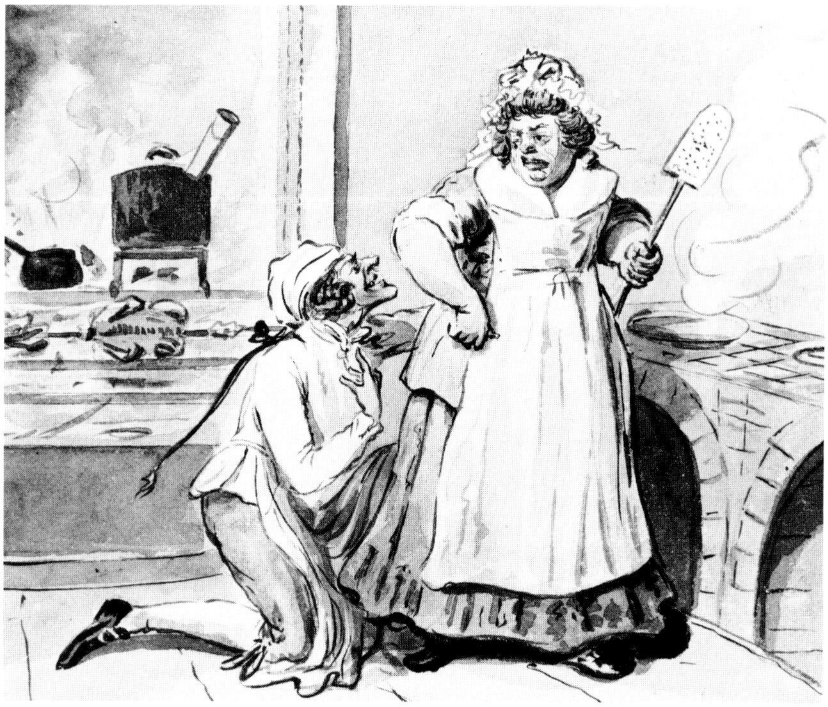

1794
Pen and watercolor over pencil
$7^1/_8$ x $8^3/_8$ inches
(17.9 x 21.2 cm.)
Verso: pencil sketches of an oven and stove, two profile sketches of a man
Annotated verso: I. Cruikshanks / A French Emigrant Cook / begging for a piece of English Roast Beef / Eyes where all the graces play, all the Loves are met, / In Pity cease to turn away / From me ma Belle Coquette.
Published: March 1, 1794, by Robert Sayer
Biblio: L & W, 109; Wark, 21
Impression: WMC

Voltaire once remarked "England has a hundred religions and only one sauce, and the French have just the reverse."[1] This view of cuisine was shared by English aristocrats, who regarded it essential for their social position to employ French cooks. But such a status symbol had its drawbacks: by reputation, French cooks were impossible to satisfy; they demanded unheard-of privileges and were usually in conflict with the English cooks with whom they worked.[2] In the English view the typical Frenchman was vain, pretentious, given to excess in fashion and manners, and disposed to intrigue in love and politics.[3] The French cook's appearance in this drawing reflects this attitude. In the accompanying text, he uses flattery, a "French" ploy, to persuade his British counterpart. The endearing term "ma belle coquette" (my beautiful flirt), obviously inappropriate, reveals the Frenchman's insincerity. The English woman's apparent refusal to be coaxed mocks French vanity.

National identity gained political and social significance in Cruikshank's time as a result of English opposition to the French Revolution, and the drawing carries out this theme with the commonplace caricatures of the French and British.[4] The skinny French cook, humbled by the oppressive political system of his country, appeals to the generosity of the fat English cook. The woman, a John Bull type of figure, projects national prosperity based on political liberty. The request for roast beef, the stereotypical English dish, recalls William Hogarth's *O the Roast Beef of Old England* (1749), depicting a massive joint of beef as the symbol of English pride amidst French misery under the ancien régime.[5]

The drawing is also up-to-date in its details of Georgian interiors. In 1790, Thomas Robinson invented a new kitchen fire which was the first to boast an oven at the side and an adjustable heat source on the top.[6] The equipment depicted suggests a connection between technical progress and a liberal political system. Pencil sketches of the stove on the verso attest to the importance of this element in Cruikshank's conception.

Mary-Kay Lombino

1. Gerald Newman, *The Rise of English Nationalism: A Cultural History, 1740-1840* (New York: St. Martin's Press, 1987), p. 15.
2. E. S. Turner, *What the Butler Saw: Two Hundred and Fifty Years of the Servant Problem* (New York: St. Martin's Press, 1962), pp. 154-56.
3. Herbert M. Atherton, *Political Prints in the Age of Hogarth* (Oxford: Clarendon Press, 1974), p. 85.
4. Ibid.
5. Derek Jarrett, *England in the Age of Hogarth* (New York: Viking Press, 1974), p. 194.
6. Bayne-Powell, *Eighteenth-Century London Life*, p. 337.

33 *Snow Balls – or the Old Buck in Distress*

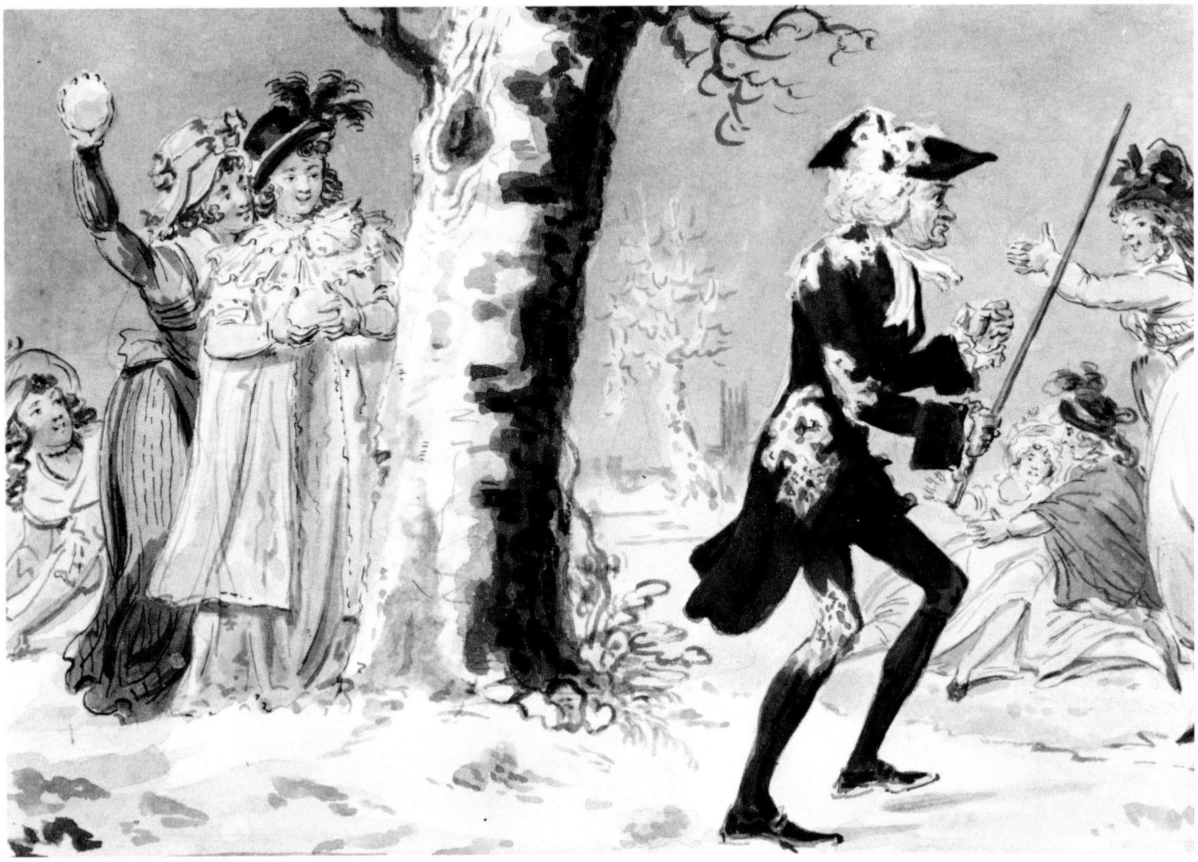

1794
Pen and watercolor over pencil
6¾ x 9¼ inches (17.3 x 24.4 cm.)
Annotated verso: Snow Balls / I. Cruikshanks
Published: May 12, 1794, by Laurie & Whittle (111)
Biblio: George, 8578; Wark, 28
Impression: BM, LWL

Three women are throwing snowballs at a thin and elderly man while others play in the snow. Clearly angry, the man holds his cane in a threatening position and clenches his fist. Dressed in a conservative black outfit, he is probably a clergyman but could be also a lawyer or a doctor. In any case, he is a member of one of the "learned professions," which were often satirized in the eighteenth century.[1] The three women, unescorted in the park, are clearly acting in an inappropriate fashion for respectable young ladies.

As the drawing suggests, gardens and parks brought together high and low segments of English society. Ladies of questionable reputation and a "learned man" could, as here, come together. What is peculiar about this image of playing in the snow is that it was published in May. Therefore, the main focus of the drawing is the comic depiction of the "easy jostling of high and low"[2] rather than a timely sketch of an event. The stuffy old man becomes an object of ridicule for both the women and the artist, and vigorous youth gets the better of old age.

Mar Martinez-Perez

1. M. D. George, *Hogarth to Cruikshank: Social Change in Graphic Satire* (New York: Walker and Co., 1967), p. 85.
2. Bayne-Powell, *Eighteenth-Century London Life*, p. 374.

34 A Box - Lobby Challenge †

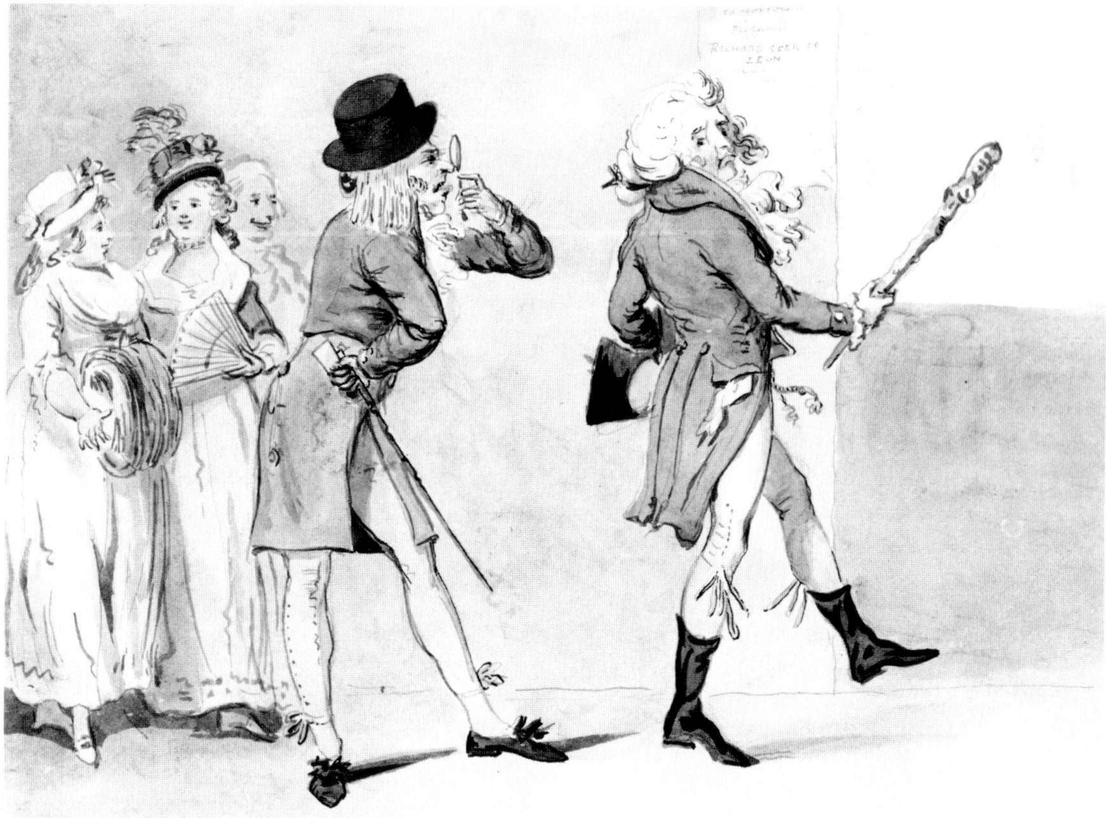

1794
Pen and watercolor over pencil
6¾ x 9 inches (17.2 x 22.9 cm.)
Inscribed recto: Performed . . . Richard Coeur de Leon
Annotated verso: A Box-Lobby Challenge / I. Cruikshanks
Published: May 12, 1794, by Laurie & Whittle (115); below the title is engraved: "Who are you Sir? – "Who am I!—Phoo / "All the World knows me Sir! Damme who are you? / "Meet me tomorrow Morning in Hyde Park, / "I am Mr Plumb the Bankers fifteenth Clerk.
Biblio: Krumbhaar, A.18; Wark, 30
Impression: WMC

A man strutting toward his box at the theater is asked to identify himself by another who observes him critically through a quizzing glass. He indignantly replies that everyone knows that he is the banker's fifteenth clerk. By dismissing the inquiry, the younger man cuts his opponent, a regular practice among social climbers in England at the time. Both figures reveal an inflated sense of their own importance.

Undoubtedly Cruikshank got his title and idea from *The Box-Lobby Challenge*, a comedy by Richard Cumberland that played at the Haymarket Theatre in the winter and spring of 1794. The drawing represents a scene from the prologue in which the antagonists are attending a performance of *Richard Coeur de Leon*, a popular drama in London that played twenty-one times at Drury Lane during the 1791-92 season.[1] (The identification of the play on the sign above the young man's head does not appear in the print after this watercolor.) Perhaps Cruikshank chose this title to satirize the scene and action. The characters represented here are anything but brave and valiant, unlike Richard Coeur de Leon (King Richard I), whose stature was no pretense.

Going to the theater was a popular pastime. People of differing classes would attend, the least expensive seats being in the gallery and the most costly in the boxes. There was often disorder in the foyer and noisy disputes and even riots if the audience was bored or unhappy with the performance. "Box lobbies" were areas where men and women who had box seats could socialize, and such is the setting for the dispute Cruikshank depicts.

Kathleen Kelly

1. Schneider, comp., Index to *The London Stage*, p. 209.

35 "Luck in the Lottery"

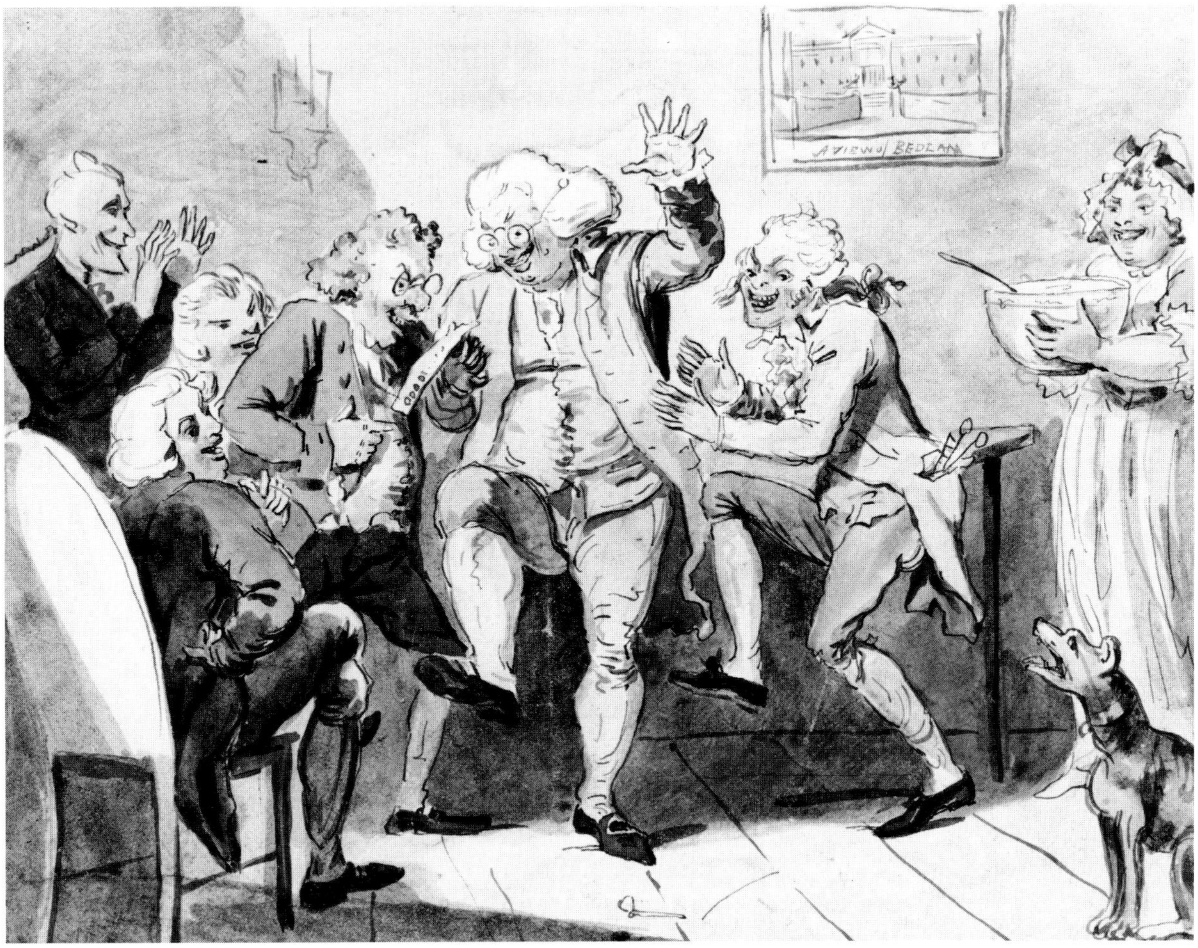

c. 1794
Pen and watercolor over pencil
7 x 8 7/8 inches (17.6 x 22.5 cm.)
Inscribed recto: A View of Bedlam
Annotated verso: Luck in the Lottery
Biblio: L & W, 117 (?); Wark, 45

In *Luck in the Lottery* one encounters six men who seem to be in a hysterical state. They are laughing, kicking up their heels, and jumping up and down with flushed faces. Undoubtedly the cause for the outburst is a winning lottery ticket, held by the central figure. A woman enters on the right carrying a bowl of punch, in all probability to celebrate his good fortune.

Cruikshank, in fact, extends the implications of this outburst by introducing *A View of Bedlam* on the back wall. Bedlam, short for St. Mary of Bethlehem in London, was an institution for the insane, and the group's delirium at their success in the lottery is being equated to behavior found in a mental asylum.

No print after this image has been located to date; however, a listing for a print with this title appears in Laurie & Whittle's 1795 catalogue.

Mari-Tere Alvarez

36 *Great Plenty and Little Waste* †

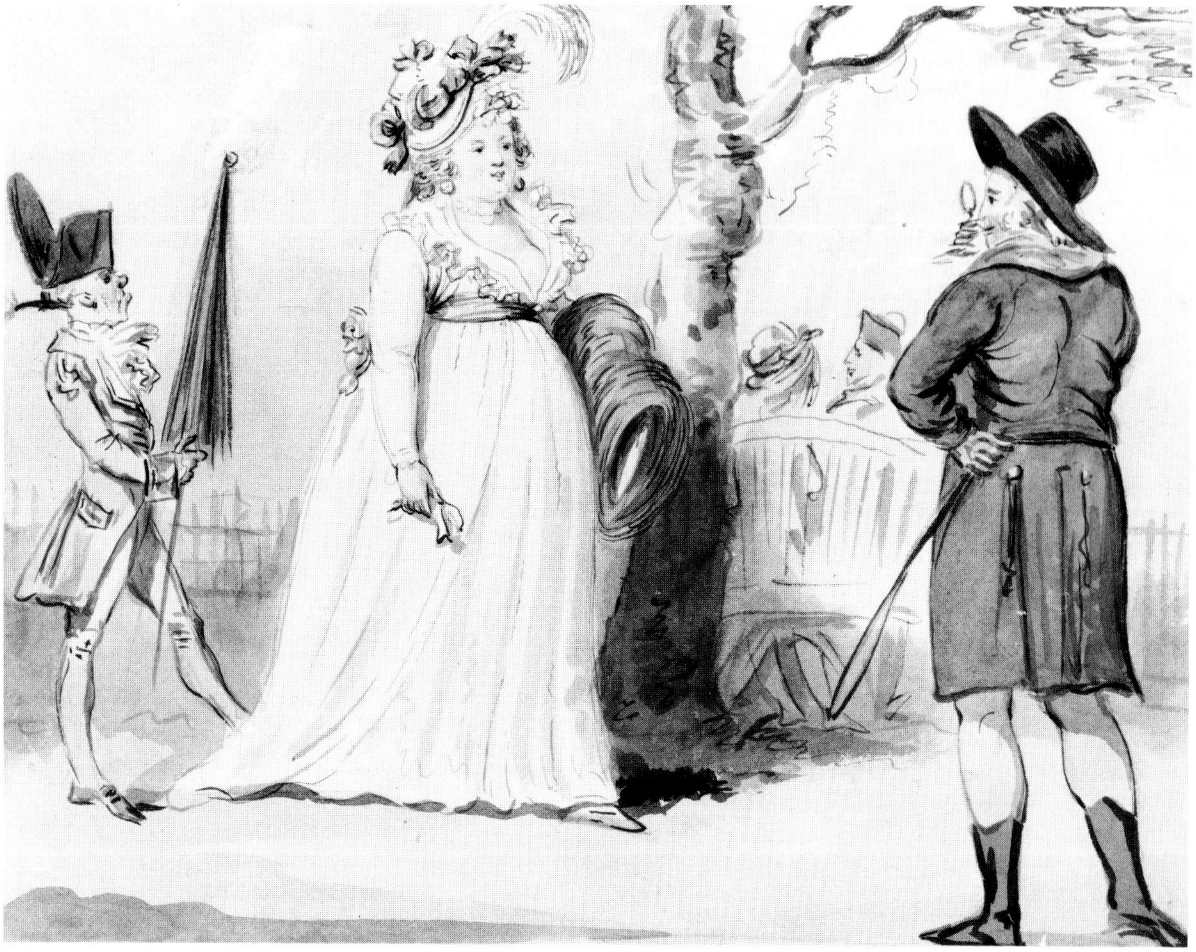

1794
Pen and watercolor over pencil
7 x 8¾ inches (17.4 x 22.3 cm.)
Verso: pencil sketch of a duel
Annotated verso: Great Plenty and no Waste / I. Cruikshanks
Published: June 12, 1794, by Laurie & Whittle (119)
Biblio: George, 8582; Krumbhaar, 464; Wark, 31
Impression: BM

Parks and pleasure gardens in the eighteenth century provided Londoners with recreation and amusement.[1] Particularly during the spring and summer months, people promenaded as both spectators and spectacles in places such as Vauxhall and Ranelegh gardens.[2] The portly lady illustrated here saunters through a park, as a dandy, carrying a crop, peers at her through his quizzing glass. Fashionably attired, she wears a high-waisted dress with flowing skirt and plunging neckline, a hat with a feather and flowers, and a pearl necklace. She carries a feathered muff on her left arm and in her right hand a glove. Her fashionable apparel establishes her social position, as does the footman, who was considered as necessary an ornament as a necklace and muff.[3]

Dressed extravagantly in a livery uniform made to compliment the colors in his mistress's costume, the footman was perhaps the clearest indicator of a lady's position in society.[4] While his primary function was to add luster, he performed a few practical duties as well. His job included simple tasks such as carrying a parasol (at a precise angle and distance from the ground). He was also expected to act as her protector, to stay close to his mistress "to prevent any idle or mischievously inclined persons from rudely interfering with or insulting her." If a stranger advanced, the footman was to close the gap, thereby alerting the other party of his intention to serve as his mistress's defender. This helps explain the proximity of the footman to the edge of the lady's dress in Cruikshank's composition.[5] If the lady depicted had felt uncomfortable with the man staring at her, she would have ordered her footman to step between them and say a few words. The footman's continued rear position suggests that she does not need his protection and is, indeed, pleased with the attention she is getting.

Although the title was undoubtedly understood by Cruikshank's contemporaries, its meaning is lost on today's viewer. "Great Plenty and Little Waste" may refer to the well-endowed lady and her small footman, or perhaps it sheds light on the encounter between the woman and her admirer. The dandy's intense gaze and her accepting response might suggest that this voluptuous woman will neither be ignored nor "wasted," but will amply satisfy his appetite.

Rhonda Howard

---

1. A. E. Richardson, *Georgian England: A Survey of Social Life, Trades, Industries, and Art from 1700 to 1820* (London: Charles Scribner's Sons, B. T. Batsford, Ltd., 1931), p. 20.
2. Plumb, *Georgian Delights*, p. 46.
3. Burton, *Pageant of Georgian England*, p. 326.
4. Celina Fox, *Londoners* (London: Thames and Hudson, 1987), p. 129.
5. William James, *The Footman's Guide* (London, Dean, and Mundey, [1833?]), p. 182. See also Mary Hallowell Perkins, *The Servant Problem in English Literature* (Boston: Richard G. Badger, 1928), p. 104.

37 "The Irish Wedding"

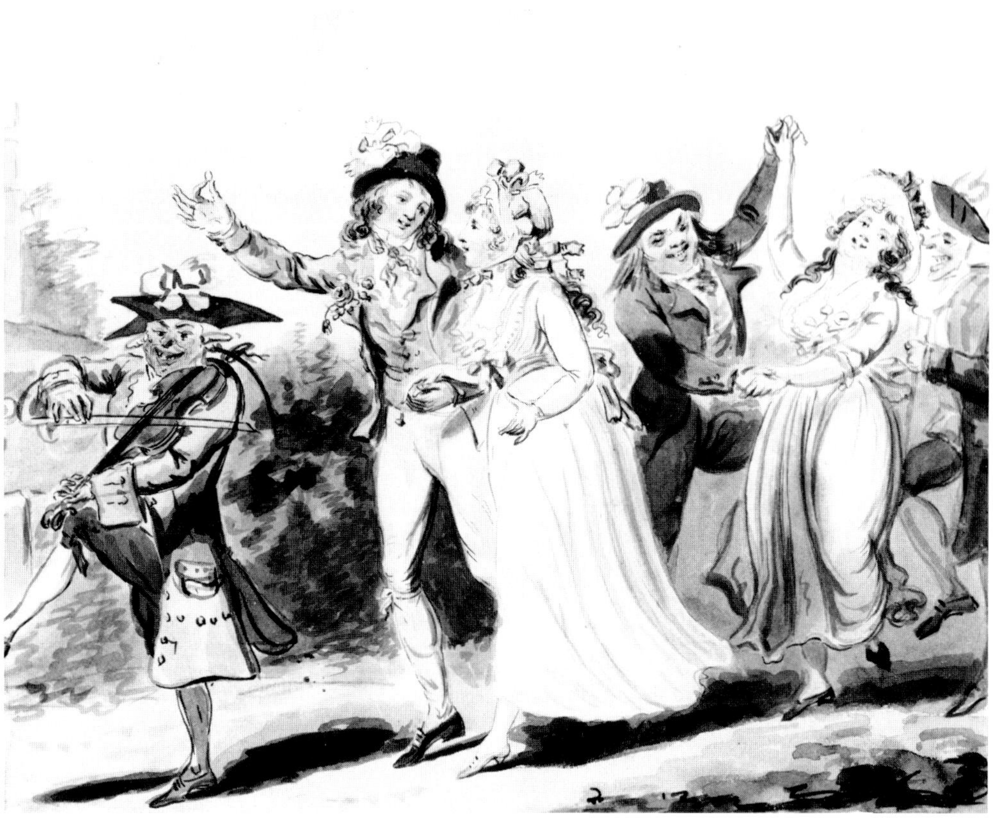

c. 1794
Pen and watercolor over pencil
6 7/8 x 8 3/4 inches (17.4 x 22.3 cm.)
Annotated verso:
The Irish Wedding / I. Cruikshanks
Biblio:
Wark, 43

Although no print after this drawing has been located, it may be a study for a work entitled *Country Wedding*, published in 1795.[1] The scene is set in the country, perhaps in Ireland, and depicts a religious processional. Dancing country folk accompany the loving young couple in the center of the image. The men's hats, with their decoration resembling the symbol on an Irish wedding ring, and the ring itself, held up by the groom, both identify the occasion and suggest its festivity.

Though no specific reference is made to Catholicism, the church in the background suggests the nature of the ceremony. The Marriage Act of 1753 made the religious celebration of Catholic marriages a felony in England. The law required Catholic couples seeking marriage either to go through an Anglican ceremony or treat the ceremony as a purely civil affair.[2] (It was not until 1836 that Catholics in England were allowed religious weddings.) The exuberance of the party, as well as the public display, would have been a sharp contrast to the subdued or clandestine Catholic weddings held in London during this period.

Ruled by England under Poyning's Law from 1495 until 1782, the Irish were often treated as children in need of parental guidance. Even in the years prior to the Anglo-Irish Union in 1800, Irish independence was not taken seriously by the British.[3] As the descendants of the Celts, the Irish were viewed by the English as a primitive and picturesque race.[4] These attitudes are evident here in the elated expressions of the country folk, their carefree manner, and the look of naiveté of the young bride, all of which add to the picturesque quality of the scene and emphasize the unsophisticated nature of the people.

The strong decorative effect of the drawing is typical of Cruikshank's works of the mid-1790s, when he created many lively and vigorous scenes like this one.[5] The brilliant coloring of the costumes and faces contributes to the charm of this delightful composition.

Mary-Kay Lombino

1. Wark (*"Drawings for Drolls,"* no. 43) refers to a print of this title which is grouped with other prints issued in 1794 in Laurie & Whittle, p. 98, no. 120.
2. John Bossy, *The English Catholic Community, 1570-1850* (London: Darton, Longman, and Todd, 1975), pp. 139-40
3. Richard Faber, *The High Road to England* (London: Faber and Faber, 1985), p. 60.
4. Richard O'Connor, *The Irish: Portrait of a People* (New York: G. P. Putnam's Sons, 1971), p. 367.
5. Wark, *"Drawings for Drolls,"* p. 16.

38 *The Farmer's Return – or News from London*

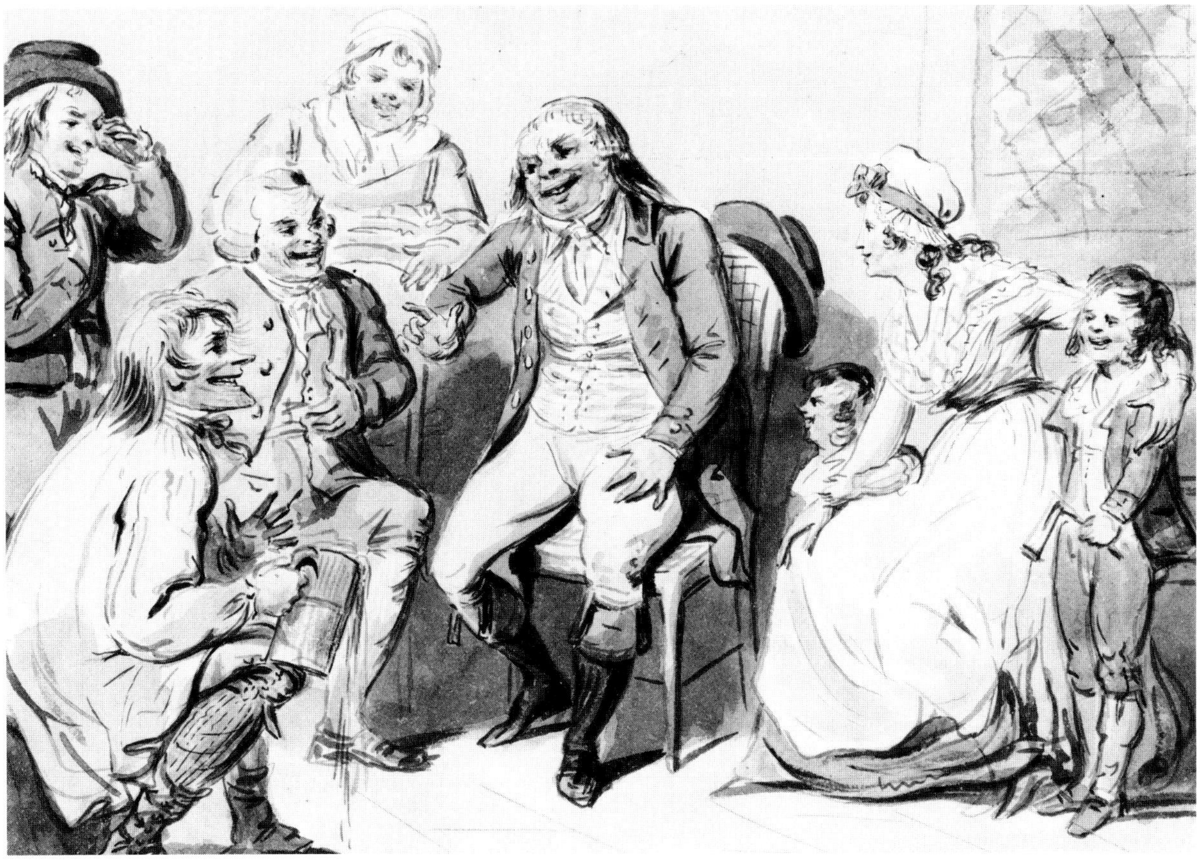

1794
Pen and watercolor over pencil
$6^{7}/_{8}$ x $8^{7}/_{8}$ inches (17.5 x 22.6 cm.)
Inscribed recto: IC
Annotated verso: The Farmer's return from London / I. Cruikshanks
Published: July 21, 1794, by Laurie & Whittle (121)
Biblio: George, 8583; Krumbhaar, 362; Wark, 32
Impression: BM, LWL, WMC

The subject of this composition was a popular one in eighteenth-century Britain. A farmer, having returned from London, regales his family and friends with tales of the experiences he has had in the city. The stage-like composition, with its arrangement of figures, recalls both William Hogarth's and Johan Zoffany's portrayal of David Garrick in *The Farmer's Return*, an interlude written by the actor as a benefit for Mrs. Pritchard and first performed in 1762. Garrick's play concerns a farmer who comes home from London after the coronation of George III in 1760 full of descriptions of the event as well as of life in the city. The work was repeatedly revived until the early 1780s; its last recorded performance was on May 23, 1781, at Covent Garden. Cruikshank's image is clearly not directly related to Garrick's play. However, the subject was a common one in contemporary literature and Cruikshank's audience, some of whom could well have known the play or images of Garrick in the role, would have generally been familiar with the theme.

Cruikshank underscores the farmer's role as a storyteller by having all eyes focused on him. He is the center of attention and of the composition. His success as a raconteur is confirmed by the actions of the farmhand in the lower left, who is so absorbed in the tale that he is unaware that he is spilling his beer.[1]

Edward J. Nygren

1. For a discussion of the portrayal of absorption in art and its relationship to the French theater of the eighteenth century, see Michael Fried, *Absorption and Theatricality* (Chicago: University of Chicago Press, 1980).

39 *A Card Party*

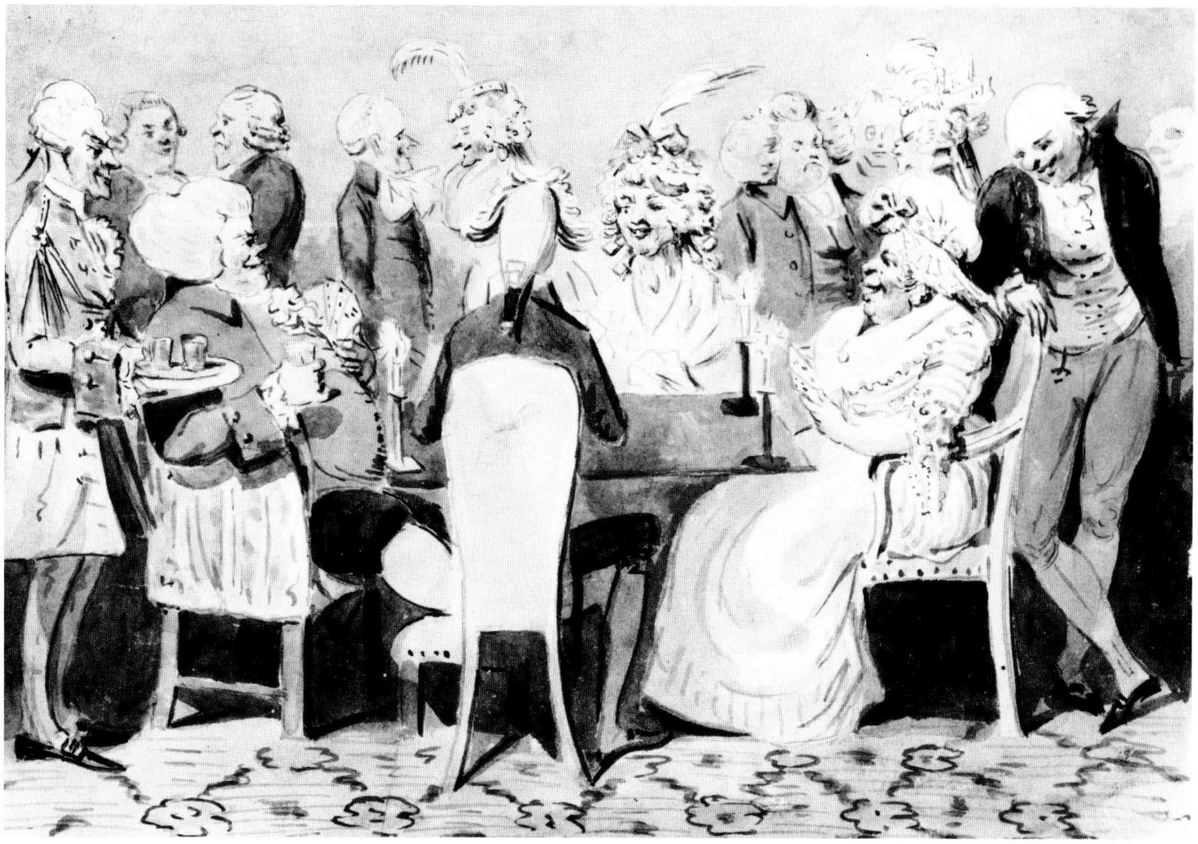

1798
Pen and watercolor
6 7/8 x 8 7/8 inches (17.5 x 22.5 cm.)
Annotated verso: A Whist Party / I. Cruikshanks
Published: August 16, 1794, by Laurie & Whittle (122)
Biblio: George, 8584; Krumbhaar, 129; Wark, 34
Impression: BM, LWL

All classes gambled. Women as well as men were inveterate cardplayers. As one writer remarked at the time: "Conversation among people of fashion is almost annihilated by universal card playing, insomuch that I have heard it given as a reason, why it is impossible for the present writers to succeed in the dialogue of genteel comedy, that the people of quality scarce ever meet but to game."[1]

In *A Card Party*, four unattractive characters are engaged in a pantomime, carefully staged by Cruikshank for our amusement. These individuals with animated faces are seated at a table playing Whist, oblivious to the large party taking place in the background. While the candles are burning themselves out and the room itself is filled with chattering guests, the cardplayers are caught up in the game. In fact, they do not even pause to notice the footman bringing refreshments to the table. Whist was very popular in the eighteenth century, and partners could gamble large sums, as much as two thousand pounds in gold. As a consequence, many individuals from good families lost fortunes, some even ending up in debtor's prison.[2]

Mari-Tere Alvarez

1. R. Cowpre, *Connoisseur* (1756), no. 6, p. 56.
2. Edmond Hoyle, *Hoyle's Improved Edition of the Rules for Playing Fashionable Games* (New York, 1830), pp. 186-88.

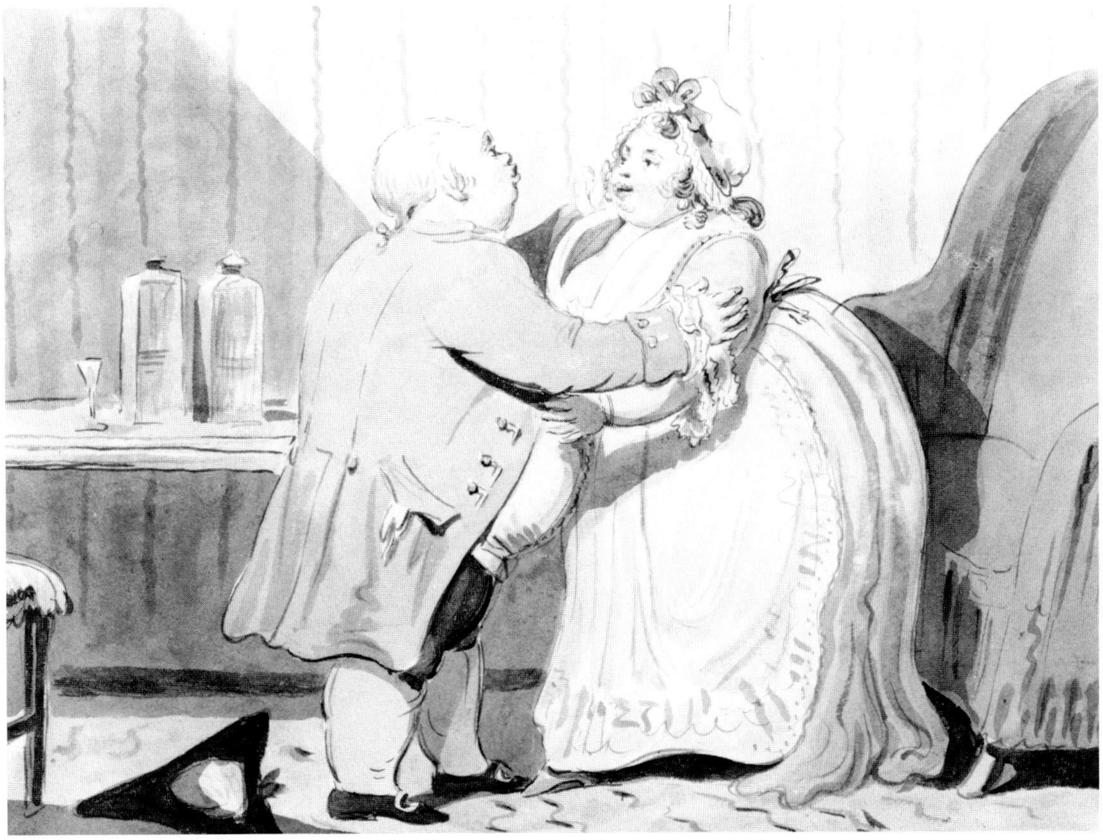

1794
Pen and watercolor over pencil
6 7/8 x 9 1/4 inches (17.7 x 23.3 cm.)
Annotated verso: A Difficult Kiss / I. Cruikshanks
Published: August 20, 1794, by Laurie & Whittle (123)
Biblio: Krumbhaar, A.29; Wark, 35
Impression: LWL, WMC

The intent behind this depiction of a physical encounter between a well-fed male and an equally contented female is unclear. It is uncertain whether this is a courting couple or a husband and wife. However, the man's hat on the floor indicates that he has just arrived and, in an amorous moment, has rushed to embrace his beloved. From the difficulties they are having, it would appear that their good fortune has hindered their ability to be affectionate toward one another. The man and woman resemble in size "John Bull," the symbol for the prosperous nation. In the eighteenth century, there was a strong feeling that Great Britain was "peculiarly free and peculiarly prosperous," a conviction which was not confined to the upper classes. England's self-reliance strengthened its confidence in its own superiority.[1]

Because overeating and heavy drinking were indulged in among all social classes during this period, the image may have been intended as a gentle satire directed at the British population in general, particularly appropriate when Britain was at war with France. Even in lower-income households, the standards for living and eating were high in comparison with those on the Continent. This is especially true of the period following the French Revolution, during which the French were stereotyped in illustrations as emaciated and impoverished. This emphasis on English prosperity at the expense of other countries served to bolster national pride.[2] Cruikshank's image pokes fun at this idea of prosperity by suggesting it may produce unforeseen difficulties.

Jennifer Katell

1. Linda Colley, *Britons: Forging the Nation, 1707-1837* (New Haven, Conn.: Yale University Press, 1992), pp. 31-43; quotation on p. 33.
2. Dorothy Marshall, *English People in the Eighteenth Century* (London: Longmans, Green, and Co., 1956), pp. 128-29, 160.

41 *The Dancing Master's Ball* †

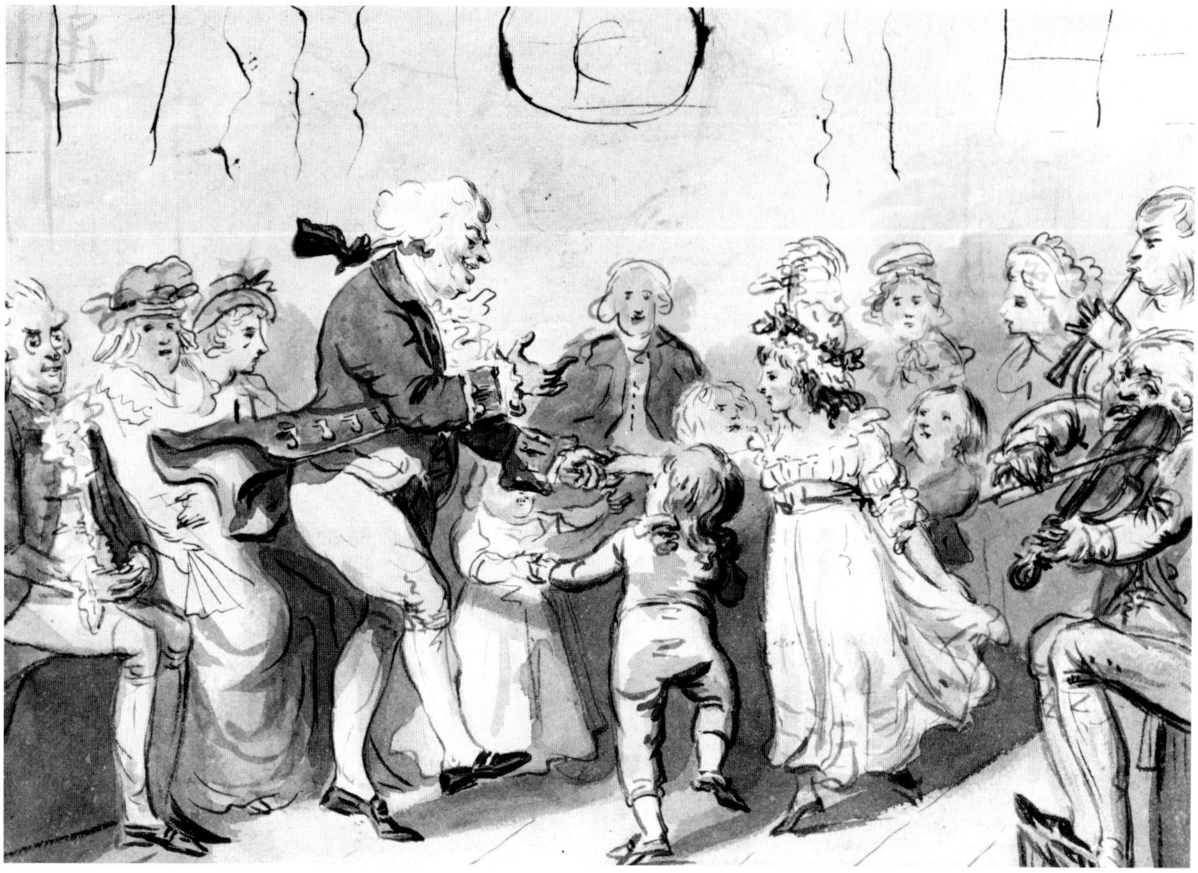

1794
Pen and watercolor over pencil
6 7/8 x 8 3/4 inches (17.5 x 22.3 cm.)
Annotated verso: The Dancing master's Ball / I. Cruikshanks
Published: August 12, 1794, by Laurie & Whittle (124)
Biblio: Wark, 36
Impression: LWL

Festive and filled with joyful energy, this drawing portrays an activity customary among middle-class families: dancing lessons for children, which could be had for a shilling an hour from "music masters, [who could] be found in droves in London."[1] This group of children, accompanied by a fiddler and a man playing a wind instrument (with a grimace expressing anything but contentment), are guided by their instructor while parents look on. The drawing vividly captures the enthusiasm of the children; yet instead of observing the performers, four of the attending adults are looking outward, as if to exchange glances with us, the audience, outside the picture plane.

Cruikshank usually makes his point with facial features, gestures, and postures, all of which express the attitudes of the figures. In this drawing, color is used additionally to focus on the prime subject: the dancing master. His coat of intense red, with a pink collar and brass buttons, dominates the scene. The coat swings out, and so does the master's long wig-tail with its luxuriant black velvet bow. The children are central to the composition, but their presence is secondary in terms of costume and color. The humor in this scene seems directed at the dancing master, who has apparently grown fat on the money he earns. But it may also be commenting on the parental ambitions and pretensions that encourage these activities.

Maria L. Brendel

1. Plumb, *Pursuit of Happiness*, p. 17.

42 “A Pair of Pretty Ones”

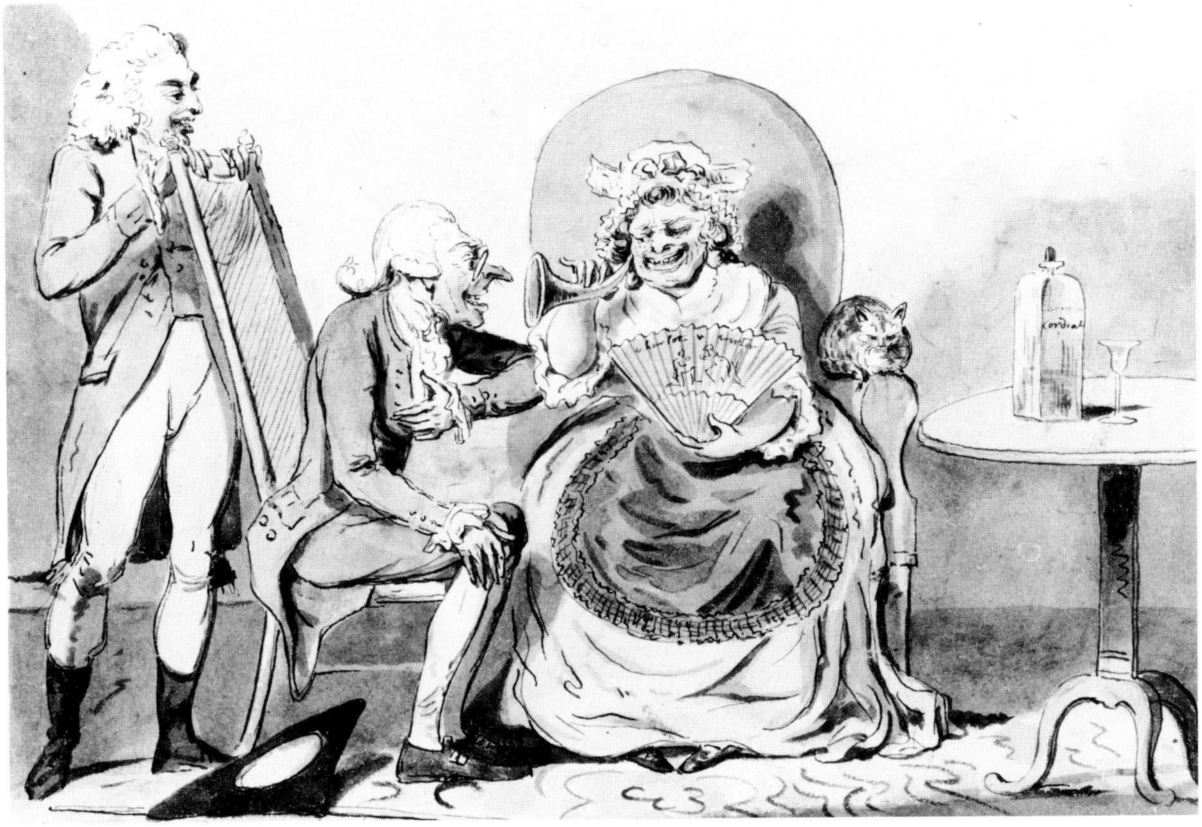

c. 1794
Pen and watercolor over pencil
6 3/8 x 9 1/4 inches (16.4 x 23.1 cm.)
Inscribed verso: Charlotte & Werter; cordial
Annotated verso: A Pair of Pretty Ones / I. Cruikshanks
Biblio: L & W, 125; Wark, 44

Although no print after this image has been found, a work of the same title is listed in the 1795 catalogue of Laurie & Whittle. Robert Wark has based the date of this composition on stylistic similarities with other images created around 1794. Heavy outlines with bright, bold use of color are characteristic of Cruikshank’s drawings from this period (see *The Difficult Kiss*, 40, and *The Finishing Touch*, 43).[1]

An unattractive elderly woman sits in a large armchair, listening through an earhorn to an equally unattractive elderly gentleman. The woman holds a fan with an image of two figures—a man on bended knee and a woman leaning forward in her chair. An inscription above the figures on the fan refers to Charlotte and Werther, the star-crossed lovers from Goethe’s popular novel *The Sorrows of Young Werther* (1774). A play by Frederick Reynolds on the subject was produced in London in 1786, 1789, and 1795.[2] The fan may well be an allusion to one of the many souvenir items produced in response to the novel, which enjoyed wide popularity in England (see *A Visit to the Boarding School*, 67).

The image on the fan and the reference to *Werther* indicate that a romantic interlude is under way. It is not clear if the seated gentleman is pleading on behalf of the young man standing behind his chair or for himself. In either case, it is possible that what is portrayed here is the negotiation for an arranged marriage.

While any interpretation must be speculative until a text for this image is located, the reference to Werther and Charlotte is ironic since theirs was an unrequited love that ended tragically. The cheerful if somewhat strange mood of this image, given the people depicted, is at odds with the reference to the tortured lovers. Even the title seems to be ironic since these figures are hardly “pretty.”

Jennifer Katell

1. Wark, *“Drawings for Drolls,”* p. 16.
2. Hogan, ed., *The London Stage*, pt. 5, p. 1578.

43 *The Finishing Touch* †

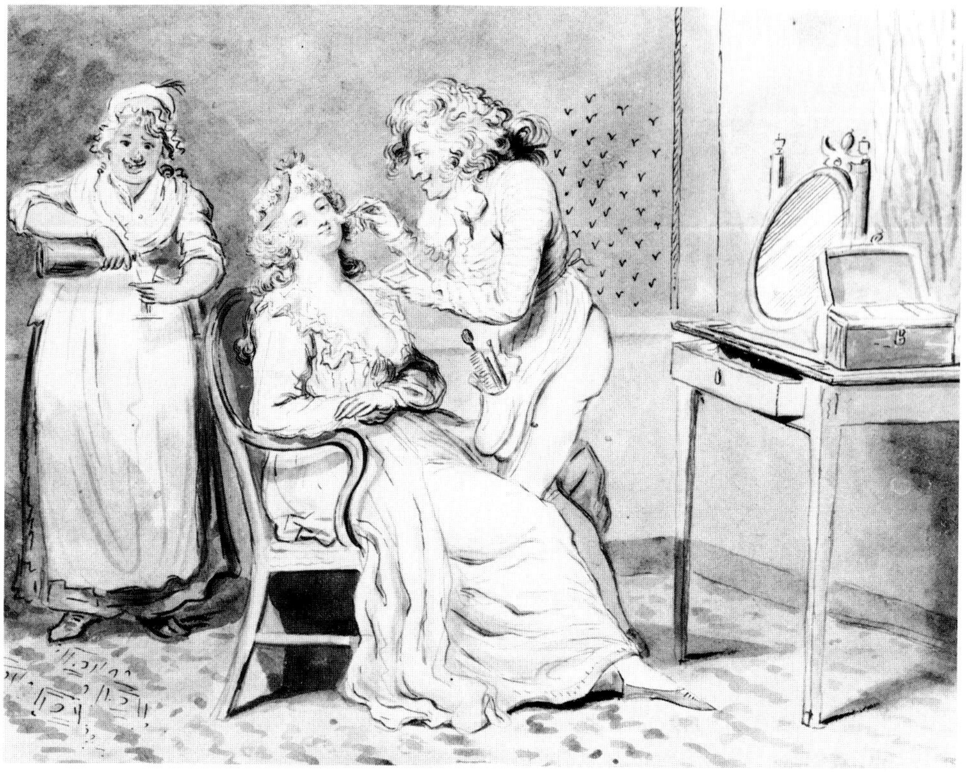

1794
Pen and watercolor over pencil
$6^5/_8$ x $9^1/_4$ inches (16.8 x 23.5 cm.)
Annotated verso: The finishing Touch / I. Cruikshanks
Published: October 13, 1794, by Laurie & Whittle (127)
Biblio: George, 8586; Krumbhaar, 370; Wark, 37
Impression: BM, LWL

An attractive young woman glances sidelong at the viewer while a male hairdresser applies cosmetics to her face. The objects—the unlocked jewelry chest and open drawer—suggest availability or emptiness; the mirror signifies vanity. Her dressing gown has been draped to reveal décolletage and ankle, while her hair is disarmingly disheveled.[1]

These stratagems are seemingly employed to enhance her appeal to the viewer/client for whom, presumably, the toothless maidservant pours a glass of spirits, identified in the print as "Holland." The label refers to a type of gin produced in the Netherlands. The old hag recalls the ubiquitous disheveled servant, or procuress, found in seventeenth-century Dutch genre paintings. Besides lending an air of bawdiness to the scene, she serves as a foil to the voluptuous beauty presented for the delectation of the viewer. Grinning almost lasciviously, the cosmetician leans forward, his legs provocatively placed between those of the courtesan. Although the looks and actions of the maid and mistress engage the client, who sits outside the picture plane, the hairdresser serves as the viewer's surrogate.

The use of cosmetics was not confined to courtesans. Aristocratic ladies and gentlemen employed a wide range of preparations, including mouse skin eyebrows, silk tie wigs, and mineral powders. Sir Walter Elliot, a character in *Persuasion* (1815), comments on the practice,[2] and Maria Cosway in *The Progress of Female Virtue; The Progress of Female Dissatisfaction* (1800), speaks of the feminine ideal of unselfconscious beauty, modesty, and chastity, which is set against the fashionable, artificial, and corrupt.

In the 1795 catalogue by Laurie & Whittle, the title of the print was given as "The Finishing Touch of an Impure's Face." Prostitutes were commonplace in the life of a gentleman, but so, too, was the disease often associated with sexual license or promiscuity. It is thus not simply the moral depravity of the courtesan to which the term "an impure's face" may refer. Cruikshank, however, seems less the critic of licentiousness than the satirist of society's foibles. He seems to accept, if not embrace, the hedonism of the age.

Deanne Shey

1. See Donald Posner, *Watteau: "A Lady at Her Toilet"* (London: Allen Lane, 1973) for a discussion of the eroticism inherent in depicting a female subject in deshabille at her toilette.
2. See *Persuasion*, chap. 4.

44 *Attraction*

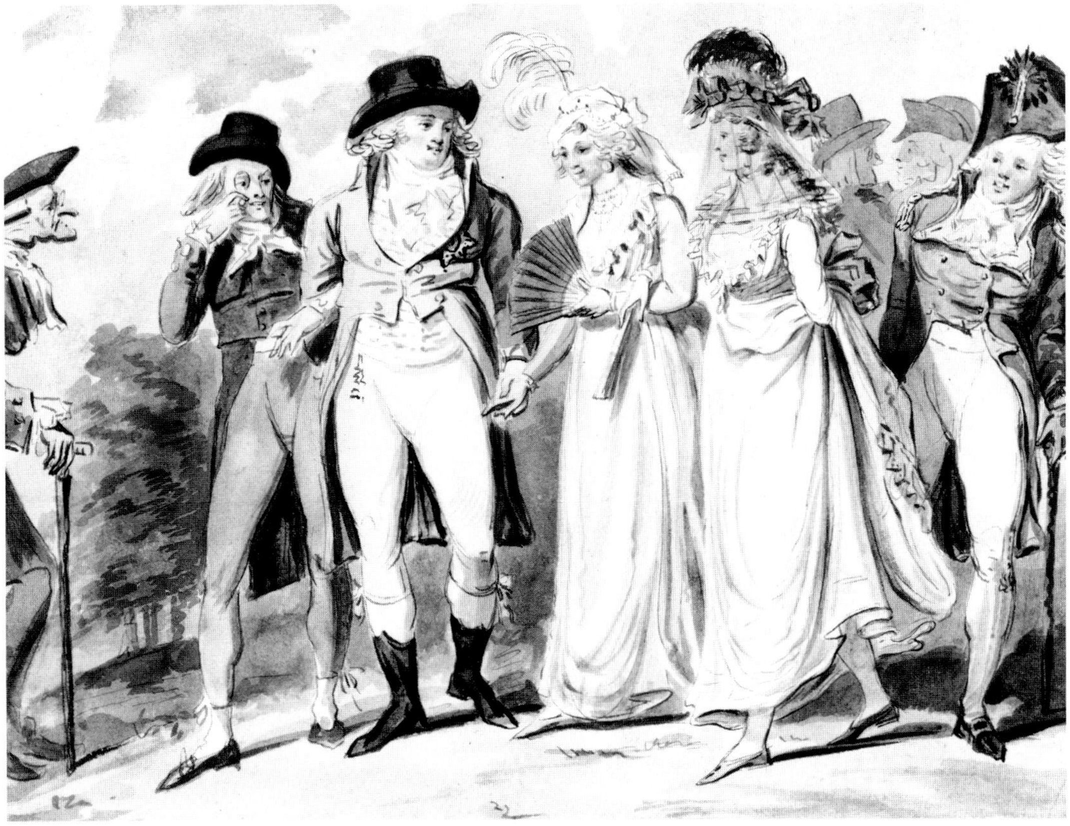

1794
Watercolor and pen
7 x 8⅞ inches (17.8 x 22.5 cm.)
Annotated verso: St. James' Park / I. Cruikshanks
Published: November 1, 1794, by Laurie & Whittle (129); below the title is engraved: Lovely Woman—There is in you all that We believe of Heaven
Biblio: Wark, 38

A group of attractive and fashionably attired young men and women stroll through a park. The pre-dinner promenade in formal evening dress through St. James or Green Park was integral to London's social life, an opportunity to see and be seen, and to exchange witticisms, malicious gossip, and delicious flirtations. Fashionable ladies and gentlemen, with montebanks and the current sirens of the stage mingling among them, would circle around each other either on foot or in carriages. It was here, in this stylish theater of seduction, that fashions were created, social allegiances displayed, and reputations made, only to be broken.[1]

The identity of these promenaders has not been established; however, the gentleman at the left center is undoubtedly a member of the nobility, as indicated by the emblem on his jacket. He may even be the Prince of Wales, who had a reputation for high living, and whose private life was the subject of journalistic commentary. Though somewhat idealized, his facial features suggest a resemblance to other depictions of the prince by Cruikshank.

In *Attraction,* all eyes seem to be directed at the beautiful turbaned lady in the center. On the print is inscribed, "Lovely Woman—There is in you all that We believe of Heaven." Perhaps this comment is directed only at the leisured classes, who find their inspiration in earthly beauty. However, if the capitalized "We" is meant to suggest the royal form of self-address, then the phrase suggests that the future king, a known womanizer, believes in nothing more divine than the visage of an attractive woman. The censorious scowl of the gentleman on the left registers a strong objection to the proceedings, regardless of whether the prince himself is involved.

Deanne Shey

1. On the social activities of the leisured classes, see Boulton, *Amusements of Old London.*

45 *Blindman's Buff*†

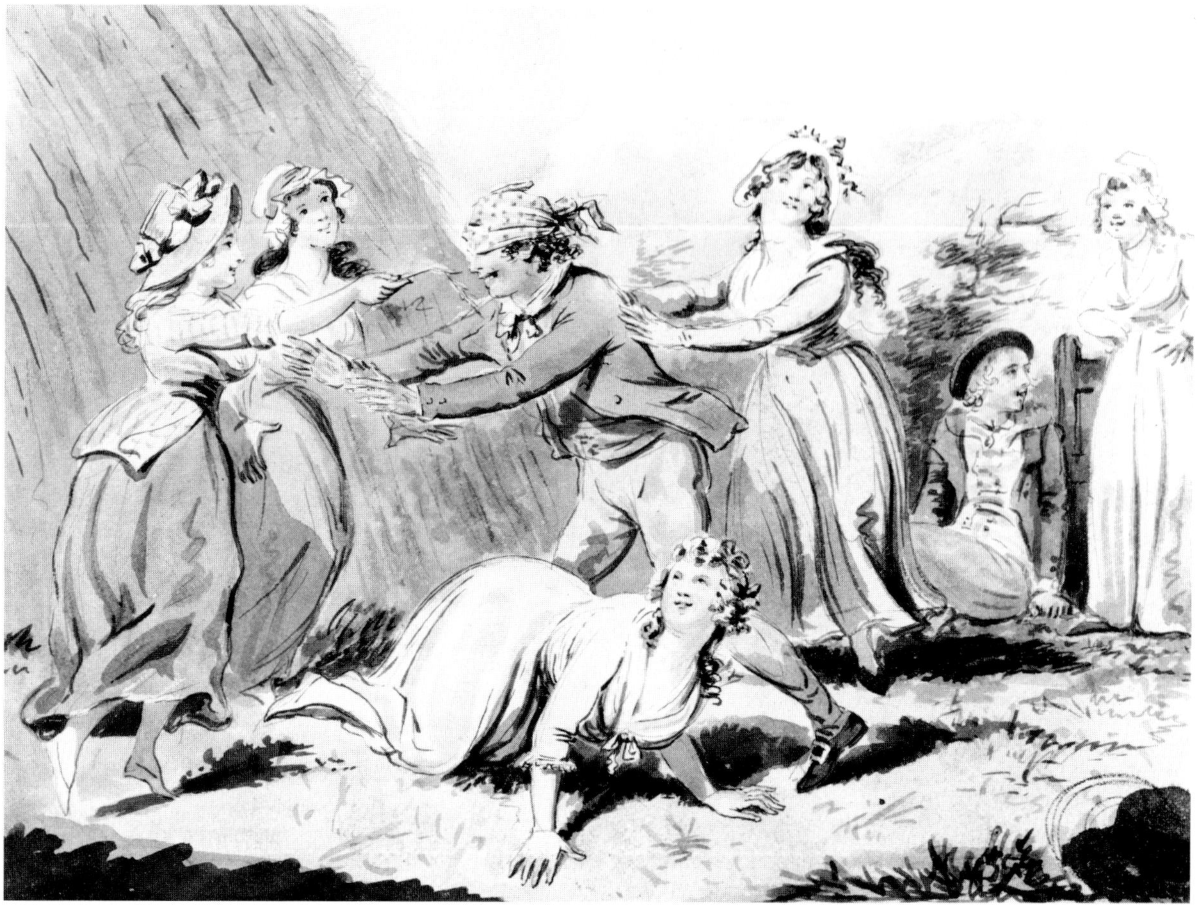

1794
Pen and watercolor over pencil
$6^3/_4$ x 9 inches
(17.15 x 22.86 cm.)
Verso: Ink drawings of heads and figures
Annotated verso: Blindman's Buff / I. Cruikshanks
Published: December 1, 1794, by Laurie & Whittle (131)
Biblio: Wark, 39
Impression: LWL

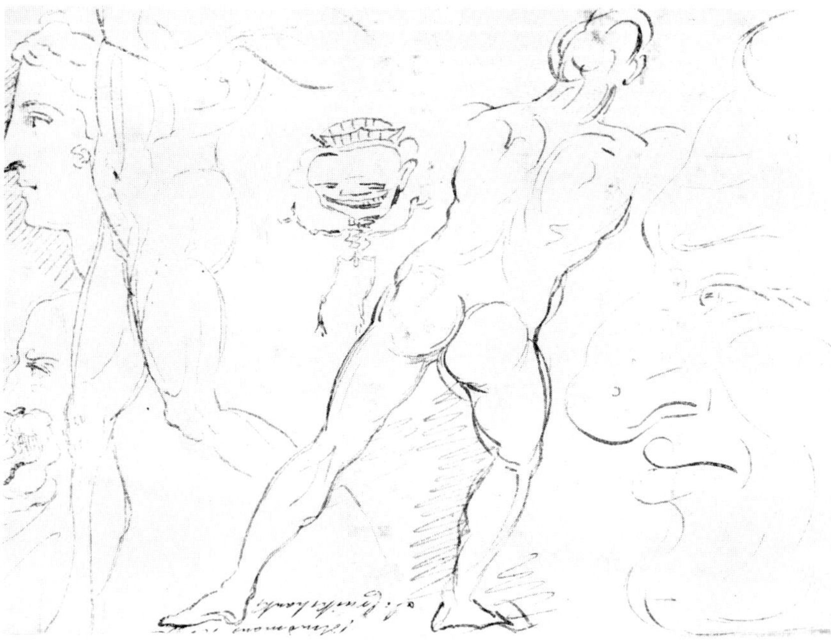

A group of frolicsome young women play the game of blindman's buff with a country youth. The object of the game is for the person whose eyes are covered to catch and identify one of the players, who then receives a kiss and becomes the "blindman." The young women are not dressed in the height of London fashion for the year 1794 but are properly hatted for country gentlefolk. As they romp with abandon, their demure dresses and prim kerchiefs, called "bosom friends," are swept up to reveal ankles, slim waists, and décolletage. The impetuous revelry depicted seems highly charged. The fluid use of line and wash contribute to the overall expression of movement, breathless activity, and lighthearted play.

Blindman's Buff, a bourgeois parlor game in the nineteenth century, is mentioned as early as 1643 in connection with rural May Day celebrations.[1] As is typical of most folk customs and festivals marking the change of seasons, there is a sense of inversion, of the crossing of boundaries, and an expression of the moment of transition.[2] In Cruikshank's drawing, the young women are indeed depicted at a period hovering between girlhood and marriage, engaged in a flirtatious game in which they are the instigators of the action, a role allowed them in play but not in real-life courtship.[3] Appropriate to the mood of inversion is the youth who is captured at the moment before he will fall and become entangled in so many feminine skirts and petticoats.

The open gate serves symbolically as both a boundary to be crossed and an entrance, underscoring the theme of youth at the threshold of adulthood. The arena of play is dominated by a haystack, an appropriate symbol of transience; a common expression of the period referred to the ephemeral nature of life that passes as quickly as grass into hay.

It is interesting to note that although the thematic content of this drawing is associated with youth and the season of springtime, the drawing was not actually published by Laurie & Whittle until December. Though perhaps the connection is unintentional, it provides an appropriate pendant to another drawing by Cruikshank, *Snow Balls – or the Old Buck in Distress* (33), published in May of the same year, depicting an aging gentleman being pelted with snowballs by a bevy of young women as he walks across a barren snow-covered field. Consonant with the theme of inversion, it is almost as if the scenes had been switched. Instead of a robust young lad who finds himself the object of charming feminine attention, it is a gaunt, rather severe old man who discovers he is the victim of its mirthful pranks.

Deanne Shey

1. For a fuller analysis of the practice of folk customs and their function as symbolic enactments of liberty, see Leah S. Marcus Shinangolou, *The Politics of Mirth* (Chicago: University of Chicago Press, 1986).
2. For another work by Cruikshank dealing with folk customs and inversion, see *Leap Year* (102).
3. See Natalie Zemon Davis, "Women on Top: Symbolic Sexual Inversion and Political Disorder in Early Modern Europe," reprinted in *The Reversible World: Symbolic Inversion in Art and Society* (Ithaca, N.Y.: Cornell University Press, 1978), pp. 147-90.

46 *Tipping All Nine*

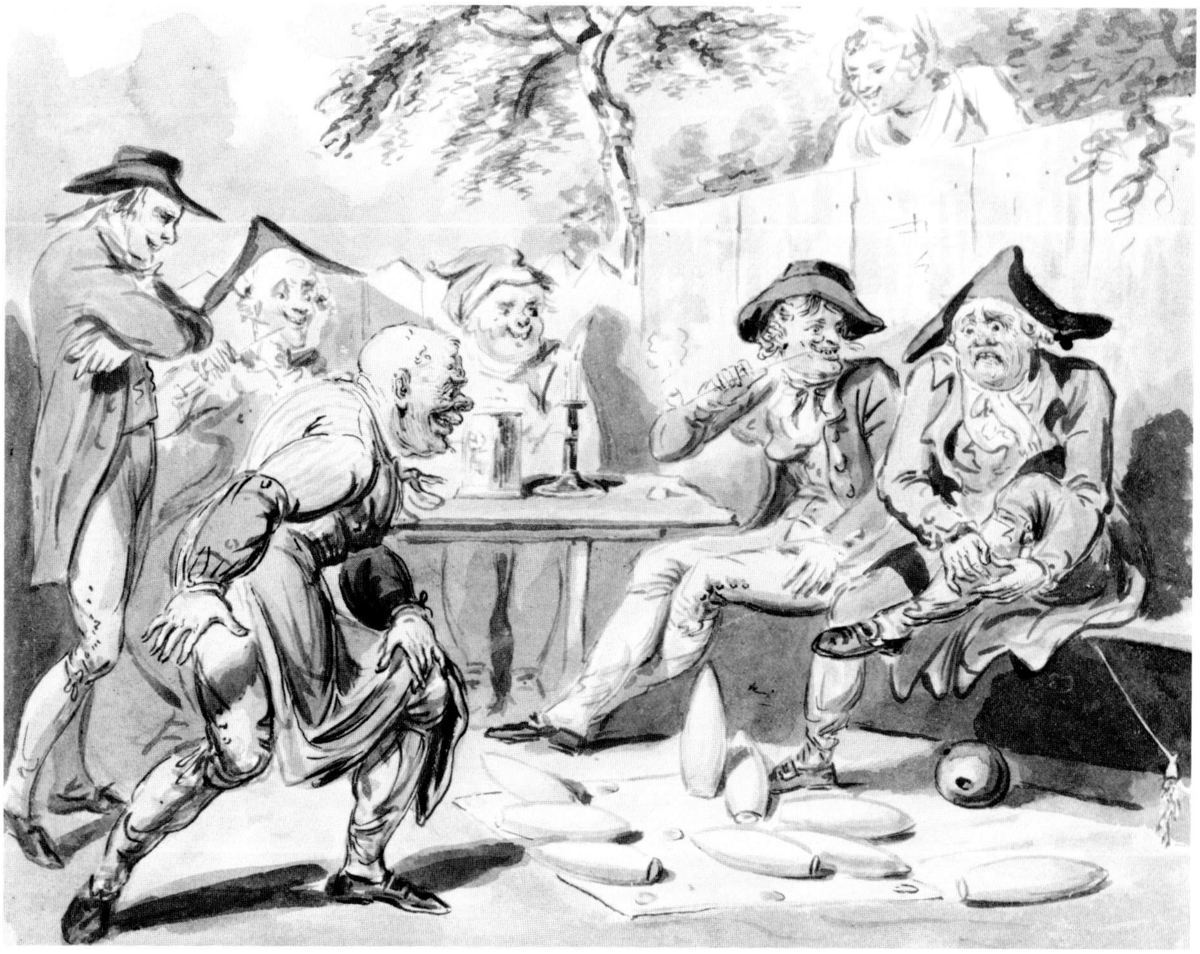

1794
Pen and watercolor over pencil
7 3/8 x 8 3/4 inches (18.8 x 22.2 cm.)
Annotated verso: Tipping All Nine / I. Cruikshanks
Published: December 1, 1794, by Laurie & Whittle (132)
Biblio: Wark, 40
Impression: LWL

Similar to modern American bowling but played informally outside an alehouse, often after work on a summer evening, ninepins was popular with the English working class.[1] The exclusion of women from this sport, as well as from pubs, may explain why a female is peering over the fence instead of entering this male-dominated space.

All the men in this "droll group" are laughing at the fellow rubbing his shin, who became a tenth pin by placing himself behind the line of fire. Again, in 1803, Cruikshank used a similar setting; however, in that case the game took on political overtones. Each of the nine pins resembled a French officer—if not Napoleon himself.[2]

Tim D. Wright

1. Robert W. Malcolmson, *Popular Recreations in English Society, 1700-1850* (Cambridge: Cambridge University Press, 1973), pp. 34, 43.
2. Krumbhaar, *Catalogue Raisonné*, p. 88.

47 *Doctors Differ and Their Patients Die* †

1794
Pen and watercolor over pencil
7 x 9 inches (17.8 x 22.8 cm.)
Annotated verso: Doctors differ and their Patients Die / I. Cruikshanks
Published: December 24, 1794, by Laurie & Whittle (143)
Biblio: George, 8590; Krumbhaar, 283; Wark, 41
Impression: BM, LWL, WMC

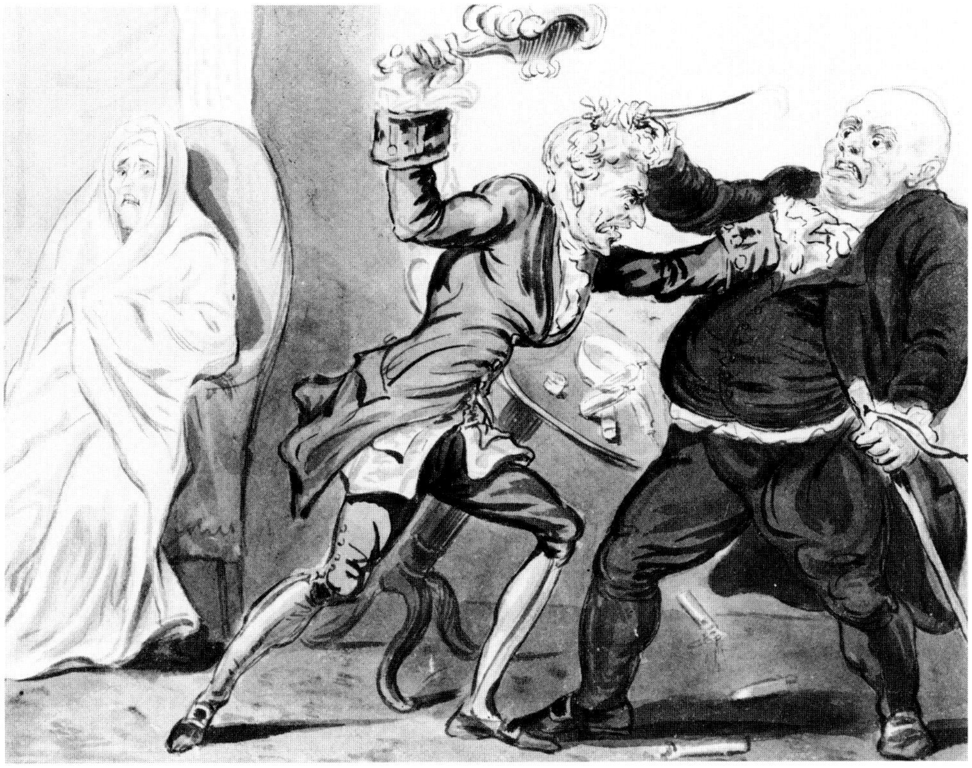

In eighteenth-century England, doctors often consulted on a case, and generally, they disagreed. As a rule, the junior was supposed to give way to the senior. If this did not happen, a third doctor would be called in.[1] Doctors used to meet in their patients' homes and "talk of the weather, or scandal and politics," and their studies "were directed to indulge the passions, rather than check disease."[2] Because medicine was often practiced by those with little training, people distrusted doctors' prescriptions, and writers ridiculed their pretensions.[3]

Cruikshank capitalizes here on the common view of doctors as argumentative, a theme also treated by William Hogarth, among others.[4] The doctors are so vehement in their respective points of view that they have come to blows, knocking over a table loaded with medication in the process. The patient looks on, horrified. Cruikshank contrasts the health and energy of the physicians with the sickness and immobility of the patient, who is clearly a victim of their differences of opinion. The attire of the doctors emphasizes their disagreement. The fat one wears an old-fashioned long black jacket. The thin man sports a more fashionable outfit. Despite their differences, however, they have in common their gross physiognomies: their rolling eyes, twisted eyebrows, and low foreheads convey not only anger but limited intelligence.

Mar Martinez-Perez

1. George, *Social Change in Graphic Satire*, p. 92.
2. Henry Angelo, *The Reminiscences of Henry Angelo*, 2d ed., 2 vols. (London: K. Paul, Trench, Trübner, and Co., Ltd., 1904), 1:97.
3. Fox, *Londoners*, p. 239; see also Bayne-Powell, *Eighteenth-Century London Life*, p. 239.
4. See *Harlot's Progress*, pl. 5.

48 *Foggy Weather* †

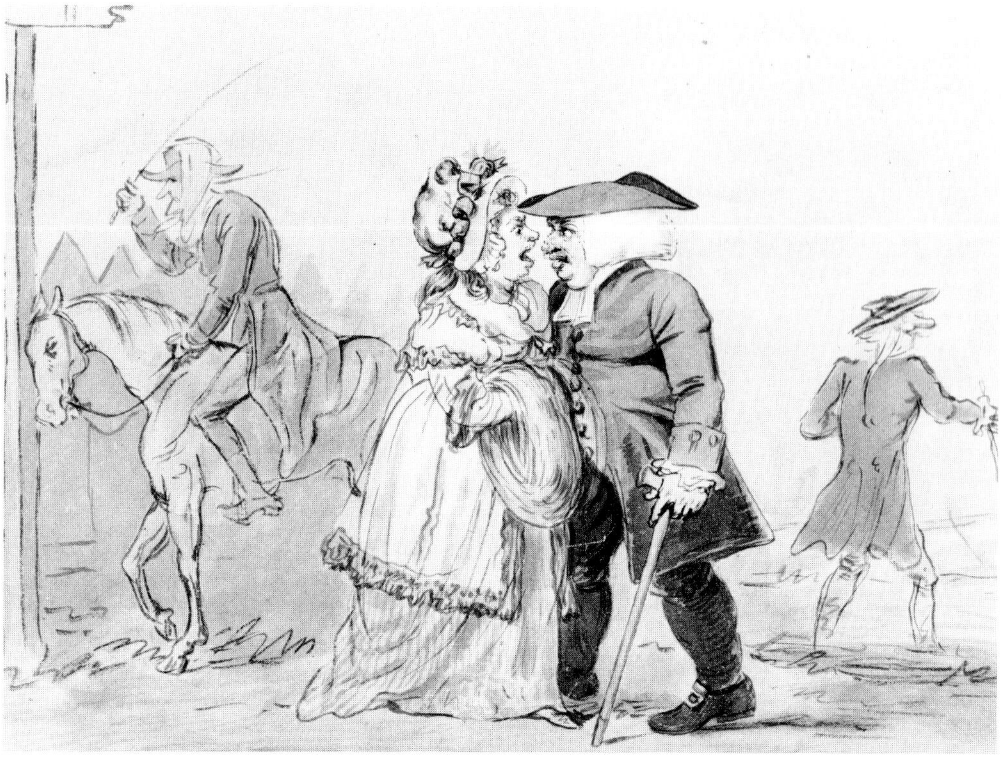

1794
Pen, watercolor, and wash over pencil
6 5/8 x 8 3/4 inches (16.8 x 22.7 cm.)
Annotated verso: Foggy Weather / I. Cruikshanks
Published: December 22, 1794, by Laurie & Whittle (144)
Biblio: George, 8591; Krumbhaar, 382; Wark, 42
Impression: BM, LWL, WMC

Fogs in London could be very dense. The marshes were still undrained and, in addition, coal fires in houses and factories produced heavy smoke, then nearly synonymous with fog.[1] The situation was particularly bad in December 1794 and January 1795 because of terrible frosts. Undoubtedly, these conditions prompted Cruikshank to take up the subject when he did.

Foreigners thought of London as a city of Cimmerian darkness, in which men groped their way for eight or nine months of the year. One remarked, "the smoke gains ground every day; if the increase of London proceeds as far as it may the inhabitants must at last bid adieu to all hopes of ever seeing the sun." Another complained that fogs, smoke, and rain "scarce left a possibility of distinguishing objects at four paces."[2] Although Cruikshank similarly exaggerates the existing conditions, this image would have struck a responsive chord in his audience.

The artist constructs his composition as a symmetrical narrative around an axis of two figures of the same height and shape. They have clearly collided because of their inability to see each other through the thick fog. The woman reacts with an aggressive gesture, and the clergyman does not look happy either. The parson's runny nose, bulging with carbuncles, looks like it is about to go into the woman's mouth. Behind them on the left, a man urges his horse forward into a pole; on the right, another walks into a stream. The foggy weather is effectively conveyed by the artist's sparing use of color. Because the two main figures are close to the viewer, they are accentuated with color, while the men behind, realized with gray washes, appear as shadowy forms seen through a mist.

Mar Martinez-Perez

1. N. Bailey, *An Universal Etymological English Dictionary* (London: J. Darby, A. Bettesworth, F. Fayram, 1793).
2. Quoted in Bayne-Powell, *Eighteenth-Century London Life*, p. 379.

49 *Foot Pad's – Or Much Ado about Nothing* †

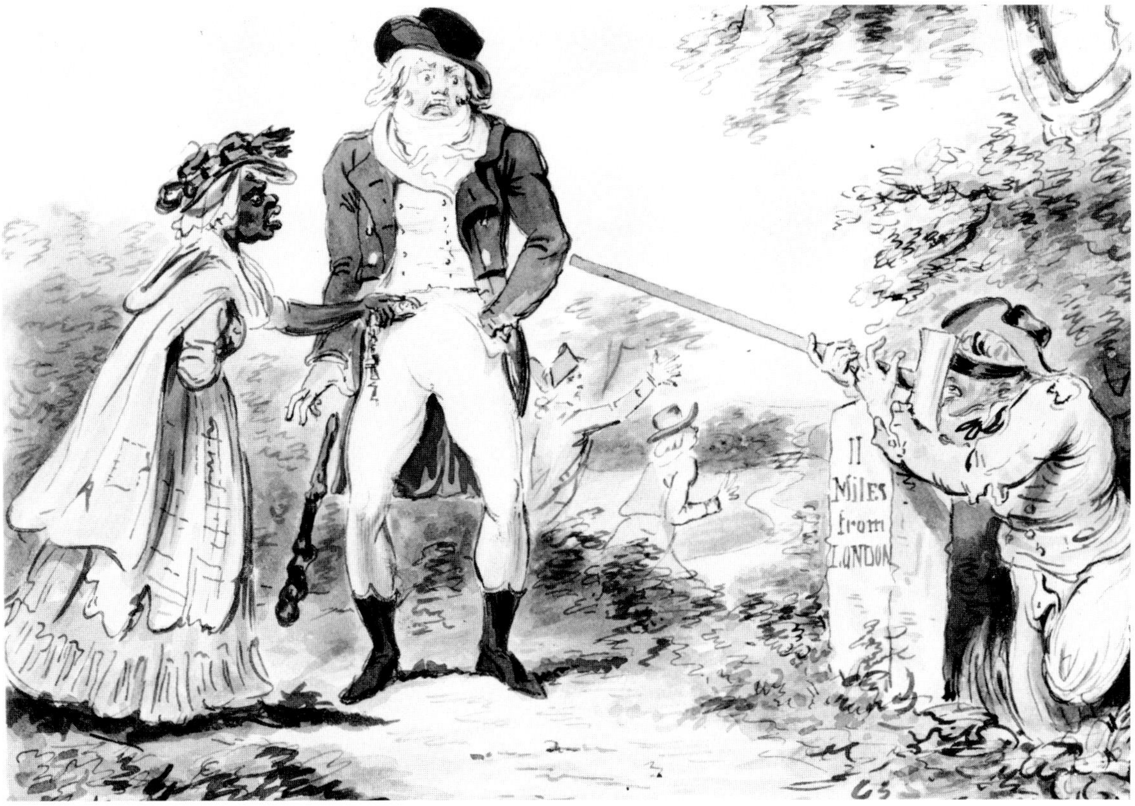

1795
Pen and watercolor over pencil
$6^{1}/_{2}$ x $9^{3}/_{8}$ inches (16.5 x 23.7 cm.)
Inscribed recto: II Miles from London
Annotated verso: Gypsy Robbers / I. Cruikshanks
Published: May 4, 1795, Laurie & Whittle (150); below the title is engraved: Buck's [*sic*] with Truncheons swagger and knock down, / Insult the Sober Peasants when they're out of Town, / But met by Lame Beggars, & a Mottley Crew, / Their Courage fails them, & down they go.
Biblio: Krumbhaar, A.39; Wark, 46
Impression: LWL, WMC

A well-built and fashionably attired man—a "buck"—drops his club, terrified by a blind, one-legged beggar kneeling behind a tombstone who aims his crutch like a gun. The beggar's partner, a black woman in tattered clothes, lifts the gentleman's pocket watch. In the background, two other men flee in fear. If the gentleman had used his club, the robbers would have been no match for him.

The road marker indicates the attack is taking place on the outskirts of London. The area surrounding the city was neither attractive nor safe. Adjacent land was often filled with refuse heaps. Vagrants lived and slept in these areas, cooking their food in kilns. In 1751, it was remarked that "the roads around London had greatly improved as of late. However, footpads [highway men and/or women who robbed on foot] and vagrants made the roads and fields around London unsafe, except on Sundays, when the number of people going to tea gardens and pleasure resorts provided some degree of safety."[1] Conspicuous among London beggars and pickpockets, blacks were often known as "St. Giles Black Birds," so named after a poor parish district in London where many of them lived.

Mari-Tere Alvarez

1. Quoted in M. Dorothy George, *London Life in the Eighteenth Century* (New York: Harper and Row, 1965), p. 105.

50 *Debating Society* †

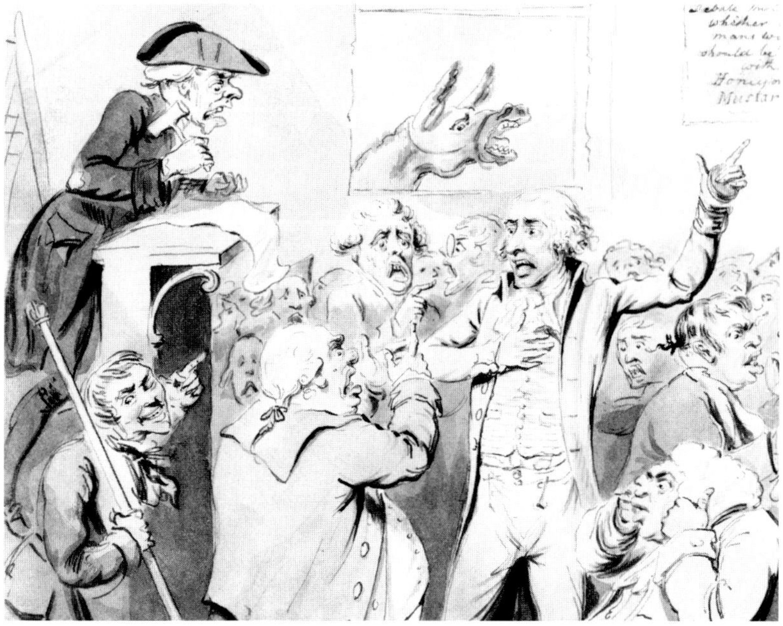

1795
Pen and watercolor
$6\frac{5}{8}$ x $9\frac{3}{8}$ inches
(16.7 x 23.9 cm.)
Inscribed recto: Thelwall; Debate this Evening whether a mans wig should be Drest with Honey or Mustard!!
Annotated verso: The Debating Society / I. Cruikshanks
Published: May 5, 1795, by Laurie & Whittle (152); below the title is engraved: (Substitute for Hair Powder) Silence Gentlemen! to Order! to Order, Only ten Speak at a time! for if you all Bray together, it's impossible to decide on this important Question.
Biblio: George, 8771; Krumbhaar, A.28; Wark, 47
Impression: BM, LWL, WMC

War with France brought great expense, and the government explored various ways to raise money. One of the most notorious was a tax passed by Parliament in 1795 affecting persons who powdered their hair—a fashion then universal among respectable people. Not surprisingly, the use of hair powder declined, but it also took on political significance. Members of the Whig faction stopped using powder and started wearing their hair cut short behind. Tories, who continued using it, were called "guinea-pigs" since one guinea was the amount of the tax.[1]

The hair-powder tax was the subject of many songs and several caricatures. Published the day before the tax came into effect, this image simultaneously draws attention to the new tax and satirizes the practices of debating societies. As a matter of fact, "there was probably no period in English history when men knew so little about politics, and cared so much for them,"[2] and in every coffee house and tavern in the city, groups of working people met to discuss the affairs of state. On special occasions separate rooms were set aside for these meetings. Cruikshank exaggerates the confusion of such gatherings, showing the men all speaking at the same time. He also draws a parallel between the braying ass and the man on the rostrum, who calls for order with a raised hammer. A sign on the wall—"Debate this Evening whether a man's wig should be Drest with Honey or Mustard!"—alludes to the edible character of the hair-dressing, which, in fact, was flour. It has been estimated that soldiers consumed 6,500 tons per annum powdering their hair.[3] The physical attributes of the men—thick eyebrows, projecting rolling eyes, short forehead—would have been recognized at the time as indicative of dullness and intolerance.[4] Between the legs of the central figure is written "Thelwall," a notation that does not appear in the print. Robert Wark has suggested it may well be a reference to John Thelwall (1764-1834), a reformer and lecturer famous for his declamatory powers.

Mar Martinez-Perez

1. Wright, *Caricature History of the Georges,* pp. 494-95. For contemporary comments, see John Ashton, *Old Times: A Picture of Social Life at the End of the Eighteenth Century* (London: John C. Nimmo, 1885), pp. 129-131.
2. Quoted in Bayne-Powell, *Eighteenth-Century London Life,* p. 121.
3. Alexander Andrews, *The Eighteenth Century* (London: Chapman and Hall, 1861), pp. 25-26.
4. Johann Caspar Lavater, *Essays on Physiognomy* (London: William Tegg, 1862), p. 208.

51 *Charms of Precedence* †

1795
Pen and watercolor over pencil
7 x 9 inches
(17.8 x 22.9 cm.)
Annotated verso: Charms of Precedence / I. Cruikshanks
Published: August 7, 1795, by Laurie & Whittle (155); below the image is engraved: "Sir will you please Walk before?" / "No, pray, Sir—you are next the door.." / "Upon mine honor I'll not Stir." / "Sir, I'm at home; consider Sir." / "Excuse me, Sir; I'll not go first."/ "Well, if I must be rude, I must / "But yet I wish I could evade it / "'Tis strangely Clownish, be perswaded."
Biblio: Wark, 48
Impression: LWL

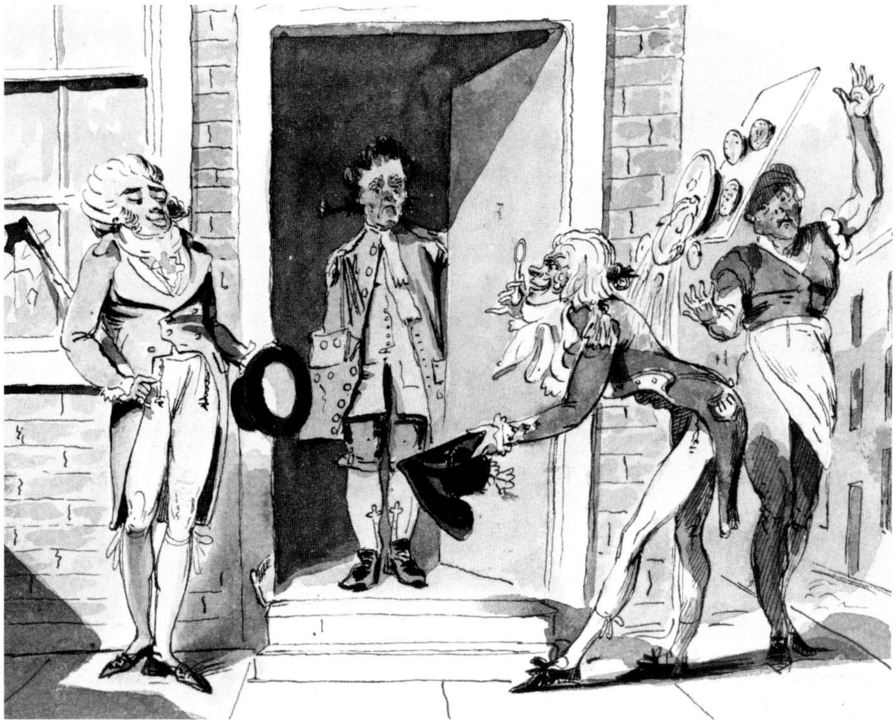

Two men encounter each other at the entrance of the residence of one of them. The exaggerated actions and expressions of the figures are presented like those of a comedy, or farce, in which Cruikshank appears to be poking fun at "fops," that is, well-dressed men who mistake style for intelligence. In their clumsy attempt to adopt gestures intended to demonstrate politeness and refinement, one figure bows and bumps into a delivery man, causing him to drop his tray of goods, while the other breaks a windowpane with his walking stick. The fact that the two men introduce themselves at the rear and not the main entrance of the house adds to the humor of the situation. The servant appears surprised and confused by the havoc. A similar theme is explored in a series of images etched by Cruikshank for G. M. Woodward's *Eccentric Excursions*.[1]

The affected manner in which the two gentlemen comport themselves, the poses that they strike, and the clothing and accessories they wear were fashionable among the dandies of the period and were indicative of social status. Both men wear white wigs, close-fitting breeches, and pointed shoes with laces. The breeches were closed in front by means of a flap, and in order to conceal the openings gentlemen often wore on either side of this flap a watch chain covered in trinkets. They were expected to produce a pretty jingle with these chains and could obtain special instructions in this art in Paris.[2]

The red coat with epaulettes and the three-cornered hat with a cockade worn by the figure on the right indicate that he is in the military. There was an elite guard whose members were assigned duties in the cities and towns, therefore enjoying the status and prestige of being in the military without having to risk their lives. These men were often satirized, and here, Cruikshank has portrayed the figure with a very red face, making fun of the use of rouge by gentlemen. While these two men are under the impression that they are quite chic, they are, in fact, pretentious clowns.

Kathleen Kelly

1. Published in 1796, the series was entitled "Six Different Methods of Carrying a Stick with the Effects"; see Woodward, *Eccentric Excursions*, pp. 8-9.
2. Max Von Boehn, *Modes and Manners* (Philadelphia: J. B. Lippincott Co., 1932), pp. 225-26.

52 *A Scotch Reel* †

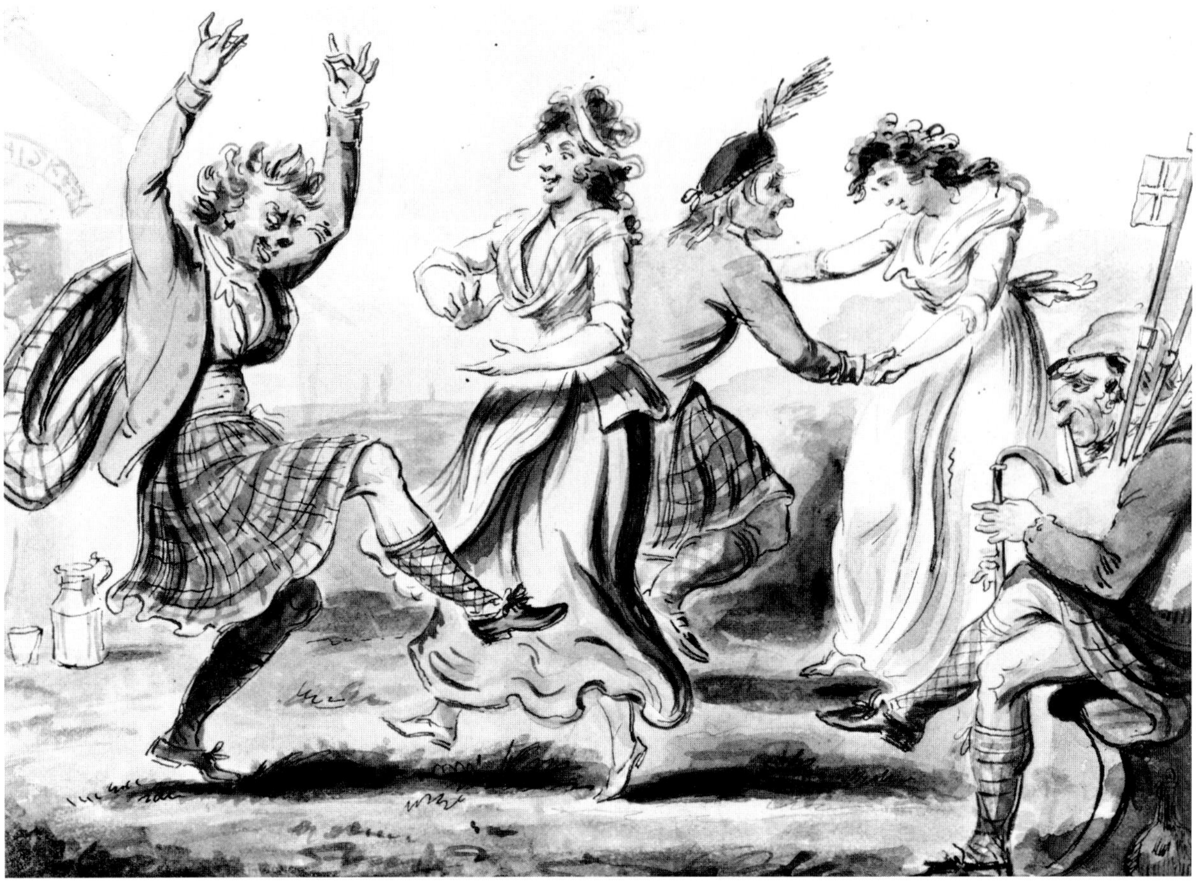

1795
Pen and watercolor
7 x 9⁷⁄₈ inches (17.9 x 25 cm.)
Inscribed recto: Whiskey
Annotated verso: St. Andrew's Day / I. Cruikshanks
Published: August 26, 1795, by Laurie & Whittle; below title is engraved: 'Twas on Christmas day, / Father he did Wed; / Three months after that, / my Mother was brought to Bed. / Tira a lira la—Tira a lira la.
Biblio: Krumbhaar, A.87; Wark, 68
Impression: WMC

Although Cruikshank was Scottish, his images of his countrymen reflected English stereotypes. This scene depicts a celebration of a holiday in the Highlands of Scotland. The inscription on the back indicates it is St. Andrew's Day, but this is not confirmed by external or internal evidence. The whiskey sign in the background and the characters' red faces as well as their exuberant demeanor suggest the common view of Scots as drunkards. Tobias Smollett's popular novel *The Expedition of Humphry Clinker* (1771) expressed British perceptions of Highlanders. In Smollett's words "The Highlanders regale themselves with whisky; a malt spirit, as strong as geneva (gin) which they swallow in great quantities."[1]

The title of the published print recalls a play by John O'Keefe entitled *The Highland Reel,* which was performed at Covent Garden for several seasons beginning in October 1792.[2] The play, a comic musical, enlivened rural scenes with ludicrous sketches in which the main character was a jovial Scottish fellow who kept a whiskey shop and often sang a verse exalting drink and dancing.[3] The reel is a form of country dance unique to the Highlands, but it is likely that the word *reel* in the title puns on the effects of drinking. The accompanying text also suggests that such moments of abandon could have other consequences.

Cruikshank's depiction of country folk here contrasts with the grim people in *St. Andrew's*

Day (see 103). The contrast indicates the distinction made between the people of the Lowlands, where he was born, and Scots of the Highlands, his wife's homeland. The dress is a traditional Highland costume that originated as an army uniform. The plaid on a kilt or shawl identified the wearer's clan. During the eighteenth century, the kilt evolved into civilian dress for a minority of Highlanders. By late in the century it was worn by Scots around the world and eventually came to symbolize Scottish patriotism and dignity.[4] Customs such as dance, music, and costume developed as distinguishing attributes of the Scots after the Union of 1707.

Despite efforts by the conservative Scottish church to stamp out activities such as folk music and dancing, popular culture reemerged from the underground and flourished after 1702.[5] The prominence of such customs was probably part of a determined effort to preserve the genuine culture and national identity of the Scottish people in the face of English domination.[6] Proud of their distinct culture, emigrants from the Highlands played bagpipes and dressed in kilts even in London.[7] These actions were subject to ridicule and caricature.

Mary-Kay Lombino

---

1. Smollett, *Humphry Clinker*, ed. James L. Thorson (New York: W. W. Norton and Co., 1983), p. 222.
2. Hogan, ed., *The London Stage*, pt. 5, p. 1411.
3. John O'Keefe, "The Highland Reel," in *Cumberland's British Theatre,* 22 vols. (London: John Cumberland, 1828), 18:72.
4. John Telfer Dunbar, *The Costume of Scotland* (Glasgow: B. T. Batsford, 1981), p. 154.
5. R. A. Houston and I. D. Whyte, *Scottish Society, 1500-1800* (Cambridge: Cambridge University Press, 1989), p. 34.
6. Faber, *The High Road to England*, p. 176.
7. Henry Mayhew, *London Labour and the London Poor*, 4 vols. (London: Griffin, Bohn, and Co., 1861), 1:170.

53 *The Disagreeable Intrusion, or Irish Fortune Hunter Detected* †

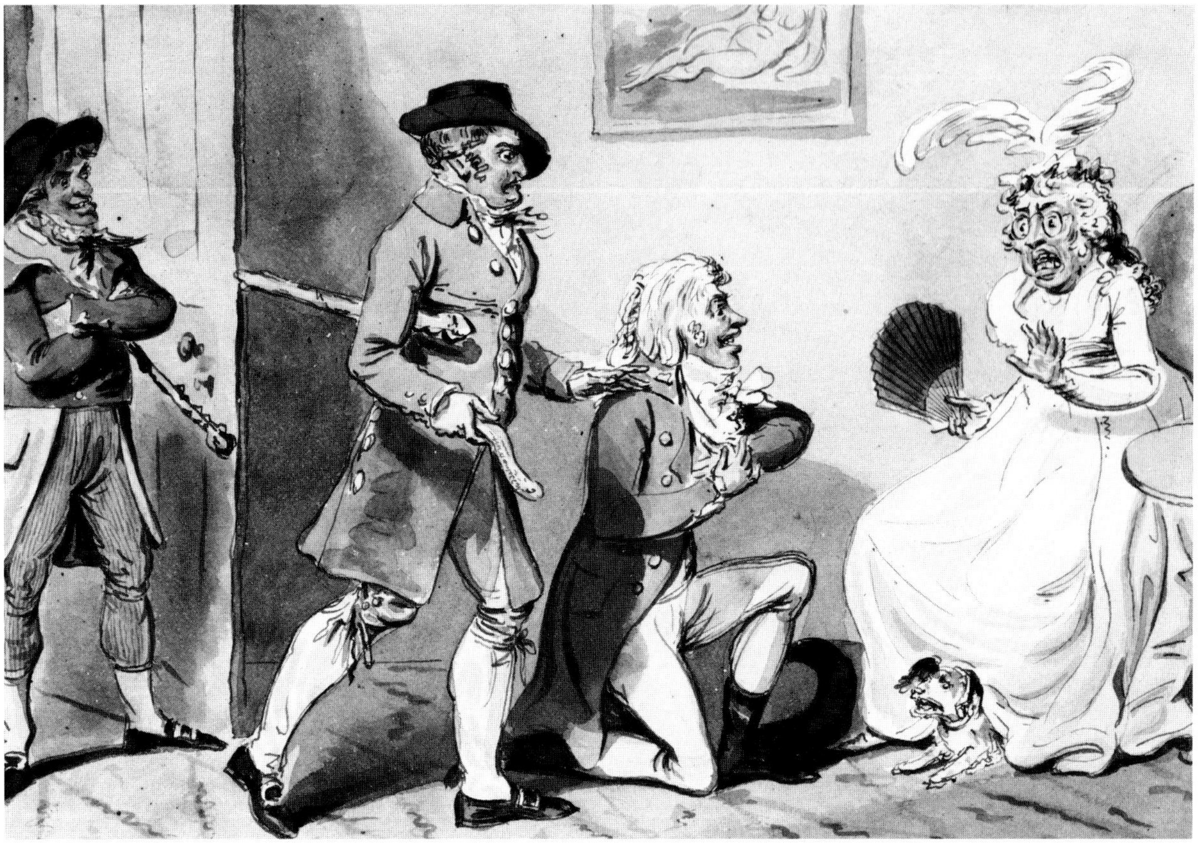

1795
Pen and watercolor over pencil
$6^5/_8$ x $9^5/_{16}$ inches (16.8 x 23.7 cm.)
Inscribed recto: Middlesex to wit (?)
Annotated verso: The Fortune Hunter / I. Cruikshanks
Published: September 4, 1795, by Laurie & Whittle (160); below the title is engraved: On my knees Dear Lady let me intreat you to Appoint the happy Day – Pray Dear Sir rise it is too much for me to see you in such an humble situation – Bailiff – Pray rise and go along with us. We'll provide a Lodging for you – Murder—Thieves—Fire—Oh—Seize um Pomp-p-Oh-O-O.
Biblio: Kruumbhaar, A.30; Wark, 49
Impression: LWL, WMC

According to a late eighteenth-century definition, a fortune hunter was "a man whose employment it is to hunt or enquire after women with great portions, to enrich himself by marrying them."[1] Irish or not, this fortune hunter of lore makes frequent appearances in novels and plays of the period. Cruikshank, along with other contemporary writers and artists, treats such characters on several occasions.

In this drawing a young Irish "gentleman," desperate for financial prosperity, seems to be caught by the bailiffs in the act of preying on an old and unattractive spinster. However, what is actually represented is a sequence of events: the declaration of the fortune hunter to the lady; her response; the apprehension of the man by the bailiff and his companion; and the reaction of the lady to the arrest. This image, capturing the sequential moments in a narrative, seems a visual equivalent of a dramatic situation in a comic play or story. In any event, the butt of the joke here is the woman, whose proposal of marriage appears doomed. Her advanced age and unattractiveness are emphasized by direct comparison with a classic image of sensual beauty, the reclining nude, in the picture above her head. The dog, closely resembling in behavior as well as expression the characteristics of its mistress, barks at the intruders.

The fortune hunter is presumably being taken into custody for making the marriage proposal, as agreeable as it might be to the spinster. In the early eighteenth century, marriage was valid without a license, at any time or place, and without the presence of a clergyman. As M. Dorothy George states, in *London Life in the Eighteenth Century:* "Entries in the Fleet [Street Prison] registers could always be forged, antedated or expunged. The practice was a direct incitement to bigamy, fictitious marriage for purposes of seduction, or marriage as the result of a drunken frolic. By persuasion, force, or fraud, women were taken to the purlieus of the Fleet, and there married, to be stripped of their fortune and deserted."[2] One man was even reported to have married as many as four times in fourteen months. The practice was effectually stopped by Lord Hardwicke's Marriage Act of 1753.[2] In the drawing, the law protects the lady from a union she clearly desires.

Julie Joyce

---

1. Johnson and Walker, *The Peoples' Pronouncing Dictionary*
2. George, *London Life in the Eighteenth Century* (Chicago: Academy, 1984), p. 305.

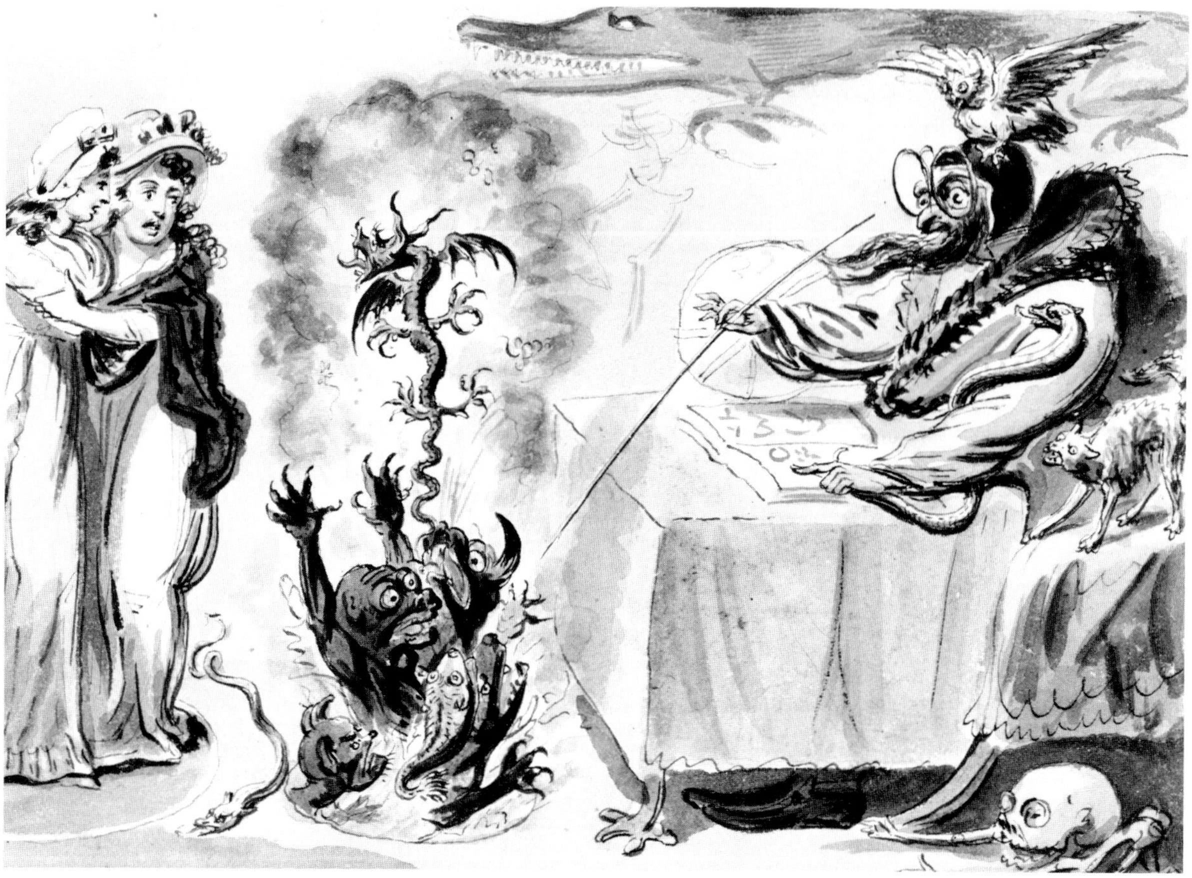

1795
Pen and watercolor over pencil
$6^{5}/_{8}$ x $9^{1}/_{8}$ inches (16.7 x 23.3 cm.)
Annotated verso: The Fortune Teller / I. Cruikshanks
Published: November 20, 1795, by Laurie & Whittle (164)
Biblio: George, 8777; Krumbhaar, 970; Wark, 50
Impression: BM, LWL, WMC

The Gothic novel, which both fostered and relied upon an interest in magic and sorcery, was very popular at the end of the eighteenth century. Typical plots included "hypnotic trances, telepathic communications, visionary experiences, and extrasensory perceptions [which] reveal the secret recesses of the mind or powers of increased mental transmission and reception."[1]

As was the case with the romance, the audience for the Gothic novel was made up primarily of middle- and upper-class women who had the leisure time to read. Here, as in *Telling Fortunes in Coffee Grounds* (3), Cruikshank seems to be making a satirical comment on the pastimes of women, in particular their reading habits—their fascination with the occult and delight in terror. In the watercolor, two young ladies stand fearfully looking on as a wizard raises demons and ghouls from fiery flames. In the print after this image, the woman on the left is replaced by a man whose country attire and physical appearance (his hair stands on end) indicate that he is both unsophisticated and frightened.[2] Therefore, the satire is perhaps directed not strictly at women but at those susceptible to Gothic sentimentality.

Jennifer Katell

1. Linda Bayer-Berenbaum, *The Gothic Imagination: Expansion in Gothic Literature and Art* (London: Associated University Press, 1982), pp. 31-32.
2. George Cruikshank, Isaac's son, treated a similar subject. See Photo Archives, Art Reference Library, the Huntington.

55 *Snap Dragon* †

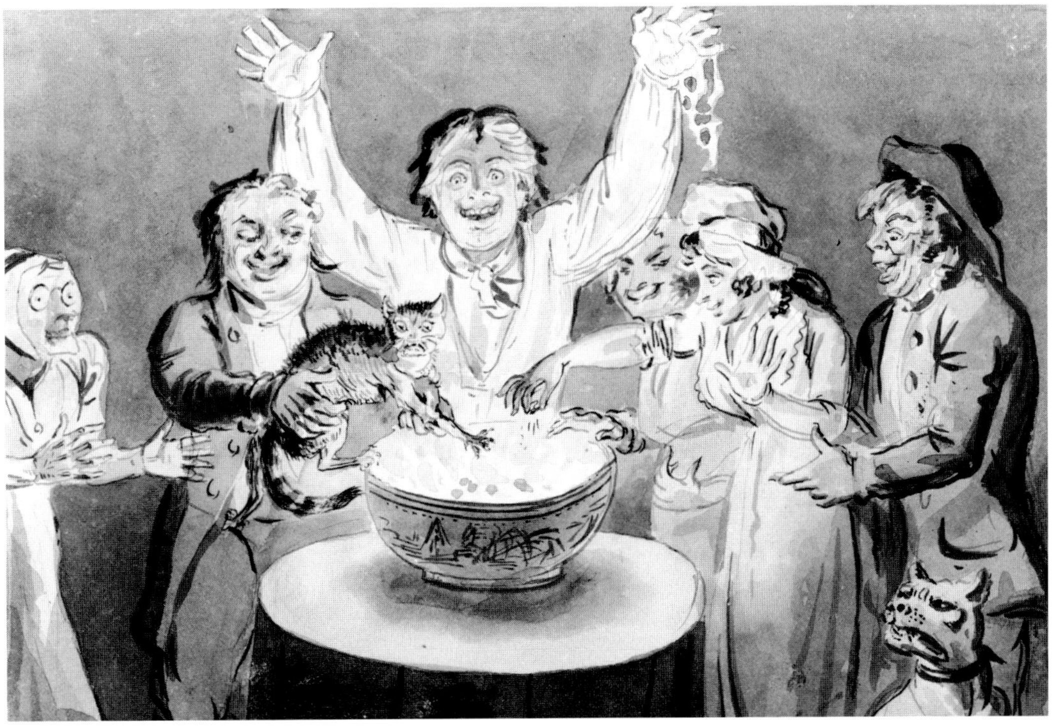

1795
Pen, gray and blue wash and watercolor over pencil
6 11/16 x 9 inches (17 x 23 cm.)
Verso: pencil sketch of a standing nude male figure in a classical pose
Annotated verso: Snap Dragon / I. Cruikshanks
Published: December 12, 1795, by Laurie & Whittle (165)
Biblio: George, 8778; Krumbhaar, 1117; Wark, 51
Impression: BM, LWL

Snapdragon, described by Robert Chambers in *The Book of Days,* was an amusement associated with the Christmas season: "A quantity of raisins are deposited in a large dish or bowl (the broader and shallower this is, the better), and brandy or some other spirit is poured over the fruit and ignited. The bystanders now endeavor, by turns, to grasp a raisin, by plunging their hands through the flames; and as this is somewhat of an arduous feat, requiring both courage and rapidity of action, a considerable amount of laughter and merriment [are] evoked at the expense of the unsuccessful competitors."[1]

Since the game was played in the dark, a lurid glare emanated from the bowl. The blue tint Cruikshank uses to capture it adds to the bizarre atmosphere of the scene, which is heightened further by the entranced expressions of the participants. Chambers suggests that in this amusement players experience a trace of the "fiery ordeal of the middle ages, and also of the Druidical fire-worship of a still remoter epoch."[2] The name of this folly may have evolved from the popular English legend surrounding St. George and the mythical slaying of a dragon named "Snap."

The fun in Snapdragon lies in the fact that the losers, or the slower players, obtain a handful or mouthful of fire before the flaming raisin can be extinguished. Yet the point of this depiction may lie in the player's treatment of the clearly terrified cat. A participant mischievously takes the animal's paw in hand as if to use it for playing the game. The hysterical amusement of the players brings to light an issue Cruikshank may or may not have been mindful of: cruelty to animals. Although the first law protecting animal rights was not enacted until 1821,[3] such issues were a social and political concern at the time of this image's publication.

Julie Joyce

1. Chambers, ed., *The Book of Days,* 2 vols. (London and Edinburgh: W. and R. Chambers, Ltd., 1932), 2:738.
2. Ibid.
3. Wellesley Pain, *Richard Martin (1754-1834)* (London: Leonard Parsons, 1925), pp. 45-76.

56 *Monsieur Tonson: A Tale* †

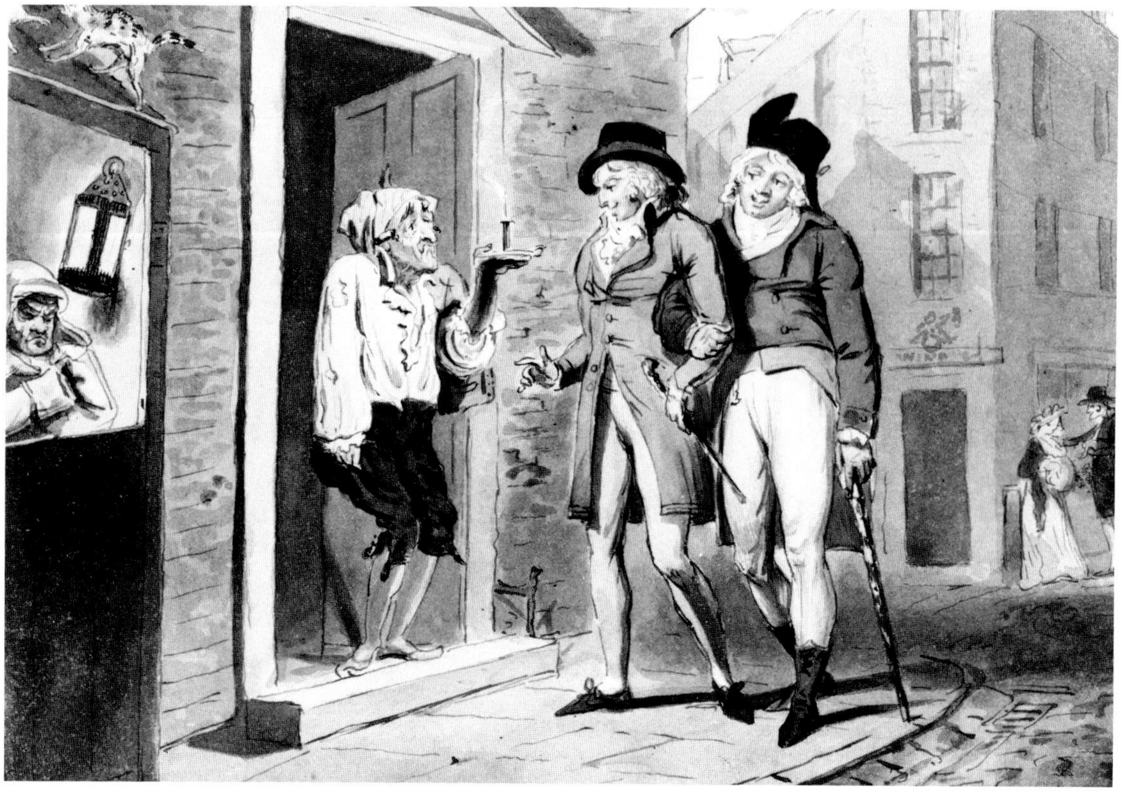

1795
Pen and watercolor over pencil
6⁷/₈ x 8⁷/₈ inches (17.5 x 22.5 cm.)
Inscribed recto: WINE
Annotated verso: Monsieur Tonson / I. Cruikshanks
Published: December 22, 1795, by Laurie & Whittle; below the title is engraved: Written by John Taylor, Esq. It was recited by Mr. Fawcett at Covent-Garden Theatre, and the Readings, at Free-Mason's Hall; followed by 28 stanzas of verse.
Biblio: Krumbhaar, A.72; Wark, 52
Impression: WMC

The poem *Monsieur Tonson,* written by the playwright John Taylor, was recited for public entertainment in the Covent Garden Theatre by the actor and dramatist John Fawcett in May of 1795 and at the Readings at Free-Mason's Hall. (The Free-Mason's Hall was rented out for plays and recitals from time to time.) It was subsequently the basis of a play by W. T. Montcrieff, which was performed in September of 1821 at Drury Lane.

The story is about a prankster and his companion—two dandies—who for a joke continually call at a particular house in the middle of the night asking for an imaginary Mr. Thompson. The occupant is French, which explains the title "Monsieur Tonson." The building is located in a quarter of London where foreigners escaping persecution in their homeland settled. Ironically, as a result of the continuous harassment by the Englishman, the Frenchman is driven from the place where he has sought refuge, never to be heard from again. Cruikshank's drawing, an interpretation of stanzas 4-10, reflects the lack of sympathy for refugees in eighteenth-century London.

To the left of the doorway is one of the many night-watchmen put on the streets of London in 1640 by King Charles I. Popularly known as "Charlies" after the king, they were frequently depicted as senile and venal incompetents. They became the victims of bucks, who would push their booths over, trapping them inside. At night, these fashionable young men would go out on "sprees" in search of fun and pleasure. After spending an evening drinking with friends, they might play pranks such as the one illustrated here.[1]

Kathleen Kelly

1. Pierce Egan, *Life in London* (London: Sherwood, Neeley, and Jones, 1821).

Monsieur Tonson

There liv'd, as Fame reports, in days of yore,
At least some fifty years ago, or more,
　　A pleasant Wight on town, yclep'd Tom King,
A fellow that was clever at a joke,
Expert in all the arts to teaze and *smoke,*
　　In short, for strokes of humour, quite *the thing.*

To many a jovial Club this King was known,
With whom his active wit unrivall'd shone—
　　Choice Spirit, grave Free Mason, Buck, and Blood,
Would crowd his Stories and *Bon Mots* to hear,
And none a disappointment e'er could fear,
　　His humour flow'd in such a copious flood.

To him a frolic was a high delight—
A frolic he would hunt for day and night,
　　Careless how Prudence on the sport might frown:
If e'er a pleasant mischief sprang to view,
At once o'er hedge and ditch away he flew,
　　Nor left the game 'till he had run it down.

One night our Hero, rambling with a friend,
Near fam'd St. Gile's chanc'd his course to bend,
　　Just by that spot the Seven Dials hight;
'Twas silence all around, and clear the coast,
The watch, as usual, dozing on his post,
　　And scarce a lamp display'd a twinkling light.

Around this place there liv'd the num'rous clans,
Of honest, plodding, Foreign Artizans,
　　Known at that time by the name of Refugees—
The rod of Persecution from their home
Compell'd the inoffensive race to roam,
　　And here they lighted, like a swarm of Bees.

Well! Our two friends were saunt'ring through the street,
In hopes some food for humour soon to meet,
　　When, in a window near, a light they view;
An though a dim and melancholy ray,
It seem'd the prologue to some merry play,
　　So tow'rds the gloomy dome our Hero drew.

Strait at the door he gave a thund'ring knock,
(The time we may suppose near two o'clock)
　　"I'll ask," says King, "if Thompson lodges here."
"Thompson," cries t'other, "who the devil is he?"
"I Know not," King replies, "but want to see
　　"What kind of animal will now appear."

After some time a little Frenchman came,
One hand display'd a rush-light's trembling flame,
　　The other held a thing they call *culotte;*
An old strip'd woollen night-cap grac'd his head,
A tatter'd waistcoat o'er one shoulder spread,
　　Scarce half awake, he heav'd a yawning note.

Though thus untimely rouz'd, he courteous smil'd,
And soon address'd our Wag in accents mild,
　　Bending his head politely to his knee—
"Pray, Sare, vat vant you, dat you come so late?
"I beg your pardon, Sare, to make you vait;
"Pray, tell me, Sare, vat your commands vid me?"

"Sir," replied King, "I merely thought to know,
"As by your house I chanc'd to-night to go—
　　"But, really, I disturb'd your sleep, I fear—
"I say, I thought that you perhaps could tell,
"Among the folks who in this street may dwell,
　　"If there's a Mr. Thompson lodges here?"

The shiv'ring Frenchman, though not pleas'd to find
The business of this unimportant kind,
　　Too simple to suspect 'twas meant in jeer,
Shrug'd out a sigh that thus his rest should break,
Then, with unalter'd courtesy he spake—
　　"No, Sare, no Monsieur Tonson lodges here."

Our Wag begg'd pardon, and tow'rds home he sped,
While the poor Frenchman crawl'd again to bed;
　　But King resolv'd, not thus to drop the jest;
So the next night, with more of whim than grace,
Again he made a visit to the place,
　　To break once more the poor old Frenchman's rest.

He knock'd, but waited longer than before,
No footstep seem'd approaching to the door;
　　Our Frenchman lay in such a sleep profound—
King, with the knocker, thunder'd then again,
Firm on his post determin'd to remain;
　　And oft, indeed, he made the door resound.

At last, King hears him o'er the passage creep,
Wond'ring what fiend again disturb'd his sleep:
　　The Wag salutes him with a civil leer;
Thus drawling out, to heighten the surprize,
(While the poor Frenchman rubb'd his heavy eyes)
　　"Is there a—Mr. Thompson—lodges here?"

The Frenchman faulter'd, with a kind of fright—
"Vy, Sare, I'm sure, I tell you, Sare, Last night—
　　(And here he labour'd with a sigh sincere)
"No Monsieur Tonson in de varld I know,
"No Monsieur Tonson here—I told you so;
　　"Indeed, Sare, dere no Monsieur Tonson here."

Some more excuses tender'd, off King goes,
And the old Frenchman sought once more repose.
　　The rogue next night pursu'd his odd career—
'Twas long indeed before the man came nigh,
And then he utter'd, in a piteous cry,
　　"Sare, 'pon my soul, no Monsieur Tonson here!"

Our sportive wight his usual visit paid,
And the next night came forth a prattling Maid,
　　Whose tongue, indeed, than any jack went faster—
Anxious she strove his errand to enquire;
He said, "'Tis vain her pretty tongue to tire,
　　"He should not stir till he had seen her Master."

The Damsel then began, in doleful state,
The Frenchman's broken slumbers to relate,
　　And begg'd he'd call at proper time of day—
King told her, she must fetch her Master down,
A chaise was ready—he was leaving Town,
　　But first had much of deep concern to say.

Thus urged, she went the snoring man to call,
And long indeed was she oblig'd to bawl,
Ere she could rouze the torpid lump of clay.
At last he wakes—he rises—and he swears,
But scarcely had he totter'd down the stairs,
When King attacks him in the usual way.

The Frenchman now perceiv'd 'twas all in vain
To this tormentor mildly to complain,
And strait in rage begun his crest to rear—
"Sare, vat the devil make you treat me so?
"Sare, I inform you, Sare, tree nights ago,
"Got tam, I swear, no Monsieur Tonson here."

True as the night, King went, and hears a strife
Between the harras'd Frenchman and his Wife,
Which should descend to chase the fiend away:
At length to join their forces they agree,
And strait impetuously they turn the key,
Prepar'd with mutual fury for the fray.

Our Hero, with the firmness of a rock,
Collected to receive the mighty shock,
Utt'ring the old enquiry, calmly stood—
The *name* of Thompson rais'd the storm so high,
He deem'd it then the safest plan to fly,
With—"Well, I'll call when you're in a gentler mood."

In short, our Hero, with the same intent,
Full many a night to plague the Frenchman went—
So fond of mischief was the wicked wit:
They threw out water—for the watch they call,
But King, expecting, still escapes from all—
Monsieur at last was forc'd his house to quit.

It happen'd that our Wag about this time,
On some fair prospect sought the Eastern clime;
Six ling'ring years were there his tedious lot:
At length, content, amid his rip'ning store,
He treads again on Britain's happy shore,
And his long absence is at once forgot.

To London, with impatient hope he flies,
And the same night, as former streaks arise,
He fain must stroll, the well known haunt to trace.
"Ah! here's the scene of frequent mirth," he said:
"My poor old Frenchman, I suppose, is dead—
"Egad! I'll knock, and see who holds his place."

With rapid strokes he makes the mansion roar,
And while he eager eyes the op'ning door,
Lo! who obeys the knocker's rattling peal?
Why e'en our little Frenchman, strange to say,
He took his abode that very day—
Capricious turn of Sportive Fortune's Wheel!

Without one thought of the relentless foe,
Who, fiend-like, haunted him so long ago,
Just in his former trim he now appears;
The waistcoat and the nightcap seem'd the same,
With rush-light as before, he creeping came,
And King's detected voice astonish'd hears.

As if some hideous spectre struck his sight,
His senses seem'd bewilder'd with afright;
His face, indeed, bespoke a heart full sore—
Then, starting, he exclaim'd, in rueful strain,
"Begar! here's Monsieur Tonson come again!"
Away he ran—and ne'er was heard of more.

57 *"The Pickpockets"* †

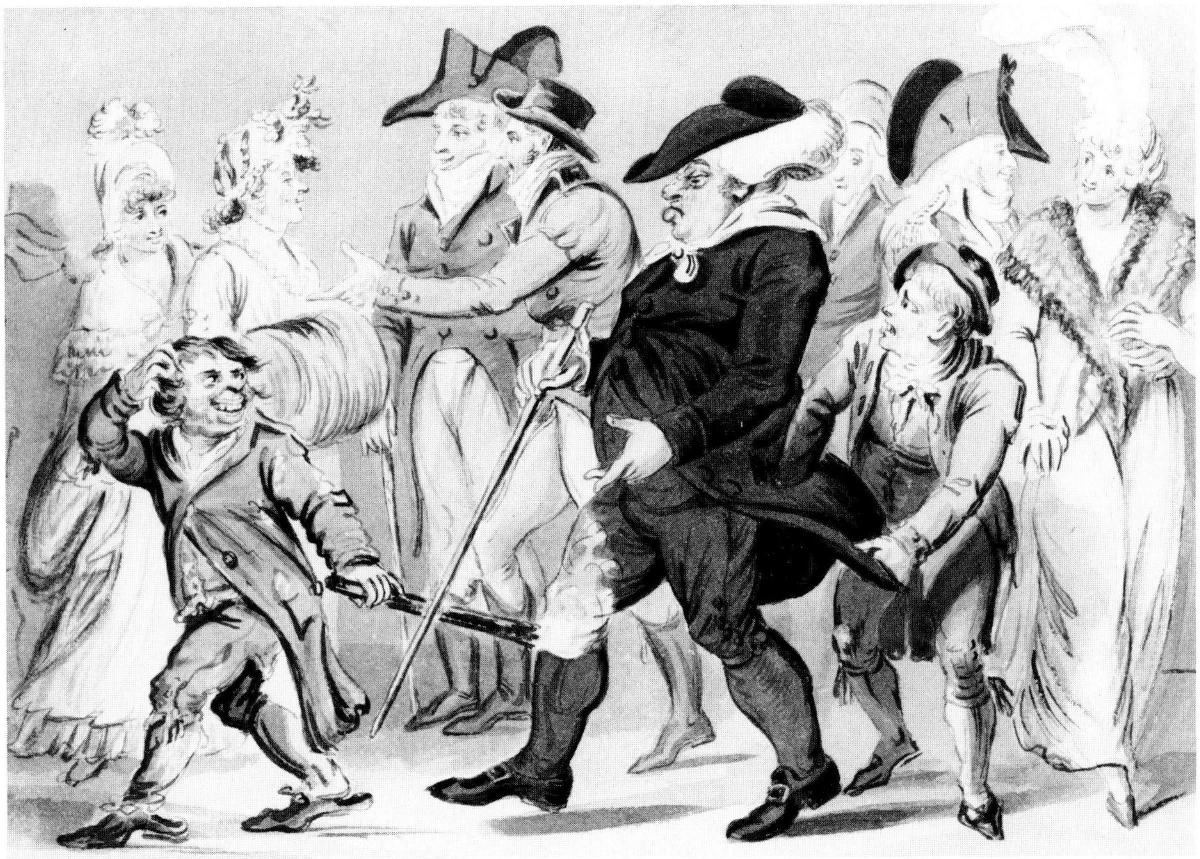

c. 1795
Pen and watercolor over pencil
$6\frac{1}{2}$ x $9\frac{1}{8}$ inches (16.5 x 23.1 cm.)
Annotated verso: I. Cruikshanks
Biblio: Wark, 53

Life in London was filled with activity but fraught with danger. On this bustling street a ragamuffin distracts a cleric by putting a torch to his knee as his youthful partner in crime picks the clergyman's pocket. In the background, Londoners are going about their business. On the left two men seem to be propositioning girls, possibly streetwalkers. The amorous couple on the right is oblivious to the surrounding action. Only one male figure, wearing a green coat, sees the robbery taking place.

Cruikshank does not seem to be making moral judgments but simply observing a London street scene. Still, his depiction reveals his awareness of civic problems. In fact, in eighteenth-century London this type of scene would not have been unusual; the viewer would have been all too aware of the large number of children that were left to make their own way on the streets. No print after this image has been located to date.

Mari-Tere Alvarez

58 "Courtship" †

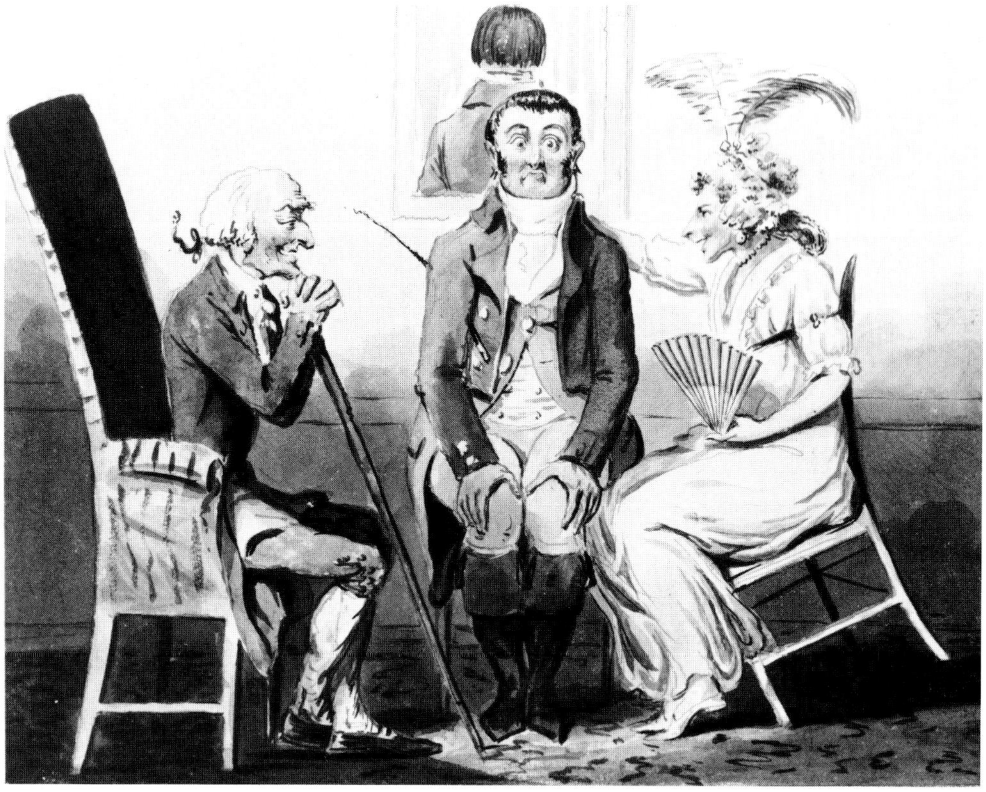

c. 1795
Pen and watercolor over pencil
6 1/2 x 8 5/8 inches (16.5 x 21.9 cm.)
Annotated verso:
Courtship / I. Cruikshanks
Biblio:
Wark, 54

A hapless man appears startled and overwhelmed by an enthusiastic and aggressive spinster, who places her arm on his shoulder. Her beady eyes, pointed nose, and open-mouthed smile indicate her eagerness. Leaning forward at a precarious angle, she touches her rather doltish, perhaps reluctant, suitor. Her movement underscores her "forwardness" in the courtship. Such assertive demeanor would have been unseemly in a world in which courtship was conducted under the watchful eye of a chaperone. Feminine perfection, as articulated by Maria Cosway in her illustrated book of manners, *The Progress of Female Virtue* (1800), was a combination of unselfconscious modesty, chastity, and graceful restraint. Perhaps Cruikshank is satirizing this rather idealized standard.

Though fashionably dressed, the young man is clearly a dullard. The wall mirror reflects this "block" head and suggests he doesn't know whether he's coming or going, at least in this situation. The old man, presumably the woman's father, seems pleased with the possible union. His high-backed chair and authoritative walking stick suggest his position in society. In contrast, the small riding crop held askew by the younger man conveys his awkwardness and, perhaps, ineffectuality in the situation. The open fan of the woman aptly signifies her receptivity. The young man and the eager spinster may be social equals, but it seems the odd courtship would bring together an ill-matched couple.

No print after this image has yet been located. Robert Wark assigned a date of 1795 based on stylistic similarities to other works of the period.[1] Certainly the strong black outlines, drawn with a coarse reed pen, which are typical of this phase, serve aptly to delineate the distinct positions of each character. The vigorous and lively line expresses the eagerness of the woman, while it serves to underscore the barely subdued anxiety of her would-be beau. The larger-scale figures, careful application of color over large areas, and highly finished rendering mark this image as characteristic of Cruikshank's vintage style.

Deanne Shey

1. Wark, *"Drawings for Drolls,"* p. 16.

59 *"Leading Apes in Hell"* †

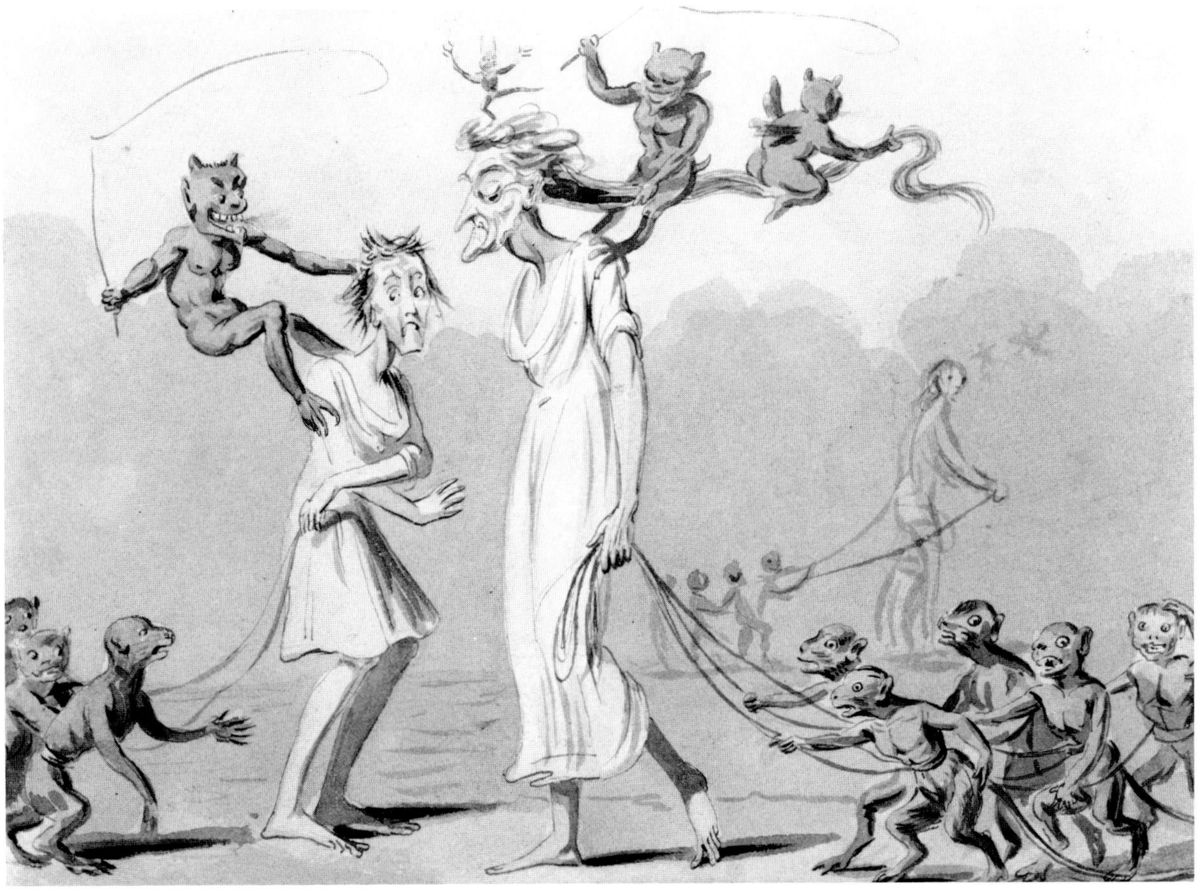

c. 1795
Pen and watercolor over pencil
6¾ x 9⅛ inches (17.7 x 23.2 cm.)
Annotated verso: Leading Apes in Hell / I. Cruikshanks
Biblio: Wark, 5

"Leading apes in hell" was a phrase that referred to "the unenviable lot of spinsters in the after-life."[1] In eighteenth-century Britain, a woman needed wealth or beauty in order to marry well. If she had money, she did not need to worry about her looks. However, if she was unfortunate enough to lack both, she would never marry and therefore her position in society could not be secured.

The importance of marriage for women in Georgian England was reflected in the pastimes enjoyed by young ladies and in the literature of the time. Many ladies consulted fortune-tellers to find out what fate had in store for them, particularly in regard to marriage. "Wise women" were paid to study astrological charts and to read palms or coffee grounds (see *Telling Fortunes in Coffee Grounds*, 3). An advantageous union was seen as the most desirable condition for a woman, and the pursuit of one became a central preoccupation in the novels of the time, from Richardson's *Pamela* to Austen's *Pride and Prejudice.*

Spinsterhood was of course viewed as a state to be shunned. In this image, Cruikshank stresses the unattractiveness of the women to justify their fate. Certainly, he seems to be suggesting here that unmarried and ugly old maids might just as well be hags walking through hell.

Jennifer Katell

1. Burton, *Pageant of Georgian England*, p. 313.

60 *Claiming the Flitch of Bacon*

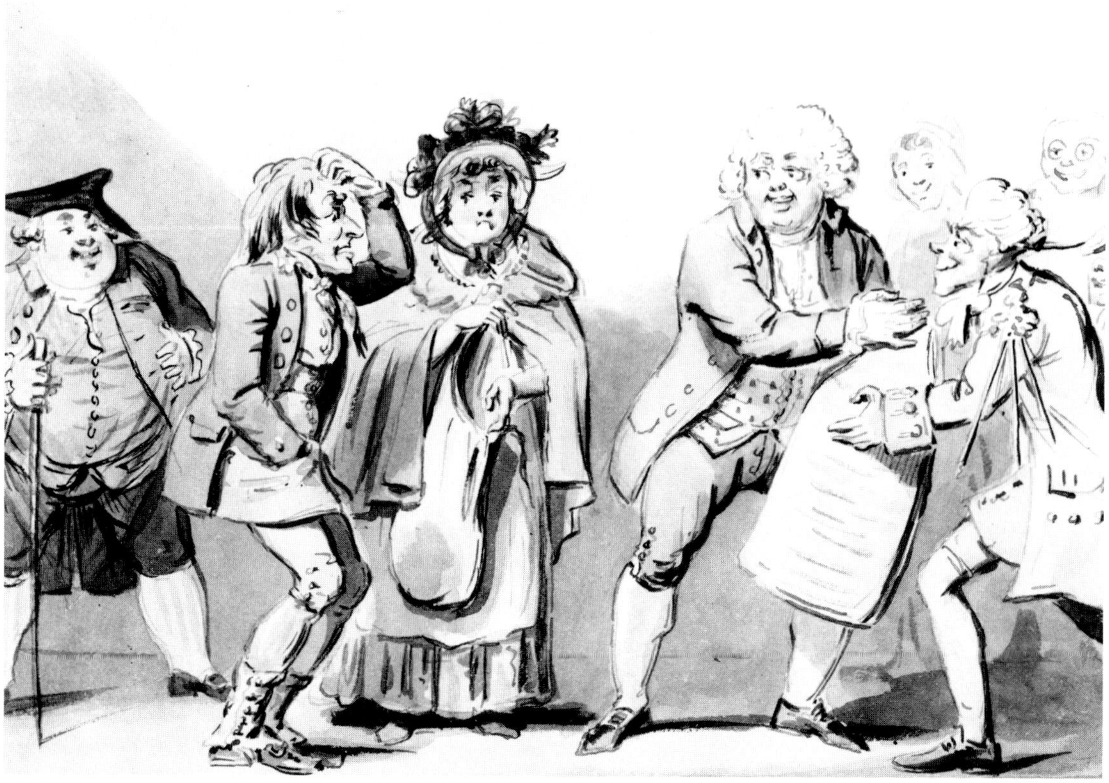

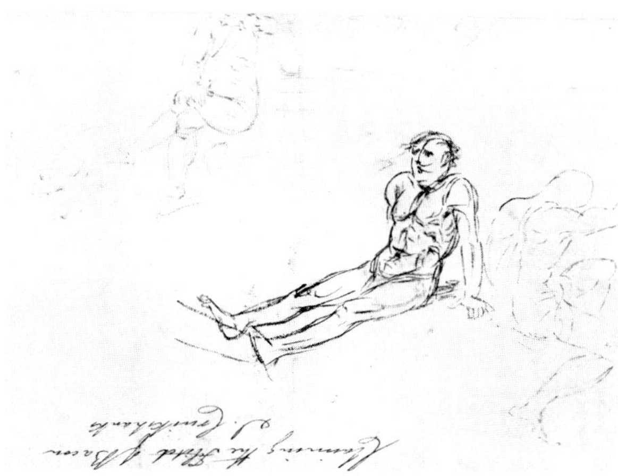

1796
Pen and watercolor over pencil
6 1/2 x 9 1/4 inches (16.5 x 23.5 cm.)
Verso: sketches of male figures
Annotated verso: Claiming the Flitch of Bacon / I. Cruikshanks
Published: February 8, 1796, by Laurie & Whittle (167); below the image is engraved: Justice – Well, then you avou you have been Married Seven Years and never quarrell'd. If so you are entitled to the Flitch of Bacon, but I think that Bag is too small to hold it – Husband – So I told my Wife before we came from home and she has been abusing me like a Pickpocket ever since, an be rot'to her – Justice – Oh! no, if that is the case. Here John hang up the Bacon again, lest she shou'd abuse you in carrying it home on account of its being too Heavy.
Biblio: Wark, 56
Impression: LWL

Thomas Morton's comedy *The Way to Get Married,* produced in 1796, was typical of eighteenth-century spoofs on marriage, popular at the time; Cruikshank's print is part of that tradition. According to the text that accompanied the print, the flitch, or side, of bacon was to go to a husband and wife who had never quarreled during seven years of marriage.

As bystanders in this scene look on, the wife, in the center, holds a large bag, ready to take the bacon home, while her husband has a puzzled look as he scratches his head. It is clear from this image and its accompanying text that this particular married couple does not have a claim to the bacon since they argued before they left home and are on the verge of having another disagreement. Much to the amusement of the stout man with the cane, this couple has already forfeited their right to the prize.

Mari-Tere Alvarez

61 *Loo* †

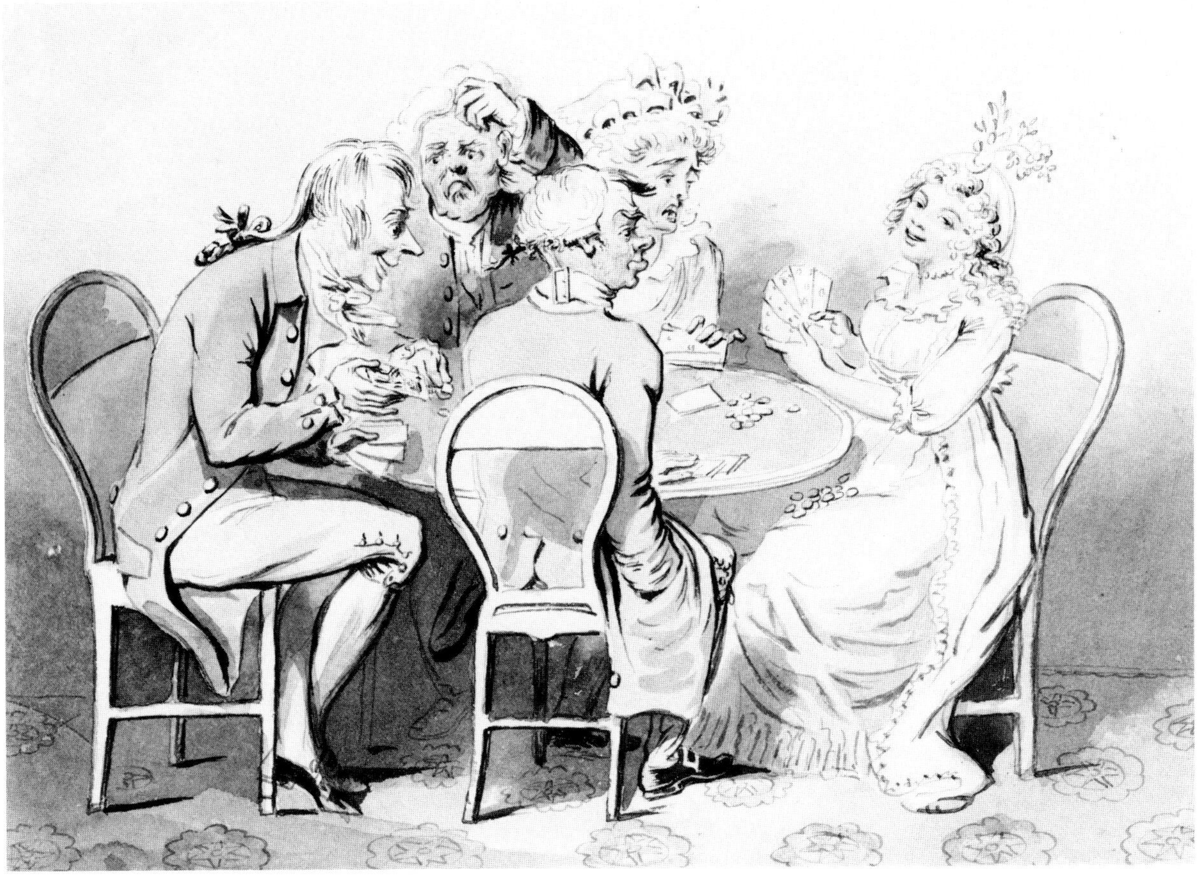

1796
Pen and watercolor
$6\frac{3}{4} \times 9\frac{1}{8}$ inches (17 x 23.1 cm.)
Annotated verso: Five Card Loo – Pam saves me / I. Cruikshanks
Published: February 20, 1796, by Laurie & Whittle (168)
Biblio: George, 8922; Krumbhaar, 668; Wark, 57
Impression: BM, LWL

Images of cardplaying are common throughout the eighteenth century. Artists developed infinite variations on the theme, including that of being cheated, in all probability the subject of this work. Here, five people are playing a game known as Loo, which Hoyle described in 1830 as a game where the trump card is the Jack of Clubs, referred to as "Pam." Loo was so popular that games would go on all night and well into the morning.[1]

The woman on the right, smiling at the viewer, holds a flush. From the amount of money on the table and in her lap, we see that she has enjoyed good fortune. Several of her companions seem perplexed by this run of luck, in particular the gentleman who scratches his head. The only person who does not seem amazed by her winning is the man directly opposite, who holds Pam, or the trump card. Allowing the woman to win yet again, he seems to be her accomplice in duping the other players.

Mari-Tere Alvarez

1. *Hoyle's Games*, pp. 138-53.

62 *Sound Argument – A Dispute Betwixt Wine & Water* †

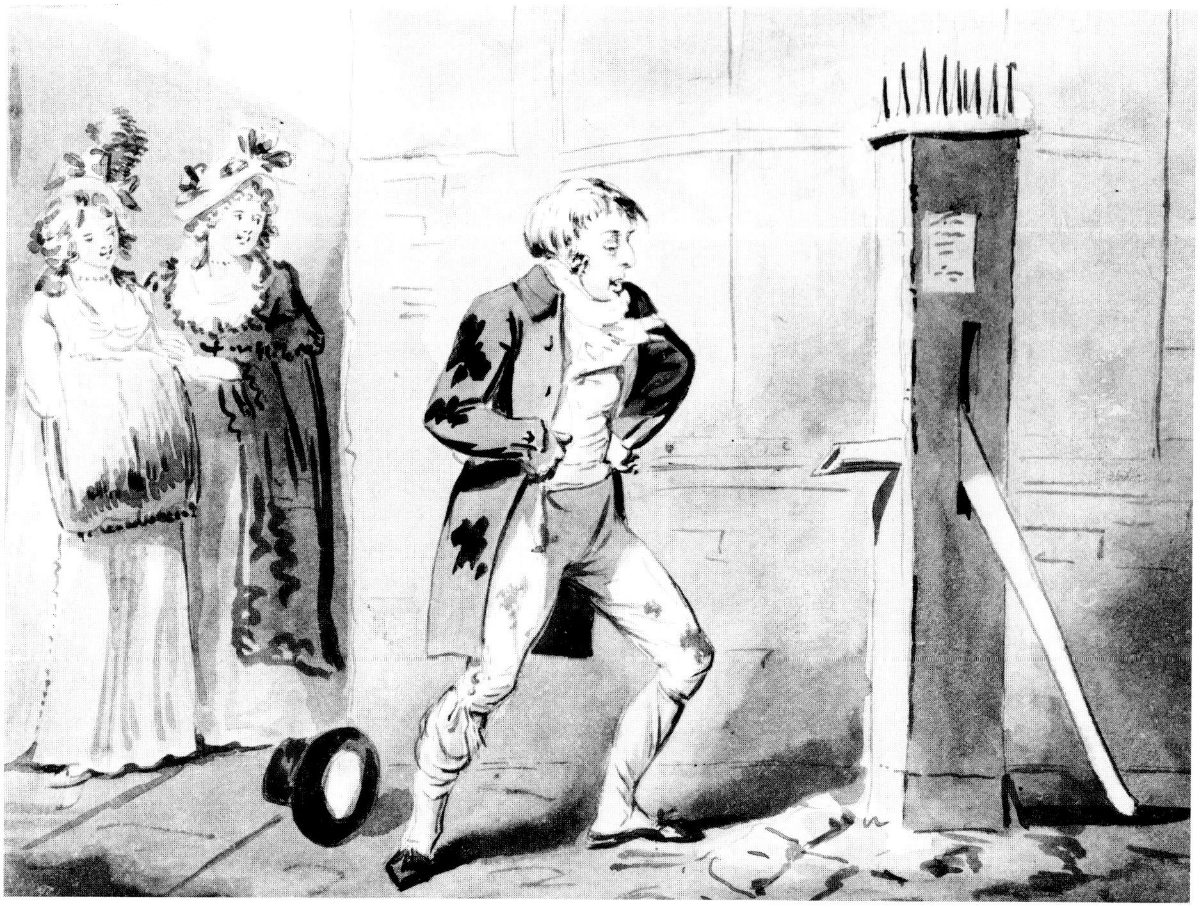

1796
Pen and watercolor over pencil
6 7/8 x 9 3/16 inches (17.5 x 23.3 cm.)
Annotated verso: Damit what are you about you are beating a Post – damme how should I know it was the Post. Why didn't he blow his Horn / I. Cruikshanks
Published: May 12, 1796, by Laurie & Whittle; below the image is engraved: You Rascal D-d-demme. How dare you run against a Gemman —I suppose you mean to-to-to Rob me. Curse you —but I'll take care of you-you-you Scoundrel. I'll have you sent on Bo-Board the Hulks ye Dog. Insult a Gemman hay-hay what do ye mean you Watery Rascal.
Biblio: Krumbhaar, A.91; Wark, 58
Impression: WMC

Late eighteenth-century London had the world's most advanced plumbing system, reaching—with the exception of certain isolated courts, alleys, and streets—throughout the entire city.[1] Therefore, the presence of the water pump suggests that this scene is set in an area off the beaten path. The gentleman, whose judgment and vision are distorted by alcohol, mistakes the pump for a "rascal" who has run into him and knocked off his hat. He even threatens to have his assailant, the pump, impressed into naval service and sent to sea. The title, as well as the text, satirizes the man's state. Like the two well-coiffed ladies, the viewer is amused as the disheveled gentleman proceeds to rebuke the pump for "his" affronting behavior. Through their common association with water, Cruikshank cleverly connects the pump, the sea, and the watery rascal.

Tim D. Wright

1. J. Ralph, *A Critical Review of Public Buildings in and about London* (London: Chatto and Windus, 1878), p. 3.

63 *The Adventures of Young Whipstitch: A Tale* †

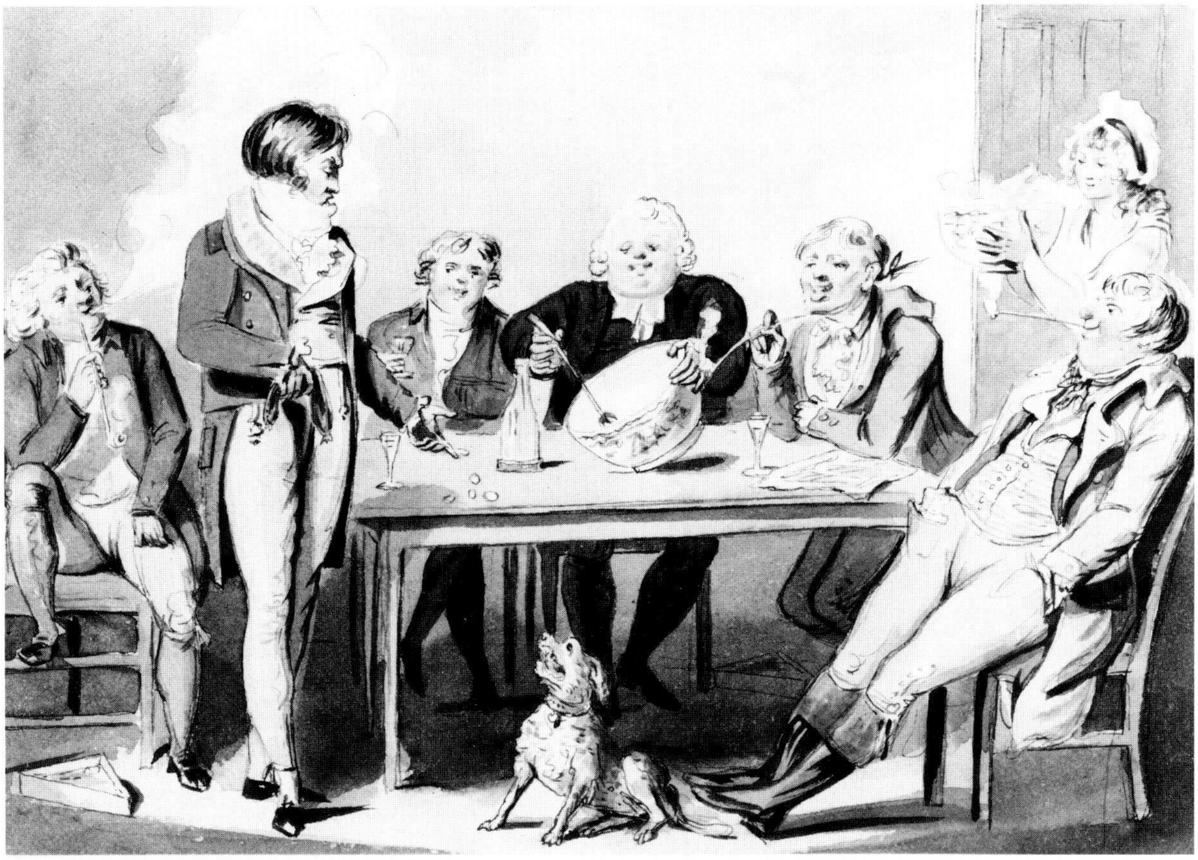

1796
Pen and watercolor over pencil
6 1/2 x 8 3/4 inches (16.5 x 24 cm.)
Inscribed verso: Adventures of Young Whipstitch / I. Cruikshanks
Published: August 12, 1796, by Laurie & Whittle; below the title are engraved 84 lines of verse.
Biblio: Krumbhaar, 5; Wark, 59
Impression: LWL, WMC

Accompanying the engraving for this drawing are verses relating the story of a tailor's son who inherits a large amount of money from his father. Disdainful of his origins, the young man travels to new places where he encounters people who talk as if they knew about his humble birth. The cleric seated in the center drinks from a bowl; a woman enters with fresh steaming punch. The men appear to be listening to the young man, whose dress is quite at odds with theirs, with a mixture of interest and good humor as they drink and smoke. The fashionably dressed young man, on the other hand, is clearly irritated by some slight he believes has occurred. He flings some money onto the table. Wealth did not assure social position, since one's status at the time was based more on family connections than on money. This emphasis on social prestige is apparently the reason that our tailor's son concocts a fictitious background for himself, and that he is quick to assume others know his secret, as they do in the tale.

Mari-Tere Alvarez

A London Taylor

A London Taylor, (as 'tis said,)
By buckram, canvas, tape, and thread,
Sleeve linings, pockets, silk and twist,
And all the long expensive list,
With which their uncouth bills abound,
Tho' rarely in the garment found:
By these and other arts in trade,
Had soon a pretty fortune made;
And did what few had ever done,
Left thirty-thousand to his son.
The son a gay young swaggering blade,
Abhorr'd the very name of trade;
And lest reflection should be thrown
On him, resolv'd to leave the town,
And travel where he was not known.
In gilded coach and liveries gay,
To Oxford first he took his way;
There Beau and Belles his taste admire,
His equipage and rich attire:
But nothing was so much ador'd
As his fine silver hilted sword;
Tho' short and small 'twas vastly neat,
The sight was deemed a perfect treat.
Beau Banter begg'd to have a look,
But when the sword in hand he took,
He swore by Gad it was an *odd* thing,
And look'd much like a taylor's *bodkin.*
His pride was hurt by this expression,
Thinking they knew his sire's profession;
Sheathing his sword he sneak'd away,
And drove for Glo'ster that same day.
There soon he found new cause for grief,
For dining on some fine roast beef,
One asked which did he prefer,
Some *cabbage* or a cucumber.
The purse-proud coxcomb took the hint,
Thought it severe reflection meant;
His stomach turn'd, he could not eat,
So made an ungenteel retreat;
Next day left Glo'ster in great wrath,
And bid his coachman drive to Bath.
There he suspected fresh abuse,
Because the dinner was roast *goose*;
And that he might no more be jeer'd,
Next day to Exeter he steer'd;
There with some bucks he drank about,
Until he fear'd they'd found him out;
His glass not fill'd as was the rule,
They said 'twas not a *thimble* full:
The name of thimble was enough,
He paid his reck'ning and went off.
He then to Plymouth took a trip,
And put up at the Royal Ship,
Which then was kept by Caleb *Snip.*
The host by name was often call'd,
At which his guest was so much gall'd,
That soon to Cambridge he remov'd,
There too he unsuccessful prov'd:
For tho' he fill'd his glass or cup,
He did not always drink it up.
The scholars mark'd how he behav'd,
And said a remnant should be sav'd.
The name of remnant gall'd him so,
That he resolv'd to York to go:
There fil'd his bumper to the top,
And always fairly drank it up:
"Well done (says Jack a buck of York)
"You go thro' *stitch* Sir, with your work."
The name of *stitch* was such reproach,
He rang the bell and call'd his coach.
But 'ere he went, enquiries made,
By what means they knew his trade;
"You put the cap on and it fits"
(Replied one of the Yorkshire Wits)
"Our words in common acceptation,
"Could not find out your occupation:
"'Twas you yourself gave us the clue,
"To find out both your trade and you.
"Vain Coxcombs and fantastic beaux,
"In every place themselves expose;
"They travel far at vast expence,
"To shew their wealth and want of sense;
"But take this for a standing rule,
"*There's no disguise can screen a fool.*"

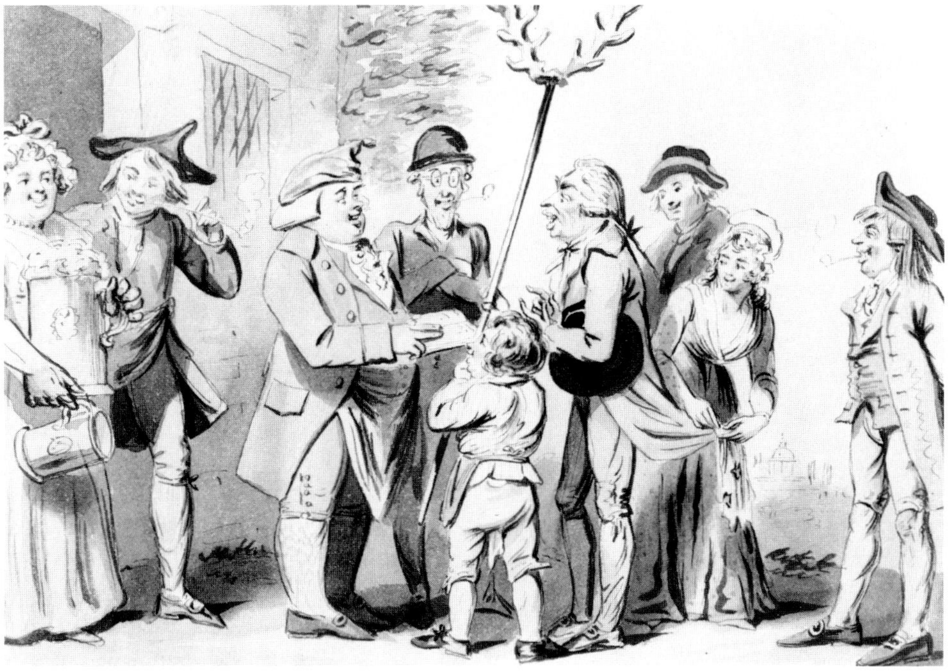

1796
Pen and watercolor over pencil
$6\frac{1}{2} \times 9\frac{1}{4}$ inches
(16.9 x 23.6 cm.)
Inscribed recto: Horns
Annotated verso: Swearing at Highgate / I. Cruikshanks
Annotated recto on mat: Swearing a Yokel Over the Horns at Highgate / an original drawing; Cruikshanks' pen . . .
Published: September 12, 1796, Laurie & Whittle; below the title is engraved: Pray Sir lay your Right Hand on this Book, and attend to the Oath. You swear by the Rules of Sound Judgement, that you will not eat Brown Bread when you can have White, except you like the Brown better, that you will not Drink Small Beer, when you can get Strong except you like the Small beer better. But you will kiss the Maid in preference to the Mistress if you like the Maid better—so help you Billy Bodkin—Turn round & fulfill your Oath.
Provenance: with J. S. Maas and Co., from whom purchased in 1968
Biblio: George, 8923; Krumbhaar, 1176a
Impression: BM, WMC

A "joke custom" initiated in the eighteenth century was practiced by several inns in the Highgate area north of London. Travelers stopping at these inns were persuaded to "Swear on the Horns" before their coaches were allowed to move on. The innkeeper would administer the oath, attended by a clerk who carried a pole with ram's horns or stag's horns attached. He would say to the traveler: "It's a custom at Highgate that all who go through, must be sworn on the horns, sir, and so, sir, must you."[1] St. Paul's is visible in the distance, indicating that the inn is some miles outside the city. All the participants appear to be having a good time with this lighthearted ceremony, which served as a boost to the local trade around the Highgate area.

In 1796, G. M. Woodward, writer and artist, published in *Eccentric Excursions* a similar subject dated August 27, drawn by him and etched by Cruikshank. In the text, the event of swearing at Highgate is described as "the ancient custom of *swearing* persons *from the country* previous to their launching into the Wiles of the metropolis." The author goes on to say that "the ceremony ends in the forfeit of a bowl of punch." Those who had been thus initiated were considered the "Freemen of Highgate." Reportedly, the oath had been composed by a blacksmith at the inn in Highgate. Despite what is stated in *Eccentric Excursions,* the ceremony was still relatively new and had only recently been codified.

Cruikshank and Woodward were friends and frequent collaborators. They treated some of the same themes in a similarly broad style. It is impossible to say who influenced whom in this particular case.

Jennifer Katell

1. Margaret Brentnall, *The Old Customs and Ceremonies of London* (London: B. T. Batsford, Ltd., 1975), p. 189.
2. Woodward, *Eccentric Excursions,* p. 27, pl. 14.

65 *Monsieur Kaniferstane: (Or, I Do Not Understand You) An Original Tale* †

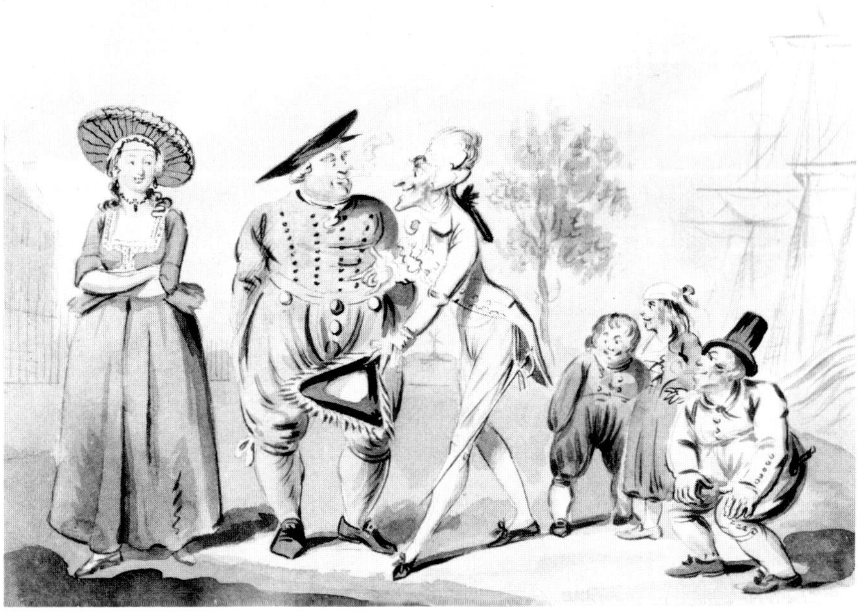

1796
Pen and watercolor over pencil (?)
6⅞ x 8¾ inches
(16.5 x 21.7 cm.)
Annotated verso: Monsieur Kaniferstain / I. Cruikshanks
Published: October 4, 1796, by Laurie & Whittle, followed by verse
Biblio: Krumbhaar, A.71; Wark, 60
Impression: LWL, WMC

Although the text accompanying the print of this drawing states that the story is set in the past, the image undoubtedly reflects the relationship between France and Holland during the 1790s, as well as the British attitudes toward these two countries at the time of publication. Revolutionary France, having invaded Holland in 1794, was willing to treat the Dutch as allies if they would first stage their own revolution and form a republic.[1] France occupied Holland for three years. The text accompanying the print satirizes both the French and the Dutch during this time, when Britain was at war with France.

The fashionable clothes and elegant manners of the Frenchman suggest his arrogance and vanity (see *A French Emigrant Cook,* 32). The English envisioned all Frenchmen as thin and affected, with sharp noses and jutting chins.[2] These traits are found here in Cruikshank's caricature of a French marquis. But Cruikshank's humor is not only directed toward the French. The Dutch were seen as oafish and well-fed, with apple cheeks and bulbous noses.[3] The Dutchman depicted fits this description; he is further caricatured by his clownish costume and awkward presence. The woman's dress, on the other hand, seems to be of an earlier date, recalling the style of clothing found in Dutch genre paintings of the seventeenth century.

The scene refers to "The Grand Tour," an established feature of aristocratic education in the eighteenth century. In France, it was referred to as a "voyage de gentilhomme." Young men traveled throughout Europe visiting foreign courts and seeing famous monuments. The purpose of the trip, aside from pleasure, was to polish manners, increase one's knowledge of the world, and sharpen character.[4] The expectation that French was to be the common language for conversation on such a tour attracted the derision of the English; an eighteenth-century saying, "Jack would be a gentleman if he could only speak French," reflected this attitude.[5]

In the accompanying text for the print of Cruikshank's drawing, the Frenchman portrayed assumes that even though he is in Holland, he can speak to everyone he meets in French. However, the exchange reveals that the people only speak Dutch. To each question the Frenchman asks, the Dutchmen reply "Ik kan Niet Verstaan" (I do not understand you). The French marquis mistakenly understands the response to be a man's name: Monsieur Kaniferstane. The repetition of the error heightens the impression of arrogance. The three Dutchmen on the right all seem to be amused by his pomposity.

Mary-Kay Lombino

1. R. R. Palmer, *The World of the French Revolution* (New York: Harper and Row, 1917), p. 166.
2. Atherton, *Political Prints in the Age of Hogarth,* p. 86.
3. Colin Holmes, ed., *Immigrants and Minorities in British Society* (London: George Allen and Unwin, 1978), p. 52.
4. Newman, *The Rise of English Nationalism,* p. 13.
5. Jarrett, *England in the Age of Hogarth,* p. 15.

Monsieur Kaniferstane: (Or, I do not understand you.) An original tale.

Once on a time a little French Marquis
For travel felt a mighty inclination;
To shew himself, and foreign parts to see,
He undertook a bold peregrination.
At Dieppe he found a sloop just under weigh,
By Dutchmen mann'd, and bound for Amsterdam;
Wind and tide serving, off he sail'd away,
And, soon sea-sick, beyond finesse or sham.
Close in the cabin he preferr'd to nestle.
There, faint and languid for a space he doz'd,
Till, from th'increas'd commotion of the vessel,
That land might be in sight he well supposed:
So to the deck he climb'd with empty maw,
And, sure enough Dutch Terra Firma saw.

While in the cabin sick and sad he lay,
Tho' a true Frenchman, he ne'er dreamt of talking:
But, when on deck, his spirits grew more gay,
And his blood 'gan to circulate with walking;
He recollected that he had a tongue,
Now, tho' a Frenchman, French with ease can jabber,
And, doubtless, thinks all others ears are hung
Like those he left at home, yet a Dutch swabber
Is apt enough no other speech to know
Than that which first he learnt from Mother Frow.

Such was the case of all the trunk-hos'd crew,
The Marquis, struck with wonder and delight,
Enraptur'd gaz'd on objects all so new.
At length a sumptuous palace caught his sight,
Which proudly rising from the water's tide,
Shew'd its new-painted front with flow'rets gay:
While trim responsive gardens spreading wide,
Displayed Dutch taste in regular array.
Anxious to know who own'd the pleasing scene,
The Marquis, bowing, with a grinning face,
Demanded of a tar in French I ween,
"To whom belong'd that most enchanting place?"
The tar, who knew as much of French as Greek,
Eye'd him at first with something like disdain;
Then, as he shifted round his quid to speak,
With growling voice cry'd "*Ik kan niet verstaan**."
"Oh, Oh," reply'd the Marquis, "does it so!"
"To Monsieur Kaniferstane; lucky man!
"The palace, to be sure, lies rather low;
"But then, the size and grandeur of the plan!
"I never saw a Chateau on the Seine,
"Equal to this of Monsieur Kaniferstane."

While he thus spoke, the sailors anchor cast,
As the Marquis descended on the Quay,
He saw a charming Frow that chanc'd to pass,
In liveliest bloom of youth, and beauty gay,
Bedeck'd with all the Amsterstam [*sic*] parade
Of gold and silver, pearls and jewels rare,
On the Marquis the much impression made:
His tender breast soon own'd a pleasing flame;
Stopping a passenger, he, bowing, said,
"Monsieur, pray tell me who's that lovely dame?"
The civil Dutchman bow'd to him again,
And gently answered, "*Ik kan niet verstaan.*"

"What Monsieur Kaniferstane's wife!" the Marquis cry'd,
"He who has got yon gay and sumptuous House;
"Well! that some men have luck can't be deny'd;
What! such an Edifice and such a Spouse!
"Ma foi! I think I never should complain,
"Had I the lot of Monsieur Kaniferstane."

As on the morrow, thro' the streets he pass'd,
Gazing on all the pretty sights about;
On a large open Hall his eyes he cast,
Where bustling crowds were going in and out.
Joining the throng, he entrance soon obtain'd,
And found the people much engag'd to see,
The numbers which the Blanks and Prizes gain'd
In their High Mightinesses Lottery.
Some laugh'd, some wept, some groan'd, and some exclaim'd,
In all the spirit of true castle-builders,
When, on a sudden, a loud voice proclaim'd
The sovereign prize of Twenty Thousand Guilders!
"And who," the Marquis cry'd to one close by,
"Who has the luck this mighty prize to gain?"
The man survey'd him with a doubtful eye,
And slowly answered, "*Ik kan niet verstaan.*"
"What! Monsieur Kaniferstan got the prize?"
The Marquis cry'd, "he's lucky on my life;
"He who has got a House of such a size,
"And such a Garden too, and such a Wife!
"Diable! you may very well be vain,
"With all these treasures, Monsieur Kaniferstane!"

A week or two elapsed, when, as he stray'd,
On novelty intent, he chanc'd to meet,
Adorn'd with solemn pomp and grave parade,
A sumptuous burial coming up the street.
"Monsieur," said he, as bowing to a baker,
Who left his shop the pageantry to see,
And just had nodded to the undertaker,
"Pray, Monsieur, whose grand burial may this be?"
The baker, as he turn'd to shop again,
Reply'd most gravely, "*Ik kan niet verstaan.*"

"Mon Dieu!" exclaimed the Marquis, "what a pity!
"Monsieur Kaniferstane! what surprise
"He had the noblest Palace in this city!
"And such a Wife! and such a glorious Prize!
"Alack! alack! good fortune smiles in vain;
"So rest in peace, good Monsieur Kaniferstan."

* This means I do not understand you.

66 *Will O' the Wisp, or Some Folkes a Little Out of the Road* †

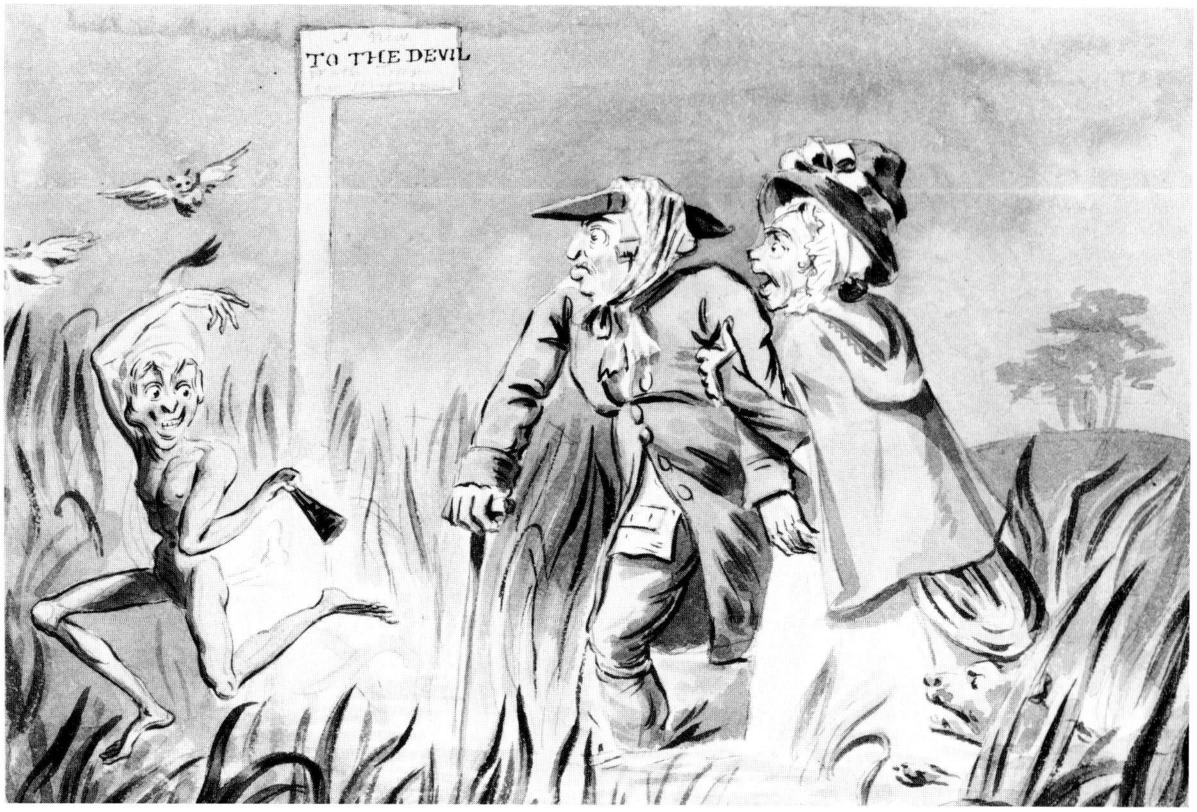

1796
Pen, gray wash, and watercolor over pencil
6 7/16 x 9 inches (16.5 x 22.9 cm.)
Inscribed recto: To the Devil, A New Water Tour
Annotated verso: A Will o' the Wisp / I. Cruikshanks
Published: December 12, 1796, by Laurie & Whittle (177); below the title is engraved: To lead poor Travellers astray, / Sad Willy still is bent on, / And while they follow, on their way / He guides them with his Lanthorn. / But having led them to a Swamp, / Bewilder'd and affrighted; / He slily did his Vapour domp, / And left them there benighted.
Biblio: Wark, 61

The title, "Will o' the Wisp," refers to something that deludes or misleads by luring one on. The expression's origin is the Latin phrase "ignis fattuus," or "friar's lantern," which is a flitting phosphorescent light seen at night, chiefly over marshy ground, and believed to be the result of spontaneous combustion of gas from decomposed matter.[1] Accordingly, this old couple is being enticed through the dark night and into a bog by a "wisp" of "golden gas" emanating from the little creature's backside.

The signpost reading "To the Devil" was altered to "The Road to Ruin" when the image was issued as a print (a pencil inscription on the drawing reads "A New Water Tour"). As the popular expression "To The Devil" suggests, this couple is literally lured on by the evil one himself. Fear is conveyed in their posture and facial expressions—even their dog seems to anticipate danger.

The print's message, "Road to Ruin," may be a reference to the popular play of the same title, which was frequently performed on the London stage from 1792 to mid-1797, particularly at Covent Garden.[2] Written by Thomas Holcroft, the comedy exposes the pitfalls of following fortune's path. In their hot pursuit of the "golden illusion," this couple is entirely unaware of their surroundings. Only the viewer and the devil see the illusory nature of their quest.

Julie Joyce

1. *The Random House Dictionary of the English Language,* 2d ed. (New York: Random House, 1987).
2. Schneider, comp., Index to *The London Stage.*

67 *A Visit to the Boarding School, the Governess Introducing little Miss to Papa and Mama* †

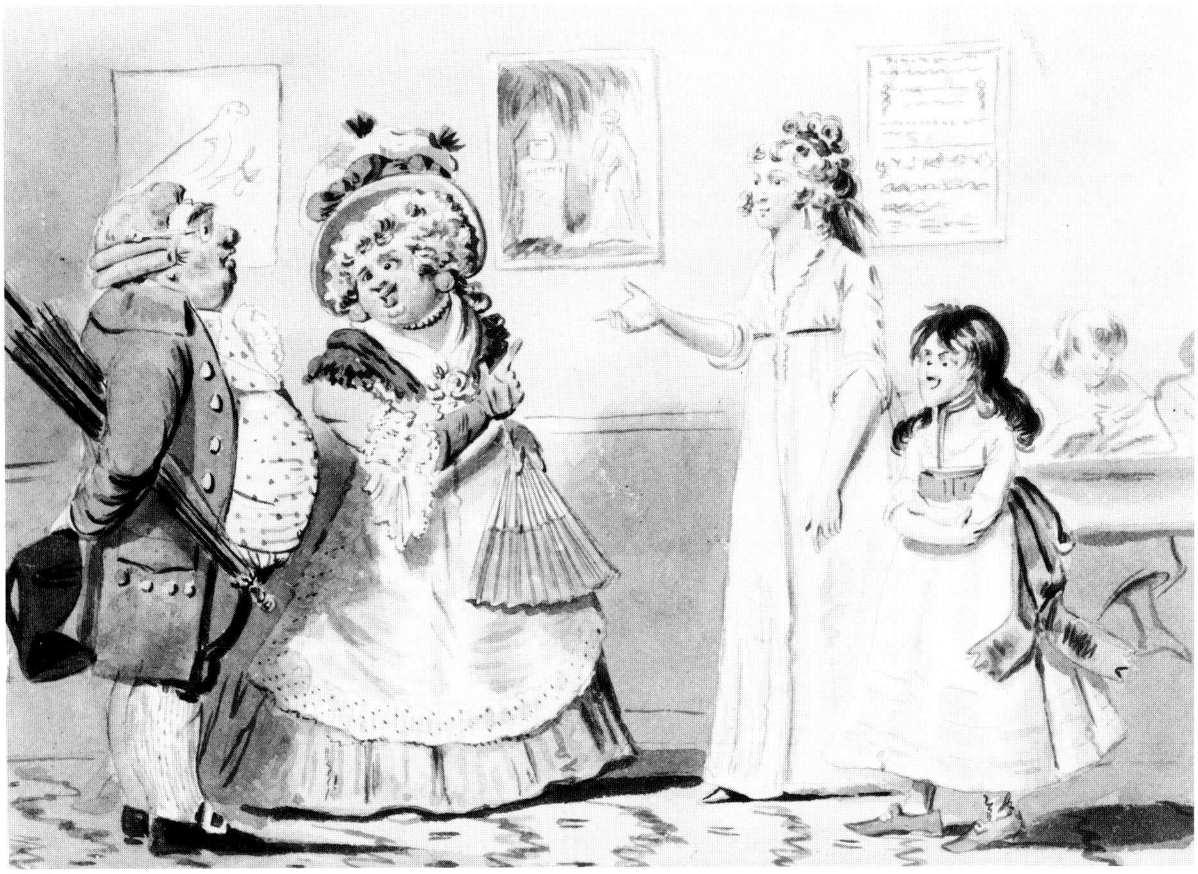

1797
Pen and watercolor over pencil (?)
6⅝ x 9⅛ inches (16.7 x 23 cm.)
Annotated verso: Charlotte at the Tomb of Werter / I. Cruikshanks
Published: June 20, 1797, by Laurie & Whittle (183); below the image is engraved: Here Mrs. Parmesan is Charlotte at the Tomb of Werter, shall Miss Dorothy work that, why I declare it looks Wastly pretty I wow – Ah; and there's the Veeping-Villow, and all so natural, well I'm sure, what think you of it Deary – why Love's, as for that there, I have no objection in the Vorld, against her Working Charlotte at the Tub of Water.
Biblio: Wark, 62
Impression: LWL

The large man and woman who speak with heavy German accents are the target of Cruikshank's humor. On visiting his daughter's boarding school, the German man has misunderstood the teacher, who mentions "Charlotte at the Tomb of Werther," an allusion to Goethe's novel, *The Sorrows of Young Werther* (1774). The story of Werther was well known in London, as the novel was adapted by Frederick Reynolds in a play performed regularly at Covent Garden beginning in 1795.[1] The man's slowness to understand this familiar reference—to a work in German, at that—is a comment on his intellectual limitation, as are his crossed eyes; the wife's are crossed as well. The young girl is also cross-eyed, implying that stupidity is an inherited national trait. The belief in such inferiority was not an uncommon English attitude toward immigrants.[2]

This drawing depicts a typical boarding school for girls. Pupils were taught to read and write, sew, and play the harpsichord. Girls were often instructed by their mothers in the crafts of keeping house, cooking, washing, baking bread, and needlework.[3] The text discusses the young girl's ability to embroider, and the image on the wall displays a typical needlework subject, the memorable final scene of the play *Werther,* in which Charlotte kneels beside her beloved Werther's tombstone in grief.[4]

Schools for young ladies often advertised in newspapers. For example, in 1798, an announcement in the *Times* read: "Mrs. Cross respectfully informs the gentry, merchants, and her friends in general that her school will recommence on Monday and that she has accommodation for five more young ladies as borders."[5] In *Emma* (1814), Jane Austen described Mrs. Goddard's boarding school as a place "where a reasonable quantity of accomplishments were sold at a reasonable price, and where girls might be sent to be out of the way and scramble themselves into a little education."[6] This minimal education was considered adequate for a future governess or wife.

In 1800, there were reportedly thirty thousand Germans living in London, probably a slight exaggeration. Many were successful in business. The elaborate dress of the German couple shown here marks them as solid middle class. After 1750, most guild regulations broke down and many London companies abolished restrictions against the employment of foreigners; German businesses flourished, often causing resentment among the English.[8] This image and its accompanying text suggest not only the inability of Germans to fit into British society but the insularity and national pride of the English.

Mary-Kay Lombino

1. Hogan, ed., *The London Stage,* pt. 5, p. 1578.
2. George, *London Life in the Eighteenth Century* (1984), p. 127.
3. Bayne-Powell, *Eighteenth-Century London Life,* p. 68.
4. Inchbald, *Inchbald's Modern Theatre,* 10 vols. (London: Longman, Hurst, Rees, Orme and Brown, 1811), 3:205.
5. Bayne-Powell, *Eighteenth-Century London Life,* p. 68.
6. Austen, *Emma* (London: T. Nelson, 1942), p. 54.
7. Holmes, ed., *Immigrants and Minorities in British Society,* p. 75.

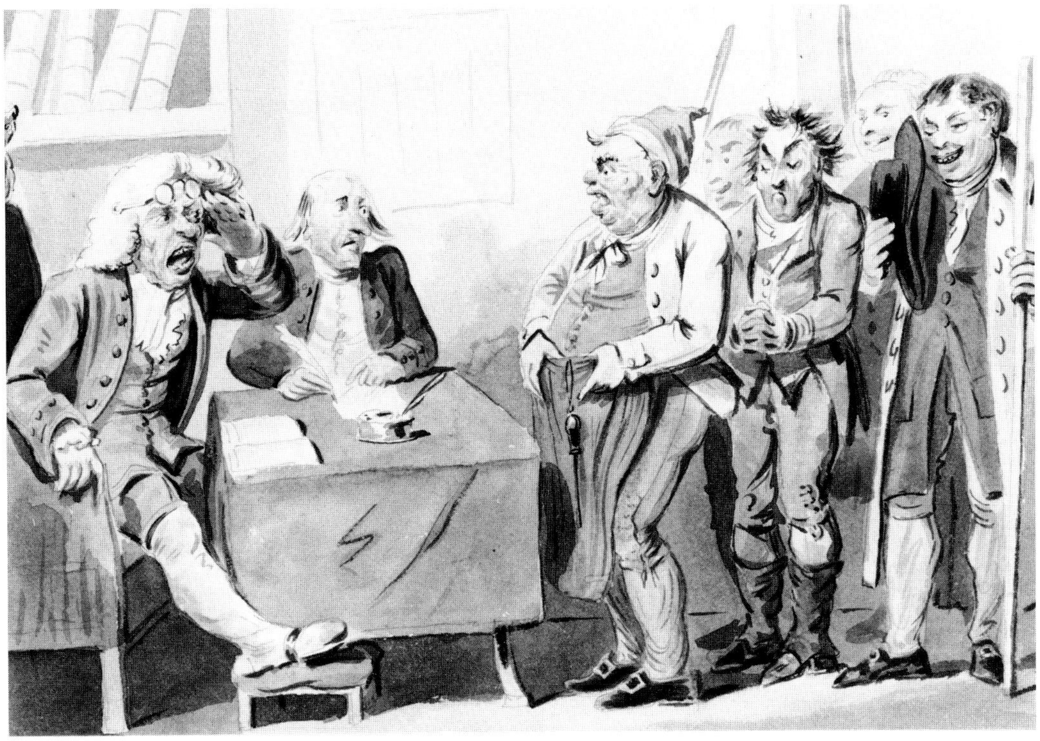

1797
Pen and watercolor over pencil
$6\frac{1}{2} \times 9\frac{1}{8}$ inches (17 x 23.3 cm.)
Annotated verso: The Deaf Justice / I. Cruikshanks
Published: September 1, 1797, Laurie & Whittle (197); below the title is engraved: Justice – Well Mr. Blunt, where was you at the time you discovered your Sheep – At Smithfield your Honor – At Smithfield: very well, and what did you do there – I went to Handle'em your Worship – Handlum, Handlum where's that, where do you say you went – I went to Handle'em an please your Honor – What have we to do with Handlum? I tell you fellow keep at Smithfield, where you began your Story, and when we want you at Handlum we'll call upon you.
Biblio: Wark, 64
Impression: LWL

The man with his foot resting on a gout stool is a justice of the peace. Petty crimes, primarily committed by the lower classes, were his jurisdiction. Although never entrusted to deal with issues of real property, justices by this time were basically autonomous, with little control by central government and no judicial review. Of the propertied class and appointed by a commission, they were unpaid and assumed a paternalistic role toward their communities.[1]

The accused, standing closest to the table, defends himself against the charge of sheep theft. Straining to amplify his hearing by putting his hand to his ear, the justice misunderstands the defendant's responses to his inquiries. The defendant protests without success that he is not the thief but rather the owner of the sheep, and that he only went to Smithfield, a livestock market in London, for the purpose of retrieving his sheep—to handle them—and not to a nonexistent place called Handlum.

The justice's incorrect use of English, his gout, and poor hearing mark him as capricious, self-indulgent, and unqualified. The owl, a symbol of wisdom, winks at the viewer as if laughing about the absence of both wisdom and justice in that courtroom, an attitude shared, it would seem, by the three smiling shepherds on the right. Perhaps because he is the real thief, the frowning man behind the accused does not find the judicial theatrics funny.

Tim D. Wright

1. Norma Landau, *Justices of the Peace* (Berkeley and Los Angeles: University of California Press, 1984), pp. 1-23, passim.

69 *Light Travelling, Only Six Inside, Children Half Price* †

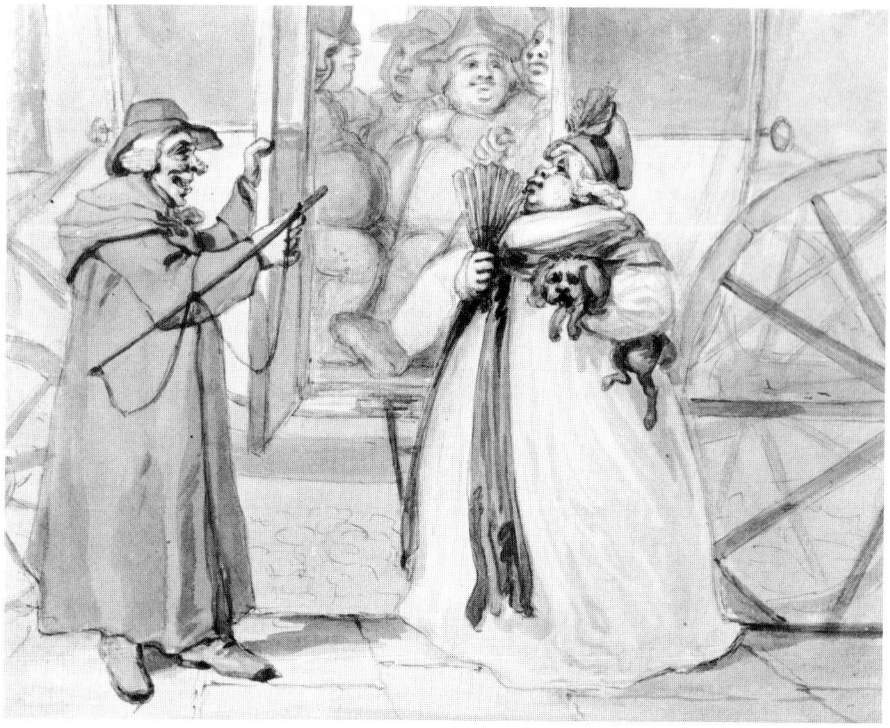

1797
Pen and watercolor over pencil
$6^{5}/_{8}$ x $8^{1}/_{2}$ inches (16.8 x 21.4 cm.)
Annotated verso: Plenty of Room Ma'am / I. Cruikshanks
Published: September 1, 1797, by Laurie & Whittle (198); below the title is engraved: Just room for one Madam – Vell I wow I have run all the way like a Lamp-lighter, till I am all over in such a Heat you can't think.
Biblio: George, 9111; Krumbhaar, 651; Wark, 63
Impression: BM, LWL

A common problem faced by the traveler in the eighteenth century was uncomfortably crowded coaches. Here, a stereotypically overweight German woman standing beside the coach is gestured inside by a coachman, though it is obvious that, with five fat men already inside, there is no room for a woman of her girth. The enormous wheel of the coach echoes her rotund figure.

The woman's heavy accent and her improper English set the tone of the caricature. Her unattractive facial features as well as size and speech are consistent with the stereotypical British view of Germans. (Earlier in the same year Cruikshank depicted a German couple who possessed the same traits [see 67].) The little dog buried in her arm looks out to the viewer with an almost human expression, as if to solicit sympathy for his impending fate. The monochrome wash, characteristic of Cruikshank's early drawings, contributes here to the dismal tone of the scene.

Accounts of stagecoach traveling in the 1780s and '90s describe the seats as meant to accommodate six persons but always rather crowded.[1] From diaries, it is known that travel could be an enjoyable or a miserable experience, depending on the weather and one's companions.[2] Summer travelers, such as those portrayed here, often complained of the intolerable heat in the coach and many men chose to ride outside to avoid the discomfort.[3] The German woman is not the type to take a place next to the driver or on the roof.

Coachmen of the time enjoyed autocracy and their commands could not be disputed.[4] The one depicted exercises such authority over the passengers. With his evil smile, he seems, in fact, to take pleasure in the prospect. Passengers of varying classes and dispositions had to tolerate each other and common suffering engendered intimacy. Owing to the cramped quarters, it was impossible for passengers to be indifferent to one another. The eager expressions of the five large men in the coach suggest that the new arrival is in for a difficult time. Although travelers had to learn to bear with each other, fatness was a hard thing to forgive.[5] A William Hogarth print entitled *Stage Coach* (1750) deals with a similar predicament.[6]

Mary-Kay Lombino

1. Violet A. Wilson, *The Coaching Era* (New York: E. P. Dutton and Company, 1922), p. 227.
2. Ibid., p. 210.
3. Charles G. Harper, *Stagecoach and Mail in the Days of Yore: A Picturesque History of the Coaching Age,* 2 vols. (London: Chapman and Hall, 1903), 2:67.
4. Turner, *The Servant Problem,* p. 75.
5. Wilson, *The Coaching Era,* p. 132.
6. Harper, *Stagecoach and Mail,* 2:56.

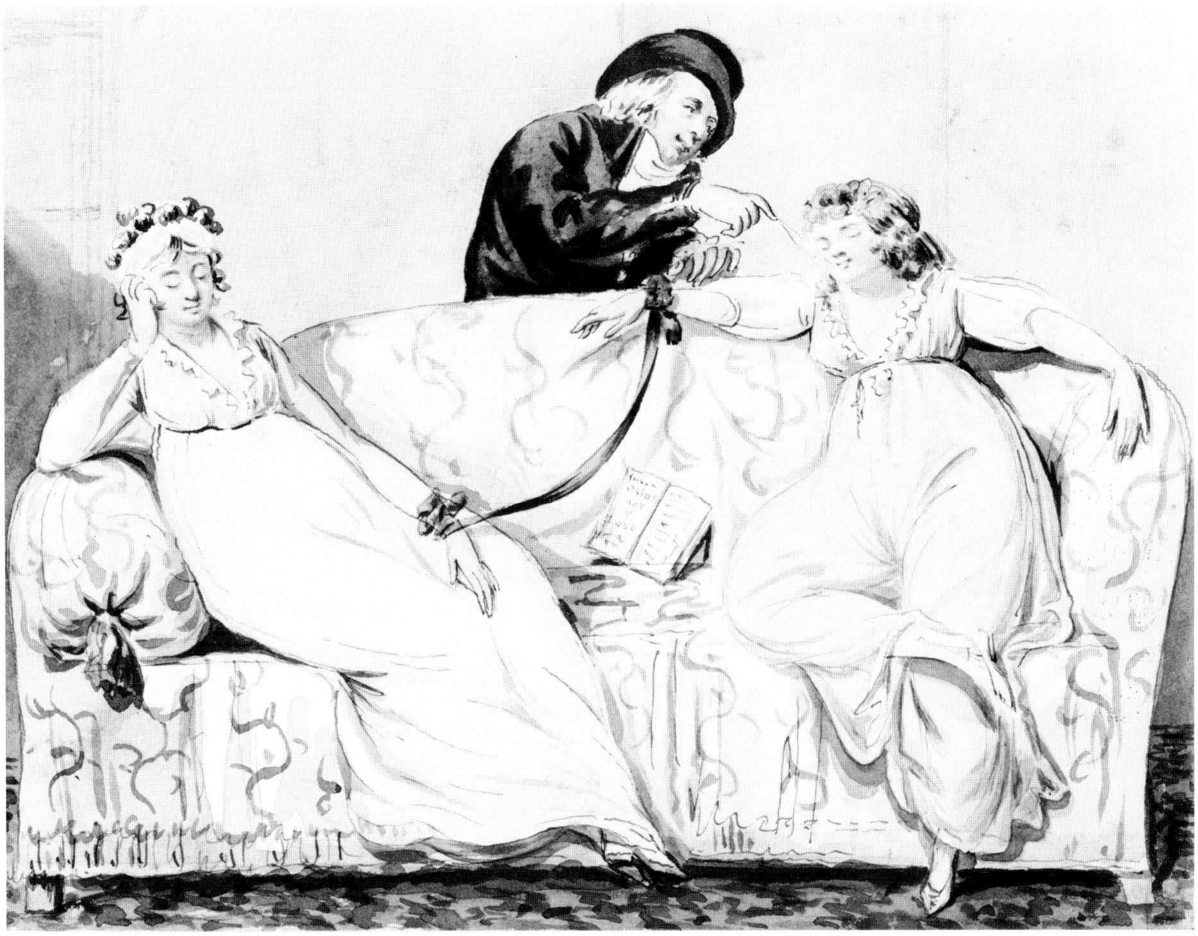

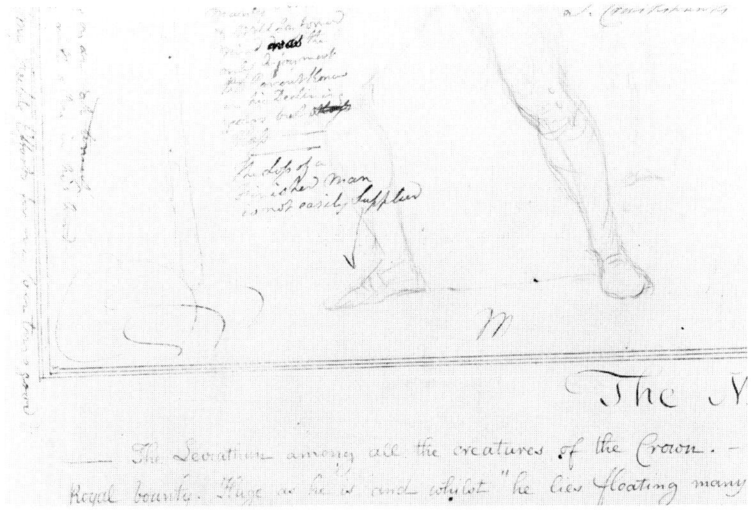

1797
Pen and watercolor over pencil
$7\frac{1}{4}$ x $9\frac{1}{4}$ inches (18.4 x 23.5 cm.)
Annotated verso: I. Cruikshanks
Verso: Pencil drawing depicting a man's forelegs in a lunging position; writing related to Cruikshank's caricature "The Modern Leviathan!!" published by Fores on March 9, 1796
Left edge along side: on ar oak time of—with a Pen in his hand / my Feeble Efforts for my countrys good
Lower edge along bottom: The M /
__ The Leviathan among all the creatures of the Crown. — royal bounty. Huge as he is and whilst "he lies floating many the very spinnacles through which he spouts a torrent of brin / and about him is from the Throne. — Is it for
Published: September 8, 1797, by Laurie & Whittle (200)
Biblio: Wark, 65
Impression: LWL, WMC

Two young women are asleep on a couch, their wrists tied together by a ribbon. A gentleman stands behind and between them tickling the nose of the lady on the right. The trio forms a triangular composition, perhaps a visual allusion to their relationship. The title, "Inseparable Friends," while clearly a reference to the young women bound together, may also have had a more specific meaning. One famous ménage-à-trois of this period was the Duke of Devonshire, his wife Georgiana, and Lady Elizabeth Foster, her friend, who married the Duke after Georgiana's death in 1809. However, they lived together happily for many years. Their living arrangement was well known by 1797, the date of this drawing, having been documented by satirists, dramatists, diarists, and gossips of London's fashionable set.[1] While Cruikshank's drawing may well be a reference to this ménage, he does not provide portraits of the individuals.

The open book placed between the two ladies is Ovid's *The Art of Love,* in which the Roman poet exhorts women to disregard societal restrictions of propriety, chastity, and monogamy, and to heed the call of sensual love, even if it led to unusual arrangements like the one portrayed here. The closed eyes of the ladies suggest they are blind to the deception that is being perpetrated upon them. Although the *Art of Love* enjoyed wide popularity in the eighteenth century, the title of the book was changed in the print to "The Fair Seducer." No work with this exact title has been found, but it may refer to a contemporary novel or operetta, or to a domestic farce of the sort popular at the time.[2]

Advice on how to inflame and ensnare a lover in a complex minuet of flirtation, avoidance, and persuasion may seem artificial and frivolous today. Yet, Cruikshank, like Ovid, seems less a critic of licentiousness or over-cultivation than a tolerant and perspicacious observer of his society's manners and morals.

Fragmentary phrases on the back of this drawing relate to and may have been a study for another Cruikshank caricature, *The Modern Leviathan,* which lampooned the Duke of Bedford's involvement in a tax scandal. Comparison of the published version of this caricature with the study on the back of "Inseparable Friends" reveals a new piece of information—the tree on which Burke sits is an oak.

Deanne Shey

1. On their relationship see Arthur Calder-Marshall, *The Two Duchesses* (New York: Harper and Row, 1978).
2. See Ernest Bernbaum, *The Drama of Sensibility: A Sketch of the History of English Sentimental Comedy and Domestic Tragedy, 1696-1780* (Cambridge, Mass.: Harvard University Press, 1925).

71 *Poor Pat, or a Present of Wild Ducks* †

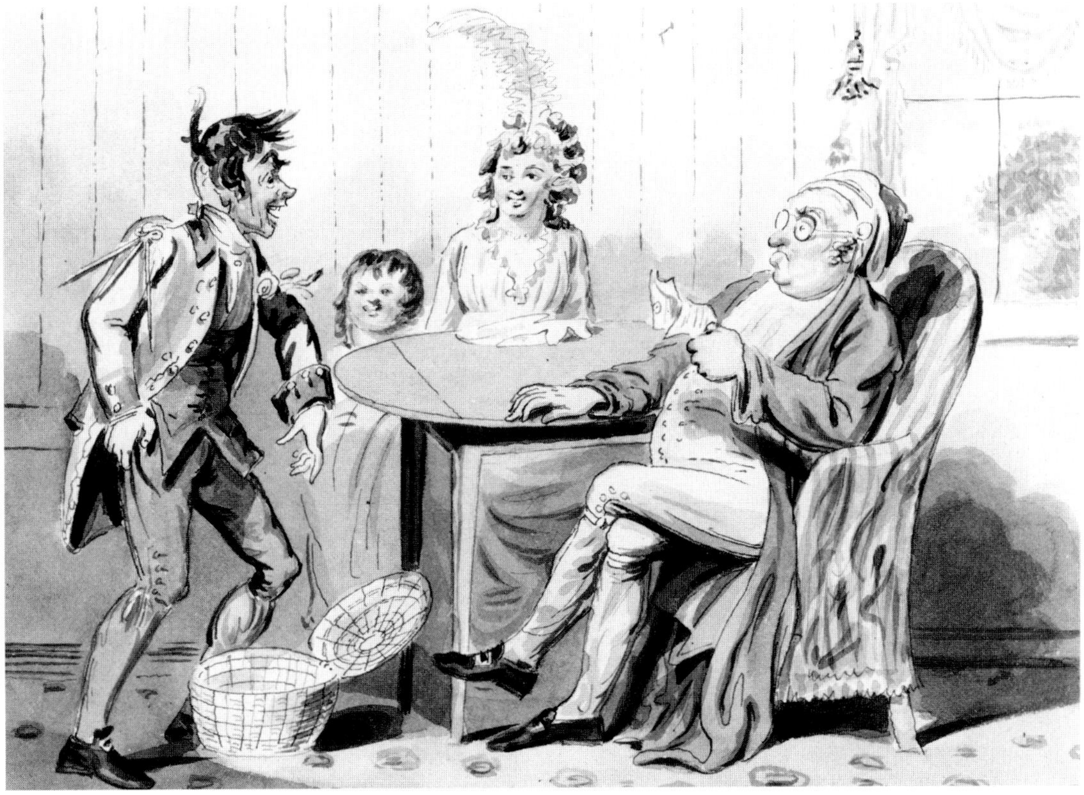

1797
Pen and watercolor over pencil
6 3/4 x 9 1/8 inches (17.1 x 23.1 cm.)
Annotated verso: A present of a pair of Ducks / I. Cruikshanks
Published: September 25, 1797, by Laurie & Whittle (201); below the title is engraved: Why Pat, I find here in the Letter, a Brace of live Wild ducks your Master has sent me – Pat – In the Letter, is it the Letter you say—By Jesus, I'm glad you found 'em there, for they flew all out of the Basket while I was Drinking a Noggin of Whiskey with Murphy O'Flanegan – Oh! Botheration – good luck to me hurra—hurra – Oh! – Your Sarvant Sir.
Biblio: Wark, 66
Impression: LWL

The Irish servant, on the left, and the seated gentleman engage in a conversation regarding a brace of ducks that had once been in the basket, visible at the former's feet. From the text added to the print, it is clear that the servant's master had ordered him to transport this basket of ducks to his friend. Tasks such as this were commonly executed by footmen, for personal delivery was considered not only polite but efficient.[1] Unfortunately, this particular footman is far from competent.

The humor in Cruikshank's tale of this inept servant's predicament relies to a large extent on ethnic stereotyping. While many servants were known to drink, Irish servants were considered especially prone to this vice. Stigmatized as drunkards, they were perceived as ignorant, illiterate, unreliable—and as great storytellers.[3] These qualities are all in evidence here. When the gentleman responds to the note with, "I find here in the letter a brace of live wild ducks," the intoxicated and ignorant footman is foolishly elated, thinking that the recipient had actually found the ducks in the letter. The woman and the child are amused as the footman congratulates himself on his personal good fortune.

Rhonda Howard

1. J. Jean Hecht, *The Domestic Servant Class in Eighteenth-Century England* (London: Routledge and KeganPaul, 1956), p. 51.
2. Marshall, *English People in the Eighteenth Century*, p. 183.
3. Sheridan Gilley, "English Attitudes to the Irish in England, " in Colin Holmes, ed. *Irish Minorities in British Society* (London: Allen and Unwin, 1987), pp. 112-13.

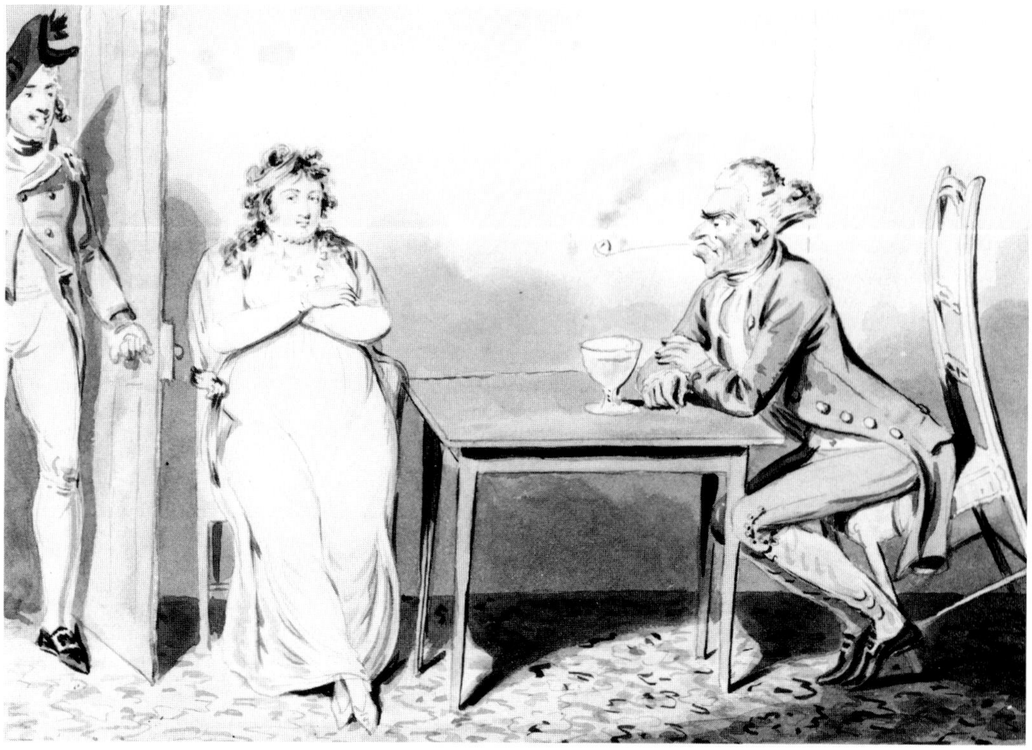

1797
Pen and watercolor over pencil
6 3/4 x 9 1/4 inches (17.5 x 23.5 cm.)
Annotated verso: Mr. Do-Nothing / I. Cruikshanks
Published: October 10, 1797, by Laurie & Whittle (202); below the title is engraved: Husband – What makes you look so thoughtful my Love, what are you puzzling your Dear Head about now – Wife – Why you said last Night at Supper that you knew every one in our Street were Cuckolds but one, And I have been Puzzling Myself ever since to find out who that one could be – Husband – Oh! Oh! Very Well, I have done.
Biblio: George, 9838; Krumbhaar, 717; Wark, 67
Impression: BM, LWL, WMC

It is an awkward moment for this married couple. From the accompanying text, it is clear that the wife has just unknowingly revealed to her husband that she has been unfaithful to him. Unpleasantly surprised, the husband leans forward and looks at his wife with an angry countenance. Unlike the viewer, he is not yet aware that her unsuspecting lover is about to enter the room. The surprise entrance, a recurring compositional device in Cruikshank's oeuvre, adds to the drama and humor of the scene.[1]

A double standard prevailed. A woman's morality and faithfulness to her marriage were both expected and valued. A man's transgressions, on the other hand, were considered uncontrollable and natural.[2] It was criminal for a woman to commit adultery while her husband, according to Boswell's *Life of Johnson,* "did not do his wife a very material injury of appetite if he steals her chambermaid."[3] The wife, in contrast, would greatly injure her husband's reputation if his peers found out that he was a cuckold. It would be a reflection on his masculinity and ability to rule in his own household.[4]

As a subject for satire and bawdy humor, cuckoldry was a popular theme. The husbands in these portrayals are usually much older than their wives, implying lack of virility and perhaps romance. This stereotypical conception of the older man as unable to please his young wife clearly underlies the humor in this work, inscribed by a later hand on the reverse side, "Mr. Do-Nothing."

Danna Freedy

1. For another example see *Folly of an Old Man Marrying a Young Wife* (5).
2. Bridget Hill, *Eighteenth-Century Women: An Anthology* (London: Allen and Unwin, 1984), p. 25.
3 Quoted ibid., p. 33.
4. Stone, *The Family, Sex, and Marriage,* pp. 503-4.

73 *The Old Cheese* †

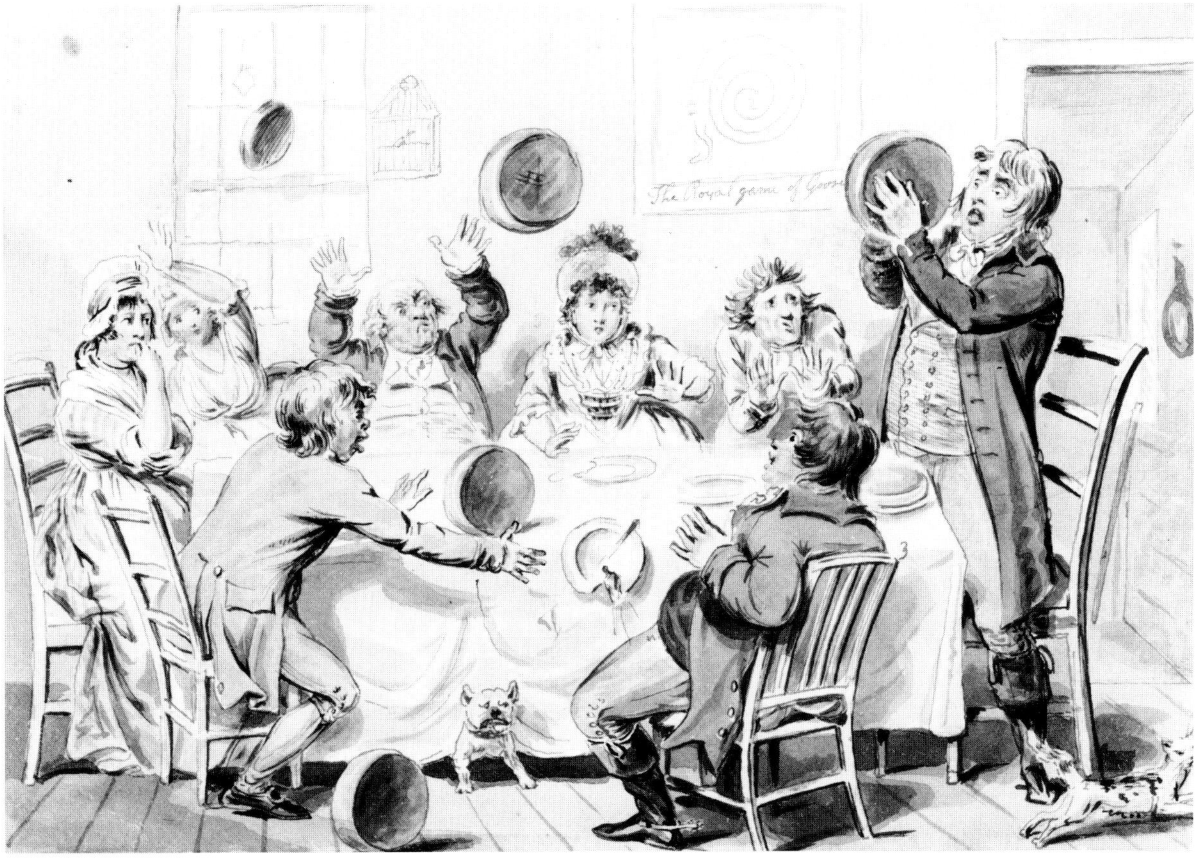

1798
Pen and watercolor over pencil
$6^{3}/_{4}$ x 9 inches (17.2 x 22.9 cm.)
Annotated verso: The old Cheese / I. Cruikshanks
Published: February 1, 1798, by Laurie & Whittle (69); below the title is engraved: An Original Tale, Recited by Mr. Fawcett, at Covent-Garden Theatre; followed by 72 lines of verse.
Biblio: George, 9332; Wark, 69
Impression: BM, LWL

This colorful scene, showing eight people gathered at a table, is Cruikshank's interpretation of a tale recited by the actor John Fawcett at Covent Garden Theatre, as the text accompanying the print states. Londoners had taken to the theater during the preceding decades as never before.[1] Performances, whether tragedy or comedy, had brief entr'acte entertainments or an afterpiece, usually a farce, and often a monologue by a major actor or actress.[2] One of the stars of the London theater was Fawcett, of whom a contemporary remarked, "there is something so effectual in the jovial hurry of his voice and the rough complacency of his concluding hems that the audience are always prepared to laugh. . . . I really know no actor who can procure so much applause."[3]

That Cruikshank designed a headpiece for the printed version of "The Old Cheese" suggests that the tale had a large following. The engraved verses, in two columns, relate the story of a witless, henpecked husband who gives an exhibition of his domestic authority to impress his guests but is finally quelled by his wife.[4] For Cruikshank, this presented an opportunity not only to express the grotesque with pen and color[5] but to address issues of gender and power in domestic relationships.

Cruikshank depicts the absurd preclimactic moment in the tale when the husband, his short-lived freedom about to end, tosses whole cheeses around with abandon. As the cheeses fly, the guests dive for cover. Even the dog reacts. The canine, as originally sketched by Cruikshank, wears a grim snarl, while in the engraving the dog emerges from beneath the cloth with clownish enthusiasm. Ignoring the mayhem he has caused, the husband is about to launch another cheese missile. His wife sits, awaiting her moment of retribution. This is the calm before the storm. She is an instant away from springing into the hallway behind her husband to beat him into submission. He has pushed her one cheese too far. At the moment depicted, she is literally holding her tongue, but will not be able to contain herself much longer. The prominently positioned wall board with the inscription of the "Royal game of Goose" (the phrase is omitted in the print) reinforces the theme of female dominance.

Maria L. Brendel

1. Plumb, *The Pursuit of Happiness,* p. 3.
2. H. Saxe Wyndham, *The Annals of Covent Garden Theatre,* 2 vols. (London: Chatto and Windus, 1906), 1:258; Hogan, ed., *The London Stage,* pt. 5, p. 81.
3. Remarks by Lamb and Hunt originally made in the eighteenth century were recorded in the early years of the nineteenth century in "Critical Essays on the Performers of the London Theatres"; see Hogan, ed., *The London Stage,* pt. 5, p. 126.
4. Wark, "*Drawings for Drolls,*" p. 69.
5. On the grotesque as part of the romantic spirit see Wark, *Ten British Pictures,* p. 68.

The Old Cheese – An Original Tale

Recited by Mr. Fawcett, at Covent-Garden Theatre.

Young Slouch, the farmer, had a jolly wife,
That knew all the conveniences of life,
Whose diligence and cleanliness supplied
The wit which Nature had to him denied;
But then she had a tongue that would be heard,
And make a better man than Slouch afraid.
This made censorious persons of the town
Say, Slouch could hardly call his soul his own;
For, if he went abroad too much, she'd use
To give him slippers, and lock up his shoes.
Talking he lov'd, and ne'er was more afflicted
Than when he was disturb'd, or contradicted;
Yet still into his story she would break
With—"'Tis not so; pray give me leave to speak."
His friends thought this was a tyrannic rule,
Not diff'ring much from calling of him fool;
Told him he must exert himself, and be,
In fact, the master of his family.
He said "That the next Tuesday noon would shew
"Whether he were the lord at home, or no;
"When their good company he would entreat
"To well-brew'd ale, and clean, if homely, meat."
With aching heart home to his wife he goes,
And on his knees does his rash act disclose;
And prays dear Sukey, that, one day at least,
He might appear as master of the feast.
"I'll grant your wish," cries she, "that you may see
"'Twere wisdom to be govern'd still by me."
The guests upon the day appointed came,
Each bowsy farmer with his simp'ring dame.
"Ho, Sue!" cries Slouch, "why do'st not thou appear?
"Are these thy manners when aunt Snap is here?
"I pardon ask," says Sue; "I'd not offend
"Any my dear invites, much less his friend."
Slouch, by his kinsman Gruffy, had been taught
To entertain his friends with finding fault,
And make the main ingredient of his treat,
His saying there was nothing fit to eat:
"The boil'd pork stinks, the roast beef is not enough,
"The bacon's rusty, and the hens are tough;
"The veal's all rags, the butter's turn'd to oil;
"And thus I buy good meat for sluts to spoil.
"'Tis we are the first Slouches ever sat
"Down to a pudding without plums or fat.
"What teeth of stomach's strong enough to feed
"Upon a goose my granum kept to breed?
"Why must old pigeons, and they stale, be drest,
"When there's so many squab ones in the nest?
"This beer is sour; 'tis musty, thick, and stale,
"And worse than any thing, except the ale."
Sue all this while many excuses made:
Some things she own'd, at other times she laid
This fault on chance, but oft'ner on the maid.
Then cheese was brought, says Slouch. "This e'en shall roll;
"I'm sure 'tis hard enough to make a bowl;
"This is skim-milk, and therefore it shall go;
"And this, because 'tis Suffolk, follow too."
But now Sue's patience did begin to waste;
Nor longer could dissimulation last.
"Pray let me rise," says Sue, "my dear; I'll find
"A cheese perhaps may be to lovy's mind."
Then in an entry standing close, where he
Alone, and none of all his friends, might see;
And brandishing a cudgel he had felt,
And far enough on this occasion smelt.
"I'll try, my joy," she cried, "if I can please
"My dearest with a taste of his Old Cheese!"
Slouch turn'd his head, saw his wife's vigorous hand
Wielding her oaken sapling of command,
Knew well the twang—"Is't the Old Cheese my dear?"
"No need, no need of Cheese," cries Slouch; "I'll swear,
"I think, I've din'd as well as my Lord Mayor!"

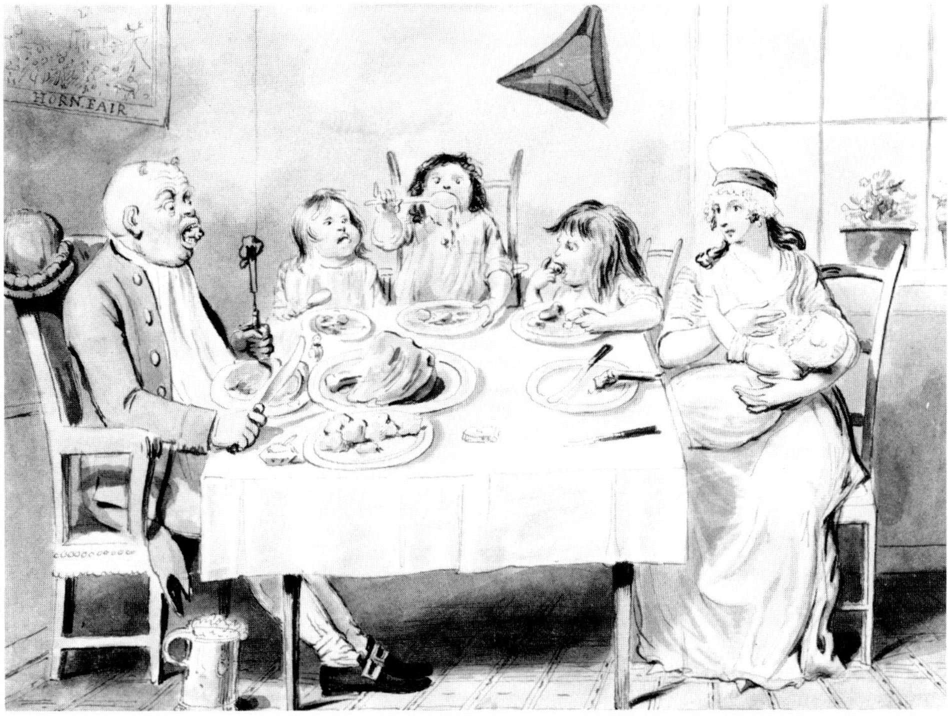

1798
Pen and watercolor over pencil
6 11/16 x 9 1/16
(17 x 23 cm.)
Inscribed recto: Horn Fair
Annotated verso: A Bone to Pick / I. Cruikshanks
Published: February 1, 1798, by Laurie & Whittle; below the title is engraved: Wife – I'll thank you for a bit more meat – Husband – No, I think you've had enough, but there's a Bone for you and be contented – Wife – Very well as this is always the case, I'll give you a Bone to Pick that's got Flesh on it. There's the four Children at the Table, and only one of them is Yours, now pick that one out and be contented.
Biblio: Krumbhaar, A.17; Wark, 70
Impression: WMC

The man's selfishness is the object of ridicule in this image of a gross husband mistreating his wife by refusing her "a bit more meat" when his plate is overflowing and his mouth is full. In retaliation for this and previous instances of abuse, the woman reveals that only one of the four children at the table is his, thereby branding him a cuckold. The tufts of hair on the man's head, suggestive of horns, as well as the image of *Horn Fair* directly above him support her claim. In the print, figures in the picture on the wall also have horns.

Both text and image offer a contrast between husband and wife. Whereas the man's remarks are thoughtless, the woman's are pointed. Despite her having borne four children probably in as many years, she appears fit. Her handsome face and figure serve as counterpoints to the gross features and body of her husband. Clues to the meaning of the man's appearance can be found in Lavater's contemporary study of physiognomy, in which a similar nose is said to be "destitute of every species of delicate sentiment"; a comparable mouth is identified as "repugnant to nature and truth"; and his kind of ear reveals "circumspection destitute of courage."[1] Like the children, the husband exhibits a lack of control in his eating habits. While their manners are in keeping with their age, his clearly are not.

Presumably the husband's past treatment of his wife led her to search for love elsewhere. Still, the woman's remarks catch the man by surprise. With eyes bulging out in disbelief, he stops chewing the food that sits between his teeth. His fork, too, is arrested in midair. Denied another morsel, the woman has given her husband a mouthful; the news is more than he can swallow.

Edward J. Nygren

1. Johann Caspar Lavater, *Essays on Physiognomy,* trans. Henry Hunter, 3 vols. in 5 (London: J. Murray, 1789-98), 5:370, 404, 413.

75 *More, Strange, and Wright*

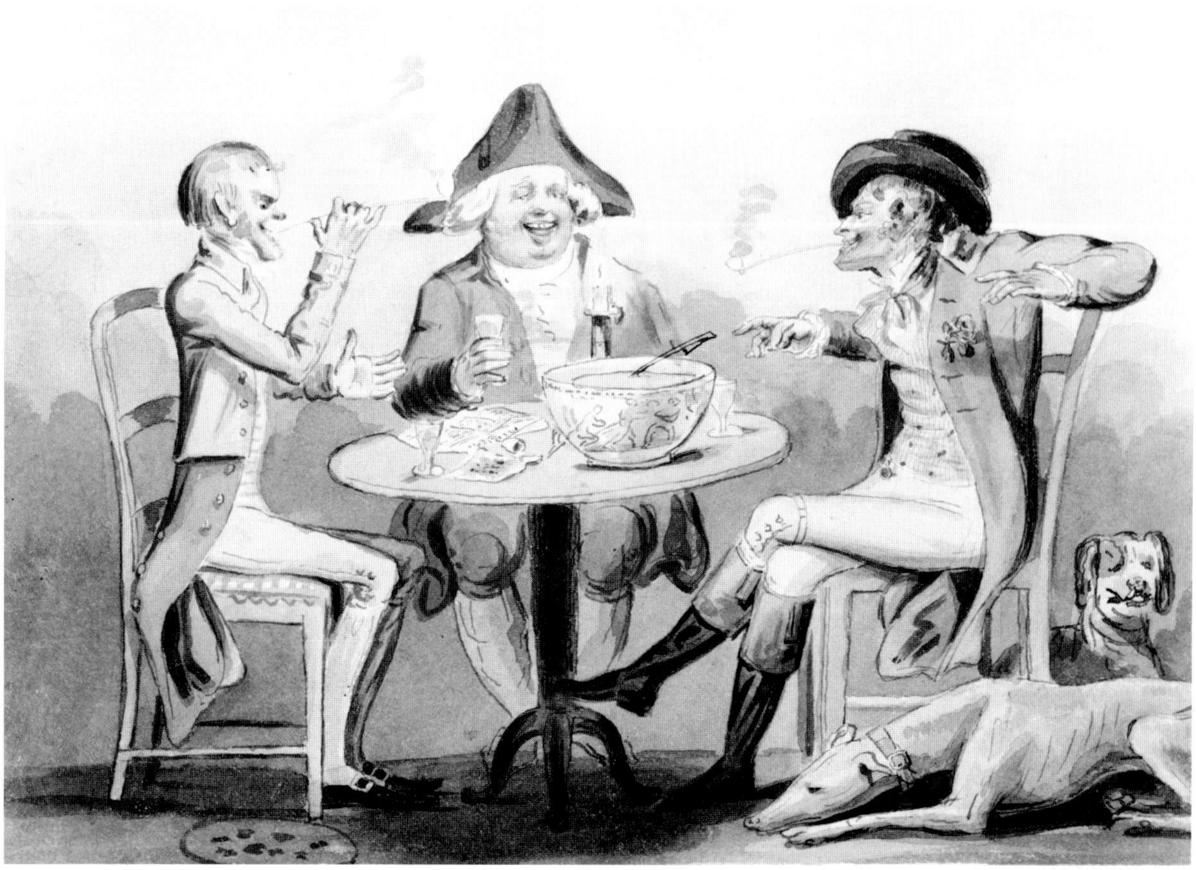

1798
Pen and watercolor over pencil
6 11/16 x 9 3/16 inches (17 x 23.3 cm.)
Annotated verso: Messrs. Moor Strange & Wright / I. Cruikshanks
Published: February 12, 1798, by Laurie & Whittle; below the title is engraved: At a Tavern one Night / Messrs More, Strange, and Wright; / Met to Drink, and good thoughts to Exchange: / Says More of us three, / The whole Town will agree; / There's only one Knave and that's Strange. / Yes says Strange rather sore, / I'm sure there's one More; / A most terrible Knave and a bite: / Who cheated his Mother, / His Sister, his Brother; / O yes replied More, that is Wright.
Biblio: Wark, 71
Impression: LWL

The gentleman to the right is fashionably dressed in a round hat and French boots, while the gentleman in the middle is in uniform. The other man is conservatively dressed.[1] Located in the foreground is a tobacco box with several holes to receive pipes. Enjoying themselves over punch—a combination of rum, lemon, and sugar—they are most likely in a rural club or tavern, as indicated by the presence of the two hunting dogs. In 1789 a typical drinker of punch was described as "indifferent to the confusion he causes. He is moreover the absolute egotist the earth contains. He conquers everything by his visible merriment and humor."[2]

The conversation of the three men is presented in iambic nonsense verse, with rhyming puns on their last names. Each attempts to identify the other as a knave or a "bite" (i.e., a cheat or scoundrel).

Tim D. Wright

1. C. W. Cunnington and P. Cunnington, *Handbook of English Costume in the Eighteenth Century*, pp. 241, 243.
2. J. M. Golby and A.W. Purdue, *The Civilization of the Crowd: Popular Culture In England, 1750-1900* (New York: Schocken Books, 1985), p. 9.

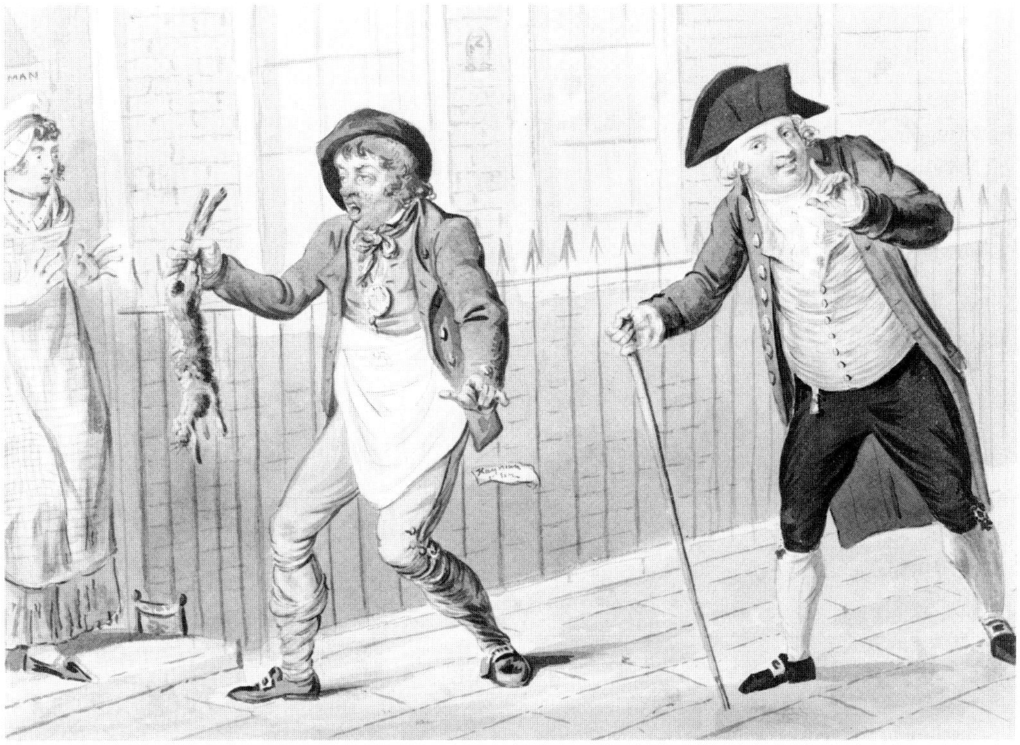

1798
Pen and watercolor over pencil
6⅝ x 9⅜ inches (17.3 x 23.9 cm.)
Inscribed recto: Hayman
Annotated verso: Frank Hayman and the Hare / I. Cruikshanks
Published: February 20, 1798, by Laurie & Whittle; below the title is engraved: Written by John Taylor, Esquire, Author of *Monsieur Tonson,* and originally intended for recitation at the Haymarket Theatre, during the Lent Season; followed by forty stanzas of verse.
Biblio: George, 9333; Krumbhaar, 393; Wark, 72
Impression: BM, LWL, WMC

Created as a headpiece for a broadside, this image illustrates an amusing story about the painter Francis Hayman (1708-76).[1] The accompanying poem of forty stanzas was written by one of the artist's former pupils ten months prior to the publication date of the print. The first half of the poem describes Hayman as a good-natured man. It continues with a lengthy account of the people, objects (primarily Hayman's paintings), and scenes commonly found in Vauxhall Garden. Near the end of the first half a man who is bored with this historical information insists upon hearing a humorous story about one of the artist's many journeys. This request produces the tale of Francis Hayman.

The second half of the poem begins with a street scene, in which Hayman sees a drunk porter with a hare slung over his back. As the porter teeters back and forth, a dog takes notice and trails close behind. Intrigued, Hayman follows in their wake. Down the road, the porter is invited into a house, but declines. Instead, he lies down on a bench. As he sleeps, the dog consumes half of the hare. Unaware of what has happened, the man continues on his way. Hayman never attempts to inform the porter of the problem. Rather, he remains out of sight, hoping that he might see the man deliver the half-eaten hare to its purchaser.

Arriving at his destination, the porter is greeted at the door by the maid, aghast at the sight of the half-eaten rabbit. Positioned to the right of the porter, the artist gestures the viewer to watch this. The drunken porter, with bright red cheeks and ruffled clothing, stands dumbfounded as he drops a paper marked "Hayman." Now, as the porter delivers the mangled animal to his address, it is clear that not having warned the man of his plight, Hayman is the victim of his own prank.

Rhonda Howard

1. The most recent study on Francis Hayman is Brian Allen, *Francis Hayman* (New Haven, Conn.: Yale University Press, 1987).

Frank Hayman; A Tale

Frank Hayman, once a Brother of the Brush,
Had talents much distinguish'd in his day,
But for his art he hardly car'd a rush,
If some odd mischief stumbl'd in his way

This Wag was deem'd by all the Social Tribe
A jovial, easy, careless, pleasant fellow,
Fond of a frolic, ready at a gibe,
And sometimes in his cups a little mellow.

There is a famous place, yclepe Vauxhall,
Where Cits, good folks, regale with merry hearts,
And oft to busy Waiters eager bawl,
For fresh supplies of Ham, and Beef, and Tarts.

There may you see of Boxes many a row,
For such as like to sup in state design'd,
With Pictures deck'd, that make a goodly show:
Now in these Pictures Hayman's skill we find.

There old Jack Falstaff, guilty of a lie,
Attempts his bragging cowardice to screen:
There, with the sage Magician, Nell we spy,
While surly Jobson low'rs with jealous spleen.

And there too rosy Remembrance fondly trace—
Ah! sweet reflections to the pensive mind,
The simple pleasures of a careless Race,
Ere yet they learn to prey upon their kind.

The Shuttle-cock that like ambition flies,
Driv'n by contending Factions to and fro;
The blinded boy, who wanders by surmise,
True emblem of our darkling state below.

And other pastimes of our early years
Recall in various scenes, life's jocund May.
Where e'en the proud Philosopher might gaze,
And envy Ignorance his thoughtless play.

Oh! Infancy, whate'er thy fortune, gay,
Whom so sad records of the past annoy,
The present rapt in frolics of the day,
And all thy future but to-morrow's joy.

But in a spacious Room, Rotunda hight,
Where all the crowd with gaping wonder roam,
There Hayman's genius wings a prouder flight,
And British triumphs decorate the Dome.

Here Asia's Tribes submit to English Bands,
While all the Blacks and Whites seem quite alive;
And here great Albion's Chief superior stands,
Meer Jaffier, a *mere nothing* to Lord Clive.

Here Amherst, too, a fav'rite Son of Fame,
Shews the true temper of a British breast,
Not more awake to Valour's active flame,
Than prompt with zeal to succour the Distrest.

And other Martial Heroes too are there;
Granby, who rears his head in naked grace—
A head that could not miss the wither'd hair,
Since the Wreaths of deathless Laurels crown the place.

There heads of Naval Heroes, wond'rous sight,
Are floating on the billows, just like fishes,
A host of heads, with powder'd locks bedight,
Borne up by Nereids, or buoyant dishes.

And not a face among them sinking dreads,
But on they glide together full of glee;
Nor need we wonder that they *raise their heads,*
Since Britons find *their element* at Sea.

At length, to dignify a train so dear,
And to complete the splendour of the scene,
A sight that ev'ry Loyal Breast must cheer,
A Patriot Monarch and a Virtuous Queen.

But now, methinks, some Critic, with a smile,
Exclaims, "But where's the Story all this while?
"Why all this tedious stuff about Vauxhall,
"When ev'ry body here has seen it all?
"What more of this Frank Hayman shall we know,
"We knew he was a Painter long ago?"

Dull Snarler, Writers for the Stage,
When they the passions would engage,
Announce, with previous art,
Some fav'rite Part,
Who when he comes is better able,
To make a figure in the Fable.
Now if this hint should not explain
Our Problem to thy torpid brain,
Stop where you are—my friend adieu—
The story was not made for you.
Yet, as some wiser folks may say,
The Prologue's longer than the Play.
'Tis the time to check the rambling Muse,
Who thus her idle Tales pursues.

Frank Hayman, tempted by a pleasant day,
After a long contention with the Gout,
A foe that oft besieg'd him, sallied out,
To breathe fresh air, and while an hour away,
It chanc'd he was strolling, void of care,
A drunken Porter pass'd him with a Hare.

The Hare was o'er his shoulder flung,
Dangling behind, in piteous plight,
And as he crept in zig-zag style,
Making the most of every mile,
From side to side poor Puffy swung,
As if each moment taking flight.

A Dog, who saw the man's condition,
A lean and hungry Politician,
On the look out was lurking close behind,
A sly and subtle chap,
Of most sagacious smell.
Like Politicians of a higher kind,
Ready to snap
At anything that fell.

The Porter stagger'd on, the Dog kept near,
Watching the lucky minute for a bite,
Now made a spring, and then drew back with fear,
While Hayman, follow'd, titt'ring at the sights.

Great was the contrast 'twixt the man and dog,
The one a negligent stupid lout
That seem'd to know not what he was about,
The other keen, observant, all agog.
Nor need it wonderment excite I ween,
That Hayman clos'd the train to mark the scene.

Through many a street our tipsey Porter reels,
Then stops, as if to solemn thought inclin'd—
The watchful dog was at his heels,
And Hayman hobbled on not far behind.

Then rolling on-again, the man survey'd
One of those happy mansions where
A cordial drop imparts it clicering aid
To all of the thirsty Sons of Care.

The sight of this refreshing place,
The scent that bails him from the door,
Arrest at once his rambling pace—
As they had often done before.

Mine Host, with accents that were wond'rous kind,
Invites him in, a jolly crew to join,
The man the gen'rous courtesy declin'd,
Merely perhaps for want of thirst—or coin.

Strait on a bench without he stretch'd along,
Regardless of the passing throng,
And soon his weary eye-lids close,
While Somnus sooths him to repose,
The Hare now prostrate at his back
This was the time to get a snack.

The Dog unable longer to refrain,
Gaz'd at the hare,
Who caus'd his care,
Jumpt and bit, jumpt and bit, jumpt and bit and bit again.
At length, when he had clear'd away the rest,
The fated spoiler finish'd on the breast.

Then having made a hearty meal,
He careless turn'd upon his heel,
Nor thought of asking "What's to pay?"
But scamper'd at his case away;
Perhaps to find some four-foot fair,
And tell the story of the Hare.

And here some Sage, with moral spleen may say,
"This Hayman should have driv'n the Dog away,
"Th' effects of vice the blameless should not bear,
"And folks who are not drunkards lose their Hare."

All this, we grant, is very true—
But in this giddy world how few
To Virtue's heights sublimely move,
Relinquishing the things they love.

Not to seem unfashionably good,
Our waggish Painter laughing stood,
In hopes more sport to find;
Dispos'd to keep in view his game,
And with th' ambitious Thane exclaims,
"The greatest is behind."
Besides, he knew, whate'er the plan
That tempts the fond pursuits of Man,
Though Pleasure may the course attend,
The Wise are heedful of *the end*.

Hence, though a mirth of lucky store,
So aptly tumbled in his way,
Yet still he linger'd after more,
And thus he said, or seem'd to say.

"How will the people fret and scold
"When they the *bony wreck* behold!
"And how the drunken rogue will flare
"When first he sees *what was the Hare!*
"The *denouement* must needs be droll—
"'Twere folly not to see the whole."
Presuming thus on future pleasure.
Hayman kept post to wait the sleeper's leisures.

At length our Porter's slumber o'er,
He jogg'd on, tottering as before;
Unconscious anybody kind
Had cas'd him in his load behind.
Now on the houses turn'd his eye,
As if his journey's end were night,
Then read the paper in his hand,
And made a stand—
Hayman drew near, with eager mien,
To mark the closing of the scene,
Expecting strait furious din,
His features ready for a grin.

And now we need but mention one thing more,
To show how well he must have lik'd the whim
Though drunk, our Porter hit at last the door,
And Hayman found the Hare was sent to Him.

MORAL

A wise old Proverb says, "To others do,
"E'en as you would those others should to you—"
Now had our Painter mark'd this rule with care,
He, not the Dog, had din'd upon the Hare.

77 *The Doctor Snatching at The Guinea After His Patient Is Dead*

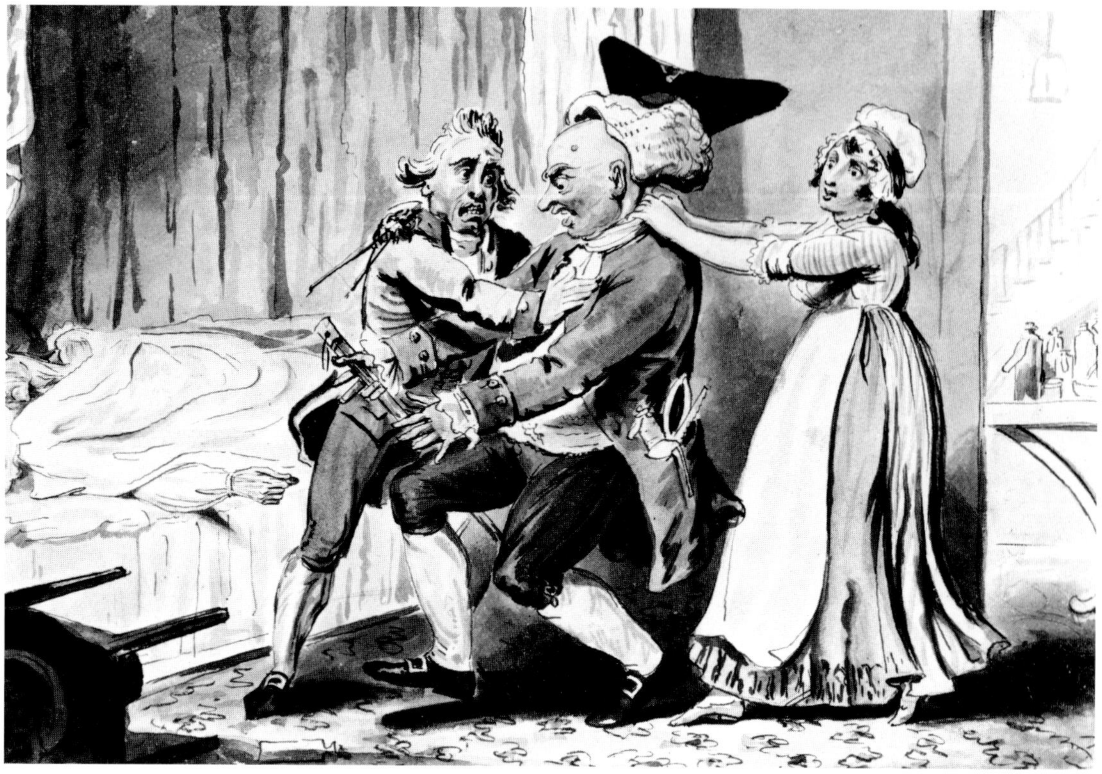

1798
Pen and watercolor over pencil
6⁵/₈ x 9¹/₈ inches (16.9 x 23.2 cm.)
Annotated verso: The Last Fee / I. Cruikshanks
Published: March 6, 1798, by Laurie & Whittle; below the title is engraved: Oh let me die in peace! Eumenes cried / To a hard Creditor at his bed-side: / How! die! roar'd Gripus, and thus your Debts evade: / By God, Sir, you shan't die till I am paid; [below the image on the right]: Vide Philosophical Transactions of T. Schamburgh.
Biblio: Wark, 73
Impression: LWL

The medical profession was harshly treated by eighteenth-century caricaturists. Despite this, medicine assumed a new importance as a profession,[1] and physicians became powerful figures in both the academic and political worlds. Walpole was attacking doctors when he wrote: "Sure the devil's three names of Satan, Beelzebub and Lucifer, were given to him in his three capacities of priest, physician and lawyer!"[2] The medical profession was regarded as lucrative, and fees were high and difficult to pay.[3] Some doctors also supplemented their income by teaching classes and delivering lectures for a general audience.[4]

Here Cruikshank depicts a doctor who is restrained by two servants when he tries to take a coin from the hand of his dying patient. His point is underscored by the physiognomic distortion and ugliness of the physician's face: bulging eyes, arched eyebrows, and short forehead.[5] In his pocket, four instruments serve as attributes of his profession: saw, clyster (or enema syringe), bottle for elixir, and scissors. The action of the servants is ambiguous. Rather than restraining the doctor from this gross act, they could, in fact, be fighting with him for the money.

Mar Martinez-Perez

1. Judy Wechsler, *The Picture of Health* (Philadelphia: University of Pennsylvania Press, 1991), p. 52.
2. Quoted in George, *Social Change in Graphic Satire*, p. 92.
3. Fox, *Londoners*, p. 239.
4. A. Calder-Marshall, *The Grand Century of the Lady* (London: Gordon and Cremonesi, 1976), pp. 101-3.
5. Lavater, *Essays on Physiognomy*, p. 208.

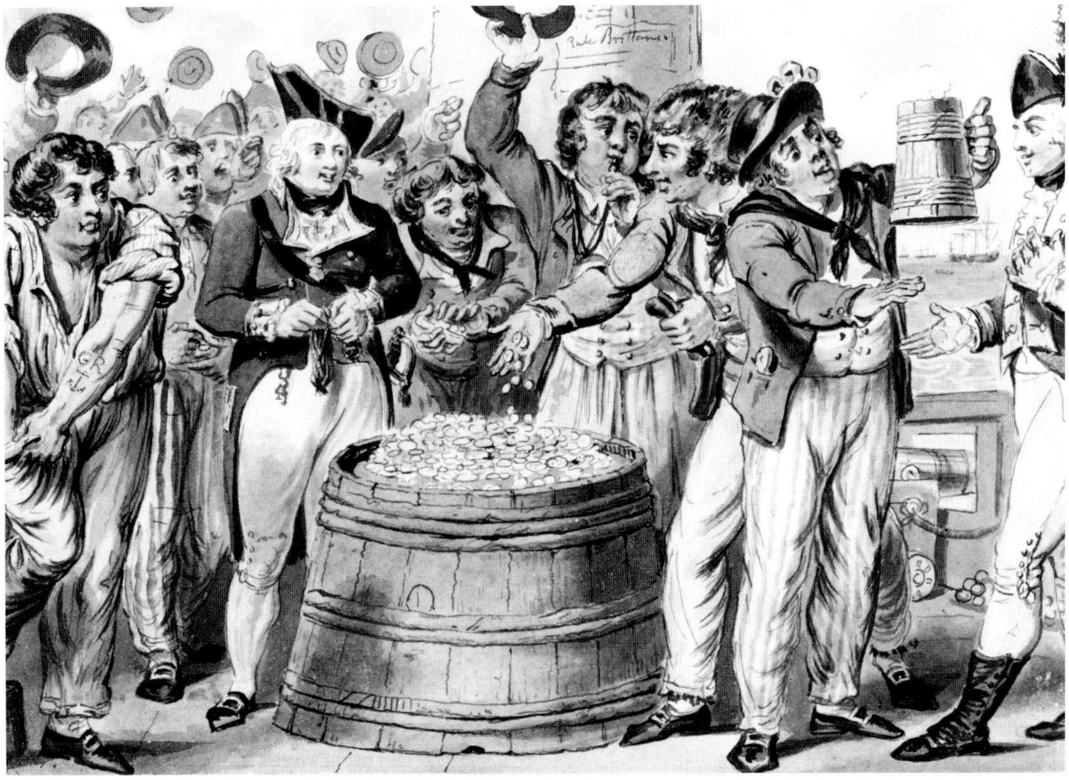

1798
Pen and watercolor over pencil
6 5/8 x 9 inches (16.9 x 22.7 cm.)
Inscribed recto: God save the King / Rule Britannia
Annotated verso: Sailors Contribution / I. Cruikshanks
Published: March 12, 1798, by Laurie & Whittle (210); below the title is engraved: Contributing Nobly against the Enemies of Old England with the Original Letter Addressed to their Commander Lieutenant P. Hue; Argonaut, Jany 31st 1798 / Sir, / We the Seamen and Marines of his Majesty's Ship Argonaut, under your command, desire to give 10s each man out of our wages, to drive before us into the sea all French scoundrels, and other blackguards that would take their parts / We are / Your faithful servants / John Mitchell, Boatswain's Mate, for Self and Ships Company / Alex. Hean, Sergeant for Self and Party / God save the King.
Biblio: George, 9185; Krumbhaar, 496; Wark, 74

With much hoopla and cheering, jovial sailors welcome a Sergeant of the Marines or an officer with open arms and a full tankard of beer. These sailors are so loyal to the king that they are contributing part of their meager salaries to defeat the French. The figure on the far left with a tattoo "G.R." on his forearm, presumably a reference to George Rex, digs deeply into his pockets to give whatever he can. On the mast hangs a sign that says "God save the King" and "Rule Britannia." This scene is set against hats flying in the air and the flinging of coins into a barrel, all in the name of England. There is a record for the *Argonaut* in the *Royal Kalendar* of 1798, indicating that it was registered as a ship in the king's commission with Lieutenant P. Hue as commander. John Mitchell signed a letter representing the men of the *Argonaut* along with their devotion and loyalty to the king and England. Mitchell was clerk in the Office of Seaman's Wages.

Sailors and naval scenes are a recurrent theme in British prints, particularly at this time, when England was at war. Often these images depicted a sailor's farewell or his return, his adventures and misadventures, or, as in this case, swearing allegiance and having a jolly time. There is usually very little satire in such works; in fact they seem to express nationalistic sentiment most of all.

Mari-Tere Alvarez

79 *Monmouth Street Mutton* †

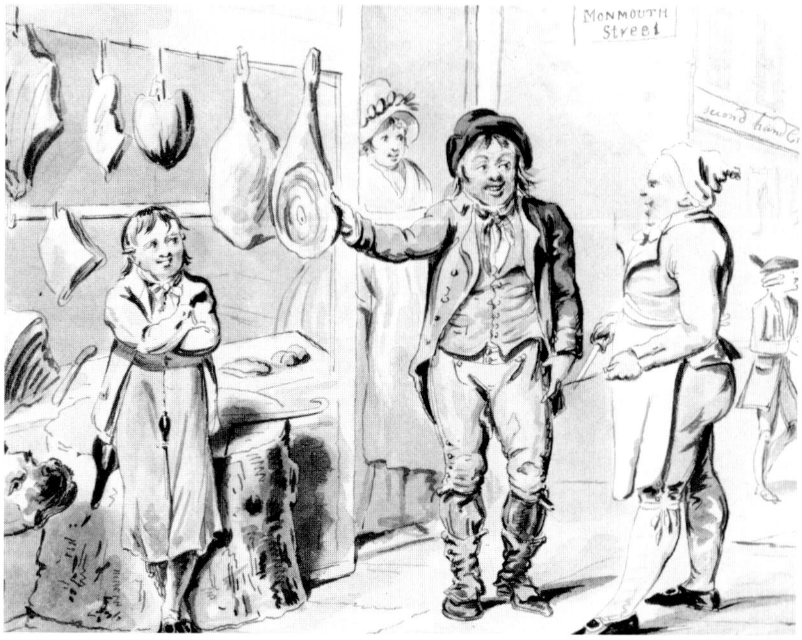

1798
Pen and watercolor over pencil
6⅝ x 9 inches (16.7 x 22.9 cm.)
Inscribed recto: Second Hand Cloath
Annotated verso: Monmouth Street Mutton / I. Cruikshanks
Published: March 16, 1798, by Laurie & Whittle (211); below the title is engraved: Pat – Hurra Measter, what do ye Ax for this here Shoulder of Mutton – Butcher – Why that there leg of Mutton, will be four and six pence. I cut it from as nice a Ship as any in Smithfield – Pat – Oh botheration, who do ye take me for, blarneying me over, wid your Ship, and your Second Hand Mutton, I can buy a New one in Fleet-Market for half that. So good Morning to your Honor, as the Devil said to the Pope.
Biblio: Wark, 75
Impression: LWL

The Irish, deemed ignorant by the British, are the focus of ridicule in this satire. In the foreground, a butcher converses with a young man named Pat. The name and the appearance of the man fit the common stereotype of a "Paddy," a slow-witted, Irish proletarian figure widely known in London as having both good and bad traits (see *Paddy and the Fireman,* 80).[1] On the one hand, "Paddy" was considered benign, humorous, and good-natured; on the other, he was held to be feckless, stupid, violent, unreliable, and drunken.[2] In the drawing, Cruikshank focuses on this negative image of the Irishman and contrasts him with the well-dressed but equally stereotypical figure of a Jew standing beneath the sign—"Second Hand Cloath." The Jew is shown in the role of a shop owner attempting to sell a used coat to a country man on Monmouth Street.

Monmouth Street is located in St. Giles, which was a poor and mainly Irish area in the eighteenth century. Considered the "sink of London," St. Giles was reputedly inhabited by vagrants and thieves living six and seven to a room in old houses cramped in the narrow, winding streets and alleys.[3] Few Irishmen in St. Giles knew how to read; they were all impoverished, and many of them frequented pubs.[4]

The accompanying text provides further evidence of Pat's ignorance. In his conversation with the butcher, he assumes that the meat is secondhand because it is being sold on Monmouth Street, the secondhand district. Like the young man on the left, Cruikshank's contemporaries, familiar with Monmouth Street's reputation, would have found the Irishman's ignorance humorous. The last line of the inscription rests on yet another stereotypical view of the Irish. Thinking that the butcher is trying to overcharge him, he retorts "Good morning to your Honor, as the Devil said to the Pope." The comment exemplifies the view that the Irish were superstitious Papists.

Mary-Kay Lombino

1. Gilley, "English Attitudes to the Irish in England," in Holmes, ed., *Immigrants and Minorities in British Society,* p. 84.
2. E. P. Thompson, *The Making of the English Working Class* (New York: Random House, 1963), pp. 429-31.
3. Thomas Burke, *The Streets of London through the Centuries* (London: B. T. Batsford, Ltd., 1949), p. 101.
4. Mayhew, *London Labour and the London Poor,* 1:104.

80 Paddy and the Fireman †

1798
Pen and watercolor over pencil
8¼ x 6⅝ inches (21 x 16.9 cm.)
Annotated verso: House on Fire / I'm only a Lodger / I. Cruikshanks
Published: March 16, 1798, by Laurie & Whittle (212); below the title is engraved: Fire Man – Get up my Friend, get up directly, the House is on Fire – Irish Man – Botheration seize you and the House both, I have no business at all, at all with it, I'm only a Lodger.
Biblio: Krumbhaar, A.74; Wark, 76
Impression: LWL, WMC

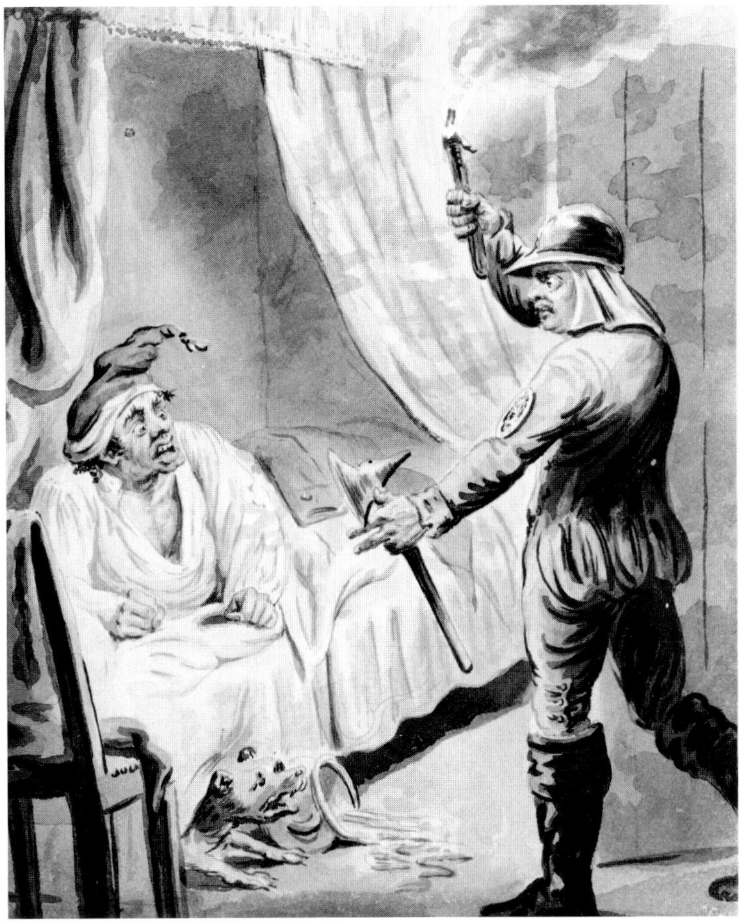

Irish immigrants, arriving in London either to stay or to stop over during their journey to America, often needed two or three days' temporary shelter. They would regularly be led by shipping agents to lodging houses, where as many as five hundred immigrants might be staying. Already resented by London's working class as a threat to their livelihood, the Irish were perceived as ignorant and lazy. Their poor living conditions only reinforced this attitude.[1]

This scene takes place in a bedroom that is unusually elaborate for an Irishman's typical lodging. The setting is rather grand, similar to those in death or dream scenes by historical painters such as Henry Fuseli, whose influence is evident here in the use of dynamic perspective as well as in the dramatic chiaroscuro and limited palette. The exaggerated facial expressions and spectacular treatment of theme also recall Fuseli's work. Even the subject—a man being awakened from his sleep in a heavily draped bed—is reminiscent of Fuseli's imagery, which Cruikshank would have known.

The fireman is attired in traditional "Sun fire-office" uniform, a suit of pink with its trademark yellow circular patch.[2] With pick-ax and firecap, he obviously startles the Irishman, who deals with the news of impending disaster by claiming it doesn't concern him since he is only a "lodger." The dog, assuming "Paddy's" characteristics, with his parallel expression and bark ("bark" was slang for Irishman),[3] knocks over the chamber pot in agitated excitement. The humor of the scene relies on the stereotypical view of the stupid and ignorant Irishman.

Londoners were well aware of the dangers of fire, the city having nearly been destroyed by conflagration five times in its history.

Julie Joyce

1. Mayhew, *London Labour and the London Poor,* 1:111-14.
2. Pyne, *The Costume of Great Britain,* pl. 4, "A Fireman."
3. George Andrewes, *Dictionary of the Slang and Cant Languages: Ancient and Modern (as used by criminals and every class of offenders)* (London: George Smeeton, 1809).

81 Ringing The Changes – Or Quizzing My Uncle †

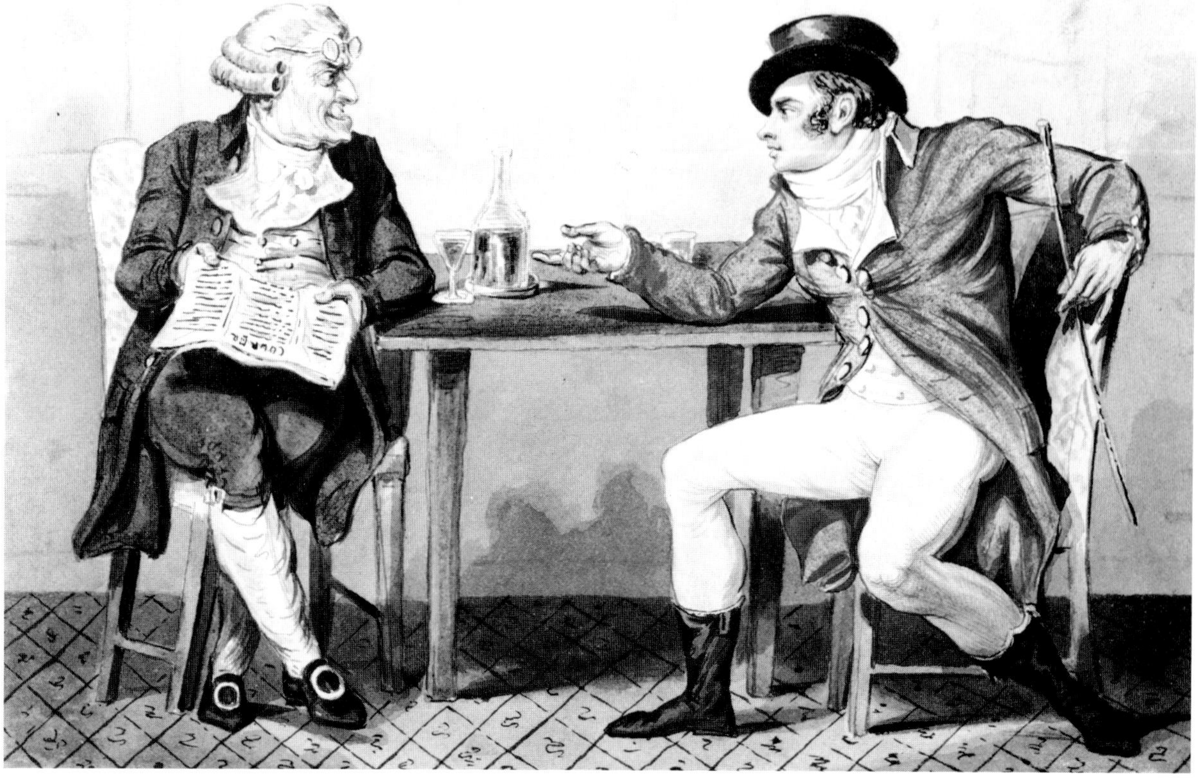

1798
Pen and watercolor with touches of bodycolor and chalk over pencil
6 5/8 x 9 1/4 inches (16.9 x 23.2 cm.)
Annotated verso: The Spendthrift / I. Cruikshanks
Published: March 20, 1798, by Laurie & Whittle (213); above the image is engraved: Old Nunke and his Hopeful Nephew; below the title is engraved: Old Gentleman (Reading) – Last Monday A Society of College Youths Rang a Peal of 4000, 500 Changes, in the Space of two Hours and twenty-Minutes, upon a Set of Treble-bob Majors, being the Shortest time ever known, what do you think of that Jack – Nephew – Mere nothing Uncle. I ring the Changes to the Tune of more than double that Sum in Half the time, on two Generals, and one Simple-Colonel, will you Lend me a Hundred Pound for two or three days Uncle.
Biblio: George, 9323; Wark, 77
Impression: BM, LWL

Probably relaxing in his club, an elderly gentleman, wearing a conservative wig and clothes,[1] reads to his nephew aloud from the *Courier*, a daily newspaper, the remarks quoted above. The article recounts a college prank in which a group of students climbed a bell tower and rang a succession of loud sounds in alternating order in a certain arrangement (treble-bob majors) and in a brief period (the shortest time ever).[2]

The nephew's attire is on the cutting edge of fashion for 1798.[3] He pretends to understand the story in order to appease his uncle and obtain a loan. However, in his haste to secure a handout, the inattentive young man misconstrues the word "major" as a reference to military rank rather than to a musical scale. His inattentiveness may very well mean he will not get the loan.

Tim D. Wright

1. C. W. Cunnington and P. Cunnington, *Handbook of English Costume in the Eighteenth Century*, pp. 241, 243.
2. Samuel Johnson, *A Dictionary of the English Language* (London: W. Strahan, 1765).
3. C. W. Cunnington and P. Cunnington, *Handbook of English Costume in the Eighteenth Century*, pp. 217, 239

Captain Wattle and Miss Roe †

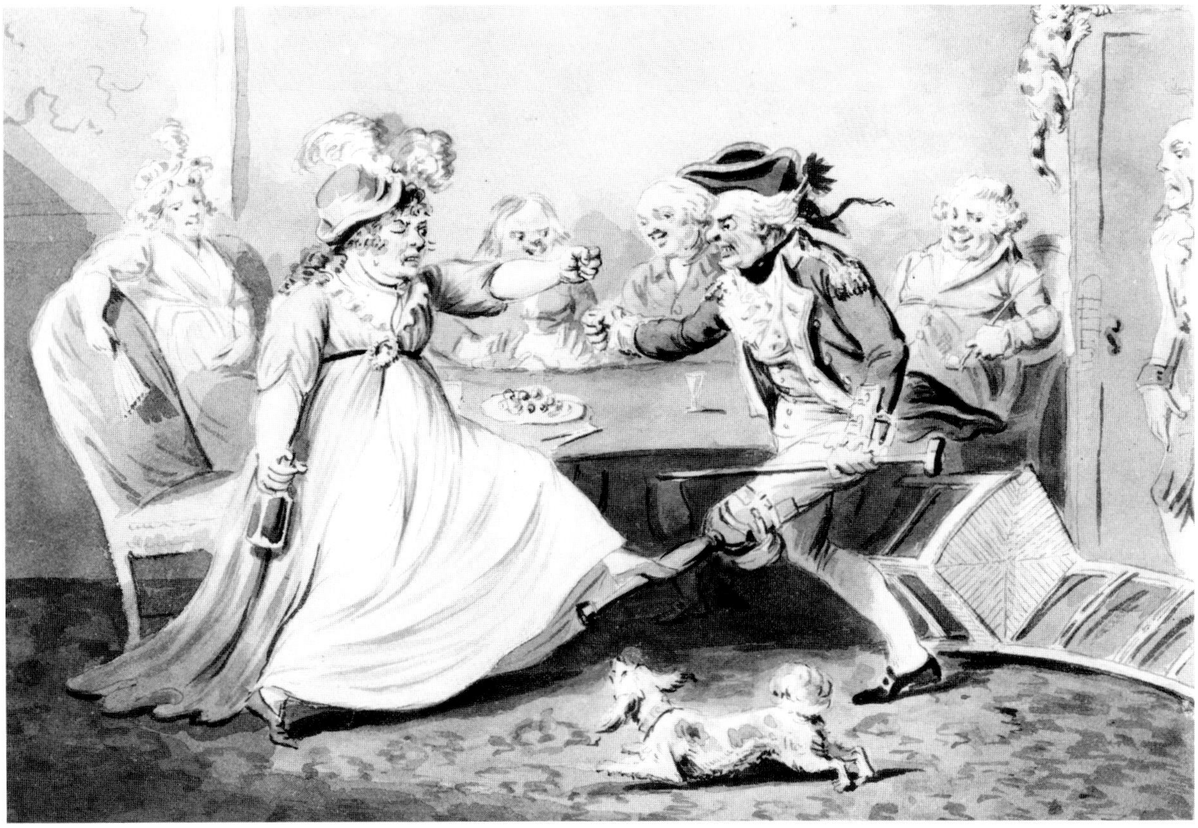

1798
Pen and watercolor over pencil
5 7/8 x 8 1/2 inches (14.9 x 21.7 cm.)
Annotated verso: Captain Wattle and Miss Roe / I. Cruikshanks
Published: April 4, 1798, by Laurie & Whittle (214); below the title are engraved three stanzas of verse.
Biblio: George, 9324; Wark, 78
Impression: BM, LWL

According to the song accompanying the print after this image, Captain Wattle was a sea captain with a great love for "the bottle" and for his mistress, Miss Roe. Once wed, he took to kicking his wife when he felt that she was too lazy and she responded by kicking him back. The closing lines of the verse suggest that it is the lot of every married couple to fight at times and at others to kiss, and it is this scene which Cruikshank illustrated. Here, the one-eyed Miss Roe, clutching the bottle of cordial she would "now and then try," returns a kick to her one-legged husband. The four seated figures in the background appear to be amused, suggesting that confrontations between Captain Wattle and Miss Roe were fairly frequent and therefore not to be taken seriously.

The image was published as part of a broadsheet containing the ballad by Charles Dibdin, performed in a solo act, *The Sphinx*, from October 1797 through April 1798. Dibdin's piece was presented during the second season of the Sans Souci Theatre, located in Leicester Square. All of the songs in *The Sphinx* were chanteys, for which Dibdin was well known. The most popular of these were published and were sung by ladies at the pianoforte as well as by sailors.[1] According to one military historian, Dibdin's songs "did more to recruit the navy than all the press gangs."[2] Issued at the end of the season, the broadsheet ballad with Cruikshank's image was a commercial venture, intended to promote the author's reputation as well as add to his income.

Jennifer Katell

1. George Hogarth, "Memoir of Charles Dibdin" in *The Songs of Charles Dibdin* (London: How and Parsons, 1842), p. xix.
2. Chambers, *Book of Days*, 2:123-24.

The Ballad of Captain Wattle and Miss Roe

Did you ever hear of Captain Wattle,
He was all for love, and a little for the bottle.
We know not though pains we have ta'en to enquire,
If gun-powder he invented or the Thames set on fire;
If to him was the center of gravity known,
The longitude or the Philosopher's stone,
Or whether he studied from Bacon or Boyle,
Copernicus, Locke, Katerfelto or Hoyle;
But this we learnt with great labour and pain,
That he loved Miss Roe and she loved him again.

Than sweet Miss Roe none e'er looked fiercer,
She had but one eye, but that one was a piercer.
We know not, for certainty, her education,
If she wrote, mended stockings, or settled the nation;
At cards if she liked whist and swabbers or voles,
Or at dinner loved pig or a steak on the coals,
Whether most of the Sappho she was of Thalestris,
Or if dancing was taught her by Hopkins or Vestris:
But for your satisfaction, this good news we obtain,
That she loved Captain Wattle and he loved her again.

When wedded he became lord and master depend on't;
He had but one leg but he'd a foot at the end on't,
Which of government when she would fain hold the bridle,
He took special caution should never lie Idle;
So, like most married folks, 'twas my plague, and my chicken,
And sometimes a Kissing, and sometimes a kicking,
Then for comfort a cordial she'd now and then try,
Alternately bunging or piping her eyes;
And these facts of this couple the history contain;
For when he kick'd Miss Roe, she kick'd him again.

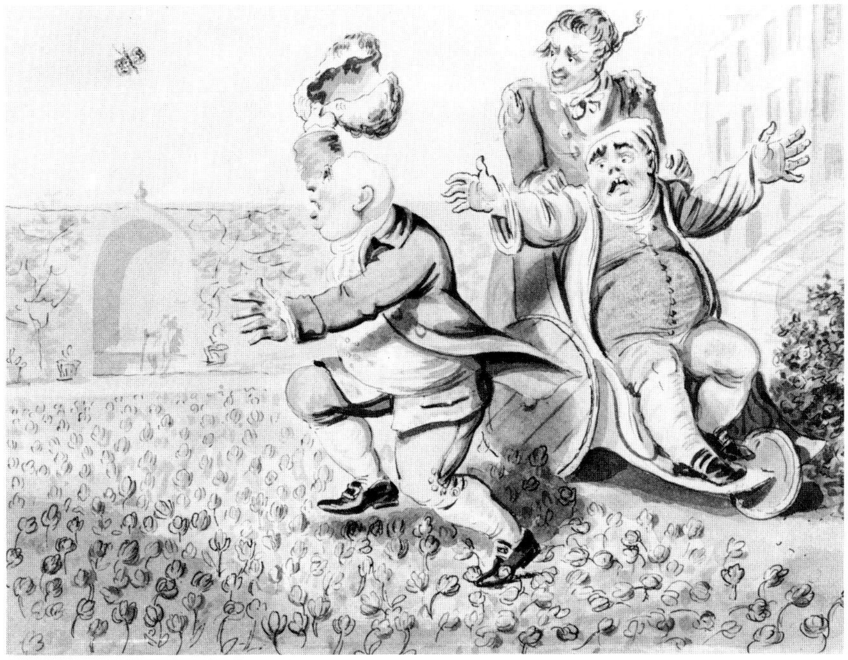

1798
Pen and watercolor over pencil(?)
6 15/16 x 8 15/16 inches (17.6 x 22.7 cm.)
Annotated verso: Morocco's Emperor by the living God / Vide, Peter Pindar / I. Cruikshanks
Published: May 24, 1798, by Laurie & Whittle (218); below the title is engraved: A Gentleman who was remarkably fond of raising fine Tulips, shewing his Collection to a Friend who was equally curious in butterflies, a scarce Fly called the Emperor of Morocco presenting itself to our Naturalist on one of the Tulips, He without any hesitation made his way over the whole Bed to seize the prize, crying out regardless of his Friends entreaties, an Emperor! an Emperor! and Emperor by all thats lucky.
Biblio: George, 9326; Krumbhaar, 794; Wark, 79
Impression: BM, LWL, WMC

Natural history became a passion of gentlemen scholars and scientists in the eighteenth century. It was a time when new systems for classifiying flora and fauna were being devised and new species of plants and animals were being discovered in all parts of the world. Cruikshank's image of two rotund gentlemen, the gardener clearly suffering from gout, pokes fun at natural history enthusiasts. The bodies of the protagonists attest to self-indulgence just as their hobbies reveal self-absorption.

The annotation on the verso of the watercolor refers to Peter Pindar, a psuedonym of John Wolcot (1738-1819), who published a poetic tale in 1788 about Sir Joseph Banks (1743-1820), president of the Royal Society, and his fascination with the Emperor of Morocco butterfly.[1] Wolcot describes how Banks, enraptured by the sight of an Emperor of Morocco, considered at the time "one of the most beautiful Flies in the Universe,"[2] chases after the insect in an effort to catch it. Unaware of his surroundings and the damage he is causing, he invades a garden, trampling over "peerless hyacinths" and through tulips and anemonies, "breaking a hundred necks at ev'ry spring." The gardener, who thinks the man mad, pursues him, but both Banks and the butterfly escape.

Although Cruikshank may well have been inspired to treat the subject by this versified tale, the incidents, though similar, are not identical and his figures are not identifiable.[3] The artist was clearly interested in looking at a general problem rather than a specific case. By so doing, he satirized the obsessiveness of collectors, which clouds their judgment and makes them oblivious to the concerns of others.

Edward J. Nygren

1. [John Wolcot], "Sir Joseph Banks and the Emperor of Morocco," in *The Works of Peter Pindar*, 3 vols. (London: John Walker, 1794), 2:187-206.
2. Moses Harris, *The Aurelian: or Natural History of English Insects; namely Moths and Butterflies* (London: Printed for the author, 1766), p. 6. "Emperor of Morocco" was the popular name for the Purple Emperor, described by Harris. According to George (9326, p. 513) it was also known as "Emperor of the Woods" and "Purple High-flyer."
3. For a treatment of a similar subject, see Thomas Rowlandson, *Butterfly Hunting* (1806), Paul Mellon Collection, Yale Center for British Art.

84 *Billing and Cooing at the Jelly Shop* †

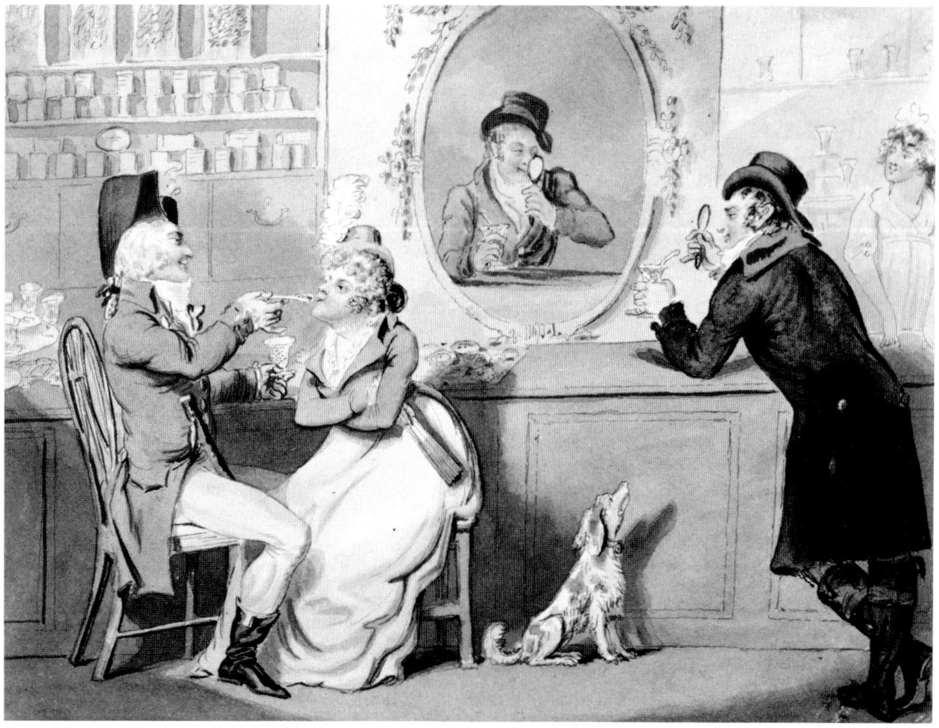

1798
Pen and watercolor over pencil
6 3/4 x 8 3/4 inches
(17.15 x 22.23 cm.)
Annotated verso: Eating Ice / I. Cruikshanks
Published: June 4, 1798, by Laurie & Whittle (219)
Biblio: George, 9327; Krumbhaar, 60; Wark, 80
Impression: BM, LWL, WMC

A man and a woman sit facing each other beside the counter of a confectioner's shop. Ices, syllabub, and jellies were the gastronomic rage during the late Georgian period. Stores selling these items suddenly appeared across London, in or near many of the fashionable public parks.[1] The sweetshop became the scene of flirtation and amorous liaison, as it provided a handy retreat to which promenaders could retire.

Confections had become increasingly popular during the eighteenth century. Hannah Glasse's *The Complete Confectioner* (1765) attests to the wide range of sweets created during the period, and *The London Magazine* (1762) describes some elaborate desserts that assumed monumental size—one sugared fantasy measured twelve by seven feet.

The phrase "billing and cooing" of course refers to the whispered murmuring and caresses of lovers. The handsome soldier, whose legs straddle his companion's, feeds her a delectable sweet in a highly suggestive manner. Each of the figures seems to consume one thing and desire another. While the lovers look at each other, deeply absorbed, the young man at the counter seems to observe them through his lorgnette, perhaps wishing to be a part of such a romance. However, the direction of this buck's gaze is ambiguous; the object may be his own reflection. The serving girl looks longingly at it while the hopeful dog at his feet eyes the sweet.

Several prints appeared in the late 1790s that were critical of the comfortable commissions obtained by those with influence. They depicted the Guards enjoying themselves at sweetshops, pleasure gardens, and other leisure entertainments, while their comrades were being killed in battle on the Continent. One such work by Gillray, published on June 9, 1797, by H. Humphrey, is *Hero's Recruiting at Kelsey's; or Guard-Day at St. James's,* in which officers indulge in jellies and sugar plums at a famous fruit shop lounge.[2] Dating from almost one year later, Cruikshank's composition belongs in the same context.

Deanne Shey

---

1. On the popularity of ice-houses as scenes of leisure activity, see Boulton, *Amusements of Old London.*
2. George, *Social Change in Graphic Satire,* p. 104.

85 The Graces Comparing Sandals †

1798
Pen and watercolor over pencil
8 1/4 x 6 3/4 inches
(22.3 x 17 cm.)
Annotated verso: The Graces comparing sandals / I. Cruikshanks
Published: July 4, 1798, by Laurie & Whittle (220)
Biblio: George, 9328; Krumbhaar, 454; Wark, 81
Impression: BM, LWL, WMC

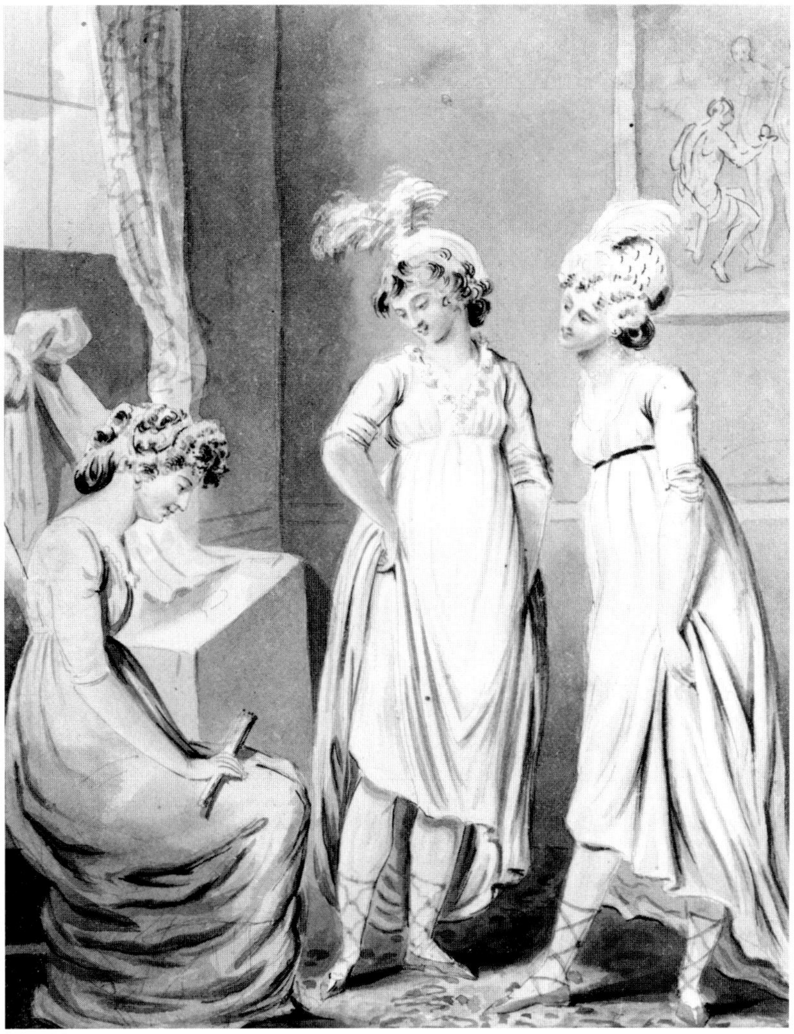

By placing a painting of the Judgment of Paris conspicuously in the background, Cruikshank pokes fun at the seriousness with which women approached questions of fashion at a time when England was at war. The point of the contrast between the repercussions of Paris's judgment—the Trojan War—and the outcome of this decision regarding sandals would not have been lost on Cruikshank's audience.[1] He sets up a clever dialogue between the scene of the three women in the foreground and the painting in the background. Both groups contain three figures similarly positioned in the composition. The neoclassical style of the dress combined with this type of elegant cross-gartering shoe reinforces the allusion to classical antiquity.

Cruikshank used the motif of the Graces similarly in the July 1794 issue of *The Sporting Magazine* to comment on the decadent nature of French styles.[2] In the earlier image, the three women are shown in dresses similar to those in this work; however, the gowns cling to their bodies and are made of a transparent fabric. The woman in the center of that composition is shown with her breasts exposed, in the fashion of the time. Ladies' attire took on political overtones at the end of the eighteenth century when Britain, then at war with France, began to promote its own styles. Heideloff's *Gallery of Fashion,* "a unique repository for English national dress for Ladies," was published from 1794 until 1822 and established England as "the arbiter of elegance" rather than France.[3] While fashion may have had a nationalistic flavor, it certainly was a source of humor for artists, including Cruikshank, who found such concerns trivial.

Danna Freedy

1. E. A. Reitan, ed., *The Best of Gentleman's Magazine, 1731-1754* (Lewiston, N.Y.: The Edwin Mellen Press, 1987), p. 145.
2. George, *Social Change in Graphic Satire,* p. 139.
3. Sitwell, *Gallery of Fashion,* pp. 1-2.

86 Helter Skelter – or A Shower on Greenwich Hill †

1798
Pen and watercolor with touches of body color over pencil
6 5/8 x 9 1/8 inches
(16.8 x 23.2 cm.)
Inscribed recto: Cruikshank 1798
Annotated verso: Shower of Rain on Greenwich Hill / I. Cruikshanks
Published: August 20, 1798, by Laurie & Whittle (221)
Biblio: George, 9329; Wark, 82
Impression: BM, LWL

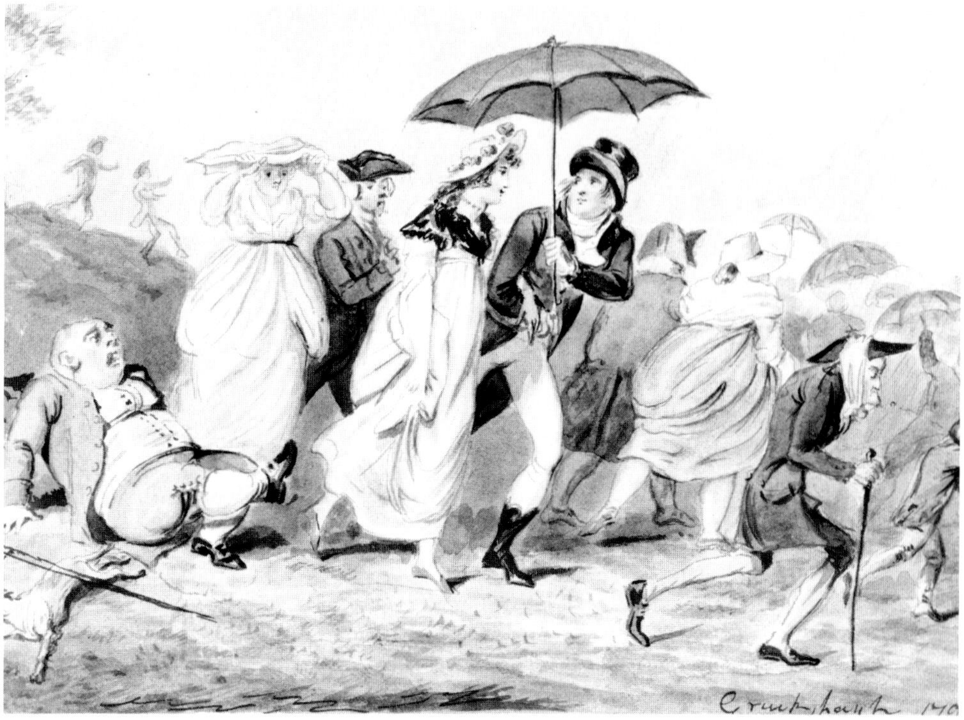

In 1800, Greenwich Hill, then part of the greater Greenwich Park in Kent, lay south of the Thames, four miles downriver from London. The panorama from the "hill where the views are beautiful beyond imagination"[1] had attracted British artists since the seventeenth century. From the park extends, "agreeably diversified with hill and dale, . . . a noble view of London and the river."[2] Cruikshank does not depict this famous vista. Instead, he focuses on the holiday makers who, surprised by a sudden shower, dash for cover. "Running down Greenwich hill" was a popular activity; however, in this scene the rain makes it a necessity.[3]

Cruikshank denotes a range of character types, contrasting young and old, thick and thin, hale and ill. A fat citizen, or "cit," wearing silver-buckled shoes, has fallen to the ground. His dropsical form, brightly colored clothes, and exaggerated facial expression bring him to prominence despite the fact that he is placed toward the left of the composition. A young couple, so absorbed in one another as to be oblivious to the rain, stride through the center. The woman is sheltered by a large umbrella held by the adoring man whose glance, together with his posture, eloquently conveys his affection. Behind them an older, conservatively dressed pair rush forward. To the right a thin, spindly man, brandishing a walking stick, attempts large strides to escape the downpour.

It was customary among all classes to promenade in the city's numerous gardens and parks; increasingly in the eighteenth century, people were encouraged to "explore the wonderful extent and variety of London."[4] Cruikshank comments acutely here on the changes in fashion that took place during the last years of the the decade. Gone were the hoop and long-waisted stays for women. Skirts and dresses became thinner. Young people gave up wigs for "shaggy hair."[5]

Maria L. Brendel

1. *Ambulator, or Pocket Companion in a Tour round London within the Circuit of Twenty-five Miles* (London: T. Gillet for J. Scatcherd, 1800), p. 89.
2. Peter Cunningham, *Murray's Guide to Modern London* (London: John Murray, 1854), p. 35.
3. *Collin's Illustrated Guide to London and Neighbourhood* (London: William Collins, Sons, and Co., Ltd., 1882), p. 76.
4. George, *London Life in the Eighteenth Century,* p. 78.
5. W. S. Lewis, "A Tour through London 1797," in *Three Tours Through London in the Years 1748, 1776, 1797* (New Haven, Conn.: Yale University Press, 1941), p. 98.

87 *Enjoying a Friend* †

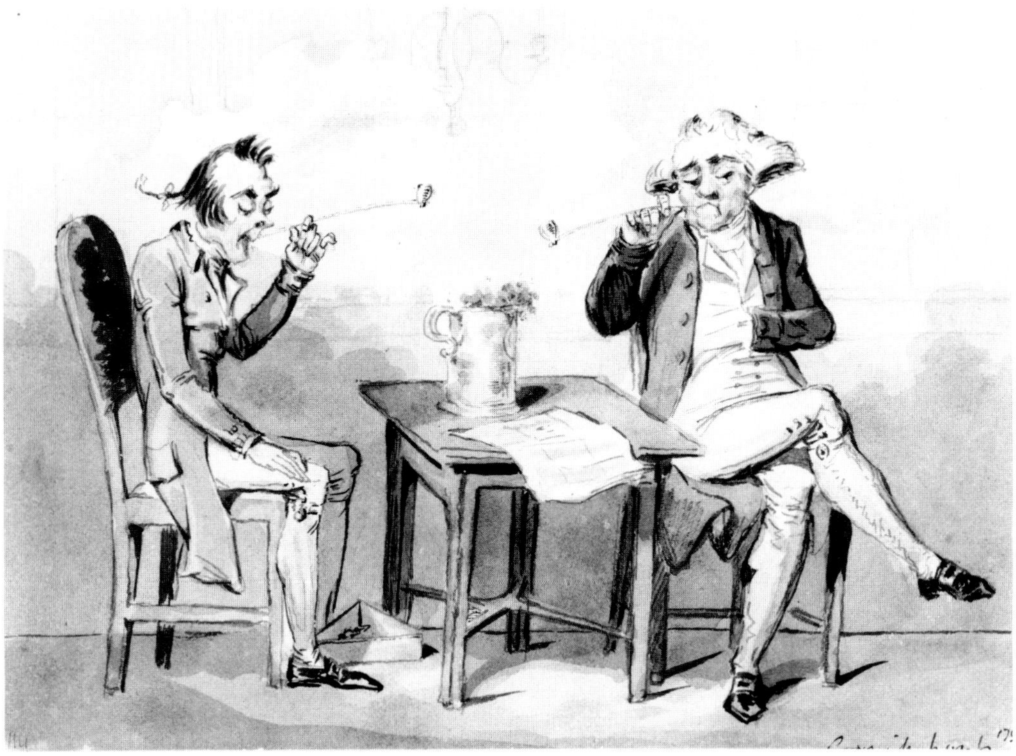

1798
Pen and watercolor
6 9/16 x 8 11/16 inches (17.6 x 23.5 cm.)
Annotated verso: Smoking Companions / I. Cruikshank
Published: August 21, 1798, by Laurie & Whittle; below the image is engraved: [on left side] Smoak is the order of the night / This, a tete a tete enjoyment / But smoaking is my friends delight / When he has no great employment / Well thus they meet to tell the news / First of friends and then their neighbors / Concerns of State and grand reviews / Present past and future labors. [on right side] Pray do admire these happy friends / Mark their attitudes and features / One says what neither comprehends / Happy dull and stupid creatures / Now they have had their story out / Two hours have past a great delay / But nothing left to talk about / They'll meet again another day.
Biblio: George, 9330; Krumbhaar, 327; Wark, 83
Impression: BM, LWL, WMC

Men gathered in clubs in eighteenth-century London to exchange news, transact business, and relax with friends. These clubs were similar in general form but varied widely in detail; they tended to encourage overindulgence in some chosen vice. However, dedication to one vice hardly resulted in exclusion of all the others.[1]

Content, and lacking any recreation to occupy their time, two men sit in silence, smoking long clay pipes. The gentleman on the left slumps forward, rests his hand on his thigh, puffs on his pipe, and exists in his own world of billowy smoke. His companion, isolated by his own pipe-smoking, places his hand in his shirt and savors the smoke that swallows up the chandelier. Neither man bothers to read the newspaper lying between them. The large container of beer on the table is probably a "peg tankard," with marks inside to measure how much each man is to drink.[2] The head is still undisturbed, suggesting that the two are engaged only in enjoying their "friend," the pipe.

Writing thirty-five years later, Thomas Carlyle captured the essence of this image when he observed two pipe smokers who "sat silently alone till midnight, and then parted, shaking hands, with congratulations on the profitable and pleasant evening they had enjoyed.[3]

Tim D. Wright

1. Jones, *Clubs of the Georgian Rakes*, p. 4.
2. John Timbs, *Clubs and Club Life In London*, 2 vols. (London: Chatto and Windus, 1899), 2:111.
3. Quoted in Compton Mackenzie, *Sublime Tobacco* (London: Chatto and Windus, 1957), p. 28.

88 *Speculation: Or, A New Way of Saving a Thousand Pounds. An Original Tale* †

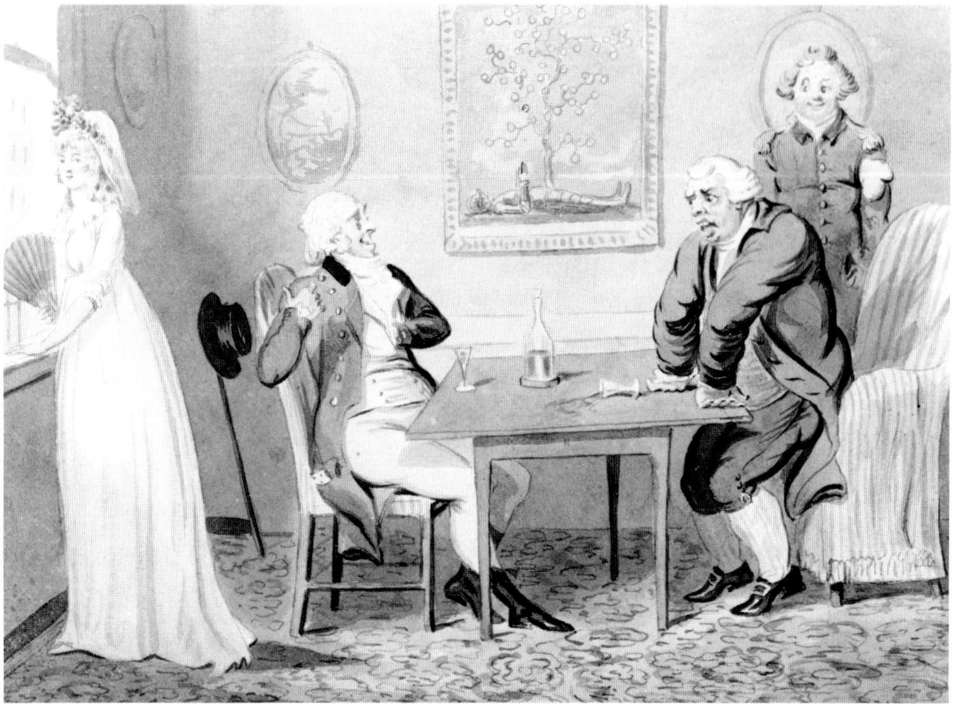

1798
Pen and watercolor over pencil
6 1/2 x 9 inches (16.5 x 22.9 cm.)
Inscribed recto: Cruikshank 179(?)
Annotated verso: How to Save £1,000 / I. Cruikshanks
Published: October 12, 1798, by Laurie & Whittle; below the title are engraved 139 lines of verse.
Biblio: Krumbhaar, 93; Wark, 84
Impression:

The print after this watercolor is accompanied by 139 lines of verse relating the story of an impoverished gambler who wangles a dinner by promising to tell his host, who has a beautiful daughter of marriageable age with a dowry of ten thousand pounds, how he can save a thousand. The gambler offers to marry the daughter for nine thousand pounds, thereby saving the father the remainder. The scene depicts the moment following the gambler's offer (lines 92-139 in the poem). The gentleman rising from his chair has just heard this insulting proposal and in anger has tipped over his glass of wine.

Parents frequently chose a suitor for an eligible daughter, taking into consideration class, social status, and wealth. This image deals with a variation on the theme, a standard one in eighteenth-century satire. The painting on the wall presents a noble family tree going back to medieval roots. For a family of such lineage, the rogue's proposal is a shock and an insult. However, in his desire to save a thousand pounds, the father has provided the gambler with a fit meal, if not a wife.

Mari-Tere Alvarez

Hazard, a careless fellow, known
At every Gambling-house in town—
Was oft in want of money, yet
Could never bear to run in debt:
Because 'tis thought, no man was willing
To give him credit for a shilling.
Dependent on Dame Fortune's will,
He threw the Dice, or well, or ill:
This Day in rags—the next in lace,
Just as it happ'd—a seize, or ace:
Was oftentimes, when not a winner,
Uncertain, where to get a dinner.

One day, when cruel Fortune's frown
Had stripp'd him of his last half-crown,
Saunt'ring along, in sorry mood,
Hungry—perhaps, for want of food,
A parlour window struck his eye;
Through which our Hero chanc'd to spy
A jolly round-fac'd personage,
Somewhat about the middle age,
Beginning a luxurious meal—
or 'twas a noble Loin of Veal;
And such a sight, I need not mention,
Quickly arrested his attention.
Surely, thought he, I know that face,
I've seen it at some other place;
I recollect 'twas at the Play,
And there I heard some people say,
"How rich this fellow was, and what
An handsome daughter he had got."

"That dinner would exactly do—
"A Loin of Veal's enough for two.
"Could not I strike out some way
"To get an introduction?—Eh!
"Most likely 'tis—I may endeavour—
"In vain!—but come, I'll try, however."

And now he meditates no more—
Thunders a rat-tat at the door,
And lest that method might not suit,
They say, he rang the bell to boot.

The party-colour'd Footman, come,
"Pray, is your Master, Sir, at home?"
"My Master, Sir's at home, but busy."
"Then he's engag'd," quoth Hazard, "Is he?"
(In voice as loud as he could bellow,)
"I'm very sorry, my good fellow,
"It happens so, because I cou'd
"Your Master, do some little good;
"A Speculation that I know
"Might save a Thousand Pounds, or so.
"No matter, friend, your Master tell,
"Another day will do as well."

"What's that you say?" the Master cries,
(With pleasure beaming from his eyes,
And napkin tuck'd beneath his chin,
Bouncing from parlour, whence within
He'd heard those joy-inspiring sounds,
Of saving him a Thousand Pounds.)
"My dear Sir, What is that you say?"
"Sir, I can call another day,
"Your dinner I've disturbed, I fear."
"Do, pray Sir, take your dinner here;
"You'll find a welcome, warm and hearty."
"I shall intrude upon your party."
"There's not a soul but I and you."
"Well then, I don't care if I do."

Our Spark's design so far compleated,
Behold him at the table seated,
Paying away, as well he might,
With some degree of appetite.

Our host, who willing would have press'd,
The Thousand Pounds upon his Guest,
Still thought it would not be genteel
To interrrupt him at his meal,
Which seem'd to fully employ him,
Talking might probably annoy him;
So thought it better he should wait
Till after dinner, the Debate.

And now "The King and Constitution,"
"With ill success to Revolution,"
And many a warm and loyal Toast
Had been discuss'd; when our good Host
Thought it was almost time to say,
"Let's move the order of the Day."
Indeed he hardly could help thinking
'Twas rather odd—his Guest was drinking;
The business not a jot the nearer,
A second bottle of Madeira;
And that he seem'd to sit and chatter
'Bout this, and that, and t'other matter,
As if he'd not the least intention
This Thousand Pounds of his to mention.
Much did he wish to give a hint,
Yet knew not how he should begin't.
At length—"Sir, you've forgot, I fear,
"The business that has brought you here.
"I think you have some intimation
"About a saving Speculation."
"Ay, Sir—you'll find it not amiss,
"My Speculation's simply this:
"I hear you have a daughter, Sir."
"A Daughter!—Well, and what of her?
"What can my Daughter have to do
"With this affair 'twixt me and you?"
"I mean to make your Daughter (craving
"Your Pardon, Sir), the means of saving
"The Sum I mention. You'll allow
"My scheme is feasible." "As How?"
"Why thus—I hear you've no objection
"To form some conjugal connection
"For this same Daughter." "No; provided
"All other matters coincided:"
"Then, Sir, I'll suit ye to a hair:
"Pray, is she not extremely fair?"
"Why, yes; there's many folks who praise her:
"But what is Beauty now a days, Sir?"
"Ay, true Sir! nothing without Wealth.
"But come, suppose we drink her health;"
"Indeed I've drank enough already."
"Oh fie! Consider, Sir, A Lady,
"By rights we should have drank her first—
"Pray fill." "Well, if I must—I must."
"And, pray, what age, Sir, may she be?"
"God bless me— She's just Twenty-three."
"Just Twenty-three! I' faith a rare age!"
"Sir, you were speaking of her Marriage."
"I was—and wish'd to know, in case
"Such an occurrence should take place,
"The Sum it might be in your power
"To give with her, by way of Dower."
"Well, Sir—Then this is my intent—
"If married with my own consent,
"I've no objection, on such grounds,
"To pay her down Ten Thousand Pounds."
"*Ten* Thousand, Sir, I think you say."
"I do."—"What, on the marriage day?"
"The whole."—"Then let her, Sir, be mine,
"I'll take her off your hands with *nine*.

89 Patience; or a Bad Job †

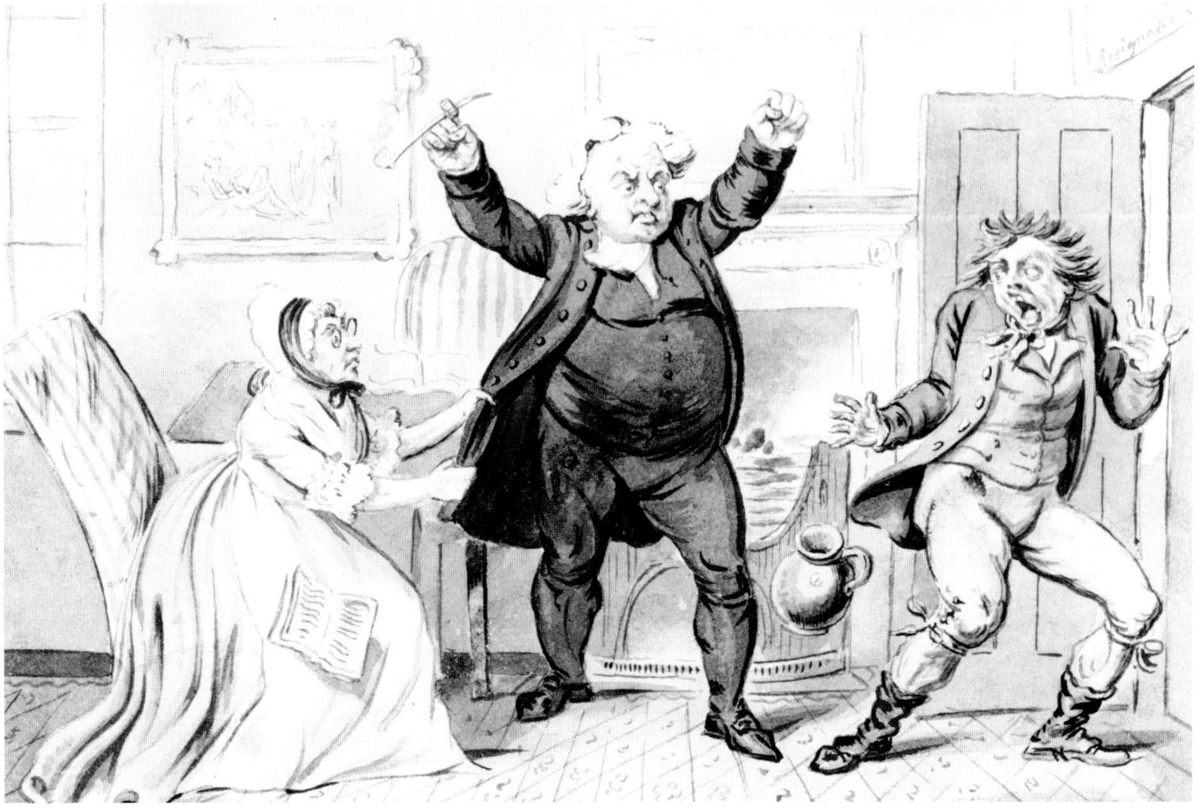

1798
Pen and watercolor over pencil
6³/₈ x 9 inches (16.2 x 22.8 cm.)
Inscribed recto: Resignation
Annotated verso: I. Cruikshanks
Published: November 20, 1798, by Laurie & Whittle; below the title is engraved: An Original Tale by the Author of Speculation; followed by text.
Biblio: George, 9335; Krumbhaar, 880; Wark, 85
Impression: BM, LWL, WMC

Although it appears that the rather large and aged clergyman standing at the center of the room is furious at his servant for dropping a jug, that is not the case. The clergyman is angry because his man, Numps, has just reported spilling a cask of ale in the cellar. This image specifically illustrates a poem entitled *Patience or a Bad Job: An Original Tale,* perhaps written by Christopher Anstey, the author of *Speculation.*[1] It tells the story of a parson who, after giving a sermon on Job, returns home to tell his wife that he is as patient and as mentally strong as Job and that women, including herself, cannot be so described.

A mockery is made of the parson's words when Numps tells the clergyman of the accident and his employer becomes enraged. The minister raises his arms in anger, his left hand clenched into a fist and his right gripping a pipe. The footman, mouth wide open and hair standing on end, throws back his arms; he drops the pitcher and crouches in self-defense. Paralyzed with fear, he is unable to run. It is the parson's wife who restrains the clergyman by grabbing his coat. The minister attempts to justify his action by saying, "Did Job e'er lose a Barrel of such Ale?"

The paintings on the wall reinforce the point of the image and the text. Over the door is *Resignation* (eliminated from the print); the composition on the far wall undoubtedly depicts Job visited by his neighbors. The clergyman, in his anger at the accident, has shown little patience or resignation. He is, in short, a "Bad Job."

Rhonda Howard

1. Although Mrs. George identifies the author of this poem as C. Anstey, Wark states that this poem does not appear in Anstey's collected works.

Patience; or, a Bad Job

'Twas at some country place, a Parson preaching,
The virtue of long sufferance was teaching;
And so pathetically did exhort
His list'ning Congregation, and in short
Discoursed so much of Job, and how he bore
With such exceeding pleasantry his woes,
Faith 'twas enough to make a man suppose
Job wished for more.

Meaning, perhaps, that since 'tis plain,
How needlessly we grieve at pain;
How would it be, if Man
Pursued a different plan,
And were to laugh and treat the matter lightly;
And not when tortur'd with the gout,
To make wry faces, roar and shout,
But look agreeable and sprightly.

"And pray d'ye think, my dearest life,"
Exclaim'd the Parson's wife,
As after Church they sat,
In courteous chat,
"That 'tis in human nature to endure
"The sad extremity of woe,
"That Job, you say, did undergo;
"'Tis more than you or I cou'd do, I'm sure."

"My dear," quoth he, "This difference,
"Shews, let me tell you, great good sense,
"A talent in your Sex we seldom see;
"And doubtless the remark is true,
"As far as it extends to you,
"Tho' not, I think, to me."

"No woman, since the world began,
"Cou'd bear misfortune like a *Man*—
"And in good truth, 'twixt you and me,
"And that without much vanity,
"I do conceive that I myself have shewn,
"That patience and that strength of mind
"Were not entirely confin'd
"To Job alone."

Thus said the modest priest, and wou'd have said much more,
But for the sudden op'ning of the door,
When out of breath, in stumps
His clownish servant, "Numps,"
With mouth wide open, on the Parson gazing—
Just like the wight,
Who drew old Priam's curtains in the night,
To tell him Troy was blazing.

"Well, Numps, the matter? speak! why look'st so pale?
"Has any thing gone wrong?" quoth Numps, "The Ale."
"What," cries the Priest, "the Ale gone sour?"
(And then his phiz began to lower.)
"Turn'd sour! No Master, no," replied the fellow;
"But just now, as I went, d'ye see,
"To tilt the Cask—away roll'd he,
"And all the Liquor spilt about the cellar."

The fact was, Numps a cask of Ale had stav'd,
Now, pray thee tell me, how the Priest behav'd?
Did he pull off his wig, or tear his hair?
Or, like the silly fellow Job,
Throw ashes on his head, or rend his robe?
Say, how did he this dire misfortune bear?
As thus, in voice of pious resignation,
He to his man address'd this *mild* oration:

"May God confound thee, thou damn'd stupid bear;"
(The best of Priests, you know will sometimes swear)
"What, you must meddle, must you,
"With the barrel, and be curst t'ye?
"I wish thy paws were in the fire—Odd rot'em—
"Get thee down stairs this instant, wretch,
"Or, by the living G_d, I'll kick thy breach
"From top to bottom."

"Nay, now, my dearest," cried the Dame,
"Is this your patience?—Fie for shame!
"I beg you'll recollect your Text,
"Job was not half so vext
"When he'd his Sons and Daughters to bewail."
"Damn all his Sons and Daughters, if you chuse,
"Answer me this, I say—Did Job e'er lose
"A Barrel of such Ale?"

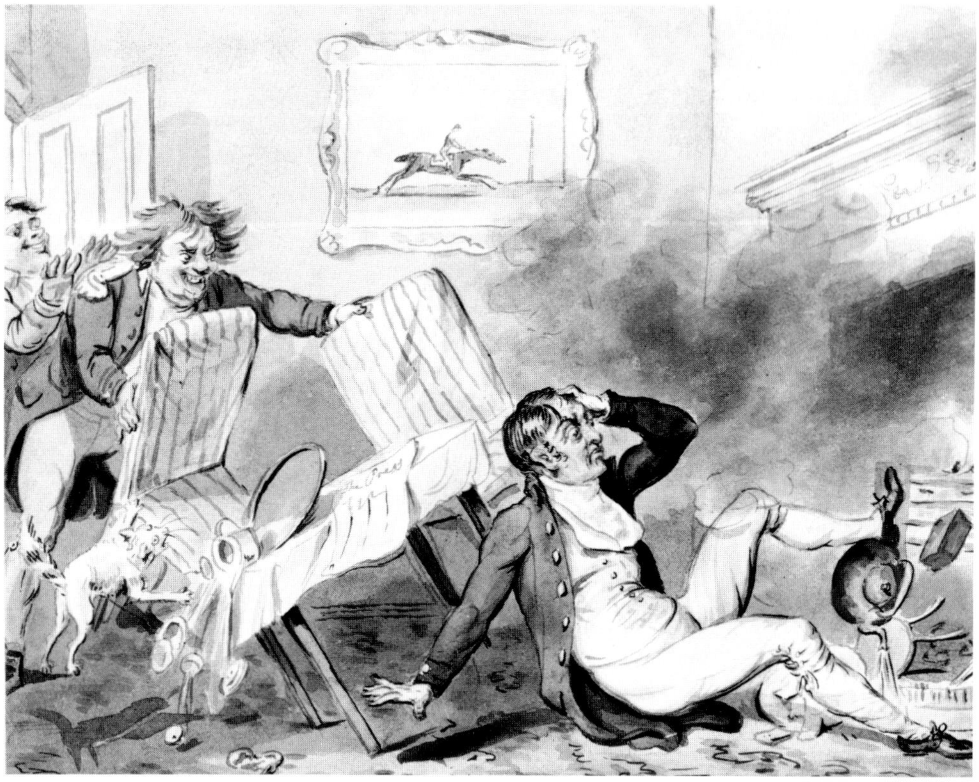

1798
Pen and watercolor over pencil
6 11/16 x 9 inches (17 x 22.9 cm.)
Annotated verso: The Smoaky Chimney / I. Cruikshanks
Published: December 18, 1798, by Laurie & Whittle (223); below the image are engraved three stanzas of verse.
Biblio: Krumbhaar, A.52; Wark, 86.
Impression: LWL, WMC

Throwing a brick down from the roof is obviously an absurd way to clean a chimney—yet another demonstration of the stupidity of the Irish. The owner of the house, whose name, "Patrick," is certainly intended to suggest his nationality, is knocked completely off his feet by the flying brick. He is the butt of the joke for having directed his Irish servant, "Dennis," to clean the chimney in this fashion. The two laughing servants clearly enjoy their master's predicament.

In general, sweeps cleaned chimneys with brooms fixed to poles or with shrubs drawn up and down with ropes. In the city of London, they climbed chimneys on the inside, acting as human brushes, a practice traceable to the late seventeenth century, when all chimneys built after the Great Fire of 1666 were made to be cleaned only in this way.[1] Sweepers were treated with extreme cruelty by their masters; many had been apprenticed as very young children from orphanages, destitute parents, or parish beadles.[2]

The humor of this image (and text in the print) is dependent on a stereotypical view of the Irish prevalent in England, which was reflective of serious underlying social tensions. Many of the Irish migrated to London for employment. Considered intruders, they were resented for taking jobs away from England's working class and for accepting lower wages.

Julie Joyce

1. Marcellus Laroon, *The Cryes of the City of London* (1711), p. 114.
2. George, *London Life in the Eighteenth Century* (1984), p. 241; and Laroon, *Cryes of the City of London,* p. 114.

When Patricks Chimney one day chanc'd to smoak,
Thought he, there's something doth ye funnel choak;
Here Dennis 'Sirrah' quick:
Up to the house top in a trice, D'ye hear,
And try if you can make the passage clear,
By thowing down a Brick.

The mean' time, in a sort of fret or fume,
He hastily pac'd up and down the room;
And oft would, little dreaming of a Blow,
His noddle up the chimney pop,
And Dawl to Dennis at the Top,
Will ye throw down a Brick or no.

And then again he'd walls, At length with ire,
Important, he ran headlong to the fire;
Dennis I say, You Thief, Odd Rot it:
Why don't ye throw a Brick bat down,
Dennis I say—Oh Christ my Crown,
Arrah! by Jasus but I've got it.

91 A Good Joke: A Groggy Parson †

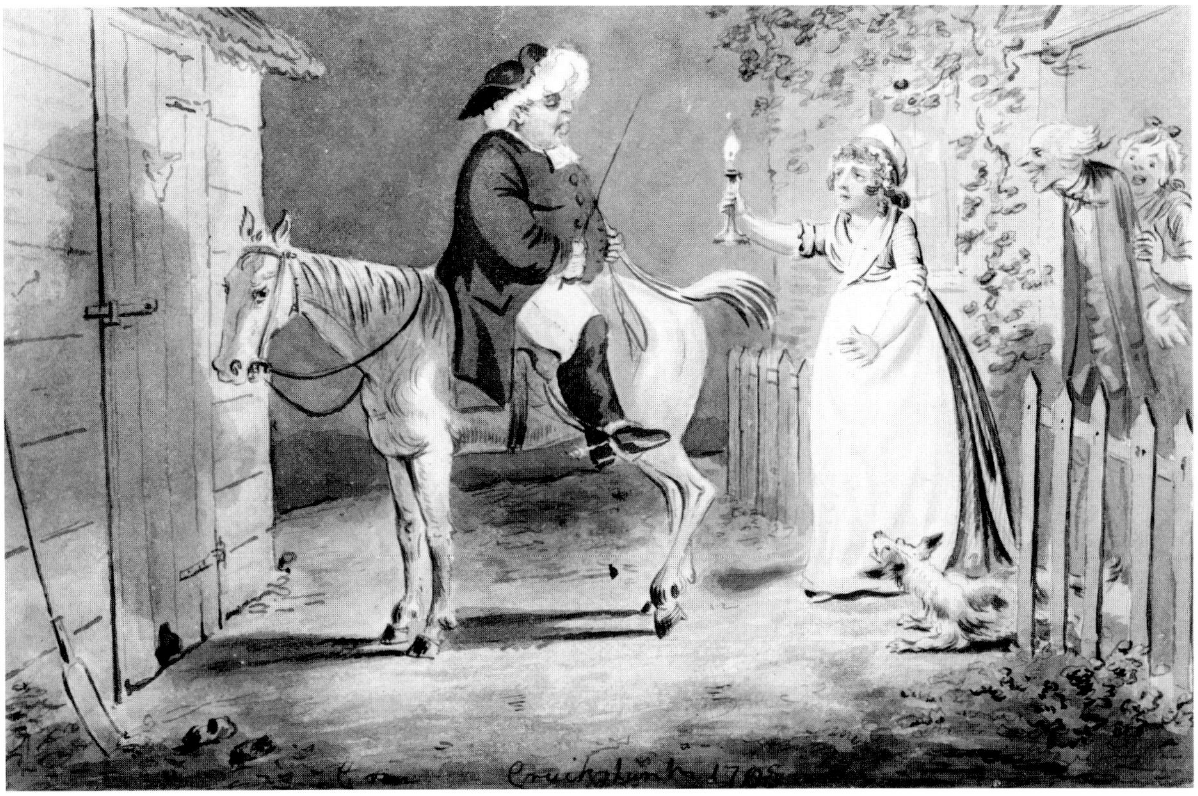

1798
Pen and watercolor over pencil
6 1/4 x 8 7/8 inches (16.2 x 22.8 cm.)
Inscribed recto: Cruikshank 1798
Annotated verso: The Parson come home rather groggy /I. Cruikshanks
Published: January 11, 1799, by Laurie & Whittle; below the title is engraved: Who had been taking his Broth rather too freely the Party resolved to play him a trick which was Accomplished by Mounting him with his face to the Horses Tail, the Old Animal went quietly home to the Stable, which brought the Wife Out with a Candle & observing her Husband in his Usual happy way Commenc'd her Attack, saying what a Sin it was for a Man of his Cloth to make such a Beast of himself, to which the Jolly Vicar replied pub! pub! my Dear never mind. Nothing grieves me but that the Plaguy Rogues should have cut my Horses Head off.
Biblio: Momus, 6; Krumbhaar, 451; Wark, 87
Impression: GC

In 1968, when Robert Wark published his catalogue of Cruikshank's drawings, a copy of the print after this watercolor had not yet been located. A recent discovery of a copy has led to the retitling of the work. The accompanying text also throws light on the scene depicted. A stout parson is seated backward on his horse, having been placed in this position by his drinking companions. He has just arrived home. His half-closed eyes indicate how far gone he is. His wife, carrying a lamp, comes out of the house and scolds him for his behavior. His absurd answer clearly amuses the servants in the doorway.

Clergymen were often satirized for their worldliness. Some were addicted to drink; others frequented theaters. However, most parsons were "ordinary good fellows, whose troubled weakness was a cowardly servility towards anyone of a powerful position."[1] The majority devoted their lives to the service of their parishioners. Still, drunkenness was widespread in the eighteenth century and the subject was treated from Hogarth to Rowlandson; a variation on this theme was the "drunken parson."[2]

Mar Martinez-Perez

1. Richardson, *Georgian England*, pp. 54-60.
2. See, for example, Rowlandson's *The Vicar and Moses*, in George, *Social Change in Graphic Satire*, p. 86.

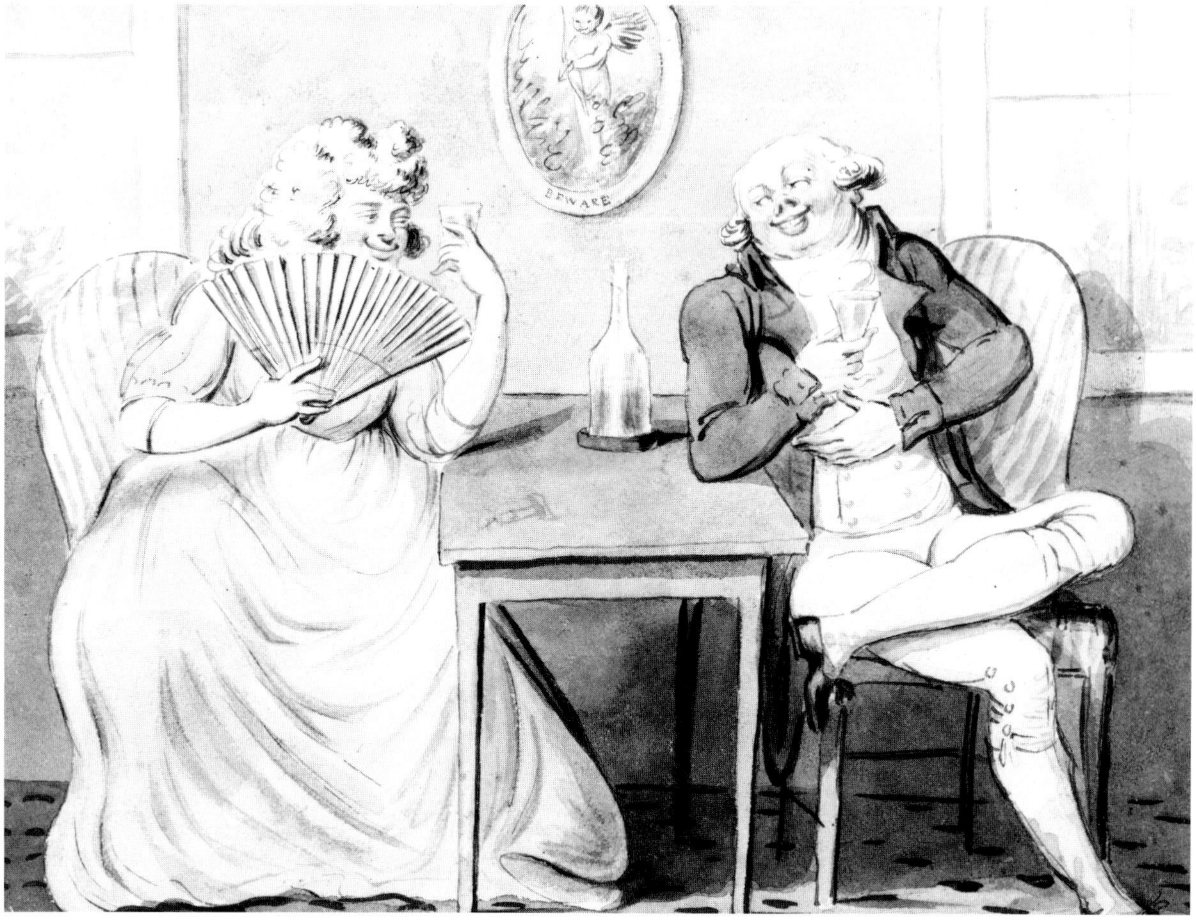

1799
Pen and watercolor over pencil
6⅞ x 9 inches (17.4 x 22.8 cm.)
Inscribed recto: Beware
Annotated verso: Drink to Me Only with Thine Eyes / I. Cruikshanks
Published: January 4, 1799, by Laurie & Whittle (224); below the image is engraved: Drink to me only with thine Eyes, / And I will pledge with mine; / Or leave a Kiss but in a Cup, / And I'll not look for Wine. / The Thirst that from the Soul doth rise / Demands a Drink Divine; / But might I of Jove's Nectar sip, / I would not change for thine.
Biblio: George, 9494; Krumbhaar, 290; Wark, 88
Impression: BM, LWL, WMC

The poem from which these lines were taken, "Song to Celia," was written by Ben Jonson and published in 1616. The ballad was set to music in 1780 by an unknown composer and became popularly known by the first line of the song, "Drink to Me Only with Thine Eyes."[1] It remains a favorite ballad even today.

The romantic sentiments of Jonson's ballad provide an ironic counterpoint to Cruikshank's rather bawdy image, in which a man and woman flirt over a bottle of wine. Although the woman holds a fan, indicative of modesty and propriety, she wears a casual dress and winks at her companion over her glass.

The wine bottle and the image of a smiling Cupid, below which the warning "Beware" is inscribed, occupy central positions in the composition. The image may have been read as a commentary on love or passion fueled by alcohol.

Jennifer Katell

1. James J. Fuld, *The Book of World Famous Music* (New York: Crown Publishers, 1966), pp. 169-171.

93 *A Cold Season* †

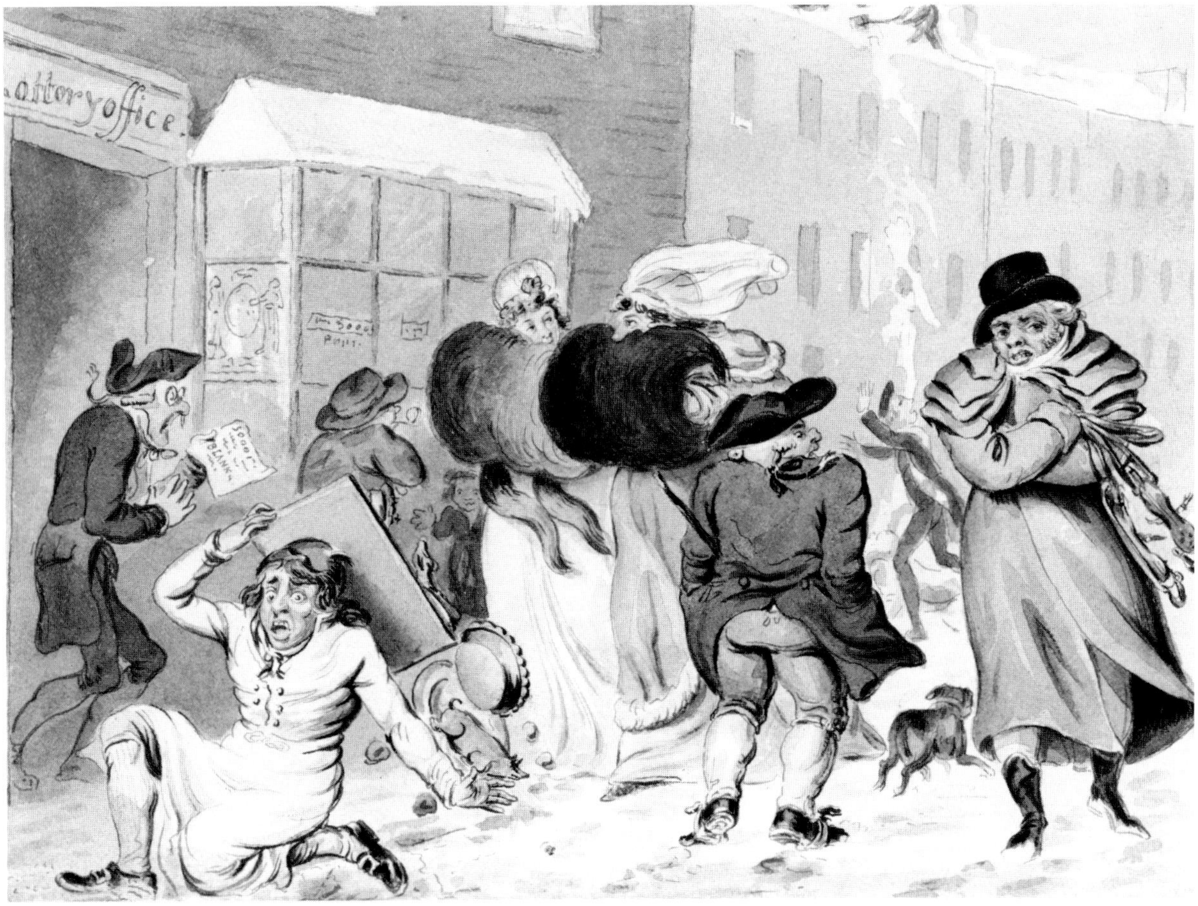

1799
Pen and watercolor over pencil
6¾ x 8⅞ inches (17 x 22.5 cm.)
Inscribed recto: Lottery Office . . . 5000 . . . Blank
Annotated verso: Snowy weather in London
Published: February 12, 1799, by Laurie & Whittle (227)
Biblio: George, 9496; Krumbhaar, 178; Wark, 89
Impression: BM, LWL, WMC

A Cold Season concerns itself with more than the weather in London. On a street, two well-dressed women stroll, their large muffs protecting their faces from the harsh wind, if not from life in general. A cook's assistant slips on the icy snow and drops the food he carries, thereby losing his potential wages. The women are in danger also. Like the boy, they could fall if they do not watch where they are going.

On the left, an old man exits the lottery office carrying a ticket marked "blank." He presumably has lost. State lotteries caused widespread financial ruin in the eighteenth century. To minimize risk, people even purchased lottery insurance, often just a scam to rob them of money.[1]

On the right, two men present contrasting pictures of the fortunes of life. One is obviously poor and improperly dressed for the season. His shoes are tied on with rags. The other is the image of affluence. The skates indicate he has leisure time to enjoy himself; however, he may be "skating on thin ice."

In the background, atop the building, two men are shoveling snow off the roof onto the people below. A passerby flees the downfall. Again there is the hint that misfortune awaits. Each figure, in his or her own way, suggests the hazards of everyday life in London where anyone, rich or poor, could lose everything in one false step.

Mari-Tere Alvarez

1. George, *London Life in the Eighteenth Century* (1965), p. 187.

94 *True Blue* †

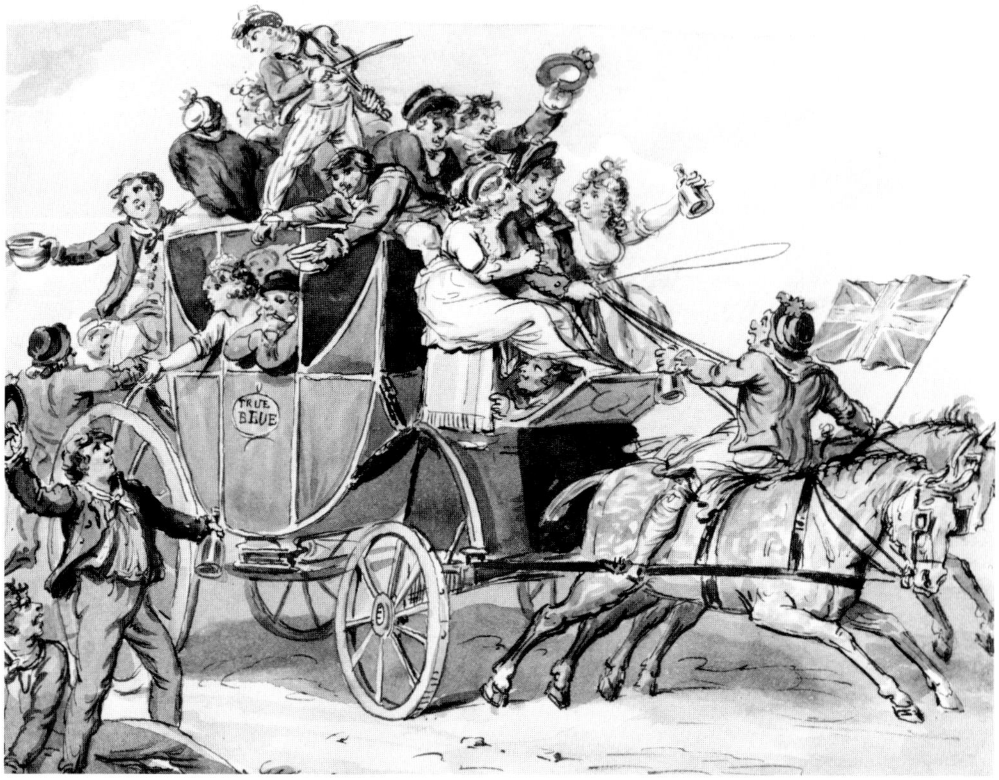

1799
Pen and watercolor
7 1/8 x 8 7/8 inches
(18 x 22.8 cm.)
Inscribed recto: True / Blue
Annotated verso: All alive at Portsmouth / I. Cruikshanks
Published: April 4, 1799, by Laurie & Whittle (228); below the title is engraved: The Jolly Tars of Old England or all alive at Portsmouth.
Biblio: Momus, 5; George, 9497; Krumbhaar, 1238; Wark, 90

In an age that saw Britain's dominance of the sea, sailors were a common feature of everyday life, particularly around major port cities such as Portsmouth. As a result, they were often depicted in prints, especially in farewells and returns. Sometimes, as here, sailors were shown drinking and having a good time.

A blue coach moves from left to right, crowded with sailors, probably celebrating their first or last few hours of liberty with wine, women, and song. There are a total of fifteen sailors, twelve of them on the coach, one on horseback, and two contemplating the scene from the ground. The overcrowded coach violates the laws of the period, which limited the number of passengers.[1] Eight of the sailors wear blue jackets, the source of their nickname.[2] The title, which also is the coach's name, alludes to both the color of their outfits and their loyalty to England. At the time of this print, British sailors were fighting gallantly against the French. Nine months earlier, during the Egyptian campaign, the British annihilated Napoleon's fleet in the Battle of the Nile.

Life at sea was very hard, marked by poor treatment and low pay,[3] but Cruikshank's picture instead radiates pleasure: one of the sailors is playing a fiddle; another looks up the skirt of a woman. The use of the basic triad—blue, yellow, red—contributes to the vibrancy of the image. It is very likely that *True Blue* served as inspiration for *Sailors on a Cruise*, a work by Isaac's son George, published in 1825 by Robins and Company, which has a similar composition.[4] *True Blue* was also reproduced in *The Cruikshankian Momus,* accompanied by several poems.

Mar Martinez-Perez

1. George, *Social Change in Graphic Satire*, pp. 140-42.
2. Richardson, *Georgian England,* p. 40.
3. N. A. M. Rodger, *The Wooden World: An Anatomy of the Georgian Navy* (Annapolis, Md.: Naval Institute Press, 1988), pp. 60-61, 124-25.
4. John Wardroper, *The Caricatures of George Cruikshank* (Boston: David R. Godine, 1978), p. 119.

95 *English Improvements on French Fashions* †

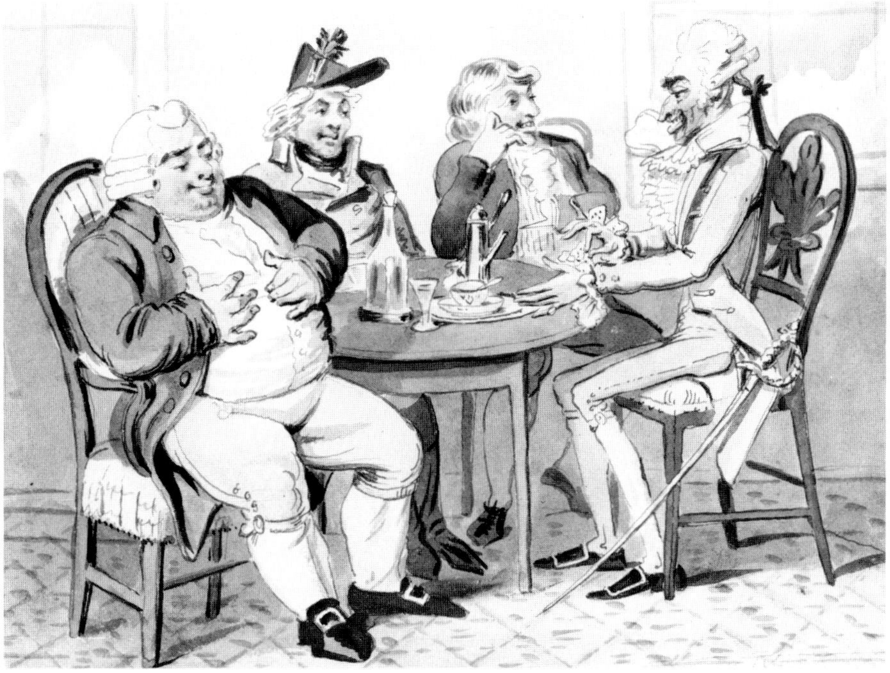

1799
Pen and watercolor over pencil
6 7/8 x 8 3/4 inches (17.5 x 22.2 cm.)
Annotated verso: A Frenchman's Story / I. Cruikshanks
Published: April 8, 1799, by Laurie & Whittle (230); below the image is engraved: Frenchman – Begar My Country be ver clever in de invention of de modes and de Fashions—dis is one, de ruffle—it be one grand ornament to de hand – Englishman – Certainly it is a great ornament to the hand, but according to custom my Country has made great improvement upon that Invention, by adding a Shirt to it.
Biblio: Wark, 91
Impression: LWL

In the 1790s the English wore clothes that were much less elaborate than those of their French counterparts. Previously, the former had looked to the latter for inspiration in design, but during this period the fashions of the English country gentleman became popular. Here, Cruikshank satirizes French frivolity by comparing it to English rationality.

The long full ruffles of which the Frenchman speaks were called *pleureuses* and were an excuse for extravagance. Louis-Sébastien Mercier remarked that a Parisian gentleman might go about in dirty shirts or no shirts at all, but he always wore costly laces. A current expression was: "One may know a man by his laces."[1]

The Frenchman recounts his story to three Englishmen at the table. It is the two figures in the foreground who are of primary importance. The stout Englishman on the left is reminiscent of John Bull, the personification of England first described in Dr. Arbuthnot's satire *Law Is a Bottomless Pit* (1712).[2] However, it was not until 1779 that he appeared in caricature and came to be known as a robust type who could be a little pig-headed but was honest and straightforward.[3]

The Englishman's stout figure reflects the current prosperity of Britain and the benefits of its political system. At this time one person in five of the world's population was a British subject. The pride the British felt and their feeling of superiority toward the French are apparent in Cruikshank's representation. Seated on the edge of his chair, the Frenchman wears a fancy wig with a ribboned queue, a shirt with an enormous bow, a very close-fitting and stiff-looking jacket, shoes with ridiculously large buckles, and a long, thin sword, clearly carried for effect since it would not have been very useful in self-defense. While the Frenchman delicately touches his ruffles, the Englishman touches his full belly, suggesting that it is more important to be well fed than fashionably dressed.

Kathleen Kelly

1. See Von Boehn, *Modes and Manners*, pp. 227-28.
2. *New Century Cyclopedia of Names* (New York: Appleton-Century-Crofts, Inc., 1954), p. 2199.
3. Leopold Wagner, *Names and Their Meanings* (London: T. Fisher Unwin, 1893), p. 24.

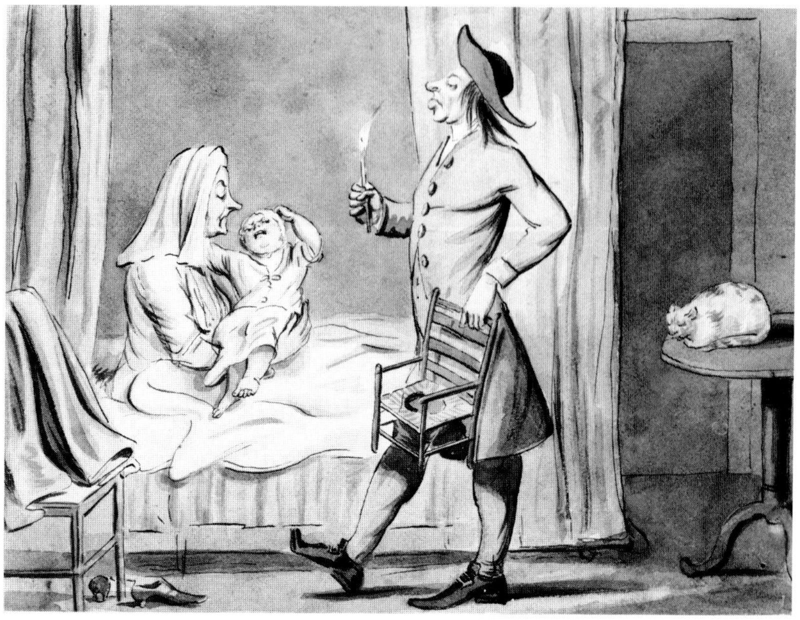

1799
Pen and watercolor
6 5/8 x 9 inches
(17 x 22.8 cm.)
Annotated verso: Nehemiahs Disaster / I. Cruikshanks
Published: April 9, 1799, by Laurie & Whittle (229); below the image is engraved: And behold about the ninth hour Tabitha the Wife of my Bosom awoke and said unto me, Arise Nathaniel speedily and make no long tarrying or delaying, but enter intc the next Room, and nigh unto tha which payeth tribute to Caesar, standeth a Wicker Chair, whereon hangeth a Garment call'd a Red Petticoat—dive in the pocket thereof and take out thence two Farthings and go to Obadiah the Tallow Chandler and buy two Candles, light one of them and bring it presently for I fear our last born Son Nehemiah, hath befouled himself—Hem—Hem.
Biblio: George, 9498; Krumbhaar, 799; Wark, 92
Impression: BM, LWL, WMC

The humor of Nehemiah's "disaster," as presented in both the image and accompanying passage, depends upon a stereotypically negative view of the Quakers and perhaps other ecclesiastical groups in England. Cruikshank is clearly making fun of their religious tone and ritual, even in dealing with the most mundane and natural incidents. In this case, the cause of a couple's exaggeratedly serious expression is that their baby's diaper is in need of a change. The characters involved wear conventional Quaker attire, the most evident article being the mother's veil. Their names, Tabitha, Daniel, and Nehemiah, are typical Quaker names, taken directly out of the Old Testament.

Although membership in the Society of Friends had increased during the eighteenth century, there were only about twenty thousand in Britain and Ireland when this watercolor was made. As Charles Frederick Holder suggests, "the period of activity of [George] Fox and [William] Penn saw some of the greatest wits in the history of England, whose temperamental characteristics were such as to make the Quaker fair game."[1] Even in the late eighteenth century, Cruikshank takes advantage of this "sport" as he satirizes the notion of perfection within contemporary Quaker doctrine, which urged that all followers, through God's assistance, were "able to bring forth fruits unto holiness and to stand perfect in their present rank."[2] What is depicted here is clearly an "imperfect" event; Nehemiah, the son of Tabitha and Daniel, has spoiled the atmosphere, along with his own diapers.

Cruikshank was not the only person to have criticized the religious practices of the Quakers. John Joseph Gurney, who hailed from a long lasting and prominent Quaker family line, nevertheless sharply details the idiosyncrasies of this group. Particularly pointed are his views on their adoption of "a higher and purer standard of action," a pretentious form of "simply complimentary and not truthful" articulation, and pedantically modest apparel.[3]

Julie Joyce

1. Charles Frederick Holder, *The Quakers in England and America* (London: The Neuner Co., 1913), p. 223; and Richard T. Vann and David Eversley, *Friends in Life and Death: The British and Irish Quakers in the Demographic Transition, 1650-1900* (Cambridge: Cambridge University Press, 1992), pp. 22-23; quotation on p. 234.
2. *A Summary of the History, Doctrine, Discipline of Friends: Written at the Desire of the Meeting for Sufferings* (London: James Phillips, George Yard, 1794), p. 16.
3. John Joseph Gurney, *Observations on the Religious Peculiarities of the Society of Friends,* 2d Amer. ed. (Philadelphia: Thomas Kite and Co., 1832.), pp. 269-70, 294.

97 *Robin & Sue*

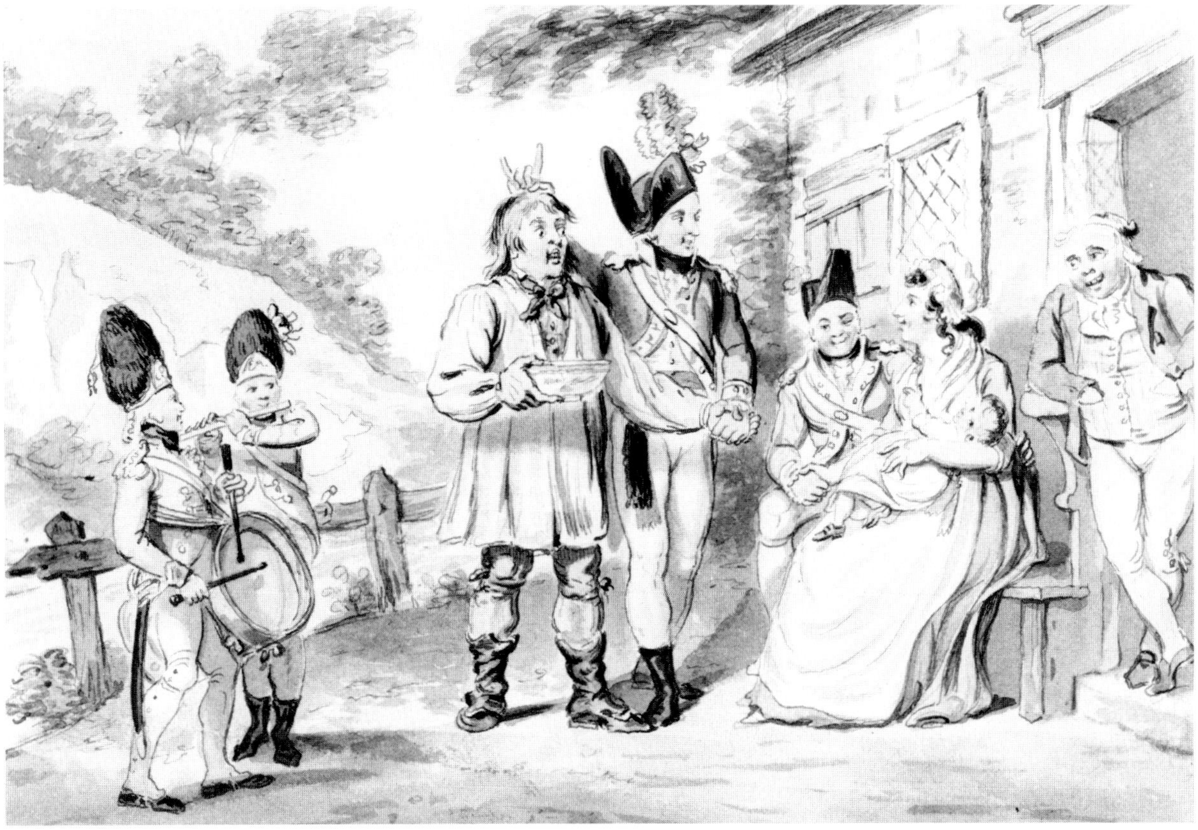

1799
Pen and watercolor over pencil
6 3/8 x 9 3/16 inches (16.2 x 23.4 cm.)
Inscribed recto: I. Cruikshanks – 1799
Annotated verso: Raising Recruits / I. Cruikshanks
Published: April 12, 1799, by Laurie & Whittle (231); below the title is engraved: I'll list for a soldier! said Robin to Sue / To avoid those eternal disputes: / Ay, ay, cried the termagent, do Robin do / Meantime I'll be raising recruits.
Biblio: Wark, 93
Impression: LWL, WMC

During the eighteenth century and into the nineteenth, Britain was at war. Military life is the background for this domestic scene of marital infidelity. Outside an inn, Robin, a country bumpkin, informs his wife Sue that he intends to join the army. A shrew, according to the the text, Sue encourages him, adding that in his absence she will be "raising recruits," referring to the child in her arms as well as to her plans to continue her adulterous relations.

It is apparent to everyone except Robin that he is already a cuckold. The recruiting sergeant next to him makes the sign over poor Robin's head in view of all save the unsuspecting husband. The grinning soldier seated next to Sue touches her with familiarity, raising doubts about the paternity of the child she holds in her lap.

Cruikshank dealt with the theme of the recruiting sergeant in other works, sometimes poking fun at the sergeant rather than the recruit. Such is the case in *The Recruiting Serjeant Taken In, or All Fair Above Board* (13).

Danna Freedy

98 Unruly Pigs †

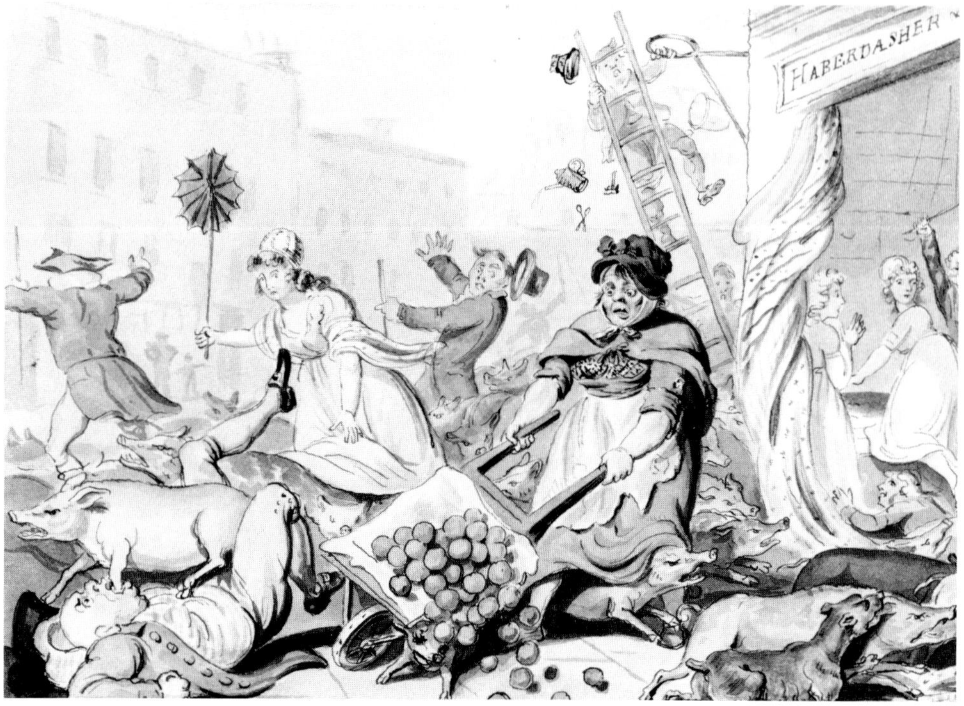

1799
Pen and watercolor over pencil
6 3/4 x 9 inches (17 x 23 cm.)
Inscribed recto: Cruikshank 1799, HABERDASHER
Annotated verso: Unruly Pigs / I. Cruikshanks
Published: May 20, 1799, by Laurie & Whittle (232)
Biblio: Wark, 94
Impression: LWL

This crowded street, flooded with rampaging pigs, is undoubtedly one of the many thoroughfares leading to Smithfield Market, at the time the greatest livestock market in London.[1] Located in the heart of the city, the area that once was Smithfield was established as a market in the twelfth century. By Cruikshank's day it was surrounded by a burgeoning metropolis. The streets leading to Smithfield, such as Aldersgate and Holborn, were utilized by drovers (one is barely visible behind the man losing his hat) for herding animals into the three-acre trading arena.[2]

In preparation for the markets held on Monday and Friday, livestock from the countryside arrived at the outskirts of London on Thursday and Sunday afternoons. In the evening the animals, in this case pigs, were driven into the city.[3] As twilight approached, lamplighters went through the streets to light the clear glass cotton-wick oil lamps.[4] Here, one clings to his ladder as it is jostled by the unruly swine.

The people scatter and panic at the stampede. Pigs run wildly between the legs and under the skirt of the woman with a parasol. On the pavement, a fat man has been toppled by a large animal, who tramples over him, putting a foot in his mouth. The owner of the haberdashery and his two female customers stare in disbelief, as another customer attempts to get up, having been brought to earth.

Although evening was thought to be the least crowded and therefore most appropriate time to drive a pack of animals through a city, Cruikshank certainly suggests it was not. With streets and shops full, the animals were a nuisance and even a danger to men and women going about their business.[5] Clearly this illustration exaggerates the situation, but the general comment on the hazards of living in a rapidly developing city is not overstated. Smithfield Market was eliminated in the nineteenth century.

Rhonda Howard

---

1. William Addison, *English Fairs and Markets* (London, B. T. Batsford, Ltd., 1953), p. 85.
2. David Hughson, *London* (W. Stratsford: Crown-Court, 1809), p. 598.
3. *Knight's Encyclopedia of London* (London: George Woodfall and Son, 1851), p. 797.
4. Pyne, *Costume of Great Britain*.
5. *Knight's Encyclopedia*, p. 797.

99 *"Robin and His Horse"*

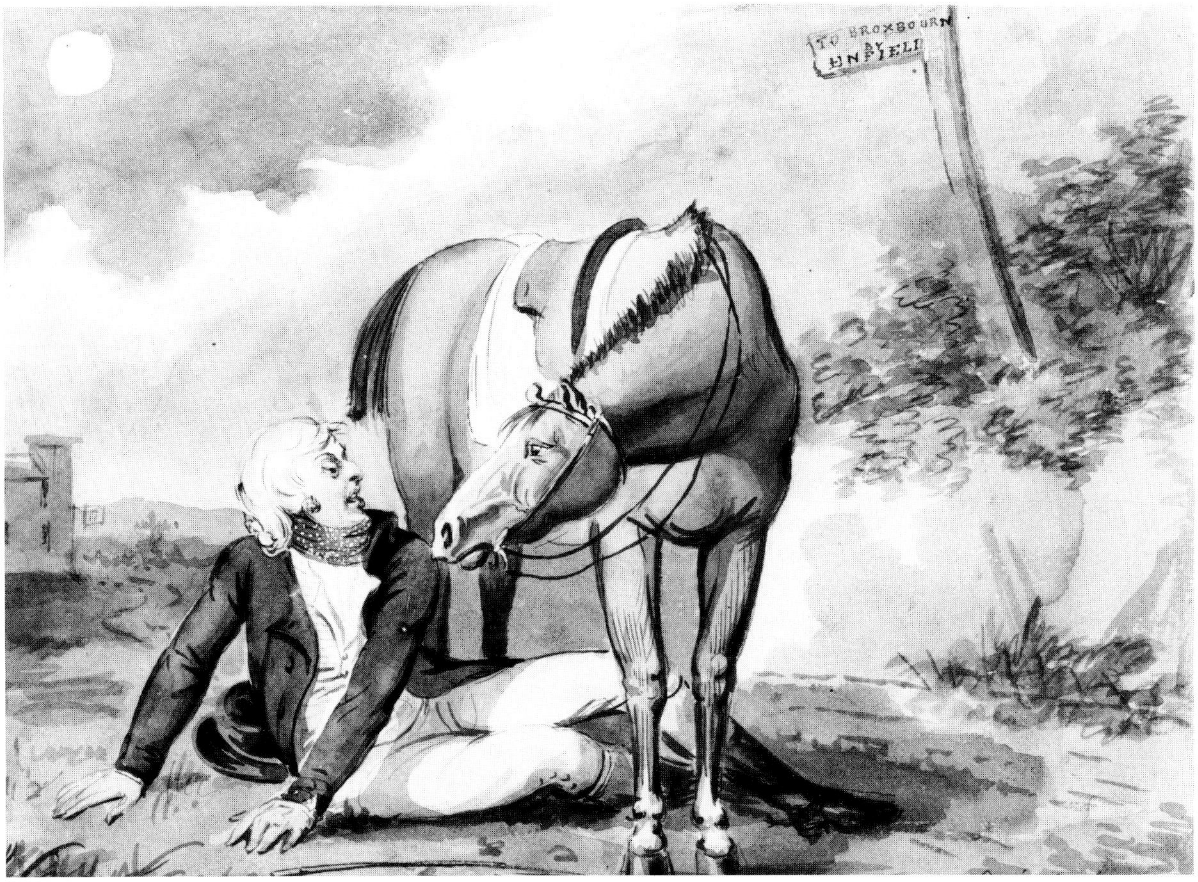

1799
Pen and watercolor over pencil
6⁵⁄₈ x 8⁷⁄₈ inches (16.8 x 22.5 cm.)
Inscribed recto: To Broxbourn by Enfield / Cruikshank 1799
Annotated verso: Robin, of the Temple of the M . . . s and his Horse Apollo / I. Cruikshanks
Biblio: Wark, 95

It is night, and the moon is high in the sky. A well-dressed man who appears to be drunk has fallen from his horse. He and the animal exchange glances as if in conversation. The scene takes place on the road to Broxbourn by way of Enfield, just north of London, the site of a racetrack.

No print after this drawing has been located. Without a title or text it is difficult to decipher the image's meaning. One can assume, however, that the specificity of the location given by Cruikshank must be important. A clue to the work's significance may be in the annotation on the verso. Apollo was the companion of the Muses, and the word beginning with "m" and ending with "s" might well be a reference to the goddesses. It could also be an indication of the identity of the fallen rider.

As Robert Wark has stated, the draftsmanship and color in this drawing are unusually crude for Cruikshank. However, since the drawing was accepted by Isaac's son George as being by his father, there is no reason to question its authenticity.

Kathleen Kelly

100 Paddy Whack's First Ride in a Sedan †

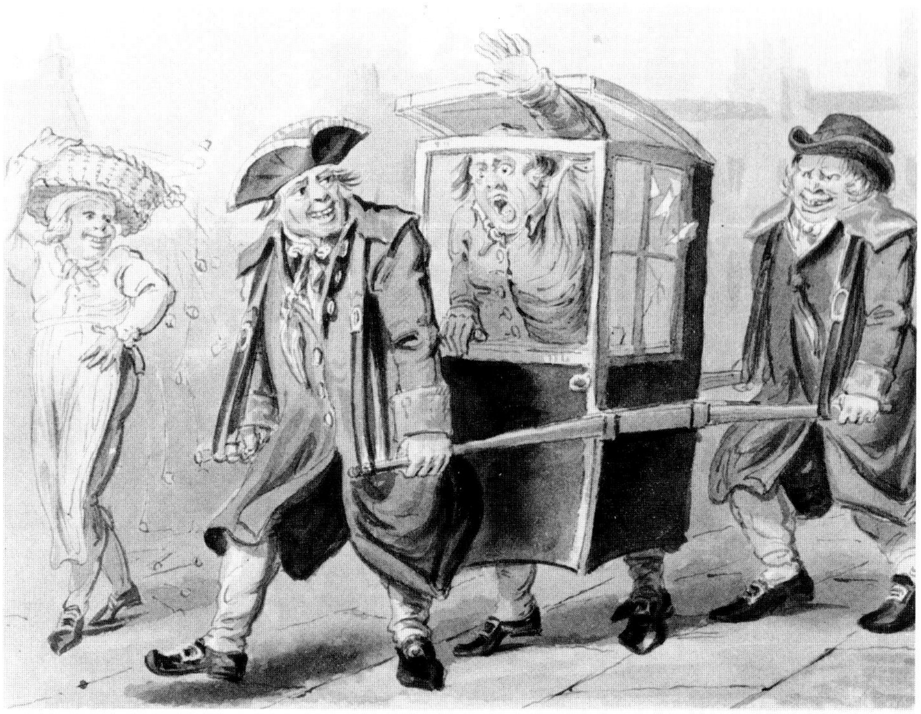

1800
Pen and watercolor over pencil
7 3/8 x 9 1/4 inches (18.7 x 23.5 cm.)
Annotated verso: Irish Chairmen / I. Cruikshanks
Published: January 28, 1800, by Laurie & Whittle (238); below the title is engraved: Arrah! my dear Honey—to be sure I'd rather walk, if it wasn't for the Fashion of the thing.
Biblio: Wark, 96
Impression: LWL

In early nineteenth-century England, and probably in some circles today, the Irish are alluded to as "Pat" or "Paddy," short for Patrick, a popular Irish given name. "Paddywhackery" is a send-up that may be described as "exaggerating Irish characteristics to the point of self-caricature, though generally the distortion gently ridicules the beholder [the Irish] rather than the subject."[1] According to slang terminology in the early nineteenth century, "pad" also had a special connotation: "To pad it" meant to walk.[2]

The Irish immigrant was perceived as a threat to the English working man. He was often held up to ridicule and portrayed as dimwitted, primitive, and lazy. Cruikshank's depiction of the central figure is nothing less than grotesque. Lavater, in his influential study of physiognomy, described a facial expression very like this one as "the transport of rage of a vulgar man, suffering, and divested of energy."[3] "Paddy" is large and clumsy, with "Irish legs" (slang for thick legs).[4] He has evidently broken the window of the sedan in whose cramped quarters he "rides," and his feet have come through the floor as well. Therefore, he is walking, completely defeating the purpose of the sedan itself.

Paddy is ridiculed by two porters, presumably English, whose pleasure is evident in their huge grins, and their hijinks are acknowledged by the laughter of a passing crier, who is chuckling with such force that his livelihood (clay pipes?) spills out from the basket perched on his head.

A symbol of status and fashion when introduced into England in the early seventeenth century, the sedan, though still in use, had lost its appeal and was employed less frequently by the time of this drawing. Fashionable or not, a sedan would not have been an appropriate means of transportation for a humble Irishman. The humor of this situation, then, lies in the fact that naive Paddy has been misled into thinking that he should travel in style, even though he is out of his element. Clearly, he is not enjoying this trip as much as his amused companions.

Julie Joyce

1. O'Connor, *The Irish*, p. 365.
2. Andrewes, *Dictionary of the Slang and Cant Languages.*
3. Lavater, *Essays on Physiognomy*, trans. Holloway and Hunter (1797-98), 2:64, pl. 11.
4. Andrewes, *Dictionary of the Slang and Cant Languages.*

101 *The Old Dog's Legacy*

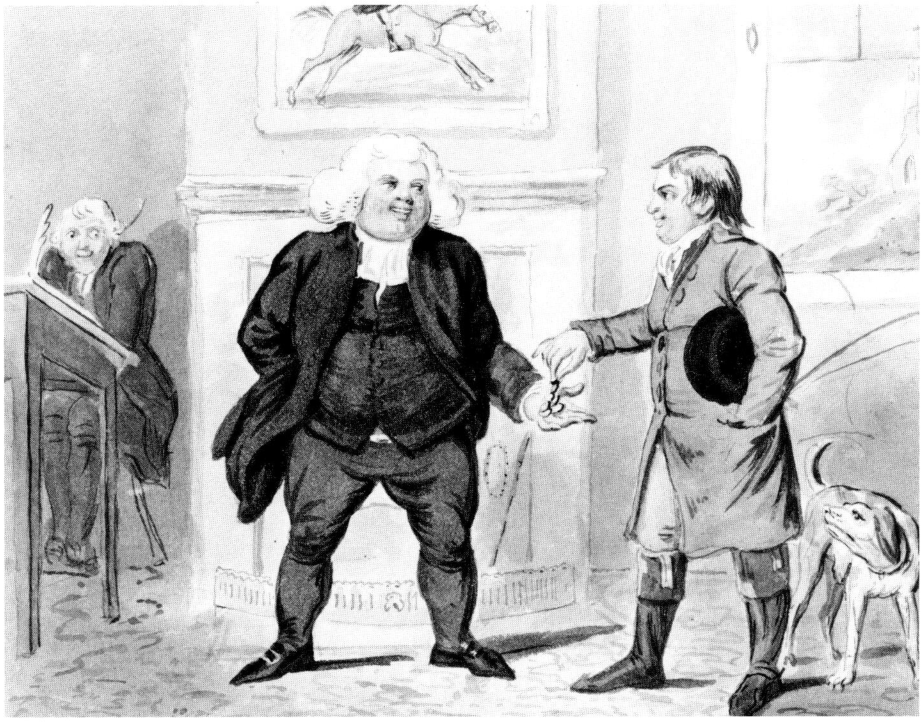

1800
Pen and watercolor over pencil
7 1/8 x 9 inches (18.2 x 23.2 cm.)
Annotated verso: Fee for Burying a Dog in the Ch. Yard / I. Cruikshanks
Published: February 1, 1800, by Laurie & Whittle (239); below the image is engraved: Vicar – How could you be so profane as to Inter your Dog in the Church Yard. You are liable to be punished in the Spiritual Court – Farmer – Why aye Doctor, but when you consider what a sensible Creature he was, you will not be so severe, the day before he died he made his Will and left you a Legacy. – Vicar – a Legacy – Farmer – Yes he left you 6 Guineas, & I'se come to give it you – Vicar – Oho if that's the case why did you not mention it before, & he might have laid inside the Church.
Biblio: Krumbhaar, A.73; Wark, 97
Impression: LWL, WMC

With oustretched hand, the fat clergyman receives money from the man dressed in riding clothes. The title plays with the word "dog," which can mean "fellow" in a negative way,[1] as well as referring to the dog in the text. Once again, the image is making fun of the venality and worldliness of clergy.

The social position of clergymen varied enormously, depending entirely upon their birth and education. The clergyman in this picture is a country parson, as indicated by the church on the hill seen through the window and by the visitor's riding clothes. Country parsons had a better life than those living in London. Like his parishioner, this one is interested in sports, as is evident from the racing picture hanging over the mantle. Many country parsons lived a life of pleasure—hunting, shooting, and drinking. Sometimes they were even accused of robbing their parishioners and seducing their daughters.[2] This kind of country parson appears in Fielding's *Tom Jones*.[3]

Dressed in a black cassock, Cruikshank's parson also wears a wig. His stoutness is a clear symptom of his prosperity; his central position in the composition suggests his sense of self-importance. His gaze rests somewhere between the countryman's eyes and the coins, which are very shiny. The clerk on the left, who keeps the books and sets down records of ceremonies, seems amused by the proceedings and the joke was presumably shared by Cruikshank's audience.

Mar Martinez-Perez

1. Richardson, *Georgian England*, p. 56.
2. Rosamond Bayne-Powell, *English Country Life in the Eighteenth Century* (London: John Murray, 1933), pp. 81-82.
3. Henry Fielding, *Tom Jones* (London: Methuen and Co., 1905), pp. 112-13.

102 *Leap Year* †

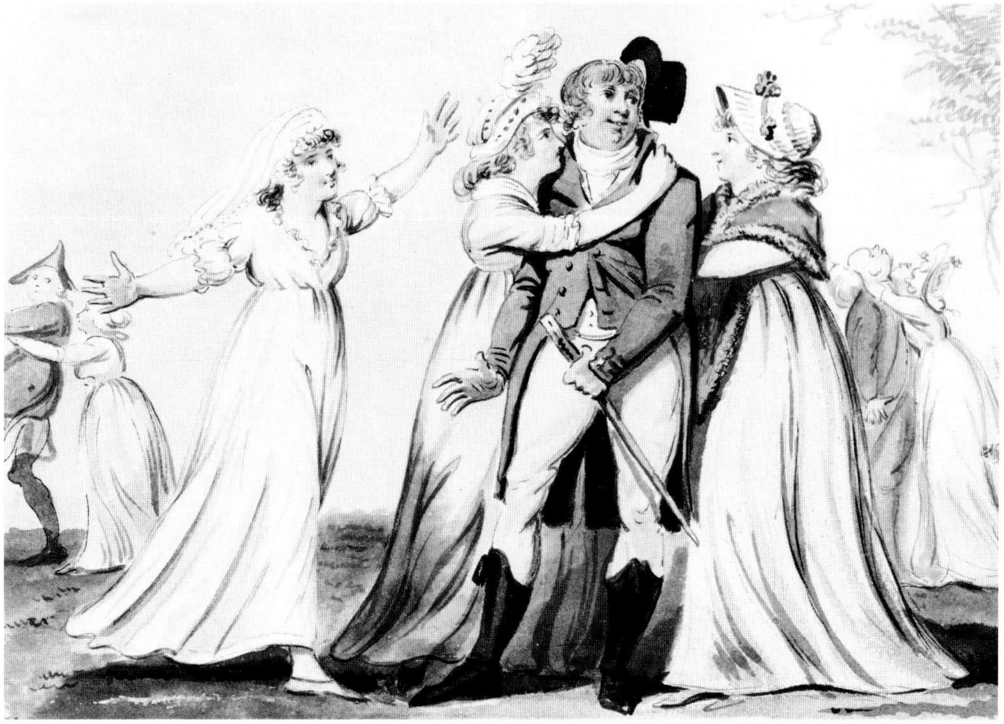

1800
Pen and watercolor over pencil
$6^3/_4$ x $9^5/_8$ inches (17.2 x 24.5 cm.)
Annotated verso: Leap Year / I. Cruikshanks
Published: March 18, 1800, by Laurie & Whittle (241)
Biblio: Wark, 98
Impression: LWL

The year 1800 was a Leap Year. Therefore, according to tradition, a woman was allowed to propose marriage to a man on February 29. In this composition, published a few weeks after that date, Cruikshank depicted eager ladies avidly pursuing prospective mates.[1] The central figure is dressed in the height of fashion. He sports the new scaramouch top hat and wide white silk scarf wrapped high on the neck and filling in the high-collared frock coat. The sides of his jacket are properly trim, a new fashion begun by Beau Brummell in the late 1790s. He would have been considered an attractive marriage prospect and, accordingly, several ladies are competing for his affections. However, even the unattractive males in the background are being pursued.

The young man, obviously delighted with the attention, maintains a firm grasp upon his walking stick which, given its position and angle, seems to assume phallic significance. As in the Judgment of Paris, a popular subject for artists, he must decide which among the three beauties is the most desirable. The composition of the drawing may be indebted to Reynolds's famous painting of Garrick between Tragedy and Comedy.

Cruikshank's interpretation of this traditional theme reflects a contemporary interest in folkloric custom. Rationalist antiquaries of the eighteenth century in England, as well as throughout Europe, sought evidence of ancient superstitions and rites as examples of pagan and papist superstition.[2] The publication of several major collections of traditions and superstitions of Old England as well as of subject peoples had piqued the popular imagination in this period.

Deanne Shey

1. On inversion and the crossing of normally accepted social boundaries see Katharine M. Briggs, *Folklore, and Folktales of England* (London: Routledge and Kegan Paul, Ltd., 1965).
2. For discussion of the English folklore movement, see Richard M. Dorson, "The First Group of British Folklorists," *Journal of American Folklore* (1955), pp. 394-416; and idem, "The Great Team of English Folklorists," in *Journal of American Folklore* (1951), pp. 1-10.

103 St. Andrew's Day †

1800
Pen and watercolor over pencil (?)
7 1/8 x 9 1/4 inches (17.9 x 23.5 cm.)
Annotated verso: St. Andrew's Day / I. Cruikshanks
Published: November 1, 1800, by Laurie & Whittle
Biblio: Krumbhaar, A.95; Wark, 99
Impression: WMC

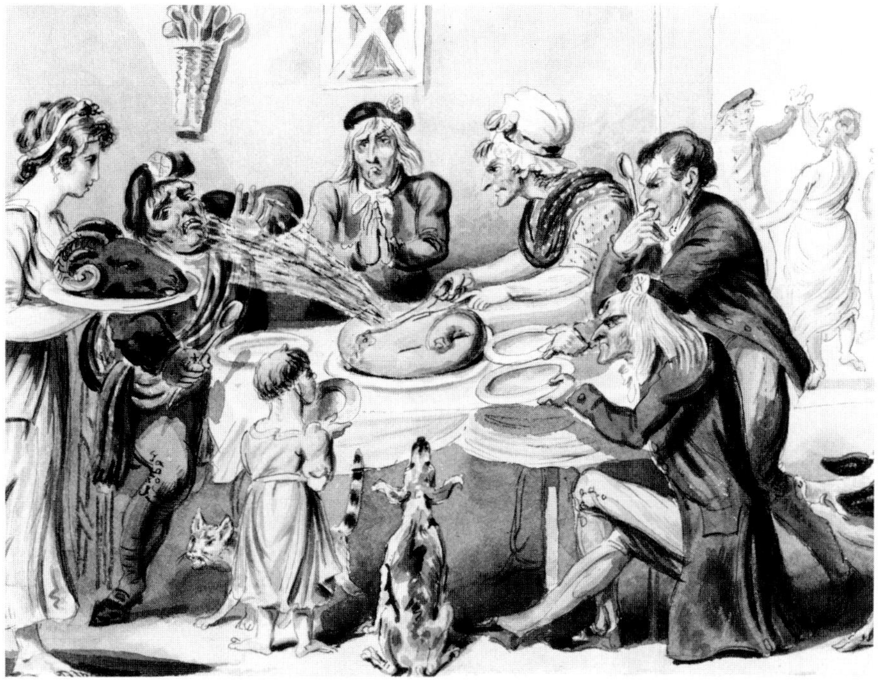

Cruikshank, who emigrated from Edinburgh around 1784, was surely attuned to the distinctive characteristics identified with the Scots by the English. Having descended from the Picts, who were known for their cruelty, they were seen as harsh by nature.[1] Although in the early eighteenth century the hostility of earlier years had been moderated by the Union of 1707, anti-Scottish prejudice was still reflected in English literature and art. Scots were portrayed as characteristically shrewd, pedantic, tough, argumentative, and lacking humor. Here Cruikshank conveys those qualities through the stern and somber expression of the people in this drawing, despite the holiday they are presumably celebrating. Except for the dancing couple in the background, the tone of the scene is set by the solemnity of the central figure.

A group of country folk have gathered on St. Andrew's Day to share traditional foods. The festival, long celebrated in Scotland, commemorates St. Andrew the Apostle, patron Saint of Scotland, whose feast day falls on November 30. The singed sheep's head on the left is a reminder of how sheep were slaughtered in the country before being brought to market (the head was left at home to be consumed). The haggis, here being cut on the table, is made from the heart, liver, brains, and other parts cooked inside the animal's stomach.[2] Elaborate dishes such as these were generally only served at special feasts.[3]

The clothes are typical of the Lowlands of Scotland. By the mid-seventeenth century, the blue hat worn by three of the men had become a national symbol. Until the 1800s, the small circular bonnets and blue coats worn by civilians were almost identical to the military uniform. A description of the uniform from 1789 describes a round signet worn on the hats as being a painted or embroidered reference to St. Andrew.[4] The saint is symbolized by an x-shape on the signet; a similar image appears in the picture on the wall. This symbol refers to the manner of the saint's death: Andrew was crucified at Patras in Archaia by being bound to a saltire or decussate (an x-shaped cross).[5] The dress of the young girl delivering the sheep's head is typical for an unmarried girl. The ribbon in her hair indicates her maidenhood.[6] In a humorous way, Cruikshank uses her action to recall depictions of Salome presenting the head of St. John the Baptist to Herod.

Mary-Kay Lombino

1. Faber, *The High Road to England,* p. 113.
2. David Daiches, ed., *A Companion to Scottish Culture* (New York: Homes and Meier Publications, 1981), p. 317.
3. Houston and Whyte, *Scottish Society, 1500-1800,* p. 251.
4. Dunbar, *The Costume of Scotland,* p. 190.
5. Herbert Thurston, S. J., and Donald Attwater, eds., *Butler's Lives of the Saints,* 4 vols. (New York: P. J. Kennedy and Sons, 1962), 4:451.
6. Dunbar, *The Costume of Scotland,* p. 125.

104 *"Irish Fortune Hunter"*

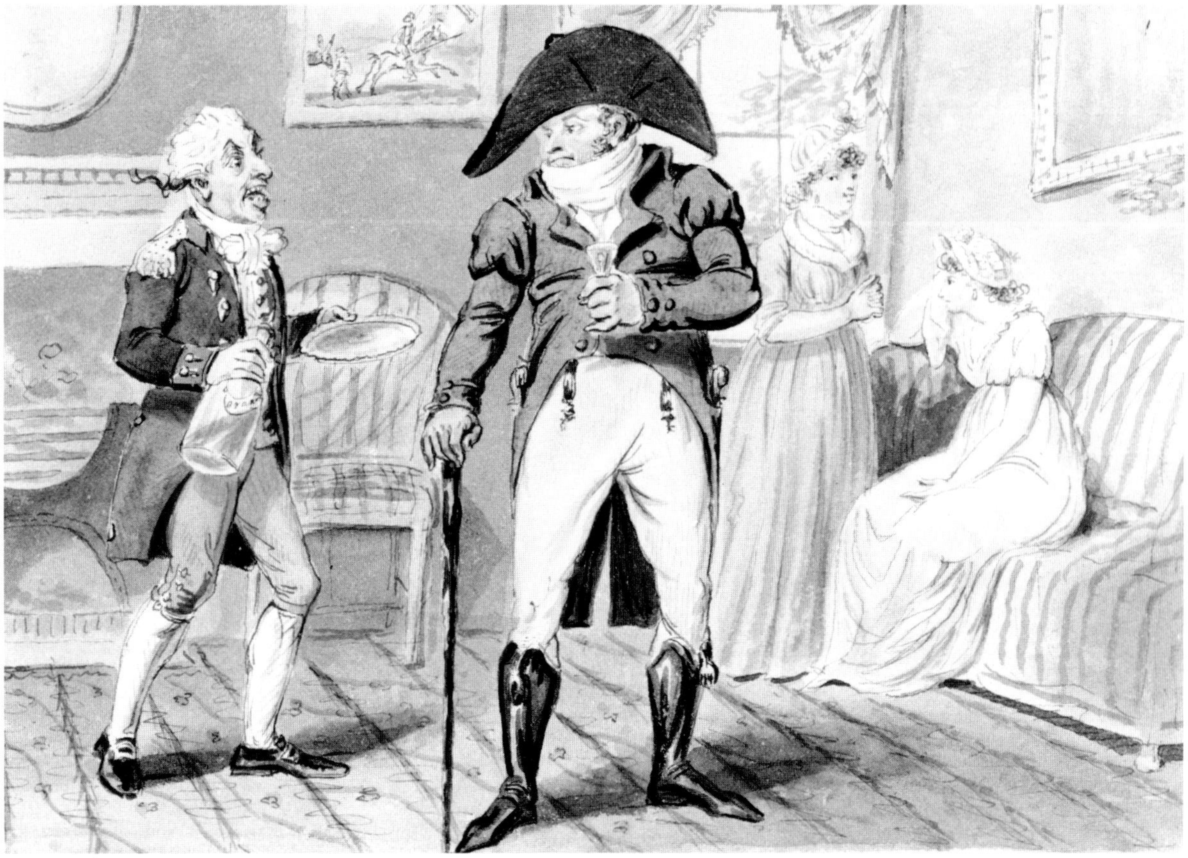

c. 1800 (?)
Pen and watercolor
6 1/2 x 9 1/8 inches (16.5 x 23 cm.)
Annotated verso: Irish Fortune Hunter / I. Cruikshanks
Biblio: Wark, 100

Although the title inscribed on the back of the drawing identifies the subject as an Irish fortune-hunter, nothing in the image seems to confirm this interpretation. In any case, something is clearly amiss. The servant seems stunned, his mouth wide open in disbelief, while on the couch sits a fearful young lady being comforted by the woman standing, presumably her mother. The central male figure, with his fashionable clothes, is the very pillar of the composition. One cannot help but think that he is, in fact, the master of the house. Like Don Quixote, whose image appears on the rear wall, the master of the house may have been imprudent or unrealistic in his ventures. Perhaps what is shown here is not an Irish fortune-hunter but a man who has lost his fortune by chasing after windmills.

Until the print for this image is discovered we can only speculate about its meaning. Robert Wark has proposed a date of circa 1800 for this drawing; however, the style of dress suggests it could be a few years earlier.

Mari-Tere Alvarez

105 *"The Poor Poet"* †

c. 1800
Pen and watercolor over pencil
6¾ x 8¾ inches (17 x 22.3 cm.)
Annotated verso: The poor Poet / I. Cruikshanks
Biblio: Wark, 101

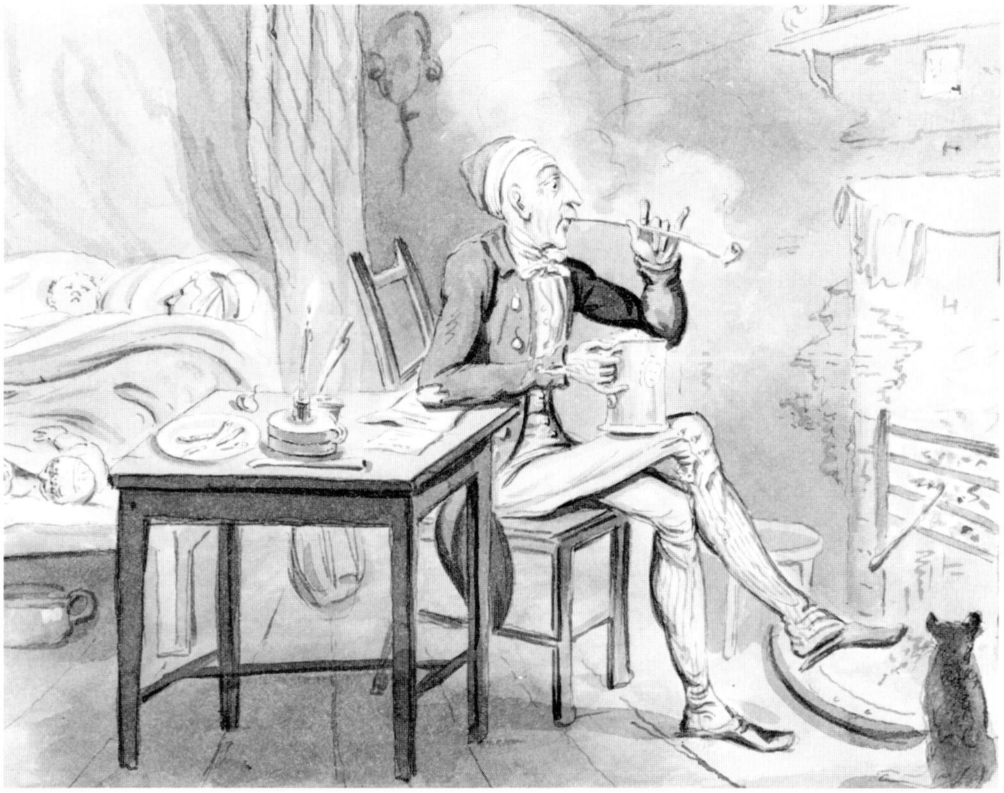

Surprisingly, no print after this image has been located, with a caption that might reveal Cruikshank's satirical intentions. The sketch presents the viewer with what had become a conventional image: the poor Romantic poet, lost in his own reveries. Robert Wark aptly describes the main figure in the drawing as "a very thin man, out at the elbows."[1]

Sitting in front of the fireplace, the versifier puffs contemplatively at his pipe as he looks into the fire, a tankard of ale in his hands. A sad face on the tankard appears to mock the poet. Clad in a nightcap, with his wig on the wall of this spartan garret, he rests his arm on the table, which is equipped with ink, quill, and paper ready for use. To judge from the poet's bemused countenance, the foolscap sheets probably are not filled with lucid verse at this late hour. Behind him, in bed, are his wife and three children, two of them with their heads at the foot. Here we are presented with a scribbler who whiles his time away by the fire, ignorant of his family and his surroundings, a poor provider at best. The sharp diagonal of the table on which the poet's elbow rests defies the law of linear perspective otherwise applied in this composition. Cruikshank, thoroughly conversant with the rudiments of perspective, probably included this distortion to heighten tension, or to suggest that the poet's sensibility, too, is askew.

The poet as a noble dreamer is a construct that emerged with positive connotations during the latter part of the eighteenth century, with the approach of what is generally regarded as the Romantic age in English letters. Earlier in the century, however, the poet appears to have been on the defensive. The prestige of poetry, for centuries regarded as the highest form of knowledge and the true educator of mankind, was jeopardized by the ethos of scientific progress. In the *Dunciad,* published in a number of editions beginning in 1728, Alexander Pope denounced the scientific learning of the age, with its false values;[3] he warned against the new learning of Bacon, Locke, and Newton.[2] Cruikshank's caricature of the pre-Romantic scribe does not have the virtues that Pope extolled. He becomes an irresponsible and laughable figure, not a source of enlightenment.

Maria L. Brendel

1. Wark, "*Drawings for Drolls,*" p. 101.
2. R. W. Harries, *Reason and Nature in the Enlightened Century* (London: Blanford Press, 1968), pp. 203-5.

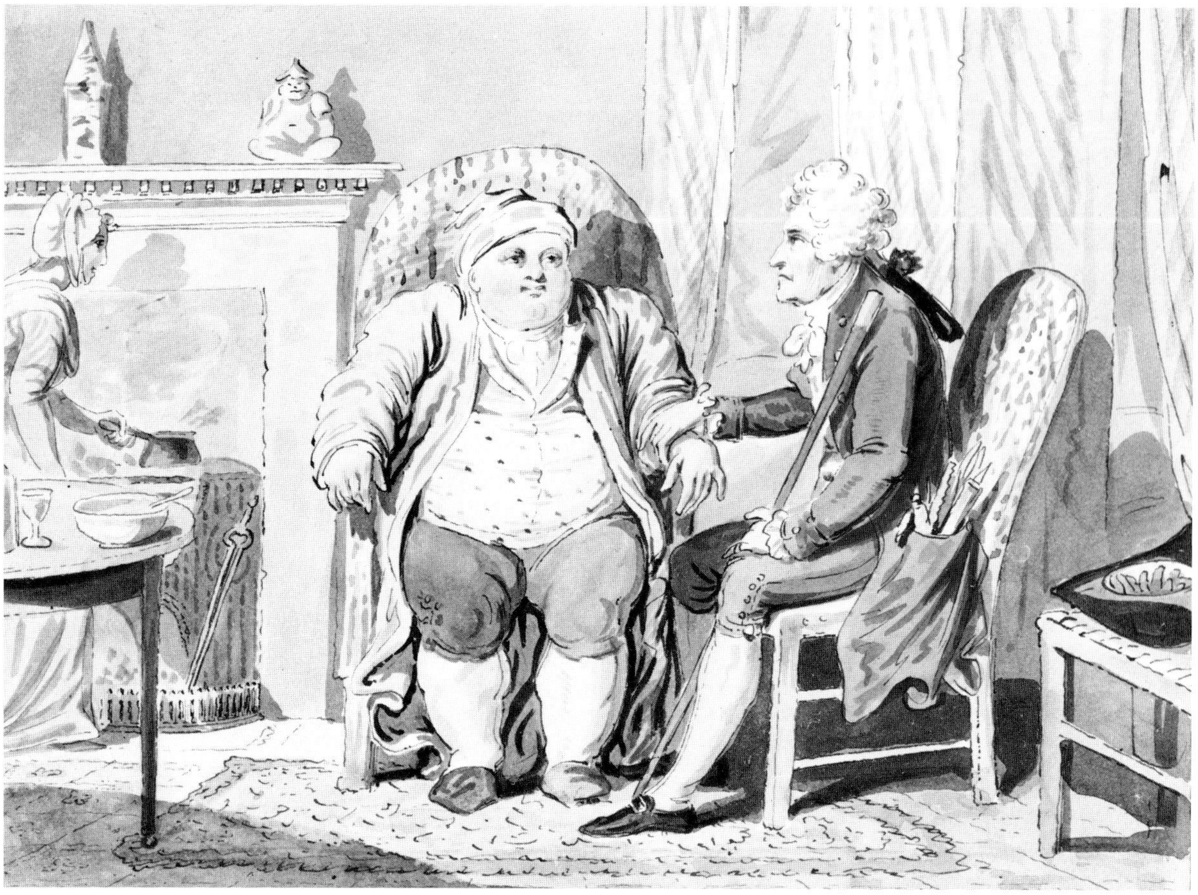

1801
Pen and watercolor
7 x 9 inches (18 x 23.2 cm.)
Annotated verso: Too Good Health / I. Cruikshanks
Published: January 20, 1801, by Laurie & Whittle (256); below the image is engraved: Oh! my dear Doctor I am very bad. I do not know what is the matter with me—I eat well, drink well, and I sleep well – Doctor – Ah! Dreadful symptoms indeed. Well well I'll give you something that shall take away all that.
Biblio: Krumbhaar, A.36; Wark, 103
Impression: LWL, WMC

Seated in a chair is a very fat man who is having his pulse taken by a physician. His size as well as the setting clearly identifies him as a prosperous middle-class citizen who can easily afford the expensive medical attention that was customary at the time[1]—even when, as the text implies, his malady is imaginary. In fact, the patient is complaining about his good life, not about an ailment—he eats well, drinks well, sleeps well. His good fortune is acknowledged by the happy Buddha perched contentedly on the mantle.

From what the patient says, he does not need a doctor. However, the physician encourages his hypochondria by considering the symptoms of eating, drinking, and sleeping well as "dreadful." With studied gravity, he promises to give his patient something to eliminate them. Fashionably dressed, the doctor wears a tie wig and a scarlet cloak. In his left hand he holds a gold-headed cane and in his pocket some of the tools to denote his profession—a bottle of elixir, saw, scissors, etc.

The image makes fun of those people who feel guilty about their good fortune and find reasons for being miserable. Concurrently, it criticizes the medical profession, a frequent butt of Cruikshank's satire (see 47 and 77).

Mar Martinez-Perez

1. Bayne-Powell, *Eighteenth-Century London Life*, p. 184.

107 *The Welsh Traveller* †

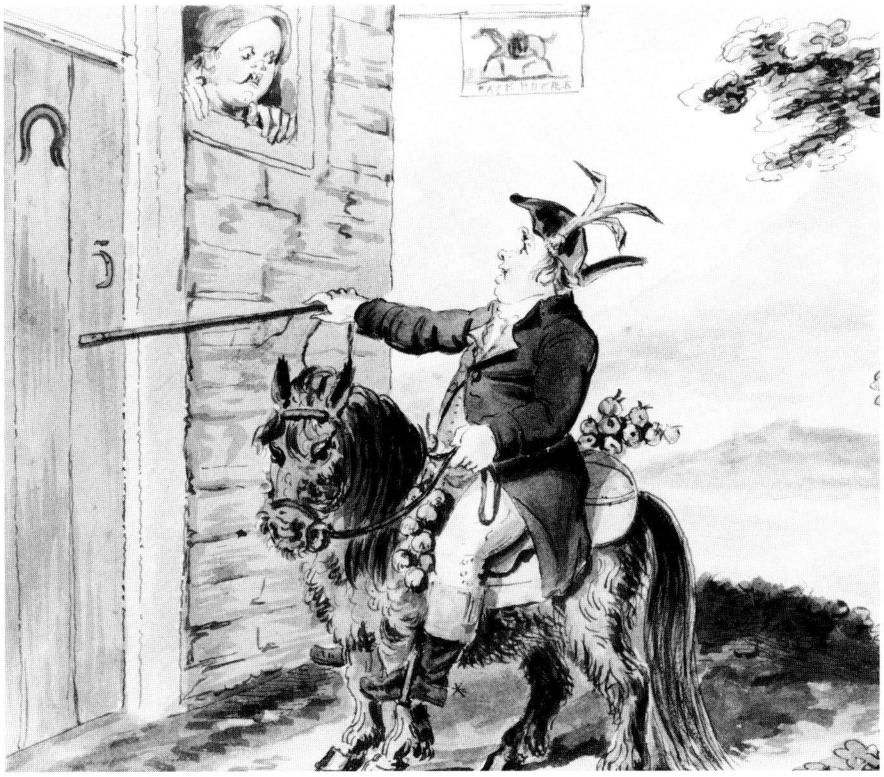

1801
Pen and watercolor over pencil
6 7/8 x 9 inches
(17.4 x 23 cm.)
Inscribed recto: Pack Horse
Annotated verso: The Welsh Ambassador / I. Cruikshanks
Published: February 4, 1801, by Laurie & Whittle (258); below the image is engraved: Open the Door directly Landlord, to shon ap Morgan - ap Shenkin - ap Jones - ap Thomas - ap Williams - ap Evans - ap Griffith - ap Owen - ap Rice - ap Morris, Shentleman of Wales - I will not open the Door, there is so many of you, my little Inn won't contain one half of you.
Biblio: Wark, 104
Impression: LWL

Much like another drawing by Cruikshank (*St. David's Day*, 111), *The Welsh Traveller* is a satire on a specific ethnic group and its customs. Here, Cruikshank exploits the reputation of the Welsh as a race obsessed with lineage.[1] In the text, the traveler, a somewhat laughable figure of a man on a small Welsh pony, demands to be granted entrance to the inn, called the Pack Horse, as he proclaims his lineage by reciting the names of his ancestors: Morgan, Shenkin, Jones, etc. All of the names are typically Welsh, and some can be linked to specific characters in the country's history. The list of names, the traveler feels, should give him stature in the eyes of the innkeeper and thus insure his admittance. Instead, on hearing the names, the innkeeper thinks there is a large group of people in need of rooms, and he responds that he cannot accommodate them all. The traveler's insignificant appearance adds humor to his attempt to make himself seem important. The leek in his hat, initially worn to distinguish friend from foe in a time of war, indicates that he is an over-zealous patriot.[2] It was often part of the dress on patriotic holidays but one would not have worn it daily or when traveling.

Although undoubtedly by a later hand, the annotation on the back of the drawing—"The Welsh Ambassador"—may be an allusion to a character in the play *The Welsh Embassador* (1623), the author of which is unknown. In the story, Penda, a Welsh soldier who rides through the country on a hobbyhorse, describes himself as a fine gentleman from as old a family as any in Wales.[3] It is not known whether Penda is depicted here, but the play expresses a view of the Welsh common in English theater and adopted by Cruikshank in this composition.[4]

Mary-Kay Lombino

1. Glanmor Williams, *Religion, Language and Nationality in Wales* (Cardiff: University of Wales Press, 1979), p. 109.
2. John Brand, *Observations on Popular Antiquities* (London: Chatto and Windus, 1913), p. 53.
3. Harold Littledale, ed., *The Welsh Embassador* (Oxford: Oxford University Press, 1920).
4. Faber, *The High Road to England*, p. 113.

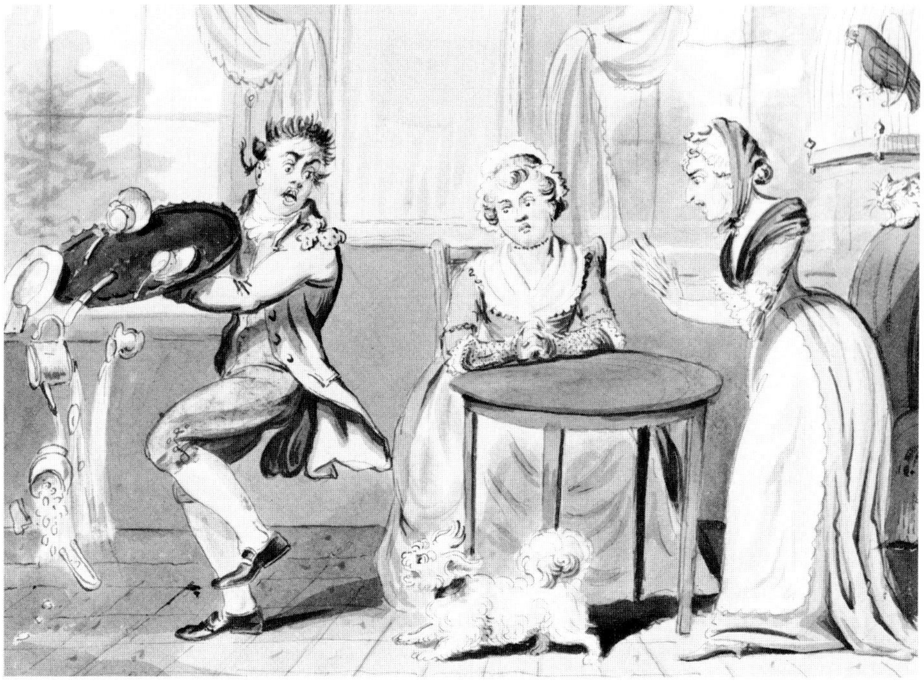

1801
Pen and watercolor over pencil
7 x 9 inches (17.4 x 22.4 cm.)
Annotated verso: The awkward Servant / I. Cruikshanks
Published: February 4, 1801, by Laurie & Whittle (259); below the image is engraved: Good lack a day John, what are you doing? you have broke all tea things – I can't help it Ma'am, that nasty cur of yours has bit my leg – Bit your leg! has he? dear me; I hope the pretty little creature won't be Sick after it!!
Biblio: Krumbhaar, A.38; Wark, 105
Impression: LWL, WMC

Defoe once remarked, "There's no such thing as a good servant in England."[1] This attitude was prevalent throughout the eighteenth century among masters and mistresses, who seldom demonstrated an appreciation for household help. The anti-servant sentiment is clearly depicted here, as all the creatures (human and animal) on the right side of the composition confront the lone footman on the left. The women, particularly the seated lady, express an annoyance with the footman for breaking the tea service.

Accused of being careless, lazy, dishonest, and insolent, servants were often charged with a variety of infractions, including breaking china.[2] Masters therefore gave them instructional books or pamphlets, such as *The Servant's Friend* or *The Footman's Guide,* which set forth their duties. One particular rule stated that servants were to be careful with their master's property "for even a little [damage to an] article was a wasteful sin."[3]

The mistress's expression of concern for her dog's health rather than for her servant's injury was typical of an age in which pets were often valued above the help.[4] The ironic title "Fellow Feeling" suggests the lack of feeling expressed by the mistress in both the image and the text to the print. In the print, the servant's left calf displays no red mark where he was bitten. The inclusion of this naturalistic detail in the watercolor plays on the viewer's sympathy for the footman, a sympathy not shown by his mistress.[5]

Rhonda Howard

1. Quoted in Perkins, *The Servant Problem in English Literature,* p. 119.
2. Ibid., p. 125.
3. *The Servant's Friend; or, The master and mistresses best gift to their servants, apprentices and workmen* [n. p., 1780?], p. 6.
4. Bayne-Powell, *Eighteenth-Century London Life,* p. 323.
5. See Jonathan Swift, *Dean Swift's Humorous Advice to Servants* (London: J. Bailey, 1810), p. 3.

109 *An Innkeeper's Daughter Shewing Town Bucks to Their Chamber*†

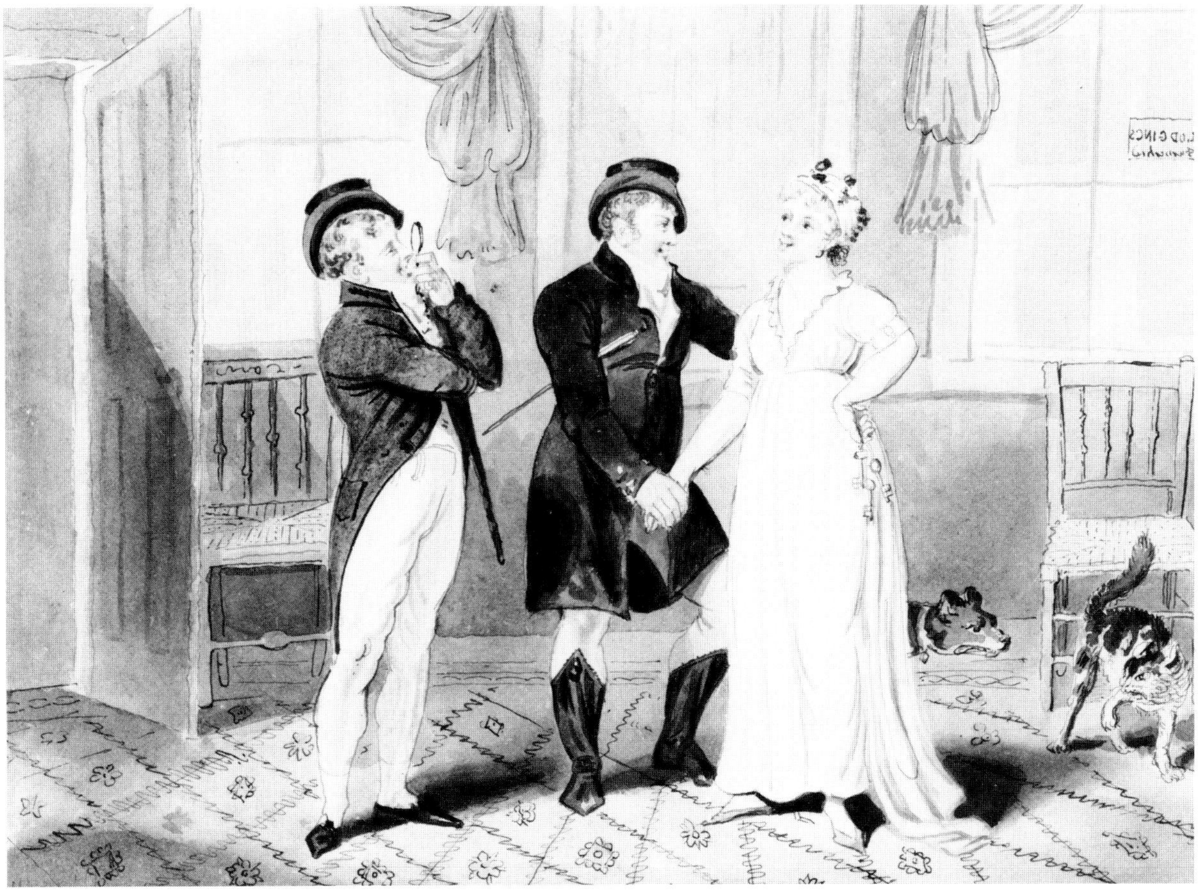

1801
Pen and watercolor over pencil (?)
$6\frac{1}{2}$ x $8\frac{3}{4}$ inches (16.5 x 22.2 cm.)
Verso: full-length pencil sketch of a young woman pulling up a stocking with a dog watching[1]
Inscribed recto [backwards]: Lodgings / furnished
Annotated verso: Lodgings to Let / I. Cruikshanks
Published: April 20, 1801, by Laurie & Whittle; below the title is engraved: Here Gentlemen is a two bedded Room, or you may have seperate Rooms. The Beds are well aired I assure you – Can I have you as a Companion my Love – Oh no Sir! But you may have my Cat, Tibby.
Biblio: Krumbhaar, 528; Wark, 106
Impression: GC, WMC

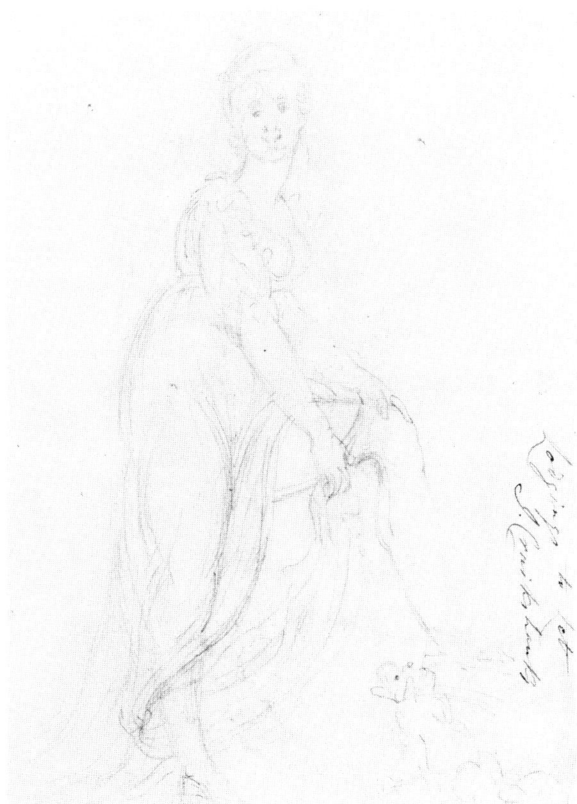

Even without the text, it is very clear that the young man, his right hand holding the woman's near his thigh and his left undoubtedly touching her back, is interested in more than renting the "furnished rooms" advertised in the window. (The sign does not appear in the print after this watercolor.) However, the exchange between the innkeeper's daughter and the "buck," a term in the early nineteenth century for a gay debauchee,[2] leaves little doubt as to the woman's ability to deal with his comments and familiarity. Undoubtedly, she has encountered similar remarks in the past. The meaning behind her reply concerning the cat is evident in Tibby's reaction to the man's dog. Clearly both hound and master should beware.

Around the turn of the century, Cruikshank produced a number of images of young men-about-town such as these two bucks.[3] Their fashionable attire as well as their demeanor and speech show them to be dandies and would-be wits, followers of Beau Brummell (1778-1840). As Ellen Moers has observed in her study of the dandy, such men had no occupation and no visible source of support.[4]

The buildings seen through the window identify the setting as urban. Given the simple good taste of the decor and the attire of the young woman, the inn could well be located in a resort such as Bath or a sporting center like Newmarket. Certainly that kind of place would attract gentlemen from London. In any case, the location is not as important as the humorous exchange of words.

Edward J. Nygren

1. Both the style of the sketch and its subject suggest that Cruikshank may well have known the drawings of Henry Fuseli (1741-1825), who became the Professor of Painting at the Royal Academy in 1801.
2. Egan, *Grose's Classical Dictionary of the Vulgar Tongue.*
3. See, for example: *Billing and Cooing at the Jelly Shop* (84) and *Bond Street Bucks and Keen Countryman* (117).
4. Ellen Moers, *The Dandy: Brummell to Beerbohm* (Lincoln and London: University of Nebraska Press, 1978), p. 18.

110 *The Unlucky Shower*

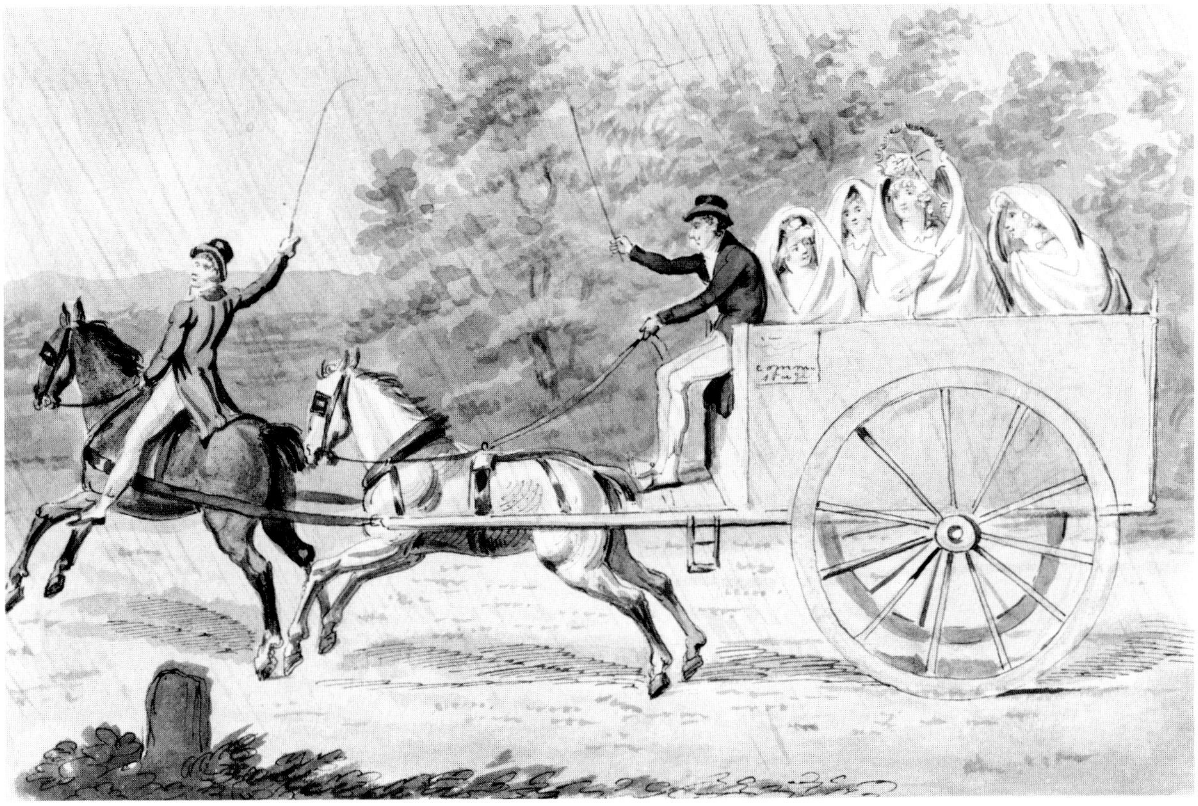

1801
Pen and watercolor over pencil
$6^{1}/_{4}$ x $9^{3}/_{8}$ inches (16.9 x 24 cm.)
Inscribed recto: Common Stage
Annotated verso: London Ladies going to a Country Dance / I. Cruikshanks
Published: May 1, 1801, by Laurie & Whittle (263)
Biblio: George, 9873; Krumbhaar, 1259; Wark, 107
Impression: BM

This drawing depicts a rainy scene in which four ladies (there are five in the print) in a wagon inscribed "common stage" are pulled by two horses, urged on by a postilion and driver. With no caption to elucidate the subject or explain the humor, the meaning of this image remains elusive. The travelers move from right to left, passing a prominently positioned milestone which in the print reads "to Croyden," a market-town in Surrey, nine and a half miles from London.[1]

Interaction occurs only between the ladies, via their glances. The two men are isolated from their passengers, with the rider turning to look outward. Interestingly, while driver and postilion are highlighted by vibrantly blue riding coats that enhance their individuality and compositional significance, the ladies, although set off by the foliage, are barely distinguishable from one another. Either seated or standing, the women huddle in this agricultural cart like soggy sacks of grain, seeking the pitiful shelter of blankets. While the two young fashionably dressed coachmen drive the horses on in an effort to escape the rain, the ladies seem indifferent to, but clearly unprepared for, the weather. The women certainly would be more at home at Almacks, the fashionable gathering place for dances in London. Obviously the satire is not carried here by caricature but by the incongruity of character and setting.

Maria L. Brendel

1. *Ambulator; or Pocket Companion in a Tour Round London*, p. 70.

111 *St. David's Day*

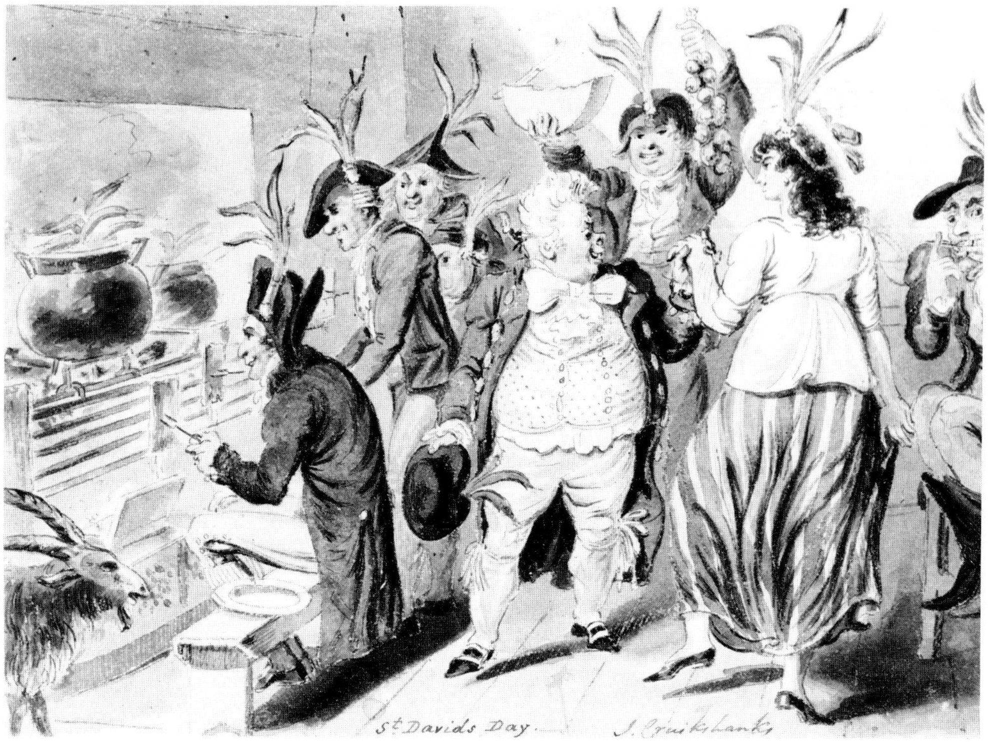

1801
Pen and watercolor over pencil
$7^1/_4 \times 9^1/_2$ inches (18.4 x 24.2 cm.)
Annotated recto: St. David's Day; / I. Cruikshanks
Published: May 1, 1801, by Laurie & Whittle
Biblio: Krumbhaar, A.96; Wark, 108
Impression: WMC

The men and woman depicted here with leeks in their hats are Welsh patriots gathered to celebrate the feast of St. David, the patron saint of Wales, on March 1, two months prior to the publication of the print after this watercolor. (The print reverses this image.) According to sixth-century legend, St. David once preached while the earth beneath him grew higher and higher until he was standing on a mountain visible to all and his voice was heard around the world.[1] By the end of the twelfth century, he was a symbol not only of Christian virtue but of patriotic pride, embodying national opposition to exploitation and subjection by the English.

In Cruikshank's day, Welsh patriotic societies flourished in London. The societies were known for extolling the glories of the Welsh past and the particular contribution of the Welsh to British history. The celebration of St. David's Day often involved a goat marching around the dinner table, an evening ball with music and dancing, the consumption of leeks, cheese, and onions, and the wearing of leeks by both sexes to symbolize national pride.[2] The importance of leeks in Welsh culture can be traced back to the sixth-century victory over the Saxons.[3] During battle, the Welsh wore leeks in their hats to show their military colors and to distinguish themselves from their enemies.[4]

Cruikshank's mild satire on Welsh pride, which depicts them as ever-faithful to their lineage and customs, is in keeping with the stereotypical view (see 107). Fluellen, the Welsh character in Shakespeare's *Henry V,* is a patriot whose everyday attire never failed to include leeks.[5] Other literary examples are found in Smollett's *The Adventures of Roderick Random* (1748), which describes Mr. Morgan as "a little proud and choleric, as all Welshmen are,"[6] and Dickens's *Bleak House* (1852), in which Mrs. Woodcourt speaks incessantly of her ancestors' greatness.[7]

Mary-Kay Lombino

1. Brand, *Observations on Popular Antiquities* (London: Chatto and Windus, 1913), p. 52.
2. Ibid., p. 53.
3. Williams, *Religion, Language, and Nationality in Wales,* p. 125.
4. T. F. Thiselton-Dyer, *British Popular Customs Present and Past* (London: George Bell and Sons, 1876), pp. 112-13.
5. Faber, *The High Road to England,* p. 113.
6. Smollett, *The Adventures of Roderick Random,* ed. Paul-Gabriel Boucé (Oxford: Oxford University Press, 1979), p. 157.
7. Faber, *The High Road to England,* p. 117.

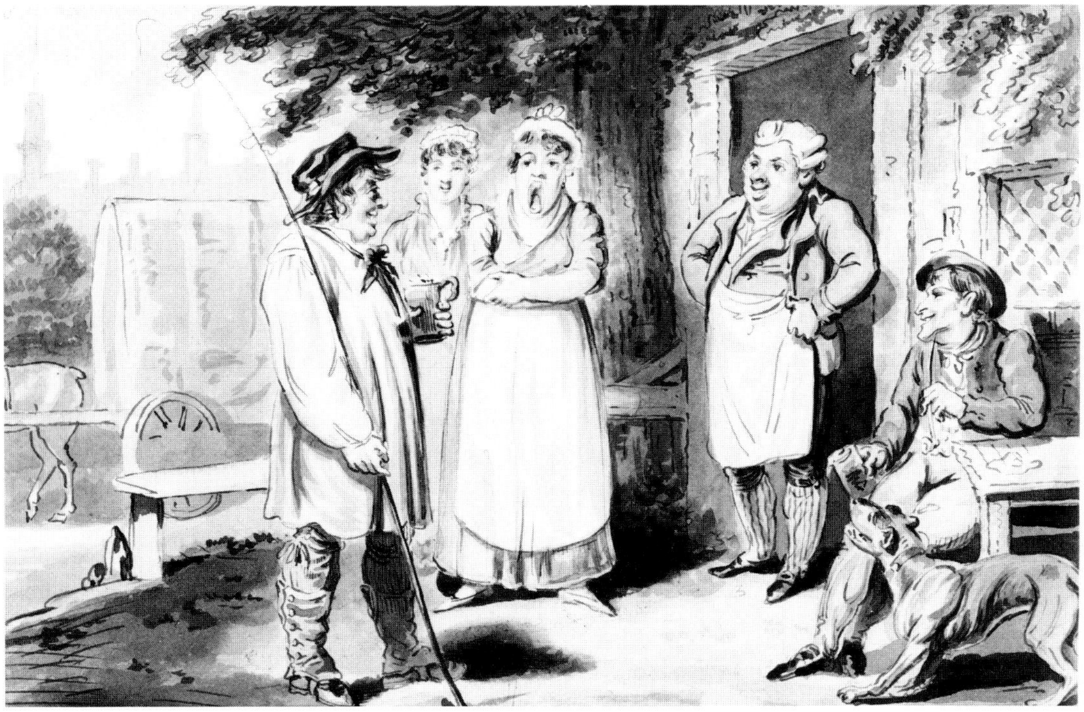

1801
Pen and watercolor over pencil
$6^3/_8$ x $9^3/_4$ inches (16.3 x 23.9 cm.)
Annotated verso: Little Mouths / I. Cruikshanks
Published: May 25, 1801, by Laurie & Whittle (265); below the image is engraved: Betty with bridled chin extends her face, / And then contracts her lips with simp'ring grace, / Cry'd hem! pray what must all the huge ones do / For husbands, when we little mouths have two? / Hold, not so fast, cry'd he, pray pardon me, / Maids with huge gaping wide mouths must have three. / Betty distorts her face with hideous squall, / And mouth a foot wide began to bawl. / Oh! ho! is't so? the case is alter'd Paul, / Is that the point? I wish the three were ten, / I warrant I'll find Mouth if they'll find Men.
Biblio: Krumbhaar, 657; Wark, 109
Impression: LWL

Outside the entrance of an inn, two women, a drayman, an innkeeper, and a customer congregate. A drayman, identified here by his horsewhip, tankard of beer, and covered wagon in the left background, transported barrels of beer to pubs and inns. It is unclear whether he is coming or going, for the drayman was known to drink on three separate occasions during the transaction: upon delivering the beer, to prove its quality; after placing the beer in the cellar, at which time he and the innkeeper pledged each other with a foaming tankard; and finally upon parting, when he had one for the road.[2]

Although the meaning of the verse that accompanies this illustration is not clear, it is obvious that there is a confrontation between the sexes, specifically between Betty—the woman with the big mouth—and the drayman, Paul. It is presumed that Paul initiated the conversation by uttering something about Betty's big mouth, for the verse begins as she is about to speak. Paul pokes fun at her and she stands with arms crossed and mouth wide open, her irritation obvious.

The play on the size of a mouth may have sexual overtones, for it could be a metaphor for the female genitalia. In the print after the watercolor, the image shows Betty with her hands clasped in front of her pelvic area, thumbs touching and fingers together in a triangular, mouth-like shape. While the exact meaning of the image is open to question, Betty's gesture and the repartee help support such an interpretation as does the expression of the three men, who are clearly amused by the exchange.

Rhonda Howard

1. The identity of Dr. King has not been determined.
2. T. L. Busby, *Costumes of the Lower Orders* (London: Baldwin and Co., 1820/19).

113 *The Wig and the Wags* †

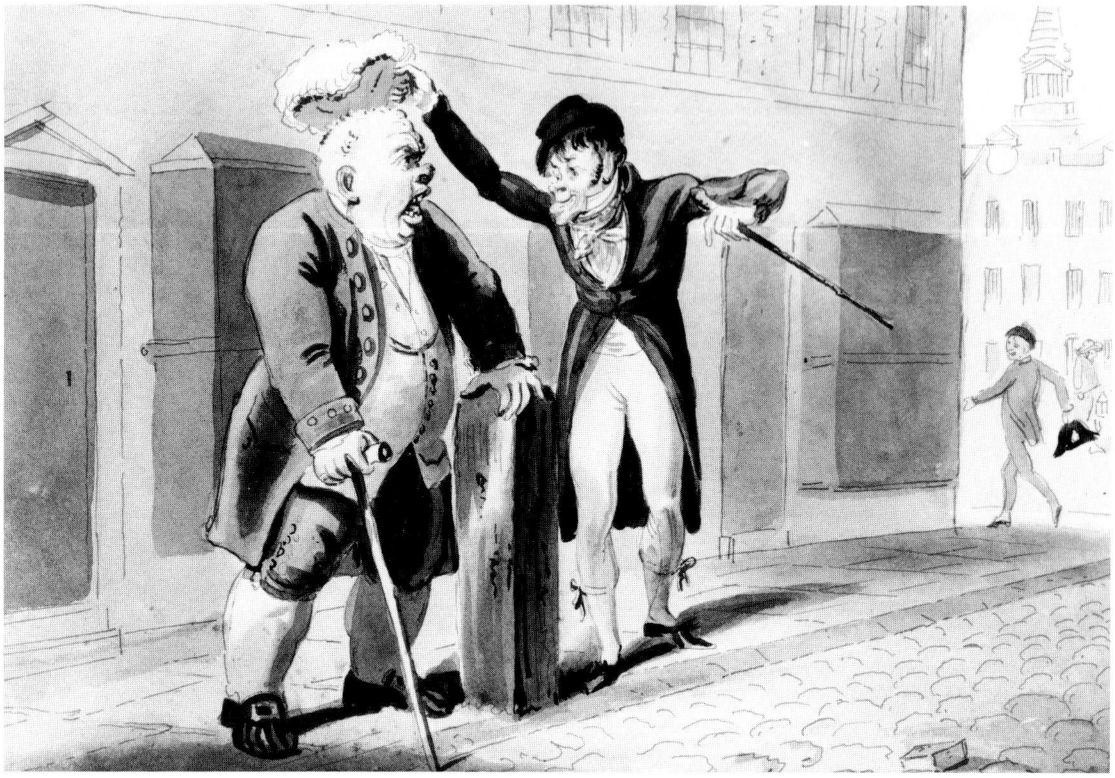

1801
Pen and watercolor over pencil
6¾ x 9⅛ inches (17.2 x 23.2 cm.)
Annotated verso: Having lost your Hat, I beg leave to take your Wig.
Published: June 24, 1801, by Laurie & Whittle; below the image is engraved: "Follow the thief," replied the stander by / "Ah! Sir" said he, "these feet will wag no more!" / "Alarm the neighborhood with hue and cry / "Alas! I've roar'd as long as lungs could roar!" / "Then" quoth the Stranger, "vain is all endeavour; / "Sans voice to call sans vigour to pursue; / "And since your hat, of course, is gone for ever / "I'll e'en make bold to take your Wig—Adieu!"
Biblio: Krumbhaar, A.113; Wark, 110
Impression: WMC

After asking the stranger for help, the stout man states that he cannot run and has cried out for help until he can cry no longer, but to no avail. The stranger responds by stating that if the victim can no longer cry for help and is too weak to pursue him, he will rob him, too. He then proceeds to take his wig. Robbed of his hat by one person, the victim is deprived of his wig by another.

The title and text play on the word *wag*. In the dialogue the word means "move quickly," but in the title it refers to the character of the wig snatcher. A wag, at the turn of the eighteenth century, was a hooligan or prankster.[1] Although people were sometimes robbed of handkerchiefs or other clothing, the items taken were generally stylish pieces that could be easily pawned or sold. In this case the victim's dress is conservative. As a result of the tax on hair powder, wigs had gone out of fashion in 1795, and were only worn by a few professionals such as judges or magistrates, who were exempt.[2] We may therefore assume that the wag is playing a prank on his victim since the latter's outdated hat and wig would not have been easily sold and he is not being robbed of his money. Moreover, the amusement expressed by two young women, who were introduced as onlookers in the place of the doorway when this image was published, confirms that the scene represents not a criminal offense but a mean practical joke.

Kathleen Kelly

1. Egan, *Grose's Classical Dictionary of the Vulgar Tongue.*
2. C. W. Cunnington and P. Cunnington, *Handbook of English Costume in the Eighteenth Century*, p. 247.

114 The Humane General

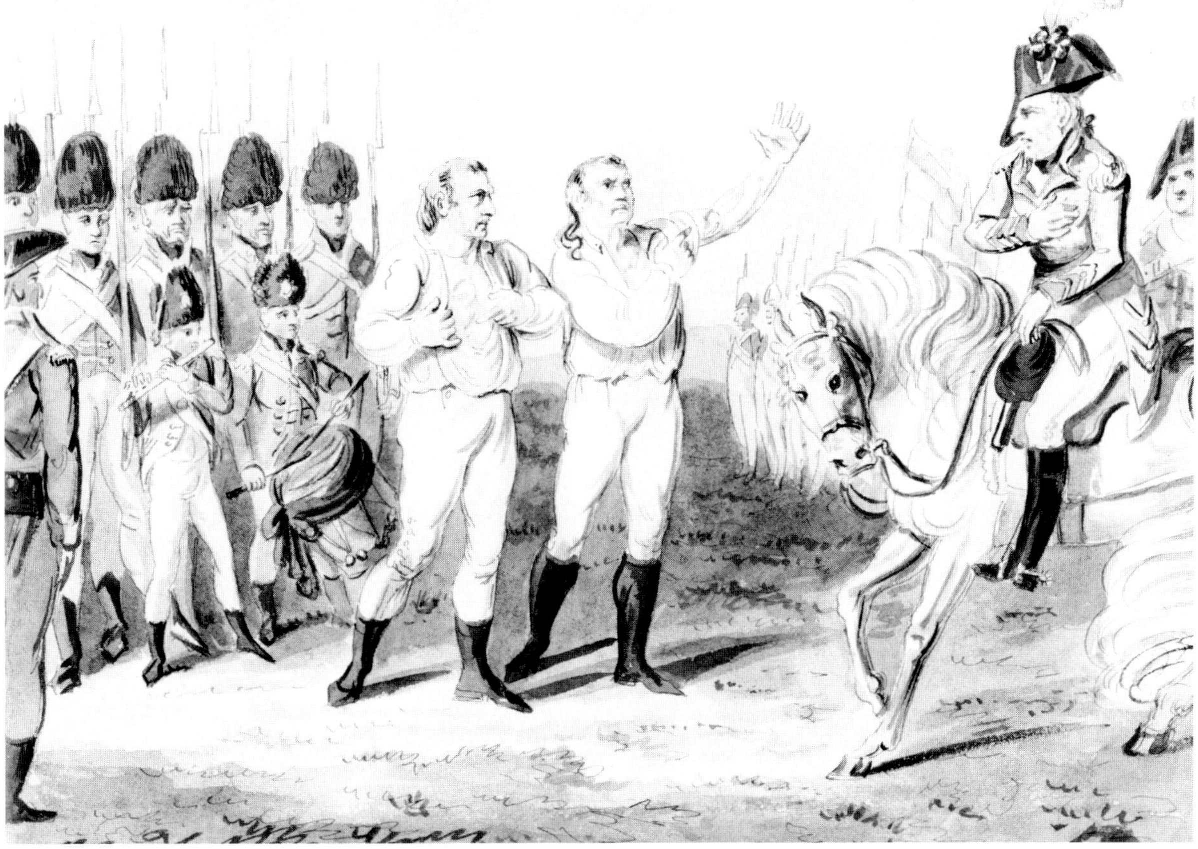

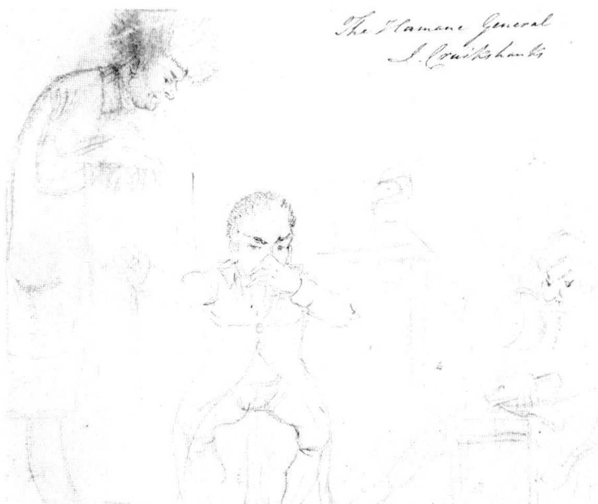

1801
Pen and watercolor over pencil
7 1/8 x 9 9/16 inches (18.1 x 24.3 cm.)
Annotated verso: The Humane General / I. Cruikshanks
Verso: Pencil sketch of three figures in a tavern
Published: July 13, 1801, by Laurie & Whittle; below the image is engraved: Two Old Soldiers sentenced to be Shot for a breach of Discipline when passing by their Noble Commander, they pointed to several Scars on their faces & breasts. What Language could come up to this!—it had the desired effect: they were instantly Pardoned. [in small type] This Story was related by General Amherst.
Biblio: Krumbhaar, A.48; Wark, 111
Impression: WMC

The source of the story has not been found. Although a positive identification of the general is not possible, Lord Jeffrey Amherst (1717-97) could well be the subject of this composition, executed and published at the height of Britain's war with France.[1] Amherst served with distinction as the commander-in-chief in North America during the late 1750s, when Britain was fighting France for control of that continent. Presumably the episode depicted occurred at that time for in 1759, Amherst commuted the sentences of three out of ten men given the death penalty.[2] Here two soldiers, stripped for execution, display their bloody wounds and scars to the general, who places his right hand on his heart in a gesture of sympathy.

At the age of 75 in 1793, Lord Jeffrey was made commander-in-chief on the outbreak of another war with France. Three years later, after retirement, he was made a field marshal. He died the following year. The subject, as a commentary on a historical military event, may well have had significance even in the early nineteenth century, when England was at war again.

Edward J. Nygren

1. For comparison with a life portrait of Amherst, see Thomas Gainsborough, *Lord Jeffrey Amherst,* National Portrait Gallery (London).
2. Fred Anderson, *A People's Army* (Chapel Hill: University of North Carolina Press, 1984), p. 123.

115 *Smothering a Rabbit with Onions* †

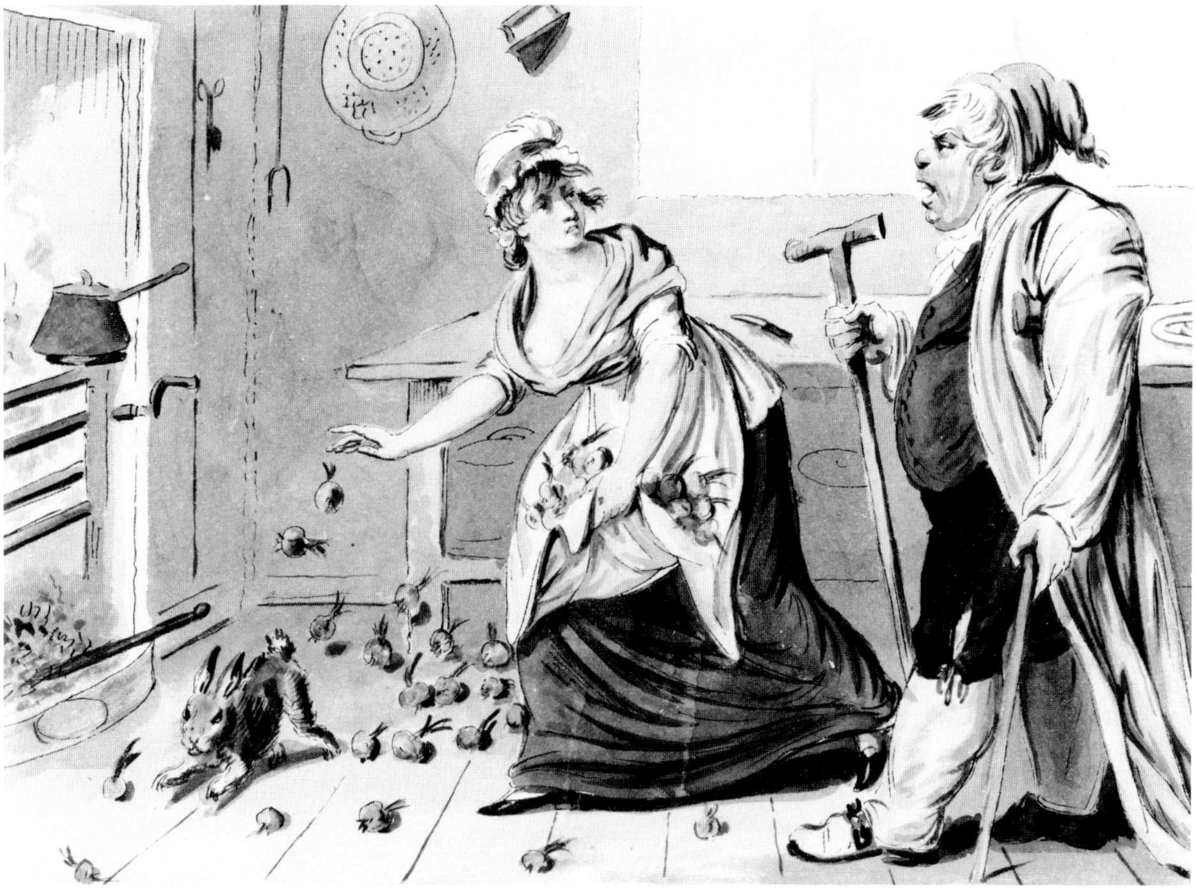

1801
Pen and watercolor
7 1/8 x 9 1/2 inches (18.2 x 24.2 cm.)
Annotated verso: Rabbit smothered with Onions / I. Cruikshanks
Published: November 23, 1801, by Laurie & Whittle; below the image is engraved: Sally, Sally what are you about, where is my Supper; where is the Rabbit smothered with Onions which I order'd an hour ago – Lord Sir I have been smothering it this half hour, till I'm sure a Broiling heat you might wring my Shirt. I have thrown all the onions in the House over twenty times, and he don't mind it at all—only see how he gallops about the kitchen as if he had been used to smothering all his life.
Biblio: Krumbhaar, A.90; Wark, 112
Impression: WMC

A cook, identified by the red ribbon around her cap,[1] attempts to prepare a "rabbit smothered with onions" by dropping onions from her apron on top of the animal's head. Her hungry master hobbles to the kitchen in search of his meal. When he arrives he finds the rabbit still alive and the onions uncut.

Women were often hired to prepare a variety of foods—roasts, rabbit, fish, vegetables, and even French cuisine.[2] This young servant, however, was probably not hired for her cooking abilities; she lacks not only culinary knowledge but common sense. She was undoubtedly employed for her master's viewing pleasure and perhaps for his extracurricular activities. Cruikshank suggests this by giving us a glimpse of her ample bosom, and the gross physiognomy of the master of the house reveals his base appetite. He follows a prevailing practice in the eighteenth century, whereby employers designated their attractive female servants as "legitimate prey."[3]

Rhonda Howard

1. E. W. Bovill. *English Country Life, 1780-1830* (New York and Toronto: Oxford University Press, 1962), p. 93.
2. Ibid., p. 100.
3. Fox, *Londoners*, p. 133; see also Katherine M. Rogers, *Feminism in Eighteenth-Century England* (Chicago, London, Urbana: University of Illinois Press, 1982), p. 19.

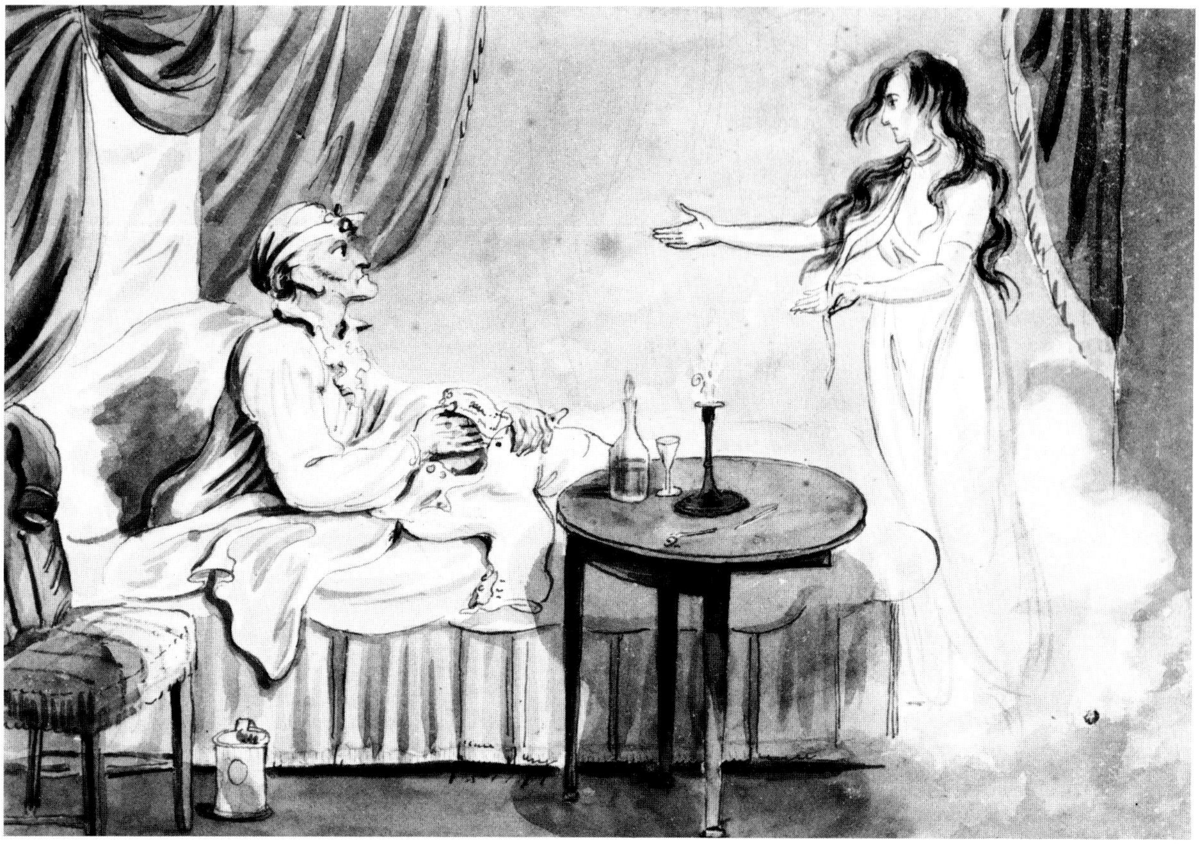

1804
Pen and watercolor over pencil
6 1/2 x 8 7/8 inches (16.5 x 22.5 cm.)
Annotated verso: Song of Miss Bailey / about 1803
Published: February 12, 1804, by Laurie & Whittle; below image is engraved: Sung by Mr. Matthews, at the Haymarket, and Mr. Fawcett, at Covent Garden: In "Love Laughs at Locksmiths," followed by verses.
Provenance: Purchased in 1962.
Biblio: Momus, p. 30; Krumbhaar, A.103; Wark, 113
Impression: WMC

When Cruikshank published this image, "Unfortunate Miss Bailey" was a song performed as part of a popular comedy, *Love Laughs at Locksmiths.* Introduced to London during the Whitby Theatre's 1803-4 season, this "farce in two acts" was written by George Colman the Younger (1762-1836), whose works dominated the Haymarket stage.[1] *Love Laughs at Locksmiths* relates the story of a courtship with nearly impossible circumstances. Captain Beldare, a gallant and important officer, falls in love with a young and beautiful lady whose image he knows only from history paintings. Lydia, the object of his desire, is enslaved as a model and kept hostage by her stepfather, the painter of these works. After several clever yet failed attempts, Captain Beldare, with the assistance of his servant Risk, sneaks into the artist's home and claims Lydia.

The song is performed during the second act, when Risk, posing as a distant relative from Yorkshire, gains entrance to the house and enhances his disguise by singing a Yorkshire "ditty." Risk intermittently repeats verses of the song not only to avoid incriminating conversation but to communicate to Lydia Captain Beldare's intentions. The verses relate the story of Miss Bailey, who took her own life after being seduced by a captain. It begins as follows: "A Captain in Halifax; that dwelt in country quarters, / Seduc'd a maid, who hang'd herself, one morning in her garters, / His wicked conscience smited him, he lost his stomach daily, / He took to drinking Batafia, and thought upon Miss Bailey." Her ghost haunts the captain, who agrees to bribe the sexton with a pound note to bury her corpse. It is this moment in the ballad that Cruikshank has chosen to illustrate.

The inscription on the print refers to the prominent actors Charles Mathews the Elder (1775-1835) and John Fawcett (1768-1837). The broadsheet with this composition was most likely published to take advantage of the popularity of the play or to promote it through the sale of the song. Isaac's son George, probably in cooperation with his father, treated this subject again, in 1807, with a different version of the ballad.[2] The title was changed to "Galvanism" and Miss Bailey miraculously recovers to marry the Captain.

Julie Joyce

1. H. Barton Baker, *History of the London Stage (and its Famous Players: 1576-1903)* (London: George Routledge and Sons, 1904), p. 225.
2. *The Cruikshankian Momus*, pp. 28-30.

Unfortunate Miss Bailey

A Captain in Halifax; that dwelt in country quarters,
Seduc'd a maid, who hang'd herself, one morning in her garters,
His wicked conscience smited him, he lost his stomach daily,
He took to drinking Batafia, and thought upon Miss Bailey.

One night betime he went to rest, for he had caught a fever,
Says he, "I am a handsome man, but I'm a gay deceiver,"
His candle just at twelve o'clock, began to burn quite palely,
A ghost step'd up to his bed side, and said, "behold Miss Bailey."

"Avaunt Miss Bailey," then he cry'd, "your face looks white and mealy,"
"Dear Captain Smith," the Ghost reply'd, "you've used me ungenteely.
"The coroner's quest goes hard with me, because I've acted fraily,
"And Parson Biggs won't buy me, tho' I am dead Miss Bailey."

"Dear Corpse," says he "since you and I, accounts must once for all close,
"I've got a One Pound Note, in my Regimentall finall clothes,
"'Twill bribe the Sexton for your grave," the Ghost then vanished gaily,
Crying "bless you wicked Captain Smith, remember poor Miss Bailey."

Next Morn his Man rapp'd at his door, "Oh! John" says he "come dress me,
"Miss Bailey's got my One Pound Note," cried John, "Good Heaven bless me!
"I shouldn't mind it if she had ta'en no more than all your Riches,
"But with your One Pound Note, by G_d! she's stol'n your leather Breeches."
"Oh! Miss Bailey, that wicked Ghost Miss Bailey."

THE MORAL

Ye wicked Captains warning take by This here sad example,
Be never Known your oaths to break, nor on your vows to trample;
Remember wicked Captain Smith, who once dress'd very gaily,
Now bare breech'd thro' the world he goes, for ruining Miss Bailey,
Oh! Miss Bailey, unfortunate Miss Bailey.

117 *Bond Street Bucks & Keen Countryman* †

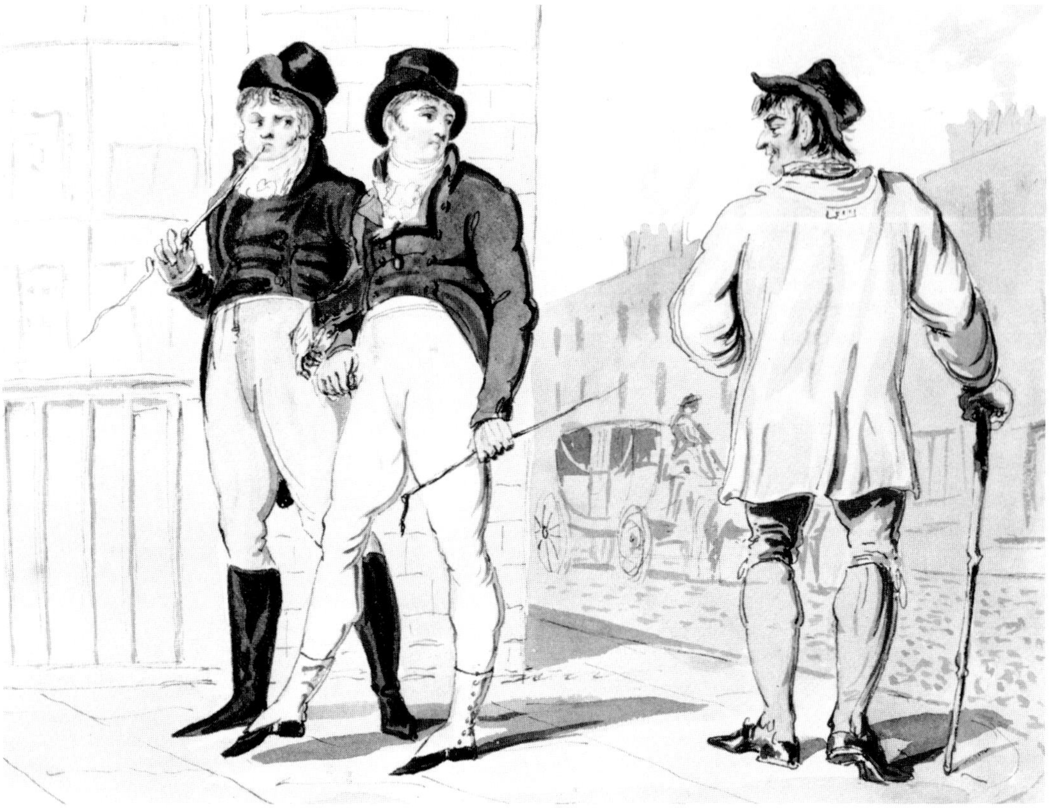

1804
Pen and watercolor over pencil
6¾ x 8⅜ inches (17.2 x 21.3 cm.)
Annotated verso: Bond Street
Published: August 20, 1804, by Laurie & Whittle (364); below the title is engraved: Two Bond Street loungers discoursing in Piccadilly, one of them said, he wish'd much to go into the Country, upon which the other made the following observation: In the Country, my Friend there is nought to be seen / But an Ass on a Common, or a Goose on a Green. A countryman passing at the time, pronounced the following impromptu: There would be in the Country them things to be seen / Were you on a Common your friend on a Green.
Provenance: Gilbert Davis Collection (1959).
Biblio: George, 10356; Krumbhaar, 82; Wark, 114
Impression: BM, WMC

Here, a young man-about-town is put in his place by a simple countryman. Cruikshank's sympathies clearly lie with the latter as, presumably, did his audience's.

In Cruikshank's day a "lounger" was an individual who spent his time idling and who was often financially independent.[1] Piccadilly stretches from Haymarket to Hyde Park, and Bond Street intersects Piccadilly. The area was (and still is) a fashionable part of London, with expensive shops and luxurious clubs frequented in the early nineteenth century by Beau Brummell and the Prince of Wales, among others.

The bucks depicted wear clothes that were the height of fashion at the turn of the century—round hat, double-breasted waistcoat, and pantaloons that extend down below the knee. Both carry riding crops, which had by then replaced walking sticks and clubs as accessories (see *A Box Lobby Challenge,* 34). Their hair is styled in a long disheveled crop known as a "Brutus Head." Natural hairstyles became popular after the fashion for wigs ended, a result of a tax on hair powder levied in 1795.[2]

Kathleen Kelly

1. Frank H. Vizetelly, *The Practical Standard Dictionary of the English Language* (New York and London: Funk and Wagnalls, Co., 1929), p. 680.
2. C. W. Cunnington and P. Cunnington, *Handbook of English Costume in the Eighteenth Century,* p. 247. Cruikshank deals with the wig tax in *Debating Society* (50).